KU-689-926

CHURCHILL

A Collection distributed by Heron Books

WINSTON S. CHURCHILL

THE SECOND WORLD WAR

BOOK III

THEIR FINEST HOUR
THE FALL OF FRANCE
May—August, 1940

Illustrations researched and selected
by Roger Jean Ségalat

Distributed by
HERON BOOKS

First published 1949
Ninth Edition, Third Impression 1970
Copyright Cassell and Company Limited
Edito-Service S.A., Geneva, Publishers

MORAL OF THE WORK

IN WAR: RESOLUTION
IN DEFEAT: DEFIANCE
IN VICTORY: MAGNANIMITY
IN PEACE: GOODWILL

PREFACE

DURING the period covered by this volume I bore a heavy burden of responsibility. I was Prime Minister, First Lord of the Treasury, Minister of Defence, and Leader of the House of Commons. After the first forty days we were alone, with victorious Germany and Italy engaged in mortal attack upon us with Soviet Russia a hostile neutral actively aiding Hitler, and Japan an unknowable menace. However, the British War Cabinet, conducting His Majesty's affairs with vigilance and fidelity, supported by Parliament and sustained by the Governments and peoples of the British Commonwealth and Empire, enabled all tasks to be accomplished and overcame all our foes.

WINSTON SPENCER CHURCHILL

Chartwell,
    Westerham,
       Kent
January 1, 1949

NOTE TO THE SECOND EDITION

A REPRINT having been called for, the opportunity has been taken to correct a few errors in detail. I am indebted to various correspondents who have drawn attention to these.

As in the case of the first volume, I have to express my appreciation of the generous reception given to the work, and I extend my cordial thanks to the many persons who have written to me concerning it.

WINSTON S. CHURCHILL

Chartwell
    January 10, 1950

ACKNOWLEDGMENTS

I MUST again acknowledge the assistance of those who helped me with the previous volume, namely, Lieutenant-General Sir Henry Pownall, Commodore G. R. G. Allen, Colonel F. W. Deakin, Sir Edward Marsh, Mr. Denis Kelly, and Mr. C. C. Wood. I have also to thank the very large number of others who have kindly read these pages and commented upon them.

Lord Ismay has continued to give me his aid, as have my other friends.

I again record my obligation to His Majesty's Government for permission to reproduce the text of certain official documents of which the Crown Copyright is legally vested in the Controller of His Majesty's Stationery Office. At the request of His Majesty's Government, on security grounds, I have paraphrased some of the telegrams published in this volume. These changes have not altered in any way the sense or substance of the telegrams.

TABLE OF CONTENTS

Chapter   *Page*

   I   THE NATIONAL COALITION   3

  II THE BATTLE OF FRANCE

          The First Week. Gamelin   25

 III THE BATTLE OF FRANCE

          The Second Week. Weygand .   .   .   47

  IV THE MARCH TO THE SEA   66

   V THE DELIVERANCE OF DUNKIRK .   .   .   87

  VI THE RUSH FOR THE SPOILS   105

 VII BACK TO FRANCE   122

VIII HOME DEFENCE. June   143

  IX THE FRENCH AGONY   157

   X THE BORDEAUX ARMISTICE .   .   .   175

  XI ADMIRAL DARLAN AND THE FRENCH FLEET. Oran .   197

 XII THE APPARATUS OF COUNTER-ATTACK. 1940 .   213

XIII AT BAY   225

XIV THE INVASION PROBLEM .   .   .   247

 XV OPERATION "SEA LION"   266

APPENDIX:

Minutes and Telegrams, May–August 1940 .   .   281

INDEX   313

MAPS AND DIAGRAMS

The Forward Movements, starting May 10 .   .   29

The Opposing Forces, May 13 .   .   .   37

TABLE OF CONTENTS

German Advances on Successive Days, May 13-17,
1940 41

Situation, Evening May 18 50

Situation, Evening May 22 59

Battle of Arras, May 21-22 63

Situation at Nightfall, May 25 75

Area of Operations, May 1940 . . *between* 77-78

Situation, May 28 85

Diagrams of Dunkirk Perimeter, May 29-June 1 93

The Opposing Forces on the Western Flank, June 5,
1940 132

The German Advance, June 5-9 . . . 133

The Last Stand of the French Army, June 1940 . 170

General Map of Western France . *between* 173-174

State of Readiness of Infantry Divisions . 239-243

Sketch Map of German Invasion Plan . . . 273

BOOK III

THEIR FINEST HOUR
THE FALL OF FRANCE

May—August, 1940

THEME OF THE BOOK

HOW THE BRITISH PEOPLE

HELD THE FORT

ALONE

TILL THOSE WHO HITHERTO HAD

BEEN HALF BLIND WERE

HALF READY

CHAPTER I

THE NATIONAL COALITION

The Beginning and the End – The Magnitude of Britain's Work for the Common Cause – Divisions in Contact with the Enemy throughout the War – The Roll of Honour – The Share of the Royal Navy – British and American Discharge of Air-bombs – American Aid in Munitions Magnifies Our War Effort – Formation of the New Cabinet – Conservative Loyalty to Mr. Chamberlain – The Leadership of the House of Commons – Heresy-hunting Quelled in Due Course – My Letter to Mr. Chamberlain of May 11 – A Peculiar Experience – Forming a Government in the Heat of Battle – New Colleagues: Clement Attlee, Arthur Greenwood, Archibald Sinclair, Ernest Bevin, Max Beaverbrook – A Small War Cabinet – Stages in the Formation of the Government, May 11–15 – A Digression on Power – Realities and Appearances in the New War Direction – Alterations in the Responsibilities of the Service Ministers – War Direction Concentrated in Very Few Hands – My Personal Methods – The Written Word – General Ismay – My Relations with the Chiefs of Staff Committee – Sir Edward Bridges – Kindness and Confidence Shown by the War Cabinet – The Office of Minister of Defence – Its Staff: Ismay, Hollis, Jacob – No Change for Five Years – Stability of Chiefs of Staff Committee – No Changes from 1941 till 1945 Except One by Death – Intimate Personal Association of Politicians and Soldiers at the Summit – The Personal Correspondence – My Relations with President Roosevelt – My Message to the President of May 15 – "Blood, Toil, Tears, and Sweat."

NOW at last the slowly-gathered, long-pent-up fury of the storm broke upon us. Four or five millions of men met each other in the first shock of the most merciless of all the wars of which record has been kept. Within a week the front in France, behind which we had been accustomed to dwell through the hard years of the former war and the opening phase of this, was to be irretrievably broken. Within three weeks the long-famed French Army was to collapse in rout and ruin, and our only British Army to be hurled into the sea with all its equipment lost. Within six weeks we were to find ourselves alone, almost disarmed, with triumphant Germany and Italy at our throats, with the whole of Europe open to Hitler's power, and Japan glowering on the other side of the globe. It was amid these facts and looming prospects that I entered upon my duties as Prime Minister and Minister of Defence and addressed myself to the first task of forming a Government of all parties to conduct His Majesty's business at home and abroad by whatever means might be deemed best suited to the national interest.

Five years later almost to a day it was possible to take a more favourable view of our circumstances. Italy was conquered and Mussolini slain. The mighty German Army had surrendered unconditionally. Hitler had committed suicide. In addition to the immense captures by General Eisenhower, nearly three million German soldiers were taken prisoners in twenty-four hours by Field-Marshal Alexander in Italy and Field-Marshal Montgomery in Germany. France was liberated, rallied, and revived. Hand in hand with our Allies, the two mightiest empires in the world, we advanced to the swift annihilation of Japanese resistance. The contrast was certainly remarkable. The road across these five years was long, hard, and perilous. Those who perished upon it did not give their lives in vain. Those who marched forward to the end will always be proud to have trodden it with honour.

* * *

In giving an account of my stewardship and in telling the tale of the famous National Coalition Government it is my first duty to make plain the scale and force of the contribution which Great Britain and her Empire, whom danger only united more tensely, made to what eventually became the Common Cause of so many States and nations. I do this with no desire to make invidious comparisons or rouse purposeless rivalries with our greatest Ally, the United States, to whom we owe immeasurable and enduring gratitude. But it is to the combined interest of the English-speaking world that the magnitude of the British war-making effort should be known and realised. I have therefore had a table made which I print on the following page, which covers the whole period of the war. This shows that until July 1944 Britain and her Empire had a substantially larger number of divisions *in contact with the enemy* than the United States. This general figure includes not only the European and African spheres, but also all the war in Asia against Japan. Till the arrival in Normandy in the autumn of 1944 of the great mass of the American Army, we had always the right to speak at least as an equal and usually as the predominant partner in every theatre of war except the Pacific and the Australasian; and this remains also true, up to the time mentioned, of the aggregation of all divisions in all theatres for any given month. From July 1944 the fighting front of the United States, as represented by divisions in contact with the enemy, became increasingly predominant, and so continued, mounting and triumphant, till the final victory ten months later.

Another comparison which I have made shows that the British and Empire sacrifice in loss of life was even greater than that of our valiant Ally. The British total dead, and missing, presumed dead, of the armed forces amounted to 303,240, to which should be added over 109,000 from the Dominions, India, and the Colonies, a total of over 412,240. This figure does not include 60,500 civilians killed in the air raids on the United Kingdom, nor the losses of our Merchant Navy and fishermen, which amounted to about 30,000. Against this figure the United States mourn the deaths in the Army and Air Force, the Navy, Marines, and Coastguard, of 322,188.* I cite these sombre Rolls of Honour in the confident faith that the equal comradeship sanctified by so much precious blood will continue to command the reverence and inspire the conduct of the English-speaking world.

On the seas the United States naturally bore almost the entire weight of the war in the Pacific, and the decisive battles which they fought near Midway Island, at Guadalcanal, and in the Coral Sea in 1942 gained for them the whole initiative in that vast ocean domain, and opened to them the assault of all the Japanese conquests, and eventually of Japan herself. The American Navy could not at the same time carry the main burden in the Atlantic and the Mediterranean. Here again it is a duty to set down the facts. Out of 781 German and 85 Italian U-boats destroyed in

---

* Eisenhower, *Crusade in Europe*, p. 1.

LAND FORCES IN FIGHTING CONTACT WITH THE ENEMY
"EQUIVALENT DIVISIONS"

	BRITISH EMPIRE			U.S.A.		
	Western Theatre	Eastern Theatre	Total	Western Theatre	Eastern Theatre	Total
Jan. 1, 1940	$5\frac{1}{8}$	—	$5\frac{1}{8}(a)$	—	—	—
July 1, 1940	6	—	6	—	—	—
Jan. 1, 1941	$10\frac{1}{3}$	—	$10\frac{1}{3}(b)$	—	—	—
July 1, 1941	13	—	13 (b)	—	—	—
Jan. 1, 1942	$7\frac{2}{3}$	7	$14\frac{2}{3}$	—	$2\frac{2}{3}$	$2\frac{2}{3}(c)$
July 1, 1942	10	$4\frac{2}{3}$	$14\frac{2}{3}$	—	$8\frac{1}{3}$	$8\frac{1}{3}$
Jan. 1, 1943	$10\frac{1}{3}$	$8\frac{2}{3}$	19	5	10	15
July 1, 1943	$16\frac{2}{3}$	$7\frac{2}{3}$	$24\frac{1}{3}$	10	$12\frac{1}{3}$	$22\frac{1}{3}$
Jan. 1, 1944	$11\frac{1}{3}$	$12\frac{1}{3}$	$23\frac{2}{3}$	$6\frac{2}{3}$	$9\frac{1}{3}$	16
July 1, 1944	$22\frac{2}{3}$	16	$38\frac{2}{3}$	25	17	42
Jan. 1, 1945	$30\frac{1}{3}$	$18\frac{2}{3}$	49	$55\frac{2}{3}$	$23\frac{1}{3}$	79

NOTES AND ASSUMPTIONS
(a) B.E.F. in France.
(b) Excludes guerrillas in Abyssinia.
(c) Excludes Filipino troops.

The dividing line between the Eastern and Western theatres is taken as a north/south line through Karachi.

The following are NOT taken as operational theatres:
N.W. Frontier of India; Gibraltar; West Africa; Iceland; Hawaii; Palestine; Iraq; Syria (except on July 1, 1941).
Malta is taken as an operational theatre; also Alaska from Jan. 1942 to July 1943.

Foreign contingents—e.g., Free French, Poles, Czechs—are NOT included.

the European theatre, the Atlantic and Indian Oceans, 594 were accounted for by British sea and air forces, who also disposed of all the German battleships, cruisers, and destroyers, besides destroying or capturing the whole Italian Fleet.

The table of U-boat losses is as follows:

U-BOAT LOSSES

Destroyed by	German	Italian	Japanese
*British Forces	525	69	9½
*United States Forces	174	5	110½
Other and unknown causes ..	82	11	10
Totals	781	85	130

Grand total of U-boats destroyed: 996

In the air superb efforts were made by the United States to come into action, especially with their daylight Fortress bombers, on the greatest scale from the earliest moment after Pearl Harbour, and their power was used both against Japan and from the British Isles against Germany.   However, when we reached Casablanca in January 1943 it is a fact that no single American bomber plane had cast a daylight bomb on Germany. Very soon the fruition of the great exertions they were making was to come, but up till the end of 1943 the British discharge of bombs upon Germany had in the aggregate exceeded by eight tons to one those cast from American machines by day or night, and it was only in the spring of 1944 that the preponderance of discharge was achieved by the United States. Here, as in the armies and on the sea, we ran the full course from the beginning, and it was not until 1944 that we were overtaken and surpassed by the tremendous war effort of the United States.

It must be remembered that our munitions effort from the beginning of Lend-Lease in January 1941 was increased by over one-fifth through the generosity of the United States. With the

* The terms British and United States Forces include Allied Forces under their operational control. Where fractional losses are shown the "kill" was shared. There were many cases of shared "kills", but in the German totals the fractions add up to whole numbers.

materials and weapons which they gave us we were actually able to wage war *as if we were a nation of fifty-eight millions instead of forty-eight.* In shipping also the marvellous production of Liberty Ships enabled the flow of supplies to be maintained across the Atlantic. On the other hand, the analysis of shipping losses by enemy action suffered by all nations throughout the war should be borne in mind. Here are the figures:

Nationality	Losses in Gross Tons	Percentage
British	11,357,000	54
United States	3,334,000	16
All other nations (outside enemy control)	6,503,000	30
	21,194,000	100

Of these losses 80 per cent. were suffered in the Atlantic Ocean, including British coastal waters and the North Sea. Only 5 per cent. were lost in the Pacific.

This is all set down, not to claim undue credit, but to establish on a footing capable of commanding fair-minded respect the intense output in every form of war activity of the people of this small Island, upon whom in the crisis of the world's history the brunt fell.

* * *

It is probably easier to form a Cabinet, especially a Coalition Cabinet, in the heat of battle than in quiet times. The sense of duty dominates all else, and personal claims recede. Once the main arrangements had been settled with the leaders of the other parties, with the formal authority of their organisations, the attitude of all those I sent for was like that of soldiers in action, who go to the places assigned to them at once without question. The Party basis being officially established, it seemed to me that no sense of Self entered into the minds of any of the very large number of gentlemen I had to see. If some few hesitated it was only because of public considerations. Even more did this high standard of behaviour apply to the large number of Conservative and National Liberal Ministers who had to leave their offices and break their careers, and at this moment of surpassing interest and excitement to step out of official life, in many cases for ever.

The Conservatives had a majority of more than one hundred

and twenty over all other parties in the House combined. Mr. Chamberlain was their chosen leader. I could not but realise that his supersession by me must be very unpleasant to many of them, after all my long years of criticism and often fierce reproach. Besides this, it must be evident to the majority of them how my life had been passed in friction or actual strife with the Conservative Party, that I had left them on Free Trade and had later returned to them as Chancellor of the Exchequer. After that I had been for many years their leading opponent on India, on foreign policy, and on the lack of preparations for war. To accept me as Prime Minister was to them very difficult. It caused pain to many honourable men. Moreover, loyalty to the chosen leader of the party is a prime characteristic of the Conservatives. If they had on some questions fallen short of their duty to the nation in the years before the war, it was because of this sense of loyalty to their appointed chief. None of these considerations caused me the slightest anxiety. I knew they were all drowned by the cannonade.

In the first instance I had offered to Mr. Chamberlain, and he had accepted, the Leadership of the House of Commons, as well as the Lord Presidency. Nothing had been published. Mr. Attlee informed me that the Labour Party would not work easily under this arrangement. In a Coalition the Leadership of the House must be generally acceptable. I put this point to Mr. Chamberlain, and, with his ready agreement, I took the Leadership myself, and held it till February 1942. During this time Mr. Attlee acted as my deputy and did the daily work. His long experience in Opposition was of great value. I came down only on the most serious occasions. These were, however, recurrent. Many Conservatives felt that their party leader had been slighted. Everyone admired his personal conduct. On his first entry into the House in his new capacity (May 13) the whole of his party—the large majority of the House—rose and received him in a vehement demonstration of sympathy and regard. In the early weeks it was from the Labour benches that I was mainly greeted. But Mr. Chamberlain's loyalty and support was steadfast, and I was sure of myself.

There was considerable pressure by elements of the Labour Party, and by some of those many able and ardent figures who had not been included in the new Government, for a purge of the "guilty men" and of Ministers who had been responsible

for Munich or could be criticised for the many shortcomings in
our war preparation. Among these Lord Halifax, Lord Simon,
and Sir Samuel Hoare were the principal targets. But this was
no time for proscriptions of able, patriotic men of long experience
in high office. If the censorious people could have had their way
at least a third of the Conservative Ministers would have been
forced to resign. Considering that Mr. Chamberlain was the
Leader of the Conservative Party, it was plain that this movement
would be destructive of the national unity. Moreover, I had no
need to ask myself whether all the blame lay on one side. Official
responsibility rested upon the Government of the time. But moral
responsibilities were more widely spread. A long, formidable list
of quotations from speeches and votes recorded by Labour, and
not less by Liberal, Ministers, all of which had been stultified by
events, was in my mind and available in detail. No one had more
right than I to pass a sponge across the past. I therefore resisted
these disruptive tendencies. "If the present," I said a few weeks
later, "tries to sit in judgment on the past it will lose the future."
This argument and the awful weight of the hour quelled the
would-be heresy-hunters.

★   ★   ★

Early on the morning of May 11 I sent a message to Mr.
Chamberlain: "No one changes houses for a month." This
avoided petty inconveniences during the crisis of the battle. I
continued to live at Admiralty House, and made its Map Room
and the fine rooms downstairs my temporary headquarters. I
reported to Mr. Chamberlain my talk with Mr. Attlee and the
progress made in forming the new Administration. "I hope to
have the War Cabinet and the Fighting Services complete to-night
for the King. The haste is necessitated by the battle. . . . As we
[two] must work so closely together, I hope you will not find it
inconvenient to occupy once again your old quarters which we
both know so well in No. 11."★ I added:

I do not think there is any necessity for a Cabinet to-day, as the
Armies and other Services are fighting in accordance with pre-
arranged plans. I should be very glad however if you and Edward
[Halifax] would come to the Admiralty War Room at 12.30 p.m.,
so that we could look at the maps and talk things over.

★ The house in Downing Street usually occupied by the Chancellor of the Exchequer.

British and French advanced forces are already on the Antwerp-Namur line, and there seem to be very good hopes that this line will be strongly occupied by the Allied armies before it can be assailed. This should be achieved in about forty-eight hours, and might be thought to be very important. Meanwhile the Germans have not yet forced the Albert Canal, and the Belgians are reported to be fighting well. The Dutch also are making a stubborn resistance.

* * *

My experiences in those first days were peculiar. One lived with the battle, upon which all thoughts were centred, and about which nothing could be done. All the time there was the Government to form and the gentlemen to see and the party balances to be adjusted. I cannot remember, nor do my records show, how all the hours were spent. A British Ministry at that time contained between sixty and seventy Ministers of the Crown, and all these had to be fitted in like a jig-saw puzzle, in this case having regard to the claims of three parties. It was necessary for me to see not only all the principal figures, but, for a few minutes at least, the crowd of able men who were to be chosen for important tasks. In forming a Coalition Government the Prime Minister has to attach due weight to the wishes of the party leaders as to who among their followers shall have the offices allotted to the party. By this principle I was mainly governed. If any who deserved better were left out on the advice of their party authorities, or even in spite of that advice, I can only express regret. On the whole however the difficulties were few.

In Clement Attlee I had a colleague of war experience long versed in the House of Commons. Our only differences in outlook were about Socialism, but these were swamped by a war soon to involve the almost complete subordination of the individual to the State. We worked together with perfect ease and confidence during the whole period of the Government. Mr. Arthur Greenwood was a wise counsellor of high courage and a good and helpful friend.

Sir Archibald Sinclair, as official Leader of the Liberal Party, found it embarrassing to accept the office of Air Minister, because his followers felt he should instead have a seat in the War Cabinet. But this ran contrary to the principle of a small War Cabinet. I therefore proposed that he should join the War Cabinet when any matter affecting fundamental political issues or party union was involved. He was my friend, and had been my second-in-command when in 1916 I commanded the 6th Royal Scots Fusiliers at Ploegsteert ("Plug Street"), and personally longed to enter upon the great sphere of action I had reserved for him. After no little intercourse this had been amicably settled. Mr. Bevin, with whom I had made acquaintance at the beginning of the war, in trying to mitigate the severe Admiralty demands for trawlers, had to consult the Transport and General Workers' Union, of which he was secretary, before he could join the team in the most important office of Minister of Labour. This took two or three days, but it was worth it. The union, the largest of all in Britain, said unanimously that he was to do it, and stuck solid for five years till we won.

The greatest difficulty was with Lord Beaverbrook. I believed he had services to render of a very high quality. I had resolved, as the result of my experiences in the previous war, to remove the supply and design of aircraft from the Air Ministry, and I wished him to become the Minister of Aircraft Production. He seemed at first reluctant to undertake the task, and of course the Air Ministry did not like having their Supply Branch separated from them. There were other resistances to his appointment. I felt sure however that our life depended upon the flow of new aircraft; I needed his vital and vibrant energy, and I persisted in my view.

* * *

In deference to prevailing opinions expressed in Parliament and the Press it was necessary that the War Cabinet should be small. I therefore began by having only five members, of whom one only, the Foreign Secretary, had a department. These were naturally the leading party politicians of the day. For the convenient conduct of business it was necessary that the Chancellor of the Exchequer and the Leader of the Liberal Party should usually be present, and as time passed the number of "constant attenders" grew. But all the responsibility was laid upon the five War Cabinet Ministers. They were the only ones who had the right to have their heads cut off on Tower Hill if we did not win. The rest could suffer for departmental shortcomings, but not on account of the policy of the State. Apart from the War Cabinet, any one could say: "I cannot take the responsibility for this or that." The burden of policy was borne at a higher level. This saved many people a lot of worry in the days which were immediately to fall upon us.

Here are the stages by which the National Coalition Government was built up day by day in the course of the great battle.

THE WAR CABINET

May 11, 1940

Prime Minister, First Lord of the Treasury, Minister of Defence, and Leader of the House of Commons	* Mr. Churchill	Conservative
Lord President of the Council	* Mr. Neville Chamberlain	Conservative
Lord Privy Seal	Mr. C. R. Attlee	Labour
Secretary of State for Foreign Affairs	* Lord Halifax	Conservative
Minister without Portfolio	Mr. Arthur Greenwood	Labour

MINISTERS OF CABINET RANK

First Lord of the Admiralty	Mr. A. V. Alexander	Labour
Secretary of State for War	* Mr. Anthony Eden	Conservative
Secretary of State for Air	Sir Archibald Sinclair	Liberal

May 12

Lord Chancellor	* Sir John Simon [becoming Lord Simon]	National Liberal
Chancellor of the Exchequer	* Sir Kingsley Wood	Conservative
Home Secretary and Minister of Home Security	* Sir John Anderson	Non-Party
Secretary of State for the Colonies	Lord Lloyd	Conservative
President of the Board of Trade	Sir Andrew Duncan	Non-Party
Minister of Supply	Mr. Herbert Morrison	Labour
Minister of Information	Mr. Alfred Duff Cooper	Conservative

May 13

Secretary of State for India and Burma	Mr. L. S. Amery	Conservative
Minister of Health	* Mr. Malcolm Macdonald	National Labour
Minister of Labour and National Service	Mr. Ernest Bevin	Labour
Minister of Food	* Lord Woolton	Non-Party

* Members in previous Administration.

May 14

Dominions Secretary and Leader of the House of Lords	* Viscount Caldecote	Conservative
Secretary of State for Scotland	* Mr. Ernest Brown	National Liberal
Minister of Aircraft Production	Lord Beaverbrook	Conservative
President of the Board of Education	* Mr. Herwald Ramsbotham	Conservative
Minister of Agriculture	* Mr. Robert Hudson	Conservative
Minister of Transport	* Sir John Reith	Non-Party
Minister of Shipping	* Mr. Ronald Cross	Conservative
Minister of Economic Warfare	Mr. Hugh Dalton	Labour
Chancellor of the Duchy of Lancaster	* Lord Hankey	Non-Party

May 15

Minister of Pensions	* Sir W. J. Womersley	Conservative
Postmaster-General	* Mr. W. S. Morrison	Conservative
Paymaster-General	Lord Cranborne	Conservative
Attorney-General	* Sir Donald Somervell, K.C.	Conservative
Lord Advocate	* Mr. T. M. Cooper, K.C.	Conservative
Solicitor-General	Sir William Jowitt, K.C.	Labour
Solicitor-General for Scotland	* Mr. J. S. C. Reid, K.C.	Conservative

*   *   *

In my long political experience I had held most of the great offices of State, but I readily admit that the post which had now fallen to me was the one I liked the best. Power, for the sake of lording it over fellow-creatures or adding to personal pomp, is rightly judged base. But power in a national crisis, when a man believes he knows what orders should be given, is a blessing. In any sphere of action there can be no comparison between the positions of number one and numbers two, three, or four. The duties and the problems of all persons other than number one are quite different and in many ways more difficult. It is always a misfortune when number two or three has to initiate a dominant plan or policy. He has to consider not only the merits of the policy, but the mind of his chief; not only what to advise, but

* Members in previous Administration.

14

what it is proper for him in his station to advise; not only what to do, but how to get it agreed, and how to get it done. Moreover, number two or three will have to reckon with numbers four, five, and six, or maybe some bright outsider, number twenty. Ambition, not so much for vulgar ends, but for fame, glints in every mind. There are always several points of view which may be right, and many which are plausible. I was ruined for the time being in 1915 over the Dardanelles, and a supreme enterprise was cast away, through my trying to carry out a major and cardinal operation of war from a subordinate position. Men are ill-advised to try such ventures. This lesson had sunk into my nature.

At the top there are great simplifications. An accepted leader has only to be sure of what it is best to do, or at least to have made up his mind about it. The loyalties which centre upon number one are enormous. If he trips he must be sustained. If he makes mistakes they must be covered. If he sleeps he must not be wantonly disturbed. If he is no good he must be pole-axed. But this last extreme process cannot be carried out every day; and certainly not in the days just after he has been chosen.

★   ★   ★

The fundamental changes in the machinery of war direction were more real than apparent. "A Constitution", said Napoleon, "should be short and obscure." The existing organisms remained intact. No official personalities were changed. The War Cabinet and the Chiefs of Staff Committee at first continued to meet every day as they had done before. In calling myself, with the King's approval, Minister of Defence I had made no legal or constitutional change. I had been careful not to define my rights and duties. I asked for no special powers either from the Crown or Parliament. It was however understood and accepted that I should assume the general direction of the war, subject to the support of the War Cabinet and of the House of Commons. The key change which occurred on my taking over was of course the supervision and direction of the Chiefs of Staff Committee by a Minister of Defence with undefined powers. As this Minister was also the Prime Minister, he had all the rights inherent in that office, including very wide powers of selection and removal of all professional and political personages. Thus for the first time the

Chiefs of Staff Committee assumed its due and proper place in direct daily contact with the executive head of the Government, and in accord with him had full control over the conduct of the war and the armed forces.

The position of the First Lord of the Admiralty and of the Secretaries of State for War and Air was decisively affected in fact though not in form. They were not members of the War Cabinet, nor did they attend the meetings of the Chiefs of Staff Committee. They remained entirely responsible for their departments, but rapidly and almost imperceptibly ceased to be responsible for the formulation of strategic plans and the day-to-day conduct of operations. These were settled by the Chiefs of Staff Committee acting directly under the Minister of Defence and Prime Minister, and thus with the authority of the War Cabinet. The three Service Ministers, very able and trusted friends of mine whom I had picked for these duties, stood on no ceremony. They organised and administered the ever-growing forces, and helped all they could in the easy, practical English fashion. They had the fullest information by virtue of their membership of the Defence Committee, and constant access to me. Their professional subordinates, the Chiefs of Staff, discussed everything with them and treated them with the utmost respect. But there was an integral direction of the war to which they loyally submitted. There never was an occasion when their powers were abrogated or challenged, and anyone in this circle could always speak his mind; but the actual war direction soon settled into a very few hands, and what had seemed so difficult before became much more simple—apart of course from Hitler. In spite of the turbulence of events and the many disasters we had to endure the machinery worked almost automatically, and one lived in a stream of coherent thought capable of being translated with great rapidity into executive action.

*　　*　　*

Although the awful battle was now going on across the Channel, and the reader is no doubt impatient to get there, it may be well at this point to describe the system and machinery for conducting military and other affairs which I set on foot and practised from my earliest days of power. I am a strong believer in transacting official business by *the Written Word*. No doubt, surveyed in the after-time, much that is set down from hour to hour under the impact of events may be lacking in proportion or may not come true. I am willing to take my chance of that. It is always better, except in the hierarchy of military discipline, to express opinions and wishes rather than to give orders. Still, written directives coming personally from the lawfully-constituted Head of the Government and Minister specially charged with defence counted to such an extent that, though not expressed as orders, they very often found their fruition in action.

To make sure that my name was not used loosely, I issued during the crisis of July the following minute:

Prime Minister to General Ismay, C.I.G.S., and
Sir Edward Bridges 19.VII.40
Let it be very clearly understood that all directions emanating from me are made in writing, or should be immediately afterwards confirmed in writing, and that I do not accept any responsibility for matters relating to national defence on which I am alleged to have given decisions unless they are recorded in writing.

When I woke about 8 a.m. I read all the telegrams, and from my bed dictated a continuous flow of minutes and directives to the departments and to the Chiefs of Staff Committee. These were typed in relays as they were done, and handed at once to General Ismay, Deputy-Secretary (Military) to the War Cabinet, and my representative on the Chiefs of Staff Committee, who came to see me early each morning. Thus he usually had a good deal in writing to bring before the Chiefs of Staff Committee when they met at ten-thirty. They gave all consideration to my views at the same time as they discussed the general situation. Thus between three and five o'clock in the afternoon, unless there were some difficulties between us requiring further consultation, there was ready a whole series of orders and telegrams sent by me or by the Chiefs of Staff and agreed between us, usually giving all the decisions immediately required.

In total war it is quite impossible to draw any precise line between military and non-military problems. That no such friction occurred between the military staff and the War Cabinet staff was due primarily to the personality of Sir Edward Bridges, Secretary to the War Cabinet. Not only was this son of a former

Poet Laureate an extremely competent and tireless worker, but he was also a man of exceptional force, ability, and personal charm, without a trace of jealousy in his nature. All that mattered to him was that the War Cabinet Secretariat as a whole should serve the Prime Minister and War Cabinet to the very best of their ability. No thought of his own personal position ever entered his mind, and never a cross word passed between the civil and military officers of the Secretariat.

In larger questions, or if there were any differences of view, I called a meeting of the War Cabinet Defence Committee, which at the outset comprised Mr. Chamberlain, Mr. Attlee, and the three Service Ministers, with the Chiefs of Staff in attendance. These formal meetings got fewer after 1941.* As the machine began to work more smoothly I came to the conclusion that the daily meetings of the War Cabinet with the Chiefs of Staff present were no longer necessary. I therefore eventually instituted what came to be known among ourselves as the "Monday Cabinet Parade". Every Monday there was a considerable gathering—all the War Cabinet, the Service Ministers, and the Minister of Home Security, the Chancellor of the Exchequer, the Secretaries of State for the Dominions and for India, the Minister of Information, the Chiefs of Staff, and the official head of the Foreign Office. At these meetings each Chief of Staff in turn unfolded his account of all that had happened during the previous seven days; and the Foreign Secretary followed them with his story of any important developments in foreign affairs. On other days of the week the War Cabinet sat alone, and all important matters requiring decision were brought before them. Other Ministers primarily concerned with the subjects to be discussed attended for their own particular problems. The members of the War Cabinet had the fullest circulation of all papers affecting the war, and saw all important telegrams sent by me. As confidence grew the War Cabinet intervened less actively in operational matters, though they watched them with close attention and full knowledge. They took almost the whole weight of home and party affairs off my shoulders, thus setting me free to concentrate upon the main theme. With regard to all future operations of importance I always consulted them in good time; but, while they gave

* The Defence Committee met 40 times in 1940, 76 in 1941, 20 in 1942, 14 in 1943, and 10 in 1944.

careful consideration to the issues involved, they frequently asked not to be informed of dates and details, and indeed on several occasions stopped me when I was about to unfold these to them.

I had never intended to embody the office of Minister of Defence in a department. This would have required legislation, and all the delicate adjustments I have described, most of which settled themselves by personal goodwill, would have had to be thrashed out in a process of ill-timed constitution-making. There was however in existence and activity under the personal direction of the Prime Minister the Military Wing of the War Cabinet Secretariat, which had in pre-war days been the Secretariat of the Committee of Imperial Defence. At the head of this stood General Ismay, with Colonel Hollis and Colonel Jacob as his two principals, and a group of specially-selected younger officers drawn from all three Services. This Secretariat became the staff of the office of the Minister of Defence. My debt to its members is immeasurable. General Ismay, Colonel Hollis, and Colonel Jacob rose steadily in rank and repute as the war proceeded, and none of them was changed. Displacements in a sphere so intimate and so concerned with secret matters are detrimental to continuous and efficient dispatch of business.

After some early changes almost equal stability was preserved in the Chiefs of Staff Committee. On the expiry of his term as Chief of the Air Staff, in September 1940, Air Marshal Newall became Governor-General of New Zealand, and was succeeded by Air Marshal Portal, who was the accepted star of the Air Force. Portal remained with me throughout the war. Sir John Dill, who had succeeded General Ironside in May 1940, remained C.I.G.S. until he accompanied me to Washington in December 1941. I then made him my personal Military Representative with the President and head of our Joint Staff Mission. His relations with General Marshall, Chief of Staff of the United States Army, became a priceless link in all our business, and when he died in harness some two years later he was accorded the unique honour of a resting-place in Arlington Cemetery, the Valhalla hitherto reserved exclusively for American warriors. He was succeeded as C.I.G.S. by Sir Alan Brooke, who stayed with me till the end.

From 1941, for nearly four years, the early part of which was passed in much misfortune and disappointment, the only change made in this small band either among the Chiefs or in the Defence staff was due to the death in harness of Admiral Pound. This may well be a record in British military history. A similar degree of continuity was achieved by President Roosevelt in his own circle. The United States Chiefs of Staff—General Marshall, Admiral King, and General Arnold, subsequently joined by Admiral Leahy—started together on the American entry into the war, and were never changed. As both the British and Americans presently formed the Combined Chiefs of Staff Committee this was an inestimable advantage for all. Nothing like it between allies has ever been known before.

I cannot say that we never differed among ourselves even at home, but a kind of understanding grew up between me and the British Chiefs of Staff that we should convince and persuade rather than try to overrule each other. This was of course helped by the fact that we spoke the same technical language, and possessed a large common body of military doctrine and war experience. In this ever-changing scene we moved as one, and the War Cabinet clothed us with ever more discretion, and sustained us with unwearied and unflinching constancy. There was no division, as in the previous war, between politicians and soldiers, between the "Frocks" and the "Brass Hats"—odious terms which darkened counsel. We came very close together indeed, and friendships were formed which I believe were deeply valued.

The efficiency of a war Administration depends mainly upon whether decisions emanating from the highest approved authority are in fact strictly, faithfully, and punctually obeyed. This we achieved in Britain in this time of crisis owing to the intense fidelity, comprehension, and whole-hearted resolve of the War Cabinet upon the essential purpose to which we had devoted ourselves. According to the directions given, ships, troops, and aeroplanes moved, and the wheels of factories spun. By all these processes, and by the confidence, indulgence, and loyalty by which I was upborne, I was soon able to give an integral direction to almost every aspect of the war. This was really necessary, because times were so very bad. The method was accepted because everyone realised how near were death and ruin. Not only individual death, which is the universal experience, stood near, but, incomparably more commanding, the life of Britain, her message, and her glory.

* * *

Any account of the methods of government which developed under the National Coalition would be incomplete without an explanation of the series of personal messages which I sent to the President of the United States and the heads of other foreign countries and the Dominions Governments. This correspondence must be described. Having obtained from the Cabinet any specific decisions required on policy, I composed and dictated these documents myself, for the most part on the basis that they were intimate and informal correspondence with friends and fellow-workers. One can usually put one's thoughts better in one's own words. It was only occasionally that I read the text to the Cabinet beforehand. Knowing their views, I used the ease and freedom needed for the doing of my work. I was of course hand-in-glove with the Foreign Secretary and his department, and any differences of view were settled together. I circulated these telegrams, in some cases after they had been sent, to the principal members of the War Cabinet, and, where he was concerned, to the Dominions Secretary. Before dispatching them I of course had my points and facts checked departmentally, and nearly all military messages passed through Ismay's hands to the Chiefs of Staff. This correspondence in no way ran counter to the official communications or the work of the Ambassadors. It became however in fact the channel of much vital business, and played a part in my conduct of the war not less, and sometimes even more, important than my duties as Minister of Defence.

The very select circle, who were entirely free to express their opinion, were almost invariably content with the drafts and gave me an increasing measure of confidence. Differences with American authorities for instance, insuperable at the second level, were settled often in a few hours by direct contact at the top. Indeed, as time went on the efficacy of this top-level transaction of business was so apparent that I had to be careful not to let it become a vehicle for ordinary departmental affairs. I had repeatedly to refuse the requests of my colleagues to address the President personally on important matters of detail. Had these intruded unduly upon the personal correspondence they would soon have destroyed its privacy and consequently its value.

My relations with the President gradually became so close that the chief business between our two countries was virtually conducted by these personal interchanges between him and me. In this way our perfect understanding was gained. As Head of the State as well as Head of the Government, Roosevelt spoke and acted with authority in every sphere; and, carrying the War Cabinet with me, I represented Great Britain with almost equal latitude. Thus a very high degree of concert was obtained, and the saving in time and the reduction in the number of people informed were both invaluable. I sent my cables to the American Embassy in London, which was in direct touch with the President at the White House through special coding machines. The speed with which answers were received and things settled was aided by clock-time. Any message which I prepared in the evening, at night, or even up to two o'clock in the morning, would reach the President before he went to bed, and very often his answer would come back to me when I woke the next morning. In all I sent him nine hundred and fifty messages, and received about eight hundred in reply. I felt I was in contact with a very great man, who was also a warm-hearted friend and the foremost champion of the high causes which we served.

* * *

The Cabinet being favourable to my trying to obtain destroyers from the American Government, I drafted during the afternoon of May 15 my first message to President Roosevelt since I became Prime Minister. To preserve the informality of our correspondence I signed myself "Former Naval Person", and to this fancy I adhered almost without exception throughout the war.

Although I have changed my office, I am sure you would not wish me to discontinue our intimate private correspondence. As you are no doubt aware, the scene has darkened swiftly. The enemy have a marked preponderance in the air, and their new technique is making a deep impression upon the French. I think myself the battle on land has only just begun, and I should like to see the masses engage. Up to the present Hitler is working with specialised units in tanks and air. The small countries are simply smashed up, one by one, like matchwood. We must expect, though it is not yet certain, that Mussolini will hurry in to share the loot of civilisation. We expect to be attacked here ourselves, both from the air and by parachute and air-borne troops, in the near future, and are getting ready for them. If necessary, we shall continue the war alone, and we are not afraid of that.

But I trust you realise, Mr. President, that the voice and force of the United States may count for nothing if they are withheld too long. You may have a completely subjugated, Nazified Europe established with astonishing swiftness, and the weight may be more than we can bear. All I ask now is that you should proclaim non-belligerency, which would mean that you would help us with everything short of actually engaging armed forces. Immediate needs are, first of all, the loan of forty or fifty of your older destroyers to bridge the gap between what we have now and the large new construction we put in hand at the beginning of the war. This time next year we shall have plenty. But if in the interval Italy comes in against us with another hundred submarines we may be strained to breaking-point. Secondly, we want several hundred of the latest types of aircraft, of which you are now getting delivery. These can be repaid by those now being constructed in the United States for us. Thirdly, anti-aircraft equipment and ammunition, of which again there will be plenty next year, if we are alive to see it. Fourthly, the fact that our ore supply is being compromised from Sweden, from North Africa, and perhaps from Northern Spain, makes it necessary to purchase steel in the United States. This also applies to other materials. We shall go on paying dollars for as long as we can, but I should like to feel reasonably sure that when we can pay no more you will give us the stuff all the same. Fifthly, we have many reports of possible German parachute or air-borne descents in Ireland. The visit of a United States squadron to Irish ports, which might well be prolonged, would be invaluable. Sixthly, I am looking to you to keep the Japanese quiet in the Pacific, using Singapore in any way convenient. The details of the material which we have in hand will be communicated to you separately.

With all good wishes and respect . . .

On May 18 a reply was received from the President welcoming the continuance of our private correspondence and dealing with my specific requests. The loan or gift of the forty or fifty older destroyers, it was stated, would require the authorisation of Congress, and the moment was not opportune. He would facilitate to the utmost the Allied Governments obtaining the latest types of United States aircraft, anti-aircraft equipment, ammunition, and steel. In all this the representations of our agent, the highly competent and devoted Mr. Purvis (presently to give his life in an air accident), would receive most favourable consideration. The President would consider carefully my suggestion that a United States squadron might visit Irish ports. About the Japanese, he merely pointed to the concentration of the American fleet at Pearl Harbour.

＊　　＊　　＊

On Monday, May 13, I asked the House of Commons, which had been specially summoned, for a vote of confidence in the new Administration. After reporting the progress which had been made in filling the various offices, I said: "I have nothing to offer but blood, toil, tears, and sweat." In all our long history no Prime Minister had ever been able to present to Parliament and the nation a programme at once so short and so popular. I ended:

You ask, What is our policy? I will say: It is to wage war, by sea, land, and air, with all our might and with all the strength that God can give us: to wage war against a monstrous tyranny, never surpassed in the dark, lamentable catalogue of human crime. That is our policy. You ask, What is our aim? I can answer in one word: Victory—victory at all costs, victory in spite of all terror; victory, however long and hard the road may be; for without victory there is no survival. Let that be realised: no survival for the British Empire; no survival for all that the British Empire has stood for, no survival for the urge and impulse of the ages, that mankind will move forward towards its goal. But I take up my task with buoyancy and hope. I feel sure that our cause will not be suffered to fail among men. At this time I feel entitled to claim the aid of all, and I say, "Come, then, let us go forward together with our united strength."

Upon these simple issues the House voted unanimously, and adjourned till May 21.

＊　　＊　　＊

Thus then we all started on our common task. Never did a British Prime Minister receive from Cabinet colleagues the loyal and true aid which I enjoyed during the next five years from these men of all parties in the State. Parliament, while maintaining free and active criticism, gave continuous, overwhelming support to all measures proposed by the Government, and the nation was united and ardent as never before. It was well indeed that this should be so, because events were to come upon us of an order more terrible than anyone had foreseen.

24

CHAPTER II

THE BATTLE OF FRANCE

The First Week.   Gamelin

May 10—May 16

Plan D – The German Order of Battle – German and French Armour
– French and British Advance through Belgium – Holland Overrun –
The Belgian Problem – Accepted Primacy of France in the Military Art
– The Gap in the Ardennes – British Difficulties during the Twilight
War Phase – Progress of Plan D – Bad News of 13th and 14th –
Kleist's Group of Armies Break the French Front – Heavy British Air
Losses – Our Final Limit for Home Defence – Reynaud Telephones
Me Morning of 15th – Destruction of the French Ninth Army Opposite
the Ardennes Gap – "Cease Fire" in Holland – The Italian Menace –
I Fly to Paris – Meeting at the Quai d'Orsay – General Gamelin's
Statement – No Strategic Reserve: "Aucune" – Proposed Attacks on
the German "Bulge" – French Demands for More British Fighter
Squadrons – My Telegram to the Cabinet on the Night of May 16 –
Cabinet Agrees to Send Ten More Fighter Squadrons.

AT the moment in the evening of May 10 when I became
responsible no fresh decision about meeting the German
invasion of the Low Countries was required from me or
from my colleagues in the new and still unformed Administration.   We had long been assured that the French and British
staffs were fully agreed upon General Gamelin's Plan D, and
it had already been in action since dawn.   In fact, by the morning
of the 11th the whole vast operation had made great progress.
On the seaward flank General Giraud's Seventh French Army
had already begun its adventurous dash into Holland.   In the
centre the British armoured-car patrols of the 12th Lancers were
upon the river Dyle, and to the south of our front all the rest of

General Billotte's First Group of Armies were hastening forward to the Meuse. The opinion of the Allied military chiefs was that Plan D, if successful, would save anything from twelve to fifteen divisions by shortening the front against Germany; and then of course there was the Belgian Army of twenty-two divisions, besides the Dutch Army of ten divisions, without which our total forces in the West were numerically inferior. I did not therefore in the slightest degree wish to interfere with the military plans, and awaited with hope the impending shock.

Nevertheless, if in the after-light we look back upon the scene, the important paper written by the British Chiefs of Staff on September 18, 1939, becomes prominent.* In this it had been affirmed that unless the Belgians were effectively holding their front on the Meuse and the Albert Canal it would be wrong for the British and French to rush to their aid, but that they should rather stand firm on the French frontier, or at the most swing their left hand slightly forward to the line of the Scheldt. Since those days of September 1939 agreement had been reached to carry out General Gamelin's Plan D. Nothing had however happened in the interval to weaken the original view of the British Chiefs of Staff. On the contrary, much had happened to strengthen it. The German Army had grown in strength and maturity with every month that had passed, and they now had a vastly more powerful armour. The French Army, gnawed by Soviet-inspired Communism and chilled by the long, cheerless winter on the front, had actually deteriorated. The Belgian Government, staking their country's life upon Hitler's respect for international law and Belgian neutrality, had not achieved any effective joint planning between their Army chiefs and those of the Allies. The anti-tank obstacles and defensive line which were to have been prepared on the front Namur–Louvain were inadequate and unfinished. The Belgian Army, which contained many brave and resolute men, could hardly brace itself for a conflict for fear of offending neutrality. The Belgian front had been, in fact, overrun at many points by the first wave of German assault, even before General Gamelin gave the signal to execute his long-prepared plan. The most that could now be hoped for was success in that very "encounter battle" which the French High Command had declared itself resolved to avoid.

* See Book II, p. 73.

On the outbreak of the war eight months before, the main power of the German Army and Air Force had been concentrated on the invasion and conquest of Poland. Along the whole of the Western front, from Aix-la-Chapelle to the Swiss frontier, there had stood forty-two German divisions without armour. After the French mobilisation France could deploy the equivalent of seventy divisions opposite to them. For reasons which have been explained, it was not deemed possible to attack the Germans then. Very different was the situation on May 10, 1940. The enemy, profiting by the eight months' delay and by the destruction of Poland, had armed, equipped, and trained about 155 divisions, of which ten were armoured ("Panzer"). Hitler's agreement with Stalin had enabled him to reduce the German forces in the East to the smallest proportions. Opposite Russia, according to General Halder, the German Chief of Staff, there was "no more than a light covering force, scarcely fit for collecting customs duties". Without premonition of their own future, the Soviet Government watched the destruction of that "Second Front" in the West for which they were soon to call so vehemently and to wait in agony so long. Hitler was therefore in a position to deliver his onslaught on France with 126 divisions and the whole of the immense armour-weapon of ten Panzer divisions, comprising nearly three thousand armoured vehicles, of which a thousand at least were heavy tanks.

These mighty forces were deployed from the North Sea to Switzerland in the following order:

> *Army Group B*, comprising 28 divisions, under General von Bock, marshalled along the front from the North Sea to Aix-la-Chapelle, was to overrun Holland and Belgium, and thereafter advance into France as the German right wing.
>
> *Army Group A*, of 44 divisions, under General von Rundstedt, constituting the main thrust, was ranged along the front from Aix-la-Chapelle to the Moselle.
>
> *Army Group C*, of 17 divisions, under General von Leeb, held the Rhine from the Moselle to the Swiss frontier.

The O.K.H. (Supreme Army Command) Reserve consisted of about forty-seven divisions, of which twenty were in immediate reserve behind the various Army Groups and twenty-seven in general reserve.

Opposite this array, the exact strength and disposition of which was of course unknown to us, the First Group of Armies, under General Billotte, consisting of fifty-one divisions, of which nine were held in G.Q.G. (Grand-Quartier-Général Réserve), and including nine British divisions, stretched from the end of the Maginot Line near Longwy to the Belgian frontier, and behind that frontier to the sea in front of Dunkirk. The Second and Third Groups of Armies, under Generals Prételat and Besson, consisting, with the reserves, of forty-three divisions, guarded the French frontier from Longwy to Switzerland. In addition the French had the equivalent of nine divisions occupying the Maginot Line—a total of 103 divisions. If the armies of Belgium and Holland became involved, this number would be increased by twenty-two Belgian and ten Dutch divisions. As both these countries were immediately attacked, the grand total of Allied divisions of all qualities nominally available on May 10 was therefore 135, or practically the same number as we now know the enemy possessed. Properly organised and equipped, well trained and led, this force should, according to the standards of the previous war, have had a good chance of bringing the invasion to a stop.

However, the Germans had full freedom to choose the moment, the direction, and the strength of their attack. More than half of the French Army stood on the southern and eastern sectors of France, and the fifty-one French and British divisions of General Billotte's Army Group No. 1, with whatever Belgian and Dutch aid was forthcoming, had to face the onslaught of upwards of seventy hostile divisions under Bock and Rundstedt between Longwy and the sea. The combination of the almost cannon-proof tank and dive-bomber aircraft which had proved so successful in Poland on a smaller scale was again to form the spearhead of the main attack, and a group of five Panzer and three motorised divisions under Kleist, included in German Army Group A, was directed through the Ardennes on Sedan and Monthermé.

To meet such modern forms of war the French deployed about 2,300 tanks, mostly light. Their armoured formations included some powerful modern types, but more than half their total armoured strength was held in dispersed battalions of light tanks, for co-operation with the infantry. Their six armoured divisions,*

* This figure includes the so-called light motorised divisions, which possessed tanks.

THE FORWARD MOVEMENTS STARTING 10 MAY

with which alone they could have countered the massed Panzer assault, were widely distributed over the front, and could not be collected together to operate in coherent action. Britain, the birthplace of the tank, had only just completed the formation and training of her first armoured division (328 tanks), which was still in England.

The German fighter aircraft now concentrated in the West were far superior to the French in numbers and quality. The British Air Force in France comprised the ten fighter squadrons (Hurricanes) which could be spared from vital Home Defence, eight squadrons of Battles, six of Blenheims, and five of Lysanders. Neither the French nor the British air authorities had equipped themselves with dive-bombers, which at this time, as in Poland, became prominent, and were to play an important part in the

29

demoralisation of the French infantry and particularly of their coloured troops.

During the night of May 9–10, heralded by widespread air attacks against airfields, communications, headquarters, and magazines, all the German forces in the Bock and Rundstedt Army Groups sprang forward towards France across the frontiers of Belgium, Holland, and Luxembourg. Complete tactical surprise was achieved in nearly every case. Out of the darkness came suddenly innumerable parties of well-armed, ardent storm troops, often with light artillery, and long before daybreak a hundred and fifty miles of front were aflame. Holland and Belgium, assaulted without the slightest pretext or warning, cried aloud for help. The Dutch had trusted to their water-line; all the sluices not seized or betrayed were opened, and the Dutch frontier guards fired upon the invaders. The Belgians succeeded in destroying the bridges of the Meuse, but the Germans captured intact two across the Albert Canal.

By Plan D, the First Allied Army Group, under General Billotte, with its small but very fine British army, was, from the moment when the Germans violated the frontier, to advance east into Belgium. It was intended to forestall the enemy and stand on the line Meuse–Louvain–Antwerp. In front of that line, along the Meuse and the Albert Canal, lay the main Belgian forces. Should these stem the first German onrush the Army Group would support them. It seemed more probable that the Belgians would be at once thrown back on to the Allied line. And this, in fact, happened. It was assumed that in this case the Belgian resistance would give a short breathing-space, during which the French and British could organise their new position. Except on the critical front of the French Ninth Army, this was accomplished. On the extreme left or seaward flank the Seventh French Army was to seize the islands commanding the mouth of the Scheldt, and, if possible, to assist the Dutch by an advance towards Breda. It was thought that on our southern flank the Ardennes constituted an impassable barrier, and south of that again began the regular fortified Maginot Line, stretching out to the Rhine and along the Rhine to Switzerland. All therefore seemed to depend upon the forward left-handed counter-stroke of the Allied Northern Armies. This again hung upon the speed with which Belgium could be occupied. Everything had been worked out in this way with the utmost detail, and only a signal was necessary to hurl forward the Allied force of well over a million men. At 5.30 a.m. on May 10 Lord Gort received a message from General Georges ordering "Alertes 1, 2, and 3"; namely, instant readiness to move into Belgium. At 6.45 a.m. General Gamelin ordered the execution of Plan D, and the long-prepared scheme of the French High Command, to which the British had subordinated themselves, came at once into action.

* * *

Mr. Colijn, when as Dutch Prime Minister he visited me in 1937, had explained to me the marvellous efficiency of the Dutch inundations. He could, he explained, by a telephone message from the luncheon table at Chartwell press a button which would confront an invader with impassable water obstacles. But all this was nonsense. The power of a great State against a small one under modern conditions is overwhelming. The Germans broke through at every point, bridging the canals or seizing the locks and water-controls. In a single day all the outer line of the Dutch defences was mastered. At the same time the German Air Force began to use its might upon a defenceless country. Rotterdam was reduced to a blazing ruin. The Hague, Utrecht, and Amsterdam were threatened with the same fate. The Dutch hope that they would be by-passed by the German right-handed swing as in the former war was vain.

However, when the blow fell the Dutch nation instantly rallied to the cause with indomitable courage. Queen Wilhelmina, her family, and the members of her Government were safely brought to England by the Royal Navy, and continued from here to inspire their people and to manage their vast empire overseas. The Queen's Navy and her great merchant fleet were placed unreservedly under British control, and played a redoubtable part in Allied affairs.

The case of Belgium requires more searching statement. Several hundreds of thousands of British and French graves in Belgium mark the struggle of the previous war. The policy of Belgium in the years between the wars had not taken sufficient account of the past. The Belgian leaders saw with worried eyes the internal weakness of France and the vacillating pacifism of Britain. They clung to a strict neutrality. In the years before they were again invaded their attitude towards the two mighty arrays which confronted each other was, officially at any rate, quite impartial. Great allowance must be made for the fearful problems of a small State in such a plight, but the French High Command had for years spoken bitterly of the line taken by the Belgian Government. Their only chance of defending their frontier against a German attack lay in a close alliance with France and Britain. The line of the Albert Canal and other water fronts was highly defensible, and had the British and French armies, aided by the Belgian Army, after the declaration of war, been drawn up on the Belgian frontiers in good time a very strong offensive might have been prepared and launched from these positions against Germany. But the Belgian Government deemed that their safety lay in the most rigid neutrality, and their only hope was founded on German good faith and respect for treaties.

Even after Britain and France had entered into war it was impossible to persuade them to rejoin the old alliance. They declared they would defend their neutrality to the death, and placed nine-tenths of their forces on their German frontier, while at the same time they strictly forbade the Anglo-French army to enter their country and make effective preparations for their defence or for forestalling counter-strokes. The construction of new lines and the anti-tank ditch during the winter of 1939 by the British armies, with the French First Army on their right, along the Franco-Belgian frontier, had been the only measure open to us. It is a haunting question whether the whole policy of Plan D should not have been reviewed upon this basis, and whether we would not have been wiser to stand and fight on the French frontier, and amid these strong defences invite the Belgian Army to fall back upon them, rather than make the hazardous and hurried forward leap to the Dyle or the Albert Canal.

* * *

No one can understand the decisions of that period without realising the immense authority wielded by the French military leaders and the belief of every French officer that France had the primacy in the military art. France had conducted and carried the main weight of the terrible land fighting from 1914 to 1918. She had lost fourteen hundred thousand men killed. Foch had been given the supreme command, and the great British and Imperial armies of sixty to seventy divisions had been placed, like the Americans, unreservedly under his orders. Now the British

The Invasion of Belgium and Holland

1 Holland flooded.
2 The Germans ford a river in Belgium.

3 A French plane shot down in Belgium, 14th May, 1940.
4 The exodus of the Belgium population.

5 The bombing of the aerodrome at Gilze-Rijen (Holland).

6 A Belgian house on fire after a bombardment.

Expeditionary Army numbered but three or four hundred thousand men, spread from the bases at Havre and along the coast forward to the line, compared with nearly a hundred French divisions, or over two million Frenchmen, actually holding the long front from Belgium to Switzerland. It was natural therefore that we should place ourselves under their command, and that their judgment should be accepted. It had been expected that General Georges would take full command of the French and British armies in the field from the moment when war was declared, and General Gamelin was expected to retire to an advisory position on the French Military Council. However, General Gamelin was averse from yielding his control as Generalissimo. He retained the supreme direction. A vexatious conflict of authority took place between him and General Georges during the eight months' lull. General Georges, in my opinion, never had the chance to make the strategic plan in its entirety and on his own responsibility.

The British General Staff and our headquarters in the field had long been anxious about the gap between the northern end of the Maginot Line and the beginning of the British fortified front along the Franco-Belgian frontier. Mr. Hore-Belisha, the Secretary of State for War, raised the point in the War Cabinet on several occasions. Representations were made through military channels. The Cabinet and our military leaders however were naturally shy of criticising those whose armies were ten times as strong as our own. The French thought that the Ardennes were impassable for large modern armies. Marshal Pétain had told the Senate Army Commission, "This sector is not dangerous." A great deal of field work was done along the Meuse, but nothing like a strong line of pill-boxes and anti-tank obstacles, such as the British had made along the Belgian sector, was attempted. Moreover, General Corap's Ninth French Army was mainly composed of troops who were definitely below the French standards. Out of its nine divisions, two were of cavalry, partly mechanised, one was a fortress division, two (61 and 53) belonged to a secondary category, two (22 and 18) were not much inferior to active divisions; only two were divisions of the permanent regular army. Here, then, from Sedan to Hirson, on the Oise, along a front of fifty miles, there were no permanent fortifications, and only two divisions of professional troops.

One cannot be strong everywhere. It is often right and necessary to hold long sectors of a frontier with light covering forces, but this of course should be only with the object of gathering larger reserves for counter-attacks when the enemy's striking-points are revealed. The spreading of forty-three divisions, or half the mobile French army, from Longwy to the Swiss frontier, the whole of which was either defended by the Maginot Line forts or by the broad, swift-flowing Rhine, with its own fortress system behind it, was an improvident disposition. The risks that have to be run by the defender are more trying than those which an assailant, who is presumably the stronger at the point of attack, must dare. Where very long fronts are concerned, they can only be met by strong mobile reserves which can rapidly intervene in a decisive battle. A weight of opinion supports the criticism that the French reserves were inadequate, and, such as they were, badly distributed. After all, the gap behind the Ardennes opened the shortest road from Germany to Paris, and had for centuries been a famous battleground. If the enemy penetrated here the whole forward movement of the Northern Armies would be deprived of its pivot, and all their communications would be endangered equally with the capital.

Looking back, we can see that Mr. Chamberlain's War Cabinet, in which I served, and for whose acts or neglects I take my full share of responsibility, ought not to have been deterred from thrashing the matter out with the French in the autumn and winter of 1939. It would have been an unpleasant and difficult argument, for the French at every stage could say: "Why do you not send more troops of your own? Will you not take over a wider sector of the front? If reserves are lacking, pray supply them. We have five million men mobilised.* We follow your ideas about the war at sea; we conform to the plans of the British Admiralty. Pray show a proper confidence in the French Army and in our historic mastery of the art of war on land."

Nevertheless we ought to have done it.

Hitler and his Generals were in little doubt as to the military views and general arrangements of their opponents. During this same autumn and winter the German factories had poured out tanks, the plants for making which must have been well

---

* The French "mobilisation" of five millions included many not under arms—*e.g.*, in factories, on the land, etc.

advanced at the Munich crisis in 1938, and bore abundant fruit in the eight months that had passed since war began. They were not at all deterred by the physical difficulties of traversing the Ardennes. On the contrary, they believed that modern mechanical transport and vast organised road-making capacity would make this region, hitherto deemed impassable, the shortest, surest, and easiest method of penetrating France and of rupturing the whole French scheme of counter-attack. Accordingly, the German Supreme Army Command planned their enormous onrush through the Ardennes to sever the curling left arm of the Allied Northern Armies at the shoulder-joint. The movement, though on a far larger scale and with different speeds and weapons, was not unlike Napoleon's thrust at the Plateau of Pratzen in the Battle of Austerlitz, whereby the entire Austro-Russian turning move was cut off and ruined and their centre broken.

* * *

At the signal the Northern Armies sprang to the rescue of Belgium and poured forward along all the roads amid the cheers of the inhabitants. The first phase of Plan D was completed by May 12. The French held the left bank of the Meuse to Huy, and their light forces beyond the river were falling back before increasing enemy pressure. The armoured divisions of the French First Army reached the line Huy–Hannut–Tirlemont. The Belgians, having lost the Albert Canal, were falling back to the line of the river Gette and taking up their prescribed position from Antwerp to Louvain. They still held Liége and Namur. The French Seventh Army had occupied the islands of Walcheren and South Beveland, and were engaged with mechanised units of the German Eighteenth Army on the line Herenthals-Bergen-op-Zoom. So rapid had been the advance of the French Seventh Army that it had already outrun its ammunition supplies. The superiority in quality though not in numbers of the British Air Force was already apparent. Thus up till the night of the 12th there was no reason to suppose that the operations were not going well.

However, during the 13th Lord Gort's headquarters became aware of the weight of the German thrust on the front of the French Ninth Army. By nightfall the enemy had established themselves on the west bank of the Meuse, on either side of Dinant and Sedan. The French G.Q.G. (Grand-Quartier-Général) were not yet certain whether the main German effort was directed through Luxembourg against the left of the Maginot Line or through Maastricht towards Brussels. Along the whole front Louvain–Namur–Dinant to Sedan an intense, heavy battle had developed, but under conditions which General Gamelin had not contemplated, for at Dinant the French Ninth Army had no time to install themselves before the enemy was upon them.

*   *   *

During the 14th the bad news began to come in. At first all was vague. At 7 p.m. I read to the Cabinet a message received from M. Reynaud stating that the Germans had broken through at Sedan, that the French were unable to resist the combination of tanks and dive-bombing, and asking for ten more squadrons of fighters to re-establish the line. Other messages received by the Chiefs of Staff gave similar information, and added that both Generals Gamelin and Georges took a serious view of the situation and that General Gamelin was surprised at the rapidity of the enemy's advance. In fact, Kleist's Group, with its immense mass of armour, heavy and light, had completely scattered or destroyed the French troops on their immediate front, and could now move forward at a pace never before known in war. At almost all points where the armies had come in contact the weight and fury of the German attack was overpowering. They crossed the Meuse in the Dinant sector with two more armoured divisions. To the north the fighting on the front of the French First Army had been most severe. The Ist and IInd British Corps were still in position from Wavre to Louvain, where our 3rd Division, under General Montgomery, had had sharp fighting. Farther north the Belgians were retiring to the Antwerp defences. The French Seventh Army, on the seaward flank, was recoiling even quicker than it had advanced.

From the moment of the invasion we began Operation "Royal Marine", the launching of the fluvial mines into the Rhine, and in the first week of the battle nearly 1,700 were "streamed".* They produced immediate results. Practically all river traffic between Karlsruhe and Mainz was suspended, and extensive damage was done to the Karlsruhe barrage and a number of

* Operation "Royal Marine" was first planned in November 1939. The mines were designed to float down the Rhine and destroy enemy bridges and shipping. They were fed into the river from French territory upstream. See Book II, App. L.

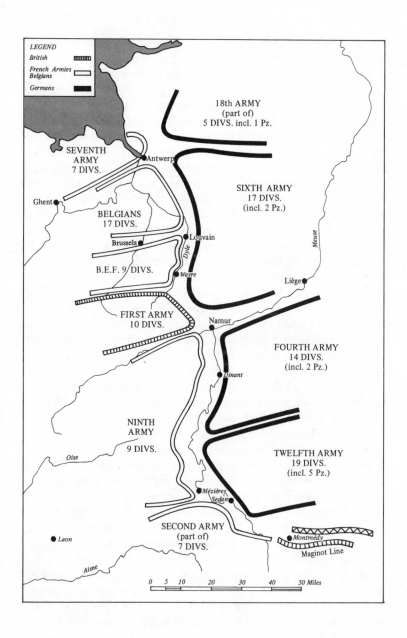

LEGEND

British

French Armies
Belgians

Germans

18th ARMY
(part of)
5 DIVS. incl. 1 Pz.

SEVENTH
ARMY
7 DIVS.

Antwerp

SIXTH ARMY
17 DIVS.
(incl. 2 Pz.)

Ghent

BELGIANS
17 DIVS.

Meuse

Louvain

Brussels

Dyle

B.E.F. 9 DIVS.

Wavre

Liège

FIRST ARMY
10 DIVS.

Namur

FOURTH ARMY
14 DIVS.
(incl. 2 Pz.)

Dinant

NINTH
ARMY

9 DIVS.

Oise

TWELFTH ARMY
19 DIVS.
(incl. 5 Pz.)

Mézières
Sedan

SECOND ARMY
(part of)
7 DIVS.

Laon

Montmédy

Maginot Line

Aisne

0   5   10   20   30   40   50 Miles

THE OPPOSING FORCES, 13 MAY

pontoon bridges. The success of this device was however lost in the deluge of disaster.

All the British air squadrons fought continuously, their principal effort being against the pontoon bridges in the Sedan area. Several of these were destroyed and others damaged in desperate and devoted attacks. The losses in the low-level attacks on the bridges from the German anti-aircraft artillery were cruel. In one case, of six aircraft only one returned from the successful task. On this day alone we lost a total of sixty-seven machines, and, being engaged principally with the enemy's anti-aircraft forces, accounted for only fifty-three German aircraft. That night there remained in France of the Royal Air Force only 206 serviceable aircraft out of 474.

This detailed information came only gradually to hand. But it was already clear that the continuance of fighting on this scale would soon completely consume the British Air Force in spite of its individual ascendancy. The hard question of how much we could send from Britain without leaving ourselves defenceless and thus losing the power to continue the war pressed itself henceforward upon us. Our own natural promptings and many weighty military arguments lent force to the incessant, vehement French appeals. On the other hand, there was a limit, and that limit if transgressed would cost us our life.

At this time all these issues were discussed by the whole War Cabinet, which met several times a day. Air Chief Marshal Dowding, at the head of our metropolitan Fighter Command, had declared to me that with twenty-five squadrons of fighters he would defend the Island against the whole might of the German Air Force, but that with less he would be overpowered. Defeat would have entailed not only the destruction of all our airfields and our air-power, but of the aircraft factories on which our whole future hung. My colleagues and I were resolved to run all risks for the sake of the battle up to that limit—and those risks were very great—but not to go beyond it, no matter what the consequences might be.

About half-past seven on the morning of the 15th I was woken up with the news that M. Reynaud was on the telephone at my bedside. He spoke in English, and evidently under stress. "We have been defeated." As I did not immediately respond he said again: "We are beaten; we have lost the battle." I said: "Surely it can't have happened so soon?" But he replied: "The front is broken near Sedan; they are pouring through in great numbers with tanks and armoured cars"—or words to that effect. I then said: "All experience shows that the offensive will come to an end after a while. I remember the 21st of March, 1918. After five or six days they have to halt for supplies, and the opportunity for counter-attack is presented. I learned all this at the time from the lips of Marshal Foch himself." Certainly this was what we had always seen in the past and what we ought to have seen now. However, the French Premier came back to the sentence with which he had begun, which proved indeed only too true: "We are defeated; we have lost the battle." I said I was willing to come over and have a talk.

On this day the French Ninth Army, Corap's, was in a state of complete dissolution, and its remnants were divided up between General Giraud, of the Seventh French Army, who took over from Corap in the north, and the headquarters of the Sixth French Army, which was forming in the south. A gap of some fifty miles had in fact been punched in the French line, through which the vast mass of enemy armour was pouring. By the evening of the 15th German armoured cars were reported to be in Liart and Montcornet, the latter sixty miles behind the original front. The French First Army was also pierced on a 5,000-yards front south of Limal. Farther north all attacks on the British were repulsed. The German attack and the retirement of the French division on their right compelled the making of a British defensive flank facing south. The French Seventh Army had retreated into the Antwerp defences west of the Scheldt, and was being driven out of the islands of Walcheren and South Beveland.

On this day also the struggle in Holland came to an end. Owing to the capitulation of the Dutch High Command at 11 a.m., only a very few Dutch troops could be evacuated.

Of course this picture presented a general impression of defeat. I had seen a good deal of this sort of thing in the previous war, and the idea of the line being broken, even on a broad front, did not convey to my mind the appalling consequences that now flowed from it. Not having had access to official information for so many years, I did not comprehend the violence of the revolution effected since the last war by the incursion of a mass of fast-moving heavy armour. I knew about it, but it had not altered my inward convictions as it should have done. There was nothing I could have done if it had. I rang up General Georges, who seemed quite cool, and reported that the breach at Sedan was being plugged. A telegram from General Gamelin also stated that although the position between Namur and Sedan was serious he viewed the situation with calm. I reported Reynaud's message and other news to the Cabinet at 11 a.m.

On the 16th the German spearheads stood along the line La Capelle–Vervins–Marle–Laon, and the vanguards of the German XIVth Corps were in support at Montcornet and Neufchâtel-sur-Aisne. The fall of Laon confirmed the penetration of over sixty miles inward upon us from the frontier near Sedan. Under this threat and the ever-increasing pressure on their own front, the First French Army and the British Expeditionary Force were ordered to withdraw in three stages to the Scheldt. Although none of these details were available even to the War Office, and no clear view could be formed of what was happening, the gravity of the crisis was obvious. I felt it imperative to go to Paris that afternoon.

*   *   *

We had to expect that the disastrous events on the front would bring new foes upon us. Although there were no indications of a change in Italian policy, the Minister of Shipping was given instructions to thin out the shipping in the Mediterranean. No more British ships were to come homewards from Aden. We had already diverted round the Cape the first convoy carrying Australian troops to England. The Defence Committee were instructed to consider action in the event of war with Italy, particularly with regard to Crete. Schemes for evacuating civilians from Aden and Gibraltar were put into operation.

*   *   *

At about 3 p.m. I flew to Paris in a "Flamingo", a Government passenger plane, of which there were three. General Dill, Vice-Chief of the Imperial General Staff, came with me, and Ismay.

It was a good machine, very comfortable, and making about 160 miles an hour. As it was unarmed, an escort was provided, but we soared off into a rain-cloud and reached Le Bourget in little more than an hour. From the moment we got out of the "Flamingo" it was obvious that the situation was incomparably worse than we had imagined. The officers who met us told General Ismay that the Germans were expected in Paris in a few

GERMAN ADVANCES ON SUCCESSIVE DAYS
13-17 MAY 1940

days at most. After hearing at the Embassy about the position, I drove to the Quai d'Orsay, arriving at five-thirty o'clock. I was conducted into one of its fine rooms. Reynaud was there, Daladier, Minister of National Defence and War, and General Gamelin. Everybody was standing. At no time did we sit down around a table. Utter dejection was written on every face. In front of Gamelin on a student's easel was a map, about two yards square, with a black ink line purporting to show the Allied front. In this line there was drawn a small but sinister bulge at Sedan.

The Commander-in-Chief briefly explained what had happened. North and south of Sedan, on a front of fifty or sixty miles, the Germans had broken through. The French army in front of them was destroyed or scattered. A heavy onrush of armoured vehicles was advancing with unheard-of speed towards Amiens and Arras, with the intention, apparently, of reaching the coast at Abbeville or thereabouts. Alternatively they might make for Paris. Behind the armour, he said, eight or ten German divisions, all motorised, were driving onwards, making flanks for themselves as they advanced against the two disconnected French armies on either side. The General talked perhaps five minutes without anyone saying a word. When he stopped there was a considerable silence. I then asked: "Where is the strategic reserve?" and, breaking into French, which I used indifferently (in every sense): "*Où est la masse de manœuvre?*" General Gamelin turned to me and, with a shake of the head and a shrug, said: "*Aucune.*"

There was another long pause. Outside in the garden of the Quai d'Orsay clouds of smoke arose from large bonfires, and I saw from the window venerable officials pushing wheel-barrows of archives on to them. Already therefore the evacuation of Paris was being prepared.

Past experience carries with its advantages the drawback that things never happen the same way again. Otherwise I suppose life would be too easy. After all, we had often had our fronts broken before; always we had been able to pull things together and wear down the momentum of the assault. But here were two new factors that I had never expected to have to face. First, the overrunning of the whole of the communications and countryside by an irresistible incursion of armoured vehicles, and secondly NO STRATEGIC RESERVE. "*Aucune.*" I was dumbfounded. What were we to think of the great French Army and its highest chiefs? It had never occurred to me that any commanders having to defend five hundred miles of engaged front would have left themselves unprovided with a mass of manœuvre. No one can defend with certainty so wide a front; but when the enemy has committed himself to a major thrust which breaks the line one can always have, one *must* always have, a mass of divisions which marches up in vehement counter-attack at the moment when the first fury of the offensive has spent its force.

What was the Maginot Line for? It should have economised troops upon a large sector of the frontier, not only offering many sally-ports for local counter-strokes, but also enabling large forces to be held in reserve; and this is the only way these things can be done. But now there was no reserve. I admit this was one of the greatest surprises I have had in my life. Why had I not known more about it, even though I had been so busy at the Admiralty? Why had the British Government, and the War Office above all, not known more about it? It was no excuse that the French High Command would not impart their dispositions to us or to Lord Gort except in vague outline. We had a right to know. We ought to have insisted. Both armies were fighting in the line together. I went back again to the window and the curling wreaths of smoke from the bonfires of the State documents of the French Republic. Still the old gentlemen were bringing up their wheelbarrows, and industriously casting their contents into the flames.

There was a considerable conversation in changing groups around the principals, of which M. Reynaud has published a detailed record. I am represented as urging that there should be no withdrawal of the Northern Armies, that on the contrary they should counter-attack. Certainly this was my mood. But here was no considered military opinion.* It must be remembered

* As other accounts of what passed have appeared, I asked Lord Ismay, who was at my side throughout, to give his recollection. He writes:

"We did not sit round a table, and much may have been said as we walked about in groups. I am positive that you did not express any 'considered military opinion' on what should be done. When we left London we considered the break-through at Sedan serious, but not mortal. There had been many 'break-throughs' in 1914-18, but they had all been stopped, generally by counter-attacks from one or both sides of the salient.

"When you realised that the French High Command felt that all was lost, you asked Gamelin a number of questions, with, I believe, the dual object, first of informing yourself as to what had happened and what he proposed to do, and secondly of stopping the panic. One of these questions was: 'When and where are you going to counter-attack the flanks of the Bulge? From the north or from the south?' I am sure that you did not press any particular strategical or tactical thought upon the conference. The burden of your song was: 'Things may be bad, but are certainly not incurable.' "

that this was the first realisation we had of the magnitude of the disaster or of the apparent French despair. We were not conducting the operations, and our army, which was only a tenth of the troops on the front, was serving under the French command. I and the British officers with me were staggered at the evident conviction of the French Commander-in-Chief and leading Ministers that all was lost, and in anything that I said I was reacting violently against this. There is however no doubt that they were quite right, and that the most rapid retreat to the south was imperative. This soon became obvious to all.

Presently General Gamelin was speaking again. He was discussing whether forces should now be gathered to strike at the flanks of the penetration, or "Bulge", as we called such things later on. Eight or nine divisions were being withdrawn from quiet parts of the front, the Maginot Line; there were two or three armoured divisions which had not been engaged; eight or nine more divisions were being brought from Africa and would arrive in the battle zone during the next fortnight or three weeks. General Giraud had been placed in command of the French army north of the gap. The Germans would advance henceforward through a corridor between two fronts on which warfare in the fashion of 1917 and 1918 could be waged. Perhaps the Germans could not maintain the corridor, with its ever-increasing double flank-guards to be built up, and at the same time nourish their armoured incursion. Something in this sense Gamelin seemed to say, and all this was quite sound. I was conscious however that it carried no conviction in this small but hitherto influential and responsible company. Presently I asked General Gamelin when and where he proposed to attack the flanks of the Bulge. His reply was: "Inferiority of numbers, inferiority of equipment, inferiority of method"—and then a hopeless shrug of the shoulders. There was no argument; there was no need of argument. And where were we British anyway, having regard to our tiny contribution—ten divisions after eight months of war, and not even one modern tank division in action?

This was the last I saw of General Gamelin. He was a patriotic, well-meaning man and skilled in his profession, and no doubt he has his tale to tell.*

* * *

* His book entitled *Servir* throws little light either upon his personal conduct of events or generally upon the course of the war.

The burden of General Gamelin's, and indeed of all the French High Command's subsequent remarks, was insistence on their inferiority in the air and earnest entreaties for more squadrons of the Royal Air Force, bomber as well as fighter, but chiefly the latter. This prayer for fighter support was destined to be repeated at every subsequent conference until France fell. In the course of his appeal General Gamelin said that fighters were needed not only to give cover to the French Army, but also to stop the German tanks. At this I said: "No. It is the business of the artillery to stop the tanks. The business of the fighters is to cleanse the skies [*nettoyer le ciel*] over the battle." It was vital that our metropolitan fighter air force should not be drawn out of Britain on any account. Our existence turned on this. Nevertheless it was necessary to cut to the bone. In the morning, before I started, the Cabinet had given me authority to move four more squadrons of fighters to France. On our return to the Embassy, and after talking it over with Dill, I decided to ask sanction for the dispatch of six more. This would leave us with only the twenty-five fighter squadrons at home, and that was the final limit. It was a rending decision either way. I told General Ismay to telephone to London that the Cabinet should assemble at once to consider an urgent telegram which would be sent over in the course of the next hour or so. Ismay did this in Hindustani, having previously arranged for an Indian Army officer to be standing by in his office. This was my telegram:

9 p.m. 16th May, 1940

I shall be glad if the Cabinet could meet immediately to consider following. Situation grave in the last degree. Furious German thrust through Sedan finds French armies ill-grouped, many in north, others in Alsace. At least four days required to bring twenty divisions to cover Paris and strike at the flanks of the Bulge, which is now fifty kilometres wide.

Three [German] armoured divisions with two or three infantry divisions have advanced through gap and large masses hurrying forward behind them. Two great dangers therefore threaten. First that B.E.F. will be largely left in the air to make a difficult disengagement and retreat to the old line. Secondly, that the German thrust will wear down the French resistance before it can be fully gathered.

Orders given to defend Paris at all costs, but archives of the Quai d'Orsay already burning in the garden. I consider the next two, three, or four days decisive for Paris and probably for the French Army.

45

Therefore the question we must face is whether we can give further aid in fighters above four squadrons, for which the French are very grateful, and whether a larger part of our long-range heavy bombers should be employed to-morrow and the following nights upon the German masses crossing the Meuse and flowing into the Bulge. Even so results cannot be guaranteed; but the French resistance may be broken up as rapidly as that of Poland unless this Battle of the Bulge is won. I personally feel that we should send squadrons of fighters demanded (*i.e.*, six more) to-morrow, and, concentrating all available French and British aviation, dominate the air above the Bulge for the next two or three days, not for any local purpose, but to give the last chance to the French Army to rally its bravery and strength. It would not be good historically if their requests were denied and their ruin resulted. Also night bombardment by a strong force of heavy bombers can no doubt be arranged. It looks as if the enemy was by now fully extended both in the air and tanks. We must not underrate the increasing difficulties of his advance if strongly counter-attacked. I imagine that if all fails here we could still shift what is left of our own air striking force to assist the B.E.F. should it be forced to withdraw. I again emphasise the mortal gravity of the hour, and express my opinion as above. Kindly inform me what you will do. Dill agrees. I must have answer by midnight in order to encourage the French. Telephone to Ismay at Embassy in Hindustani.

The reply came at about eleven-thirty. The Cabinet said "Yes." I immediately took Ismay off with me in a car to M. Reynaud's flat. We found it more or less in darkness. After an interval M. Reynaud emerged from his bedroom in his dressing-gown and I told him the favourable news. Ten fighter squadrons! I then persuaded him to send for M. Daladier, who was duly summoned and brought to the flat to hear the decision of the British Cabinet. In this way I hoped to revive the spirits of our French friends, as much as our limited means allowed. Daladier never spoke a word. He rose slowly from his chair and wrung my hand. I got back to the Embassy about 2 a.m., and slept well, though the cannon fire in petty aeroplane raids made one roll over from time to time. In the morning I flew home, and, in spite of other preoccupations, pressed on with the construction of the second level of the new Government.

CHAPTER III

THE BATTLE OF FRANCE
The Second Week.   Weygand
May 17—May 24

The Battle Crisis Grows – The Local Defence Volunteers – Reinforcements from the East – My Telegrams to the President of May 18 and May 20 – General Gamelin's Final Order No. 12, May 19 – French Cabinet Changes – General Weygand Appointed – First Orders to the Little Ships, May 20 – Operation "Dynamo" – Weygand Tours the Front – Billotte Killed in a Motor Accident – French Failure to Grapple with German Armour – Ironside's Report, May 21 – Parliament Votes Extraordinary Powers to the Government – My Second Visit to Paris – Weygand's Plan – Peril of the Northern Armies – Fighting round Arras – Correspondence with M. Reynaud – Sir John Dill Chief of the Imperial General Staff.

THE War Cabinet met at 10 a.m. on the 17th, and I gave them an account of my visit to Paris, and of the situation so far as I could measure it.

I said I had told the French that unless they made a supreme effort we should not be justified in accepting the grave risk to the safety of our country that we were incurring by the dispatch of the additional fighter squadrons to France. I felt that the question of air reinforcements was one of the gravest that a British Cabinet had ever had to face. It was claimed that the German air losses had been four or five times our own, but I had been told that the French had only a quarter of their fighter aircraft left. On this day Gamelin thought the situation "lost", and is reported to have said: "I will guarantee the safety of Paris only for to-day, to-morrow [the 18th], and the night following." In Norway it appeared that Narvik was likely to be captured by us at any moment, but Lord Cork was informed that in the light of the news from France no more reinforcements could be sent to him.

The battle crisis grew hourly in intensity. At the request of General Georges the British Army prolonged its defensive flank by occupying points on the whole line from Douai to Péronne, thus attempting to cover Arras, which was a road-centre vital to any southward retreat. That afternoon the Germans entered Brussels. The next day they reached Cambrai, passed St. Quentin, and brushed our small parties out of Péronne. The French Seventh, the Belgian, the British, and the French First Army all continued their withdrawal to the Scheldt, the British standing along the Dendre for the day, and forming the detachment "Petreforce" (a temporary grouping of various units under Major-General Petre) for the defence of Arras.

At midnight (May 18–19) Lord Gort was visited at his headquarters by General Billotte. Neither the personality of this French General nor his proposals, such as they were, inspired confidence in his allies. From this moment the possibility of a withdrawal to the coast began to present itself to the British Commander-in-Chief. In his dispatch published in March 1941 he wrote: "The picture was now [night of the 19th] no longer that of a line bent or temporarily broken, but of a besieged fortress."

As the result of my visit to Paris and the Cabinet discussions I already found it necessary to pose a general question to my colleagues.

Prime Minister to Lord President   17.V.40

I am very much obliged to you for undertaking to examine to-night the consequences of the withdrawal of the French Government from Paris or the fall of that city, as well as the problems which would arise if it were necessary to withdraw the B.E.F. from France, either along its communications or by the Belgian and Channel ports. It is quite understood that in the first instance this report could be no more than an enumeration of the main considerations which arise, and which could thereafter be remitted to the Staffs. I am myself seeing the military authorities at 6.30.

*   *   *

The swift fate of Holland was in all our minds. Mr. Eden had already proposed to the War Cabinet the formation of Local Defence Volunteers, and this plan was energetically pressed. All over the country, in every town and village, bands of determined men came together armed with shot-guns, sporting rifles, clubs, and spears. From this a vast organisation was soon to spring. But the need of Regulars was also vital.

Prime Minister to General Ismay, for C.O.S.   18.v.40

1. I cannot feel that we have enough trustworthy troops in England, in view of the very large numbers that may be landed from air-carriers preceded by parachutists. I do not consider this danger is imminent at the present time, as the great battle in France has yet to be decided.

I wish the following moves to be considered with a view to immediate action:

(i) The transports which brought the Australians to Suez should bring home eight battalions of Regular infantry from Palestine, properly convoyed, even at some risk, by whatever route is thought best. I hope it will be possible to use the Mediterranean.

(ii) The Australian fast convoy arrives early in June with 14,000 men.

(iii) These ships should be immediately filled with eight battalions of Territorials and sent to India, where they should pick up eight [more] Regular battalions. The speed of this fast convoy should be accelerated.

2. Everything must be done to carry out the recommendations for the control of aliens put forward by the Committee and minuted by me on another paper. Action should also be taken against Communists and Fascists, and very considerable numbers should be put in protective or preventive internment, including the leaders. These measures must, of course, be brought before the Cabinet before action.

3. The Chiefs of Staff must consider whether it would not be well to send only half of the so-called Armoured Division to France. One must always be prepared for the fact that the French may be offered very advantageous terms of peace, and the whole weight be thrown on us.

*   *   *

I also thought it necessary, with the approval of my colleagues, to send the following grave telegrams to President Roosevelt in order to show how seriously the interests of the United States would be affected by the conquest and subjugation not only of France but of Great Britain. The Cabinet pondered over these drafts for a while, but made no amendment.

Former Naval Person to President Roosevelt   18.v.40

I do not need to tell you about the gravity of what has happened. We are determined to persevere to the very end, whatever the result

SITUATION, EVENING 18 MAY

of the great battle raging in France may be. We must expect in any
case to be attacked here on the Dutch model before very long, and we
hope to give a good account of ourselves. But if American assistance
is to play any part it must be available soon.

Former Naval Person to President Roosevelt   20.V.40

Lothian has reported his conversation with you. I understand your
difficulties, but I am very sorry about the destroyers. If they were
here in six weeks they would play an invaluable part. The battle in
France is full of danger to both sides. Though we have taken heavy
toll of the enemy in the air and are clawing down two or three to one
of their planes, they have still a formidable numerical superiority.
Our most vital need is, therefore, the delivery at the earliest possible
date of the largest possible number of Curtiss P.40 fighters, now in
course of delivery to your Army.

With regard to the closing part of your talk with Lothian, our intention is, whatever happens, to fight on to the end in this Island, and, provided we can get the help for which we ask, we hope to run them very close in the air battles in view of individual superiority. Members of the present Administration would [be] likely [to] go down during this process should it result adversely, but in no conceivable circumstances will we consent to surrender. If members of the present Administration were finished and others came in to parley amid the ruins, you must not be blind to the fact that the sole remaining bargaining counter with Germany would be the Fleet, and if this country was left by the United States to its fate no one would have the right to blame those then responsible if they made the best terms they could for the surviving inhabitants. Excuse me, Mr. President, putting this nightmare bluntly. Evidently I could not answer for my successors, who in utter despair and helplessness might well have to accommodate themselves to the German will. However, there is happily no need at present to dwell upon such ideas. Once more thanking you for your goodwill . . .

*   *   *

Far-reaching changes were now made by M. Reynaud in the French Cabinet and High Command. On the 18th Marshal Pétain was appointed Vice-President of the Council. Reynaud himself, transferring Daladier to Foreign Affairs, took over the Ministry of National Defence and War. At 7 p.m. on the 19th he appointed Weygand, who had just arrived from the Levant, to replace General Gamelin. I had known Weygand when he was the right-hand man of Marshal Foch, and had admired his masterly intervention in the Battle of Warsaw against the Bolshevik invasion of Poland in August 1920—an event decisive for Europe at that time. He was now seventy-three, but was reported to be efficient and vigorous in a very high degree. General Gamelin's final Order (No. 12), dated 9.45 a.m. on May 19, prescribed that the Northern Armies, instead of letting themselves be encircled, must at all costs force their way southwards to the Somme, attacking the Panzer divisions which had cut their communications. At the same time the Second Army and the newly-forming Sixth were to attack northward towards Mézières. These decisions were sound. Indeed, an Order for the general retreat of the Northern Armies southward was already at least four days overdue. Once the gravity of the breach in the French centre at Sedan was apparent, the only hope for the Northern Armies lay in an immediate march to the Somme. Instead, under General Billotte,

51

they had only made gradual and partial withdrawals to the Scheldt and formed the defensive flank to the right. Even now there might have been time for the southward march.

The confusion of the northern command, the apparent paralysis of the First French Army, and the uncertainty about what was happening had caused the War Cabinet extreme anxiety. All our proceedings were quiet and composed, but we had a united and decided opinion, behind which there was silent passion. On the 19th we were informed (4.30 p.m.) that Lord Gort was "examining a possible withdrawal towards Dunkirk if that were forced upon him". The C.I.G.S. (Ironside) could not accept this proposal, as, like most of us, he favoured the southward march. We therefore sent him to Lord Gort with instructions to move the British Army in a south-westerly direction and to force his way through all opposition in order to join up with the French in the south, and that the Belgians should be urged to conform to this movement, or, alternatively, that we would evacuate as many of their troops as possible from the Channel ports. He was to be told that we would ourselves inform the French Government of what had been resolved. At the same Cabinet we sent Dill to General Georges' H.Q., with which we had a direct telephone line. He was to stay there for four days, and tell us all he could find out. Contacts even with Lord Gort were intermittent and difficult, but it was reported that only four days' supplies and ammunition for one battle were available.

*　　*　　*

At the morning War Cabinet of May 20 we again discussed the situation of our Army. Even on the assumption of a successful fighting retreat to the Somme, I thought it likely that considerable numbers might be cut off or driven back on the sea. It is recorded in the minutes of the meeting: "The Prime Minister thought that as a precautionary measure the Admiralty should assemble a large number of small vessels in readiness to proceed to ports and inlets on the French coast." On this the Admiralty acted immediately and with ever-increasing vigour as the days passed and darkened. Operational control had been delegated on the 19th to Admiral Ramsay, commanding at Dover, whose resources at that time comprised thirty-six personnel vessels of various sorts based on Southampton and Dover. On the afternoon of the 20th, in consequence of the orders from London, the first conference of all concerned, including representatives of the Shipping Ministry, was held at Dover to consider *"the emergency evacuation across the Channel of very large forces"*. It was planned if necessary to evacuate from Calais, Boulogne, and Dunkirk, at a rate of ten thousand men from each port every twenty-four hours. Thirty craft of passenger-ferry type, twelve naval drifters, and six small coasters were provided as a first instalment. On May 22 the Admiralty ordered forty Dutch *schuits* which had taken refuge with us to be requisitioned and manned with naval crews. These were commissioned between May 25 and May 27. From Harwich round to Weymouth sea-transport officers were directed to list all suitable ships up to a thousand tons, and a complete survey was made of all shipping in British harbours. These plans for what was called "Operation Dynamo" proved the salvation of the Army ten days later.

*   *   *

The direction of the German thrust had now become more obvious. Armoured vehicles and mechanised divisions continued to pour through the gap towards Amiens and Arras, curling westwards along the Somme towards the sea. On the night of the 20th they entered Abbeville, having traversed and cut the whole communications of the Northern Armies. These hideous, fatal scythes encountered little or no resistance once the front had been broken. The German tanks—the dreaded *"chars allemands"*—ranged freely through the open country, and, aided and supplied by mechanised transport, advanced thirty or forty miles a day. They had passed through scores of towns and hundreds of villages without the slightest opposition, their officers looking out of the open cupolas and waving jauntily to the inhabitants. Eye-witnesses spoke of crowds of French prisoners marching along with them, many still carrying their rifles, which were from time to time collected and broken under the tanks. I was shocked by the utter failure to grapple with the German armour, which, with a few thousand vehicles, was compassing the entire destruction of mighty armies, and by the swift collapse of all French resistance once the fighting front had been pierced. The whole German movement was proceeding along the main roads, which at no point seemed to be blocked.

Already on the 17th I had asked the Chief of the Air Staff:

53

Is there no possibility of finding out where a column of enemy armoured vehicles harbours during the dark hours, and then bombing? We are being ripped to pieces behind the front by these wandering columns.

I now telegraphed to Reynaud:

21.V.40

Many congratulations upon appointing Weygand, in whom we have entire confidence here.

It is not possible to stop columns of tanks from piercing thin lines and penetrating deeply. All ideas of stopping holes and hemming in these intruders are vicious. Principle should be, on the contrary, to punch holes. Undue importance should not be attached to the arrival of a few tanks at any particular point. What can they do if they enter a town? Towns should be held with riflemen, and tank personnel should be fired upon should they attempt to leave vehicles. If they cannot get food or drink or petrol, they can only make a mess and depart. Where possible, buildings should be blown down upon them. Every town with valuable cross-roads should be held in this fashion. Secondly, the tank columns in the open must be hunted down and attacked in the open country by numbers of small mobile columns with a few cannon. Their tracks must be wearing out, and their energy must abate. This is the one way to deal with the armoured intruders. As for the main body, which does not seem to be coming on very quickly, the only method is to drive in upon the flanks. The confusion of this battle can only be cleared by being aggravated, so that it becomes a *mêlée*. They strike at our communications; we should strike at theirs. I feel more confident than I did at the beginning of the battle; but all the armies must fight at the same time, and I hope the British will have a chance soon. Above is only my personal view, and I trust it will give no offence if I state it to you.

Every good wish.

Weygand's first act was to confer with his senior commanders. It was not unnatural that he should wish to see the situation in the north for himself, and to make contact with the commanders there. Allowances must be made for a general who takes over the command in the crisis of a losing battle. But now there was no time. He should not have left the summit of the remaining controls and have become involved in the delays and strains of personal movement. We may note in detail what followed. On the morning of the 20th Weygand, installed in Gamelin's place, made arrangements to visit the Northern Armies on the 21st.

After learning that the roads to the north were cut by the Germans he decided to fly. His plane was attacked, and forced to land at Calais. The hour appointed for his conference at Ypres had to be altered to 3 p.m. on the 21st. Here he met King Leopold and General Billotte. Lord Gort, who had not been notified of time and place, was not present, and no British officers were there. The King described this conference as "four hours of confused talking". It discussed the co-ordination of the three Armies, the execution of the Weygand plan, and if that failed the retirement of the British and French to the Lys, and the Belgians to the Yser. At 7 p.m. General Weygand had to leave. Lord Gort did not arrive till eight, when he received an account of the proceedings from General Billotte. Weygand drove back to Calais, embarked on a submarine for Dieppe, and returned to Paris. Billotte drove off in his car to deal with the crisis, and within the hour was killed in a motor collision. Thus all was again in suspense.

*　　*　　*

On the 21st Ironside returned and reported that Lord Gort, on receiving the Cabinet instructions, had put the following points to him:

(i) That the southward march would involve a rearguard action from the Scheldt at the same time as an attack into an area already strongly held by the enemy armoured and mobile formations. During such a movement both flanks would have to be protected.

(ii) That sustained offensive operations were difficult in view of the administrative situation, and

(iii) That neither the French First Army nor the Belgians were likely to be able to conform to such a manœuvre if attempted.

Ironside added that confusion reigned in the French High Command in the north, that General Billotte had failed to carry out his duties of co-ordination for the past eight days and appeared to have no plans, that the B.E.F. were in good heart and had so far had only about five hundred battle casualties. He gave a vivid description of the state of the roads, crowded with refugees, scourged by the fire of German aircraft. He had had a rough time himself.

Two fearsome alternatives therefore presented themselves to

55

the War Cabinet. The first, the British Army at all costs, with or without French and Belgian co-operation, to cut its way to the south and the Somme, a task which Lord Gort doubted its ability to perform; the second, to fall back on Dunkirk and face a sea evacuation under hostile air attack, with the certainty of losing all the artillery and equipment, then so scarce and precious. Obviously great risks should be run to achieve the first, but there was no reason why all possible precautions and preparations should not be taken for the sea evacuation if the southern plan failed. I proposed to my colleagues that I should go to France to meet Reynaud and Weygand and come to a decision. Dill was to meet me there from General Georges' H.Q.

$\star \quad \star \quad \star$

This was the moment when my colleagues felt it right to obtain from Parliament the extraordinary powers for which a Bill had been prepared during the last few days. This measure would give the Government practically unlimited power over the life, liberty, and property of all His Majesty's subjects in Great Britain. In general terms of law the powers granted by Parliament were absolute. The Act was to "include power by Order in Council to make such Defence Regulations making provision for requiring persons to place themselves, their services and their property at the disposal of His Majesty as appear to him to be necessary or expedient for securing the public safety, the defence of the Realm, the maintenance of public order, or the efficient prosecution of any war in which His Majesty may be engaged, or for maintaining supplies or services essential to the life of the community".

In regard to persons, the Minister of Labour was empowered to direct anyone to perform any service required. The regulation giving him this power included a Fair Wages clause, which was inserted in the Act to regulate wage conditions. Labour supply committees were to be set up in important centres. The control of property in the widest sense was imposed in equal manner. Control of all establishments, including banks, was imposed under the authority of Government orders. Employers could be required to produce their books, and Excess Profits were to be taxed at 100 per cent. A Production Council, to be presided over by Mr. Greenwood, was to be formed, and a Director of Labour Supply to be appointed.

This Bill was accordingly presented to Parliament on the afternoon of the 22nd by Mr. Chamberlain and Mr. Attlee, the latter himself moving the Second Reading. Both the Commons and the Lords with their immense Conservative majorities passed it unanimously through all its stages in a single afternoon, and it received the Royal Assent that night.

> For Romans in Rome's quarrel
> Spared neither land nor gold,
> Nor son nor wife, nor limb nor life,
> In the brave days of old.

Such was the temper of the hour.

*　　*　　*

When I arrived in Paris on May 22 there was a new setting. Gamelin was gone; Daladier was gone from the war scene. Reynaud was both Prime Minister and Minister of War. As the German thrust had definitely turned seaward, Paris was not immediately threatened. Grand-Quartier-Général (G.Q.G.) was still at Vincennes. M. Reynaud drove me down there about noon. In the garden some of those figures I had seen round Gamelin—one a very tall cavalry officer—were pacing moodily up and down. "*C'est l'ancien régime*," remarked the aide-de-camp. Reynaud and I were brought into Weygand's room, and afterwards to the map room, where we had the great maps of the Supreme Command. Weygand met us. In spite of his physical exertions and a night of travel, he was brisk, buoyant, and incisive. He made an excellent impression upon all. He unfolded his plan of war. He was not content with a southward march or retreat for the Northern Armies. They should strike south-east from around Cambrai and Arras in the general direction of St. Quentin, thus taking in flank the German armoured divisions at present engaged in what he called the St. Quentin–Amiens pocket. Their rear, he thought, would be protected by the Belgian Army, which would cover them towards the east, and if necessary towards the north. Meanwhile a new French army under General Frère, composed of eighteen to twenty divisions drawn from Alsace, from the Maginot Line, from Africa, and from every other quarter, were to form a front along the Somme. Their left hand would push forward through Amiens to Arras, and thus by their utmost efforts establish contact with the armies

57

of the north. The enemy armour must be kept under constant pressure. "The Panzer divisions must not," said Weygand, "be allowed to keep the initiative." All necessary orders had been given so far as it was possible to give orders at all. We were now told that General Billotte, to whom he had imparted his whole plan, had just been killed in the motor accident. Dill and I were agreed that we had no choice, and indeed no inclination, except to welcome the plan. I emphasised that "it was indispensable to reopen communications between the armies of the north and those of the south by way of Arras". I explained that Lord Gort, while striking south-west, must also guard his path to the coast. To make sure there was no mistake about what was settled, I myself dictated a *résumé* of the decision and showed it to Weygand, who agreed. I reported accordingly to the Cabinet, and sent the following telegram to Lord Gort:

22.V.40

I flew to Paris this morning with Dill and others. The conclusions which were reached between Reynaud, Weygand, and ourselves are summarised below. They accord exactly with general directions you have received from the War Office. You have our best wishes in the vital battle now opening towards Bapaume and Cambrai.

It was agreed—

1. That the Belgian Army should withdraw to the line of the Yser and stand there, the sluices being opened.

2. That the British Army and the French First Army should attack south-west towards Bapaume and Cambrai at the earliest moment, certainly to-morrow, with about eight divisions, and with the Belgian Cavalry Corps on the right of the British.

3. That as this battle is vital to both armies and the British communications depend upon freeing Amiens, the British Air Force should give the utmost possible help, both by day and by night, while it is going on.

4. That the new French Army Group which is advancing upon Amiens and forming a line along the Somme should strike northwards and join hands with the British divisions who are attacking southwards in the general direction of Bapaume.

It will be seen that Weygand's new plan did not differ except in emphasis from the cancelled Instruction No. 12 of General Gamelin. Nor was it out of harmony with the vehement opinion which the War Cabinet had expressed on the 19th. The Northern Armies were to shoulder their way southwards by offensive

LEGEND
British
French Armies
Belgians
German Attacks

BELGIANS

Antwerp

Ghent

Brussels

Calais

Dunkirk

Yser

Ypres

Menin

Lys

Oudenarde

Scheldt

Namur

B.E.F.

Boulogne

St. Omer

Cassel

Hazebrouck

Lille

Montreuil

Béthune

FIRST
ARMY

Maulde

Valenciennes

Hesdin

St. Pol

Douai

Arras

Cambrai

Abbeville

Doullens

(TEN GERMANY PZ. DIVISIONS)

Somme

Amiens

Péronne

Oise

St. Quentin

Serre

Sedan

SEVENTH ARMY
(Concentrating)

Chauny

Laon

Aisne

0   10   20   30   40 Miles

Oise

Soissons

SIXTH ARMY

Reims

SITUATION, EVENING 22 MAY

action, destroying, if possible, the armoured incursion. They
were to be met by a helpful thrust through Amiens by the new
French Army Group under General Frère. This would be most
important if it came true. In private I complained to M. Reynaud
that Gort had been left entirely without orders for four consecu-
tive days. Even since Weygand had assumed command three days
had been lost in taking decisions. The change in the Supreme
Command was right. The resultant delay was evil.

I slept the night at the Embassy. The air raids were trivial; the
guns were noisy, but one never heard a bomb. Very different
indeed were the experiences of Paris from the ordeal which
London was soon to endure. I had a keen desire to go to see my
friend General Georges at his headquarters at Compiègne. Our
liaison officer with him, Brigadier Swayne, was with me for some

time and gave me the picture of the French armies so far as he knew it, which was only part of the way. I was persuaded that it would be better not to intrude at this time, when this vast and complicated operation was being attempted in the teeth of every form of administrative difficulty and frequent breakdowns in communication.

In the absence of any supreme war direction events and the enemy had taken control. On the 17th Gort had begun to direct troops to the line Ruyaulcourt–Arleux and to garrison Arras, and was constantly strengthening his southern flank. The French Seventh Army, less the XVIth Corps, which had suffered heavily in the Walcheren fighting, had moved south to join the First French Army. It had traversed the British rear without serious disturbance. On the 20th Gort had informed both Generals Billotte and Blanchard that he proposed to attack southwards from Arras on May 21st with two divisions and an armoured brigade, and Billotte had agreed to co-operate with two French divisions from the First French Army. This army of thirteen divisions was gathered in an oblong some nineteen miles by ten: Maulde–Valenciennes–Denain–Douai. The enemy had crossed the Scheldt on the 20th around Oudenarde, and the three British corps, which still faced east, withdrew on the 23rd to the defences we had erected in the winter along the Belgian frontier, from which they had advanced so eagerly twelve days before. On this day the B.E.F. were put on half rations. The impression of French helplessness derived from many sources led me to protest to Reynaud.

Prime Minister to M. Reynaud   23.V.40
   (Copy to Lord Gort)
   Communications of Northern Armies have been cut by strong enemy armoured forces. Salvation of these armies can only be obtained by immediate execution of Weygand's plan. I demand the issue to the French commanders in north and south and Belgian G.H.Q. of the most stringent orders to carry this out and turn defeat into victory. Time is vital as supplies are short.

I reported this message to the War Cabinet when they met at 11.30 a.m., pointing out that the whole success of the Weygand plan was dependent on the French taking the initiative, which they showed no signs of doing. We met again at 7 p.m.

And the next day:

7 A German rifleman.

8 German infantry in action.

9 A flame-thrower.
10 Going through barbed-wire.

Prime Minister to M. Reynaud, for General Weygand 24.V.40

General Gort wires that co-ordination of northern front is essential with armies of three different nations. He says he cannot undertake this co-ordination, as he is already fighting north and south and is threatened on his lines of communications. At the same time Sir Roger Keyes tells me that up to 3 p.m. to-day (23rd) Belgian Headquarters and King had received no directive. How does this agree with your statement that Blanchard and Gort are *main dans la main?* Appreciate fully difficulties of communication, but feel no effective concert of operations in northern area, against which enemy are concentrating. Trust you will be able to rectify this. Gort further says that any advance by him must be in the nature of sortie, and that relief must come from south, as he has not (*repeat* not) ammunition for serious attack. Nevertheless, we are instructing him to persevere in carrying out your plan. We have not here even seen your own directive, and have no knowledge of the details of your northern operations. Will you kindly have this sent through French Mission at earliest? All good wishes.

* * *

Some account of the small battle fought by the British around Arras must be given here. General Franklyn, who commanded, intended to occupy the area Arras–Cambrai–Bapaume. He had the 5th and 50th British Divisions and the 1st Army Tank Brigade. His plan was to attack with this armour and one brigade of each division, the whole under General Martel, round the western and southern sides of Arras, with an immediate objective on the river Sensée. The French were to co-operate with two divisions on the east to the Cambrai–Arras road. The British divisions consisted of only two brigades each, and the tanks numbered sixty-five Mark I and eighteen Mark II, all of whose tracks, the life of which was short, were wearing out. The attack began at 2 p.m. on May 21, and soon found itself engaged with much stronger opposition than was expected. French support on the eastern flank did not materialise, and on the western was limited to one light mechanised division. The enemy armour actually consisted of about four hundred tanks of the 7th and 8th Armoured Divisions, a general named Rommel commanding the former. At first the attack prospered, and four hundred prisoners were taken, but the line of the river Sensée was not reached, and the German counter-attack, in overwhelming numbers, with full air support, caused heavy casualties. The 12th Lancers presently reported strong enemy columns moving towards St. Pol and

61

threatening to turn the western flank. During the night the Army Tank Brigade, the 13th Brigade of the 5th Division, and the 151st Brigade of the 50th Division gradually withdrew to the river Scarpe. Here three British brigades stood until the afternoon of the 22nd, and in this neighbourhood repulsed various attacks. We still held Arras, but the enemy gradually tended to swing round towards Béthune. The French light mechanised division guarding our western flank was forced from Mont St. Eloi, and the enemy tanks soon after approached Souchez. By 7 p.m. on the 23rd the British eastern flank was under heavy pressure, and the enemy reaching Lens had encircled the western flank. Thus the position was precarious. We were hopelessly outnumbered, beset by masses of armour, and almost surrounded. At 10 p.m. General Franklyn informed G.H.Q. that unless his force was withdrawn during the night its retirement would become impossible. He was told that orders to withdraw had been sent him three hours before. The operation had some temporary effect on the enemy; they recorded at the time "heavy British counter-attacks with armour", which caused them considerable anxiety.

In pursuance of the Weygand plan Gort proposed to General Blanchard, who now commanded the northern group, that two British divisions, one French division, and the French Cavalry Corps should attack southwards between the Canal du Nord and the Scheldt Canal. Two French divisions had in fact twice previously reached the outskirts of Cambrai, but on each occasion they were bombed and withdrew. In all these days this was the only offensive action of the French First Army.

*　　*　　*

In London we had no knowledge of the progress of this forlorn attempt at Arras to break the encircling line. However, during the 24th very reproachful telegrams arrived from Reynaud. The shorter of his two messages tells the story.

You wired me [he said] this morning that you had instructed General Gort to continue to carry out the Weygand plan. General Weygand now informs me that, according to a telegram from General Blanchard, the British Army had carried out, on its own initiative, a retreat of twenty-five miles towards the ports at a time when our troops moving up from the south are gaining ground towards the north, where they were to meet their allies.

BATTLE OF ARRAS, MAY 21–22

This action of the British Army is in direct opposition to the formal
orders renewed this morning by General Weygand. This retreat has
naturally obliged General Weygand to change all his arrangements,
and he is compelled to give up the idea of closing the gap and restoring
a continuous front. I need not lay any stress upon the gravity of the
possible consequences.

Up to this time General Weygand had been counting on
General Frère's army advancing northwards on Amiens, Albert,
and Péronne. They had, in fact, made no noticeable progress, and
were still forming and assembling. The following are my replies
to M. Reynaud:

25.V.40

My telegram last night told you all we knew over here, and we
have still heard nothing from Lord Gort to contradict it. But I must
tell you that a Staff officer has reported to the War Office confirming
the withdrawal of the two divisions from the Arras region, which your

63

telegram to me mentioned. General Dill, who should be with Lord Gort, has been told to send a Staff officer by air at the earliest moment. As soon as we know what has happened I will report fully. It is clear however that the Northern Army is practically surrounded and that all its communications are cut except through Dunkirk and Ostend.

25.V.40

We have every reason to believe that Gort is still persevering in southward move. All we know is that he has been forced by the pressure on his western flank, and to keep communication with Dunkirk for indispensable supplies, to place parts of two divisions between himself and the increasing pressure of the German armoured forces, which in apparently irresistible strength have successively captured Abbeville and Boulogne, are menacing Calais and Dunkirk, and have taken St. Omer. How can he move southward and disengage his northern front unless he throws out this shield on his right hand? Nothing in the movements of the B.E.F. of which we are aware can be any excuse for the abandonment of the strong pressure of your northward move across the Somme, which we trust will develop.

Secondly, you complained of heavy materials being moved from Havre. Only materials moved away were gas shells, which it was indiscreet to leave. Also some of the stores have been moved from the north to the south side of the river at Havre.

Thirdly, should I become aware that extreme pressure of events has compelled any departure from the plan agreed I shall immediately inform you. Dill, who was this morning wholly convinced that the sole hope of any effective extrication of our Army lies in the southward move and in the active advance of General Frère, is now with Gort. You must understand that, having waited for the southward move for a week after it became obvious[ly necessary], we find ourselves now ripped from the coast by the mass of the enemy's armoured vehicles. We therefore have no choice but to continue the southward move, using such flank guard protection to the westward as is necessary.

General Spears will be with you to-morrow morning, and it will probably be quickest to send him back when the position is clear.

★　　★　　★

There was a very strong feeling in Cabinet and high military circles that the abilities and strategic knowledge of Sir John Dill, who had been since April 23 Vice-Chief of the Imperial General Staff, should find their full scope in his appointment as our principal Army adviser. No one could doubt that his professional standing was in many ways superior to that of Ironside.

As the adverse battle drew to its climax I and my colleagues greatly desired that Sir John Dill should become C.I.G.S. We had also to choose a Commander-in-Chief for the British Island, if we were invaded. Late at night on May 25 Ironside, Dill, Ismay, myself, and one or two others in my room at Admiralty House were trying to measure the position. General Ironside volunteered the proposal that he should cease to be C.I.G.S., but declared himself quite willing to command the British Home Forces. Considering the unpromising task that such a command was at the time thought to involve, this was a spirited and selfless offer. I therefore accepted General Ironside's proposal; and the high dignities and honours which were later conferred upon him arose from my appreciation of his bearing at this moment in our affairs. Sir John Dill became C.I.G.S. on May 27. The changes were generally judged appropriate for the time being.

CHAPTER IV

THE MARCH TO THE SEA

May 24—May 31

Review of the Battle – General Halder's Account of Hitler's Personal Intervention – Halt of the German Armour – The Truth from the German Staff Diaries – A Separate Cause for the Halt at the Decisive Point – The Defence of Boulogne – The Drama of Calais – The Consequences of Prolonged Defence – Gort Abandons the Weygand Plan – His Decision of May 25 – Filling the Belgian Gap – Withdrawal of the British Army to the Dunkirk Bridgeheads – Extrication of the Four British Divisions from Lille – A Question to the Chiefs of Staff – Their Answer – My Message to Lord Gort – And to Admiral Keyes – General Pownall's Account of the Gort-Blanchard Meeting on the Morning of the 28th – Surrender of the Belgian Army, May 28 – Decisive Battle Fought by General Brooke and the IInd Corps, May 28 – Withdrawal to the Bridgehead – Escape by Sea of Half the French First Army.

WE may now review up to this point the course of this memorable battle.

Only Hitler was prepared to violate the neutrality of Belgium and Holland. Belgium would not invite the Allies in until she was herself attacked. Therefore the military initiative rested with Hitler. On May 10 he struck his blow. The First Army Group, with the British in the centre, instead of standing behind their fortifications, leaped forward into Belgium on a vain, because belated, mission of rescue. The French had left the gap opposite the Ardennes ill fortified and weakly guarded. An armoured inroad on a scale never known in war broke the centre of the French line of armies, and in forty-eight hours threatened to cut all the Northern Armies alike from their southern communications and from the sea. By the 14th at the latest the French High Command should have given imperative orders to these armies to make a general retreat at full speed, accepting not only risks but heavy losses of *matériel*. This issue was not faced in its brutal realism by General Gamelin. The French commander of the northern group, Billotte, was incapable of taking the necessary decisions himself. Confusion reigned throughout the armies of the threatened left wing.

As the superior power of the enemy was felt they fell back. As the turning movement swung round their right they formed a defensive flank. If they had started back on the 14th they could have been on their old line by the 17th and would have had a good chance of fighting their way out. At least three mortal days were lost. From the 17th onwards the British War Cabinet saw clearly that an immediate fighting march southwards would alone save the British Army. They were resolved to press their view upon the French Government and General Gamelin, but their own commander, Lord Gort, was doubtful whether it was possible to disengage the fighting fronts, and still more to break through at the same time. On the 19th General Gamelin was dismissed, and Weygand reigned in his stead. Gamelin's "Instruction No. 12", his last order, though five days late, was sound in principle, and also in conformity with the main conclusions of the British War Cabinet and Chiefs of Staff. The change in the Supreme Command, or want of command, led to another three days' delay. The spirited plan which General Weygand proposed after visiting the Northern Armies was never more than a paper scheme. In the main it was the Gamelin plan, rendered still more hopeless by further delay.

In the hideous dilemma which now presented itself we accepted the Weygand plan, and made loyal and persistent, though now ineffectual, efforts to carry it out until the 25th, when, all the communications being cut, our weak counter-attack being repulsed, with the loss of Arras, the Belgian front breaking and King Leopold about to capitulate, all hope of escape to the southward vanished. There remained only the sea. Could we reach it, or must we be surrounded and broken up in the open field? In any case the whole artillery and equipment of our Army, irreplaceable for many months, must be lost. But what was that compared with saving the Army, the nucleus and structure upon which alone Britain could build her armies of the future? Lord Gort, who had from the 25th onwards felt that evacuation by sea was our only chance, now proceeded to form a bridgehead around Dunkirk and to fight his way into it with what strength remained. All the discipline of the British, and the qualities of their commanders, who included Brooke, Alexander, and Montgomery, were to be needed. Much more was to be needed. All that man could do was done. Would it be enough?

* * *

A much-disputed episode must now be examined. General Halder, Chief of the German General Staff, has declared that at this moment Hitler made his only effective direct personal intervention in the battle. He became, according to this authority, "alarmed about the armoured formations, because they were in considerable danger in a difficult country, honeycombed with canals, without being able to attain any vital results". He felt he could not sacrifice armoured formations uselessly, as they were essential to the second stage of the campaign. He believed, no doubt, that his air superiority would be sufficient to prevent a large-scale evacuation by sea. He therefore, according to Halder, sent a message to him through Brauchitsch ordering "the armoured formations to be stopped, the points even taken back". Thus, says Halder, the way to Dunkirk was cleared for the British Army. At any rate we intercepted a German message sent in clear at 11.42 a.m. on May 24, to the effect that the attack on the line Dunkirk-Hazebrouck-Merville was to be discontinued for the present. Halder states that he refused, on behalf of Supreme Army Headquarters (O.K.H.), to interfere in the movement of Army Group Rundstedt, which had clear orders to prevent the enemy from reaching the coast. The quicker and more complete the success here, he argued, the easier it would be later to repair the loss of some tanks. The next day he was ordered to go with Brauchitsch to a conference.

The excited discussion finished with a definite order by Hitler, to which he added that he would ensure execution of his order by sending personal liaison officers to the front. Keitel was sent by plane to Army Group Rundstedt, and other officers to the front command posts. "I have never been able," says General Halder, "to figure how Hitler conceived the idea of the useless endangering of the armoured formations. It is most likely that Keitel, who was for a considerable time in Flanders in the First World War, had originated these ideas by his tales."

Other German generals have told much the same story, and have even suggested that Hitler's order was inspired by a political motive, to improve the chances of peace with England after France was beaten. Authentic documentary evidence has now come to light in the shape of the actual diary of Rundstedt's headquarters *written at the time*. This tells a different tale. At midnight on the 23rd orders came from Brauchitsch at O.K.H., confirming that the Fourth Army was to remain under Rundstedt for "the last act" of "the encirclement battle". Next morning Hitler visited Rundstedt, who represented to him that his armour, which had come so far and so fast, was much reduced in strength and needed a pause wherein to reorganise and regain its balance for the final blow against an enemy who, his staff diary says, was "fighting with extraordinary tenacity". Moreover, Rundstedt foresaw the possibility of attacks on his widely-dispersed forces from north and south; in fact, the Weygand Plan, which, if it had been feasible, was the obvious Allied counter-stroke. Hitler "agreed entirely" that the attack east of Arras should be carried out by infantry and that the mobile formations should continue to hold the line Lens–Béthune–Aire–St. Omer–Gravelines in order to intercept the enemy forces under pressure from Army Group B in the north-east. He also dwelt on the paramount necessity of conserving the armoured forces for further operations. However, very early on the 25th a fresh directive was sent from Brauchitsch as the Commander-in-Chief ordering the continuation of the advance by the armour. Rundstedt, fortified by Hitler's verbal agreement, would have none of it. He did not pass on the order to the Fourth Army Commander, Kluge, who was told to continue to husband the Panzer divisions. Kluge protested at the delay, but it was not till next day, the 26th, that Rundstedt released them, although even then he enjoined that Dunkirk was not yet itself to be directly assaulted. The diary records that the Fourth Army protested at this restriction, and its Chief of Staff telephoned on the 27th:

The picture in the Channel ports is as follows. Big ships come up the quayside, boards are put down, and the men crowd on the ships. All material is left behind. But we are not keen on finding these men, newly equipped, up against us later.

It is therefore certain that the armour was halted; that this was done on the initiative not of Hitler but of Rundstedt. Rundstedt no doubt had reasons for his view both in the condition of the armour and in the general battle, but he ought to have obeyed the formal orders of the Army Command, or at least told them what Hitler had said in conversation. There is general agreement among the German commanders that a great opportunity was lost.

* * *

There was however a separate cause which affected the movements of the German armour at the decisive point.

After reaching the sea beyond Abbeville on the night of the 20th, the leading German armoured and motorised columns had moved northward along the coast by Étaples towards Boulogne, Calais, and Dunkirk, with the evident intention of cutting off all escape by sea. This region was lighted in my mind from the previous war, when I had maintained the mobile Marine Brigade operating from Dunkirk against the flanks and rear of the German armies marching on Paris. I did not therefore have to learn about the inundation system between Calais and Dunkirk, or the significance of the Gravelines waterline. The sluices had already been opened, and with every day the floods were spreading, thus giving southerly protection to our line of retreat. The defence of Boulogne, but still more of Calais, to the latest hour, stood forth upon the confused scene, and garrisons were immediately sent there from England. Boulogne, isolated and attacked on May 22, was defended by two battalions of the Guards and one of our few anti-tank batteries, with some French troops. After thirty-six hours' resistance it was reported to be untenable, and I consented to the remainder of the garrison, including the French, being taken off by sea. The Guards were embarked by eight destroyers on the night of May 23-24, with a loss of only 200 men. The French continued to fight in the Citadel until the morning of the 25th. I regretted our evacuation.

Some days earlier I had placed the conduct of the defence of the Channel ports directly under the Chief of the Imperial General Staff, with whom I was in constant touch. I now resolved that Calais should be fought to the death, and that no evacuation by sea could be allowed to the garrison, which consisted of one battalion of the Rifle Brigade, one of the 60th Rifles, the Queen

Victoria Rifles, the 229th Anti-tank Battery, R.A., and a battalion of the Royal Tank Regiment, with twenty-one light and twenty-seven cruiser tanks, and an equal number of Frenchmen. It was painful thus to sacrifice these splendid, trained troops, of which we had so few, for the doubtful advantage of gaining two or perhaps three days, and the unknown uses that could be made of these days. The Secretary of State for War and the C.I.G.S. agreed to this hard measure. The telegrams and minutes tell the tale.

Prime Minister to General Ismay, for C.I.G.S.   23.V.40

Apart from the general order issued, I trust, last night by Weygand, for assuring the southward movement of the armies via Amiens, it is imperative that a clear line of supply should be opened up at the earliest moment to Gort's army by Dunkirk, Calais, or Boulogne. Gort cannot remain insensible to the peril in which he is now placed, and he must detach even a division, or whatever lesser force is necessary, to meet our force pushing through from the coast. If the regiment of armoured vehicles, including cruiser tanks, has actually landed at Calais, this should improve the situation, and should encourage us to send the rest of the 2nd Brigade of that Armoured Division in there. This coastal area must be cleaned up if the major operation of withdrawal is to have any chance. The intruders behind the line must be struck at and brought to bay. The refugees should be driven into the fields and parked there, as proposed by General Weygand, so that the roads can be kept clear. Are you in touch with Gort by telephone and telegraph, and how long does it take to send him a ciphered message? Will you kindly tell one of your Staff officers to send a map to Downing Street with the position, so far as it is known to-day, of the nine British divisions. Do not reply to this yourself.

Prime Minister to General Ismay   24.V.40

I cannot understand the situation around Calais. The Germans are blocking all exits, and our regiment of tanks is boxed up in the town because it cannot face the field guns planted on the outskirts. Yet I expect the forces achieving this are very modest. Why, then, are they not attacked? Why does not Lord Gort attack them from the rear at the same time that we make a sortie from Calais? Surely Gort can spare a brigade or two to clear his communications and to secure the supplies vital to his army. Here is a general with nine divisions about to be starved out, and yet he cannot send a force to clear his communications. What else can be so important as this? Where could a reserve be better employed?

This force blockading Calais should be attacked at once by Gort, by the Canadians from Dunkirk, and by a sortie of our boxed-up tanks.

Apparently the Germans can go anywhere and do anything, and their tanks can act in twos and threes all over our rear, and even when they are located they are not attacked. Also our tanks recoil before their field guns, but our field guns do not like to take on their tanks. If their motorised artillery, far from its base, can block us, why cannot we, with the artillery of a great army, block them? . . . The responsibility for cleansing the communications with Calais and keeping them open rests primarily with the B.E.F.

This did less than justice to our troops. But I print it as I wrote it at the time.

Prime Minister to General Ismay   24.v.40
Vice-Chief of the Naval Staff informs me that [an] order was sent at 2 a.m. to Calais saying that evacuation was decided on in principle, but this is surely madness. The only effect of evacuating Calais would be to transfer the forces now blocking it to Dunkirk. Calais must be held for many reasons, but specially to hold the enemy on its front. The Admiralty say they are preparing twenty-four naval 12-pounders, which with S.A.P.* will pierce any tank. Some of these will be ready this evening.

Prime Minister to C.I.G.S.   25.v.40
I must know at earliest why Gort gave up Arras, and what actually he is doing with the rest of his army. Is he still persevering in Weygand's plan, or has he become largely stationary? If the latter, what do you consider the probable course of events in the next few days, and what course do you recommend? Clearly, he must not allow himself to be encircled without fighting a battle. Should he [not] do this by fighting his way to the coast and destroying the armoured troops which stand between him and the sea with overwhelming force of artillery, while covering himself and the Belgian front, which would also curl back, by strong rearguards? To-morrow at latest this decision must be taken.
It should surely be possible for Dill to fly home from any aerodrome momentarily clear, and R.A.F. should send a whole squadron to escort him.

Prime Minister to Secretary of State for War and C.I.G.S.   25.v.40
Pray find out who was the officer responsible for sending the order to evacuate Calais yesterday, and by whom this very lukewarm telegram I saw this morning was drafted, in which mention is made of "for the sake of Allied solidarity". This is not the way to encourage men to fight to the end. Are you sure there is no streak of defeatist opinion in the General Staff?

* Semi-armour-piercing shell.

Prime Minister to C.I.G.S.   25.V.40

Something like this should be said to the Brigadier defending Calais: Defence of Calais to the utmost is of the highest importance to our country and our Army now. First, it occupies a large part of the enemy's armoured forces, and keeps them from attacking our line of communications. Secondly, it preserves a sally-port from which portions of the British Army may make their way home. Lord Gort has already sent troops to your aid, and the Navy will do all possible to keep you supplied. The eyes of the Empire are upon the defence of Calais, and His Majesty's Government are confident that you and your gallant regiment will perform an exploit worthy of the British name.

This message was sent to Brigadier Nicholson at about 2 p.m. on May 25.

The final decision not to relieve the garrison was taken on the evening of May 26. Till then the destroyers were held ready. Eden and Ironside were with me at the Admiralty. We three came out from dinner and at 9 p.m. did the deed. It involved Eden's own regiment, in which he had long served and fought in the previous struggle. One has to eat and drink in war, but I could not help feeling physically sick as we afterwards sat silent at the table.

Here was the message to the Brigadier:

Every hour you continue to exist is of the greatest help to the B.E.F. Government has therefore decided you must continue to fight. Have greatest possible admiration for your splendid stand. Evacuation will not (*repeat* not) take place, and craft required for above purpose are to return to Dover. *Verity* and *Windsor* to cover Commander Minesweeping and his retirement.

Calais was the crux. Many other causes might have prevented the deliverance of Dunkirk, but it is certain that the three days gained by the defence of Calais enabled the Gravelines waterline to be held, and that without this, even in spite of Hitler's vacillations and Rundstedt's orders, all would have been cut off and lost.

*   *   *

Upon all this there now descended a simplifying catastrophe. The Germans, who had hitherto not pressed the Belgian front severely, on May 24 broke the Belgian line on either side of Courtrai, which is but thirty miles from Ostend and Dunkirk.

The King of the Belgians soon considered the situation hopeless, and prepared himself for capitulation.

By May 23 the Ist and IInd Corps of the B.E.F., withdrawn by stages from Belgium, were back again on the frontier defences north and east of Lille, which they had built for themselves during the winter. The German scythe-cut round our southern flank had reached the sea, and we had to shield ourselves from this. As the facts forced themselves upon Gort and his headquarters, troops had successively been sent to positions along the canal line La Bassée–Béthune–Aire–St. Omer–Watten. These, with elements of the French XVIth Corps, touched the sea at the Gravelines water-line. The British IIIrd Corps was responsible in the main for this curled-in flank facing south. There was no continuous line, but only a series of defended "stops" at the main crossings, some of which, like St. Omer and Watten, had already fallen to the enemy. The indispensable roads northwards from Cassel were threatened. Gort's reserve consisted only of the two British divisions, the 5th and 50th, which had, as we have seen, just been so narrowly extricated from their southerly counter-attack made at Arras in forlorn fulfilment of the Weygand plan. At this date the total frontage of the B.E.F. was about ninety miles, everywhere in close contact with the enemy.

To the south of the B.E.F. lay the First French Army, having two divisions in the frontier defences and the remainder, comprising eleven divisions in no good shape, cramped in the area north and east of Douai. This army was under attack from the south-east claw of the German encirclement. On our left the Belgian Army was being driven back from the Lys canal at many places, and with their retirement northwards a gap was developing north of Menin.

In the evening of the 25th Lord Gort took a vital decision. His orders still were to pursue the Weygand plan of a southerly attack towards Cambrai, in which the 5th and 50th Divisions, in conjunction with the French, were to be employed. The promised French attack northwards from the Somme showed no sign of reality. The last defenders of Boulogne had been evacuated. Calais still held out. Gort now abandoned the Weygand plan. There was in his view no longer hope of a march to the south and to the Somme. Moreover, at the same time the crumbling of the Belgian defence and the gap opening to the north created a new

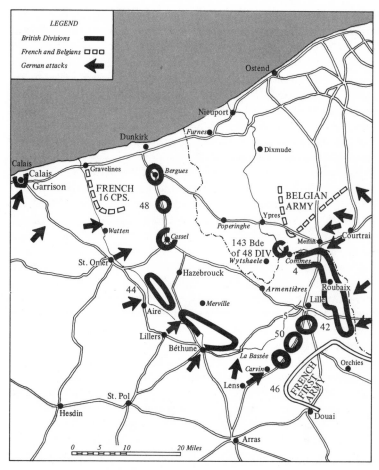

LEGEND

British Divisions

French and Belgians □□□

German attacks

Ostend

Nieuport

Furnes

Dunkirk

Dixmude

Calais

Calais Garrison

Gravelines

Bergues

FRENCH 16 CPS.

48

BELGIAN ARMY

Watten

Poperinghe

Ypres

Courtrai

Cassel

143 Bde of 48 DIV

Menin

St. Omer

Wytshaele

Commes

4

Hazebrouck

Armentières

Roubaix

44

Merville

Lille

Aire

5

Lillers

50

42

Béthune

La Bassée

Carvin

Orchies

Lens

46

FRENCH FIRST ARMY

St. Pol

Hesdin

Douai

0   5   10   20 Miles

Arras

SITUATION AT NIGHTFALL 25 MAY

peril, dominating in itself. A captured order of the German
Sixth Army showed that one corps was to march north-west-
wards towards Ypres and another corps westwards towards
Wytschaete. How could the Belgians withstand this double thrust?

Confident in his military virtue, and convinced of the complete breakdown of all control, either by the British and French
Governments or by the French Supreme Command, Gort resolved to abandon the attack to the southward, to plug the gap

which a Belgian capitulation was about to open in the north, and to march to the sea. At this moment here was the only hope of saving anything from destruction or surrender. At 6 p.m. he ordered the 5th and 50th Divisions to join the IInd British Corps to fill the impending Belgian gap. He informed General Blanchard, who had succeeded Billotte in command of the First Army Group, of his action; and this officer, acknowledging the force of events, gave orders at 11.30 p.m. for a withdrawal on the 26th to a line behind the Lys canal west of Lille, with a view to forming a bridgehead around Dunkirk.

Early on May 26 Gort and Blanchard drew up their plan for withdrawal to the coast. As the First French Army had farther to go, the first movements of the B.E.F. on the night of the 26th–27th were to be preparatory, and rearguards of the British Ist and IInd Corps remained on the frontier defences till the night of the 27th–28th. In all this Lord Gort had acted upon his own responsibility. But by now we at home, with a somewhat different angle of information, had already reached the same conclusions. On the 26th a telegram from the War Office approved his conduct, and authorised him "to operate towards the coast forthwith in conjunction with the French and Belgian armies". The emergency gathering on a vast scale of naval vessels of all kinds and sizes was already in full swing.

The reader must now look at the diagram which shows the areas held on the night of the 25th–26th by the British divisions.

On the western flank of the corridor to the sea the position remained largely unchanged during the 26th. The localities held by the 48th and 44th Divisions came under relatively little pressure. The 2nd Division however had heavy fighting on the Aire and La Bassée canals, and they held their ground. Farther to the east a strong German attack developed around Carvin, jointly defended by British and French troops. The situation was restored by the counter-attack of two battalions of the 50th Division, which were in bivouac close by. On the left of the British line the 5th Division, with the 143rd Brigade of the 48th Division under command, had travelled through the night, and at dawn took over the defence of the Ypres–Comines canal to close the gap which had opened between the British and Belgian armies. They were only just in time. Soon after they arrived the enemy attacked, and the fighting was heavy all day. Three battalions of the 1st Division in reserve were drawn in. The 50th Division, after bivouacking south of Lille, moved northwards to prolong the flank of the 5th Division around Ypres. The Belgian Army, heavily attacked throughout the day and with their right flank driven in, reported that they had no forces with which to regain touch with the British, and that they were unable to fall back to the line of the Yser canal in conformity with the British movement.

Meanwhile the organisation of the bridgeheads around Dunkirk was proceeding. The French were to hold from Gravelines to Bergues, and the British thence along the canal by Furnes to Nieuport and the sea. The various groups and parties of all arms which were arriving from both directions were woven into this line. Confirming the orders of the 26th, Lord Gort received from the War Office a telegram, dispatched at 1 p.m. on the 27th, telling him that his task henceforward was "to evacuate the maximum force possible". I had informed M. Reynaud the day before that the policy was to evacuate the British Expeditionary Force, and had requested him to issue corresponding orders. Such was the breakdown in communications that at 2 p.m. on the 27th the commander of the First French Army issued an order to his corps: *"La bataille sera livrée sans esprit de recul sur la position de la Lys."*

Four British divisions and the whole of the First French Army were now in dire peril of being cut off around Lille. The two arms of the German encircling movement strove to close the pincers upon them. Although we had not in those days the admirable map rooms of more coherent periods, and although no control of the battle from London was possible, I had for three days past been harrowed by the position of the mass of Allied troops around Lille, including our four fine divisions. This however was one of those rare but decisive moments when mechanical transport exercises its rights. When Gort gave the order all these four divisions came back with surprising rapidity almost in a night. Meanwhile, by fierce battles on either side of the corridor, the rest of the British Army kept the path open to the sea. The pincer-claws, which were delayed by the 2nd Division, and checked for three days by the 5th Division, eventually met on the night of May 29 in a manner similar to the great Russian operation round Stalingrad in 1942. The trap had taken two and a half days to close, and in that time four British divisions and a great part of the First French Army, except the Vth Corps, which was

AREA OF OPERATIONS, MAY 1940

lost, withdrew in good order through the gap, in spite of the French having only horse transport, and the main road to Dunkirk being already cut and the secondary roads filled with retiring troops, long trains of transport, and many thousands of refugees.

★　　★　　★

The question about our ability to go on alone, which I had asked Mr. Chamberlain to examine with other Ministers ten days before, was now put formally by me to our military advisers. I drafted the reference purposely in terms which, while giving a lead, left freedom to the Chiefs of Staff to express their view, whatever it might be. I knew beforehand that they were absolutely determined; but it is wise to have written records of such decisions. I wished moreover to be able to assure Parliament that our resolve was backed by professional opinion. Here it is, with the answer:

1. We have reviewed our report on "British Strategy in a Certain Eventuality" in the light of the following terms of reference remitted to us by the Prime Minister.

"In the event of France being unable to continue in the war and becoming neutral, with the Germans holding their present position and the Belgian Army being forced to capitulate after assisting the British Expeditionary Force to reach the coast; in the event of terms being offered to Britain which would place her entirely at the mercy of Germany through disarmament, cession of naval bases in the Orkneys, etc.; what are the prospects of our continuing the war alone against Germany and probably Italy? Can the Navy and the Air Force hold out reasonable hopes of preventing serious invasion, and could the forces gathered in this Island cope with raids from the air involving detachments not greater than 10,000 men; it being observed that a prolongation of British resistance might be very dangerous for Germany, engaged in holding down the greater part of Europe?"

2. Our conclusions are contained in the following paragraphs:

3. While our Air Force is in being, our Navy and Air Force together should be able to prevent Germany carrying out a serious sea-borne invasion of this country.

4. Supposing Germany gained complete air superiority, we consider that the Navy could hold up an invasion for a time, but not for an indefinite period.

5. If, with our Navy unable to prevent it, and our Air Force gone, Germany attempted an invasion, our coast and beach defences could not prevent German tanks and infantry getting a firm footing on our

shores. In the circumstances envisaged above our land forces would be insufficient to deal with a serious invasion.

6. The crux of the matter is air superiority. Once Germany had attained this she might attempt to subjugate this country by air attack alone.

7. Germany could not gain complete air superiority unless she could knock out our Air Force, and the aircraft industries, some vital portions of which are concentrated at Coventry and Birmingham.

8. Air attacks on the aircraft factories would be made by day or by night. We consider that we should be able to inflict such casualties on the enemy by day as to prevent serious damage. Whatever we do however by way of defensive measures—and we are pressing on with these with all dispatch—we cannot be sure of protecting the large industrial centres, upon which our aircraft industries depend, from serious material damage by night attack. The enemy would not have to employ precision bombing to achieve this effect.

9. Whether the attacks succeed in eliminating the aircraft industry depends not only on the material damage by bombs, but on the moral effect on the workpeople and their determination to carry on in the face of wholesale havoc and destruction.

10. If therefore the enemy presses home night attacks on our aircraft industry, he is likely to achieve such material and moral damage within the industrial area concerned as to bring all work to a standstill.

11. It must be remembered that numerically the Germans have a superiority of four to one. Moreover, the German aircraft factories are well dispersed and relatively inaccessible.

12. On the other hand, so long as we have a counter-offensive bomber force we can carry out similar attacks on German industrial centres and by moral and material effect bring a proportion of them to a standstill.

13. To sum up, our conclusion is that *prima facie* Germany has most of the cards; but the real test is whether the morale of our fighting personnel and civil population will counterbalance the numerical and material advantages which Germany enjoys. We believe it will.

This report, which of course was written at the darkest moment before the Dunkirk Deliverance, was signed not only by the three Chiefs of Staff, Newall, Pound, and Ironside, but by the three Vice-Chiefs, Dill, Phillips, and Peirse. Reading it in after years, I must admit that it was grave and grim. But the War Cabinet and the few other Ministers who saw it were all of one mind. There was no discussion. Heart and soul we were together.

*　　*　　*

I now addressed myself to Lord Gort:

27.V.40

1. At this solemn moment I cannot help sending you my good wishes. No one can tell how it will go. But anything is better than being cooped up and starved out. I venture these few remarks. First, cannon ought to kill tanks, and they may as well be lost doing that as any other way. Second, I feel very anxious about Ostend till it is occupied by a brigade with artillery. Third, very likely the enemy tanks attacking Calais are tired, and, anyhow, busy on Calais. A column directed upon Calais while it is still holding out might have a good chance. Perhaps they will be less formidable when attacked themselves.

2. It is now necessary to tell the Belgians. I am sending following telegram to Keyes, but your personal contact with the King is desirable. Keyes will help. We are asking them to sacrifice themselves for us.

3. Presume [our] troops know they are cutting their way home to Blighty. Never was there such a spur for fighting. We shall give you all that the Navy and Air Force can do. Anthony Eden is with me now and joins his good wishes to mine.

Enclosure

Prime Minister to Admiral Keyes

Impart following to your friend [the King of the Belgians]. Presume he knows that British and French are fighting their way to coast between Gravelines and Ostend inclusive, and that we propose to give fullest support from Navy and Air Force during hazardous embarkation. What can we do for him? Certainly we cannot serve Belgium's cause by being hemmed in and starved out. Our only hope is victory, and England will never quit the war whatever happens till Hitler is beat or we cease to be a State. Trust you will make sure he leaves with you by aeroplane before too late. Should our operation prosper and we establish [an] effective bridgehead, we would try, if desired, to carry some Belgian divisions to France by sea. Vitally important Belgium should continue in war, and safety [of] King's person essential.

My telegram did not reach Admiral Keyes until after his return to England on the 28th. In consequence this particular message was not delivered to King Leopold. The fact is not however important because on the afternoon of the 27th between 5 and 6 o'clock Admiral Keyes spoke to me on the telephone. The following passage is taken from his report.

At about 5 p.m. on the 27th, when the King told me his Army had collapsed and he was asking for a cessation of hostilities, a cipher telegram was sent to Gort and to the War Office by wireless. The War Office received it at 5.54 p.m. I motored at once to La Panne and telephoned to the Prime Minister. The Prime Minister was not at all surprised, in view of the repeated warnings, but he told me that I must make every endeavour to persuade the King and Queen [Mother] to come to England with me, and dictated a message which he said I ought to have received that afternoon:

27.V.40

"Belgian Embassy here assumes from King's decision to remain that he regards the war as lost and contemplates separate peace.

"It is in order to dissociate itself from this that the constitutional Belgian Government has reassembled on foreign soil. Even if present Belgian Army has to lay down its arms there are 200,000 Belgians of military age in France, and greater resources than Belgium had in 1914, on which to fight back. By present decision the King is dividing the nation and delivering it into Hitler's protection. Please convey these considerations to the King, and impress upon him the disastrous consequences to the Allies and to Belgium of his present choice."

I gave King Leopold the Prime Minister's message, but he said that he had made up his mind that he must stay with his Army and people. . . .

*　　*　　*

At home I issued the following general injunction:

(Strictly Confidential)   28.V.40

In these dark days the Prime Minister would be grateful if all his colleagues in the Government, as well as important officials, would maintain a high morale in their circles; not minimising the gravity of events, but showing confidence in our ability and inflexible resolve to continue the war till we have broken the will of the enemy to bring all Europe under his domination.

No tolerance should be given to the idea that France will make a separate peace; but whatever may happen on the Continent, we cannot doubt our duty, and we shall certainly use all our power to defend the Island, the Empire, and our Cause.

During the morning of the 28th Lord Gort met General Blanchard again. I am indebted to General Pownall, Lord Gort's Chief of Staff, for this record made by him at the time:

Blanchard's enthusiasm at the Cassel meeting had evaporated when he visited us to-day. He had no constructive suggestions or plans. We read to him the telegram ordering us to proceed to the coast with a view to embarkation. He was horrified. And that was strange; for what other reason did he think that he and Gort had been ordered to form bridgeheads? To what else could such a preliminary move lead? We pointed out that we had both received similar instructions regarding the bridgeheads. What had happened now was that we had got from our Government the next and logical step (which had no doubt been communicated to the French Government), whereas he had received as yet no such corresponding order. This pacified him somewhat, but by no means entirely. Then we said that we too, like him, wanted to keep the British and the First French Army together in this their last phase. Presumably therefore the First French Army would continue the retirement to-night, keeping aligned with us. Whereat he went completely off the deep end—it was impossible, he declared. We explained to him as clearly as the human tongue can explain the factors in the situation. The threat from the Germans on our north-eastern flank would probably not develop in strength for the next twenty-four hours (though when it did come it would be serious indeed). What was of immediate importance was the threat to our long south-western flank. There, as he well knew, advance-guards of German infantry divisions, supported by artillery, had made attacks yesterday at various points. Though the main points Wormhoudt, Cassel, Hazebrouck had held, there had been some penetration. The Germans might be relied upon to press these advantages, and we could be sure that the main bodies of the divisions would soon deploy and force themselves right across our line of withdrawal to the sea (a withdrawal which had been ordered for us, if not for him). There was therefore not a moment to be lost in getting back from the Lys, and we must get back to-night at least to the line Ypres-Poperinghe-Cassel. To wait till to-morrow night was to give *two* days to the Germans to get behind us, an act of madness. We thought it unlikely that we could get even 30 per cent. of our forces away even if we reached the sea; many indeed in forward positions would never reach it. But even if we could only save a small proportion of highly-trained officers and men it would be something useful to the continuance of the war. Everything possible must therefore be done, and the one thing that was possible, if only in part, was to get back some way to-night. . . .

Then came a liaison officer from General Prioux, now commanding the First Army. The liaison officer told Blanchard that Prioux had decided that he could *not* withdraw any farther to-night, and therefore intended to remain in the quadrangle of canals whose north-eastern corner is Armentières and south-western corner Béthune. This seemed to decide Blanchard against withdrawal. We begged him for the sake of the First Army and of the Allied cause to order Prioux to bring back at least some of his army in line with us. Not all of them could be so tired or so far away that it was impossible. For every man brought back there was at least *some* chance of embarkation, whereas every man who remained behind would certainly be eaten up. Why not *try* then? There was nothing to be gained by not trying: for those who did try there was at least *some* hope. But there was no shaking him. He declared that evacuation from the beach was impossible—no doubt the British Admiralty had arranged it for the B.E.F., but the French Marine would never be able to do it for French soldiers. It was therefore idle to try—the chance wasn't worth the effort involved; he agreed with Prioux.

He then asked, in terms, whether it was therefore Gort's intention to withdraw to-night to the line Ypres-Poperinghe-Cassel or not, knowing that in doing so Gort would be going *without* the French First Army. To which Gort replied that he *was* going. In the first place he had been ordered to re-embark, and to do so necessitated immediate withdrawal. To wait another twenty-four hours would mean that he would not be able to carry out his orders, for the troops would be cut off. In the second place, and apart from the formal aspect of obeying orders, it was madness to leave the troops forward in their present exposed positions. There they would certainly be overwhelmed very soon. For these reasons, therefore, and with great regret, it was necessary for the B.E.F. to withdraw even if the First French Army did not do so. . . .

*　　*　　*

In the early hours of the 28th the Belgian Army surrendered. Lord Gort received the formal intimation of this only one hour before the event, but the collapse had been foreseen three days earlier, and in one fashion or another the gap was plugged. I announced this event to the House in far more moderate terms than those M. Reynaud had thought it right to use.

The House will be aware that the King of the Belgians yesterday sent a plenipotentiary to the German Command asking for a suspension of arms on the Belgian front. The British and French Governments instructed their generals immediately to dissociate themselves from this procedure and to persevere in the operations in which they are now engaged. However, the German Command has agreed to the Belgian proposals and the Belgian Army ceased to resist the enemy's will at four o'clock this morning.

I have no intention of suggesting to the House that we should attempt at this moment to pass judgment upon the action of the King of the Belgians in his capacity as Commander-in-Chief of the Belgian

Army. This army has fought very bravely and has both suffered and inflicted heavy losses. The Belgian Government has dissociated itself from the action of the King, and, declaring itself to be the only legal Government of Belgium, has formally announced its resolve to continue the war at the side of the Allies.

Concern was expressed by the French Government that my reference to King Leopold's action was in sharp contrast to that of M. Reynaud. I thought it my duty, when speaking in the House on June 4, after a careful examination of the fuller facts then available, and in justice not only to our French Ally but also to the Belgian Government now in London, to state the truth in plain terms.

At the last moment, when Belgium was already invaded, King Leopold called upon us to come to his aid, and even at the last moment we came. He and his brave, efficient Army, nearly half a million strong, guarded our left flank and thus kept open our only line of retreat to the sea. Suddenly, without prior consultation, with the least possible notice, without the advice of his Ministers and upon his own personal act, he sent a plenipotentiary to the German Command, surrendered his Army, and exposed our whole flank and means of retreat.

The brave and efficient army of which I spoke had indeed conducted itself in accordance with its best traditions. They were overcome by an enemy whom it was beyond their power to resist for long. That they were defeated and ordered to surrender is no slur upon their honour or reputation.

*　　*　　*

All this day of the 28th the escape of the British Army hung in the balance. On the front from Comines to Ypres and thence to the sea, facing east and attempting to fill the Belgian gap, General Brooke and his IInd Corps fought a magnificent battle. For two days past the 5th Division had held Comines against all attacks, but as the Belgians withdrew northwards, and then capitulated, the gap widened beyond repair. The protection of the flank of the B.E.F. was now their task. First the 50th Division came in to prolong the line; then the 4th and 3rd Divisions, newly withdrawn from east of Lille, hastened in motor transport to extend the wall of the vital corridor that led to Dunkirk. The German thrust between the British and Belgian Armies was not to be prevented, but its fatal consequence, an inward turn across the Yser,

SITUATION 28 MAY

which would have brought the enemy on to the beaches behind our fighting troops, was foreseen and everywhere forestalled.

The Germans sustained a bloody repulse. Orders were given to the British artillery, both field and medium, to fire off all their ammunition at the enemy, and the tremendous fire did much to quell the German assault. All the time, only about four miles behind Brooke's struggling front, vast masses of transport and troops poured back into the developing bridgehead of Dunkirk, and were fitted with skilful improvisation into its defences. Moreover, within the perimeter itself the main east-west road was at one time completely blocked by vehicles, and a one-way track was cleared only by bulldozers hurling them into the ditches on either side.

In the afternoon of the 28th Gort ordered a general withdrawal to the bridgehead, which now ran Gravelines–Bergues–Furnes–Nieuport. On this front the British divisions stood from right to left, and from Bergues to the sea by Nieuport, in the following order: 46th, 42nd, 1st, 50th, 3rd, and 4th. By the 29th a large part of the B.E.F. had arrived within the perimeter, and by this time the naval measures for evacuation were beginning to attain their full effect. On May 30 G.H.Q. reported that all British divisions, or the remains of them, had come in.

More than half the First French Army found their way to Dunkirk, where the great majority were safely embarked. But the line of retreat of at least five divisions was cut by the German pincers movement west of Lille. On the 28th they attempted to break out westwards, but in vain; the enemy closed in upon them from all sides. All through the next three days the French in Lille fought on gradually contracting fronts against increasing pressure, until on the evening of the 31st, short of food and with their ammunition exhausted, they were forced to surrender. About fifty thousand men thus fell into German hands. These Frenchmen, under the gallant leadership of General Molinié, had for four critical days contained no less than seven German divisions which otherwise could have joined in the assaults on the Dunkirk perimeter. This was a splendid contribution to the escape of their more fortunate comrades and of the B.E.F.

* * *

It was a severe experience for me, bearing so heavy an overall responsibility, to watch during these days in flickering glimpses this drama in which control was impossible, and intervention more likely to do harm than good. There is no doubt that by pressing in all loyalty the Weygand plan of retirement to the Somme as long as we did, our dangers, already so grave, were increased. But Gort's decision, in which we speedily concurred, to abandon the Weygand plan and march to the sea was executed by him and his staff with masterly skill, and will ever be regarded as a brilliant episode in British military annals.

The Hell that was Dunkirk

11 The town after the bombardment.

12 Soldiers wading with difficulty through the water to the nearest craft.

13 The extraordinary crowding of ships in port.
14 British and French soldiers waiting their turn on the beaches for embarkation.

15 A bomb explodes at Dunkirk.
16 What was left of the town on the 4th June, 1940.

CHAPTER V

THE DELIVERANCE OF DUNKIRK

May 26—June 4

Service of Intercession and Prayer – "Hard and Heavy Tidings" – A Demonstration of Ministers – The Gathering of the Little Ships – Seven Hundred Vessels – Three Vital Factors – The Mosquito Armada – Bringing Off the French – Final Orders to Lord Gort – A Possible Consequence – Gort Transfers the Dunkirk Command to Alexander – My Third Visit to Paris, May 31 – General Spears and Marshal Pétain – The Evacuation Complete – My Statement to Parliament, June 4 – Significance of the Air Victory – Britain's Resolve.

*T*HERE was a short service of Intercession and Prayer in Westminster Abbey on May 26. The English are loth to expose their feelings, but in my stall in the Choir I could feel the pent-up, passionate emotion, and also the fear of the congregation, not of death or wounds or material loss, but of defeat and the final ruin of Britain.

* * *

It was Tuesday, May 28, and I did not again attend the House until that day week. There was no advantage to be gained by a further statement in the interval, nor did Members express a wish for one. But everyone realised that the fate of our Army and perhaps much else might well be decided before the week was out. "The House," I said, "should prepare itself for hard and heavy tidings. I have only to add that nothing which may happen in this battle can in any way relieve us of our duty to defend the world cause to which we have vowed ourselves; nor should it destroy our confidence in our power to make our way, as on former occasions in our history, through disaster and through grief to the ultimate defeat of our enemies." I had not seen many of my colleagues outside the War Cabinet, except individually, since the formation of the Government, and I thought it right to have a meeting in my room at the House of Commons of all Ministers of Cabinet rank other than the War Cabinet Members. We were perhaps twenty-five round the table. I described the course of events, and I showed them plainly where we were, and all that was in the balance. Then I said quite casually, and not treating it as a point of special significance:

"Of course, whatever happens at Dunkirk, we shall fight on."

There occurred a demonstration which, considering the character of the gathering—twenty-five experienced politicians and Parliament men, who represented all the different points of view, whether right or wrong, before the war—surprised me. Quite a number seemed to jump up from the table and come running to my chair, shouting and patting me on the back. There is no doubt that had I at this juncture faltered at all in the leading of the nation I should have been hurled out of office. I was sure that every Minister was ready to be killed quite soon, and have all his family and possessions destroyed, rather than give in. In this they represented the House of Commons and almost all the people. It fell to me in these coming days and months to express their sentiments on suitable occasions. This I was able to do because they were mine also. There was a white glow, overpowering, sublime, which ran through our Island from end to end.

* * *

Accurate and excellent accounts have been written of the evacuation of the British and French armies from Dunkirk. Ever since the 20th the gathering of shipping and small craft had been proceeding under the control of Admiral Ramsay, who commanded at Dover. On the evening of the 26th (6.57 p.m.) an Admiralty signal put Operation "Dynamo" into play, and the first troops were brought home that night. After the loss of Boulogne and Calais only the remains of the port of Dunkirk and the open beaches next to the Belgian frontier were in our hands. At this time it was thought that the most we could rescue was about forty-five thousand men in two days. Early the next morning, May 27, emergency measures were taken to find additional small craft "for a special requirement". This was no less than the full evacuation of the British Expeditionary Force.

It was plain that large numbers of such craft would be required for work on the beaches, in addition to bigger ships which could load in Dunkirk harbour. On the suggestion of Mr. H. C. Riggs, of the Ministry of Shipping, the various boatyards, from Teddington to Brightlingsea, were searched by Admiralty officers, and yielded upwards of forty serviceable motor-boats or launches, which were assembled at Sheerness on the following day. At the same time lifeboats from liners in the London docks, tugs from the Thames, yachts, fishing-craft, lighters, barges, and pleasure-boats—anything that could be of use along the beaches—were called into service. By the night of the 27th a great tide of small vessels began to flow towards the sea, first to our Channel ports, and thence to the beaches of Dunkirk and the beloved Army.

Once the need for secrecy was relaxed the Admiralty did not hesitate to give full rein to the spontaneous movement which swept the seafaring population of our south and south-eastern shores. Everyone who had a boat of any kind, steam or sail, put out for Dunkirk, and the preparations, fortunately begun a week earlier, were now aided by the brilliant improvisation of volunteers on an amazing scale. The numbers arriving on the 29th were small, but they were the forerunners of nearly four hundred small craft which from the 31st were destined to play a vital part by ferrying from the beaches to the off-lying ships almost a hundred thousand men. In these days I missed the head of my Admiralty Map Room, Captain Pim, and one or two other familiar faces. They had got hold of a Dutch *schuit* which in four days brought off eight hundred soldiers. Altogether there came to the rescue of the Army under the ceaseless air bombardment of the enemy about eight hundred and sixty vessels, of which nearly seven hundred were British and the rest Allied.

Here is the official list, in which ships not engaged in embarking troops are omitted:

BRITISH SHIPS

	Total engaged	Sunk	Damaged
A.A. Cruiser	1	—	1
Destroyers	39	6	19
Sloops, Corvettes, and Gunboats ..	5	1	1

	Total engaged	Sunk	Damaged
Minesweepers	30	5	7
Trawlers and Drifters	77	17	6
Special Service Vessels	3	1	—
Armed Boarding Vessels	3	1	1
Motor Torpedo-boats and Motor Anti-Submarine Boats ..	4	—	—
Dutch *Schuits* (British Naval Crews)	40	4	(Not recorded)
Yachts (Naval Crews)	26	3	(Not recorded)
Personnel Ships	45	8	8
Hospital Carriers	8	1	5
Naval Motor Boats	12	6	(Not recorded)
Tugs	22	3	(Not recorded)
*Other Small Craft	372	170	(Not recorded)
Total ..	693	226	

ALLIED SHIPS

	Total engaged	Sunk	Damaged
Warships (all types)	49	8	(Not recorded)
Other Ships and Craft	119	9	(Not recorded)
Total ..	168	17	
Grand Total ..	861	243	

★   ★   ★

Meanwhile ashore around Dunkirk the occupation of the perimeter was effected with precision. The troops arrived out of chaos and were formed in order along the defences, which even in two days had grown. Those men who were in best shape

★ Omitting ships' lifeboats and some other privately owned small craft, of which no record is available.

turned about to form the line. Divisions like the 2nd and 5th, which had suffered most, were held in reserve on the beaches and were then embarked early. In the first instance there were to be three corps on the front, but by the 29th, with the French taking a greater share in the defences, two sufficed. The enemy had closely followed the withdrawal, and hard fighting was incessant, especially on the flanks near Nieuport and Bergues. As the evacuation went on the steady decrease in the number of troops, both British and French, was accompanied by a corresponding contraction of the defence. On the beaches, among the sand dunes, for three, four, or five days scores of thousands of men dwelt under unrelenting air attack. Hitler's belief that the German Air Force would render escape impossible, and that therefore he should keep his armoured formations for the final stroke of the campaign, was a mistaken but not unreasonable view.

Three factors falsified his expectations. First, the incessant air-bombing of the masses of troops along the seashore did them very little harm. The bombs plunged into the soft sand, which muffled their explosions. In the early stages, after a crashing air raid, the troops were astonished to find that hardly anybody had been killed or wounded. Everywhere there had been explosions, but scarcely anyone was the worse. A rocky shore would have produced far more deadly results. Presently the soldiers regarded the air attacks with contempt. They crouched in the sand dunes with composure and growing hope. Before them lay the grey but not unfriendly sea. Beyond, the rescuing ships and—Home.

The second factor which Hitler had not foreseen was the slaughter of his airmen. British and German air quality was put directly to the test. By intense effort Fighter Command maintained successive patrols over the scene, and fought the enemy at long odds. Hour after hour they bit into the German fighter and bomber squadrons, taking a heavy toll, scattering them and driving them away. Day after day this went on, till the glorious victory of the Royal Air Force was gained. Wherever German aircraft were encountered, sometimes in forties and fifties, they were instantly attacked, often by single squadrons or less, and shot down in scores, which presently added up into hundreds. The whole Metropolitan Air Force, our last sacred reserve, was used. Sometimes the fighter pilots made four sorties a day. A clear result was obtained. The superior enemy were beaten or killed, and for all their bravery mastered, or even cowed. This was a decisive clash. Unhappily, the troops on the beaches saw very little of this epic conflict in the air, often miles away or above the clouds. They knew nothing of the loss inflicted on the enemy. All they felt was the bombs scourging the beaches, cast by the foes who had got through, but did not perhaps return. There was even a bitter anger in the Army against the Air Force, and some of the troops landing at Dover or at Thames ports in their ignorance insulted men in Air Force uniform. They should have clasped their hands; but how could they know? In Parliament I took pains to spread the truth.

But all the aid of the sand and all the prowess in the air would have been vain without the sea. The instructions given ten or twelve days before had, under the pressure and emotion of events, borne amazing fruit. Perfect discipline prevailed ashore and afloat. The sea was calm. To and fro between the shore and the ships plied the little boats, gathering the men from the beaches as they waded out or picking them from the water, with total indifference to the air bombardment, which often claimed its victims. Their numbers alone defied air attack. The Mosquito Armada as a whole was unsinkable. In the midst of our defeat glory came to the Island people, united and unconquerable; and the tale of the Dunkirk beaches will shine in whatever records are preserved of our affairs.

Notwithstanding the valiant work of the small craft it must not be forgotten that the heaviest burden fell on the ships plying from Dunkirk harbour, where two-thirds of the men were embarked. The destroyers played the predominant part, as the casualty list on pages 89–90 shows. Nor must the great part played by the personnel ships with their mercantile crews be overlooked.

* * *

The progress of the evacuation was watched with anxious eyes and growing hope. On the evening of the 27th Lord Gort's position appeared critical to the naval authorities, and Captain Tennant, R.N., from the Admiralty, who had assumed the duties of Senior Naval Officer at Dunkirk, signalled for all available craft to be sent to the beaches immediately, as "evacuation to-morrow night is problematical". The picture presented was grim, even desperate. Extreme efforts were made to meet the call, and a

DIAGRAM OF DUNKIRK PERIMETER, 29-30 MAY

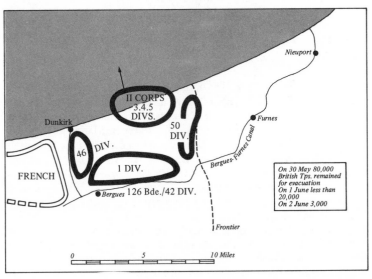

DIAGRAM OF DUNKIRK PERIMETER, 31 MAY—1 JUNE

cruiser, eight destroyers, and twenty-six other vessels were sent. The 28th was a day of tension, which gradually eased as the position on land was stabilised with the powerful help of the Royal Air Force. The naval plans were carried through despite severe losses on the 29th, when three destroyers and twenty-one other vessels were sunk and many others damaged.

There was never any question of our leaving the French behind. Here was my order before any request or complaint from the French was received:

Prime Minister to Secretary of State for War,
C.I.G.S., and General Ismay   29.V.40
    (Original to C.I.G.S.)

It is essential that the French should share in such evacuations from Dunkirk as may be possible. Nor must they be dependent only upon their own shipping resources. Arrangements must be concerted at once with the French Missions in this country, or, if necessary, with the French Government, so that no reproaches, or as few as possible, may arise. It might perhaps be well if we evacuated the two French divisions from Dunkirk, and replaced them *pro tem.* with our own troops, thus simplifying the command. But let me have the best proposals possible, and advise me whether there is any action I should take.

Prime Minister to General Spears (Paris)   29.V.40

Following for Reynaud, for communication to Weygand and Georges:

We have evacuated nearly 50,000 from Dunkirk and beaches, and hope another 30,000 to-night. Front may be beaten in at any time, or piers, beaches, and shipping rendered unusable by air attack, and also by artillery fire from the south-west. No one can tell how long present good flow will last, or how much we can save for future. We wish French troops to share in evacuation to fullest possible extent, and Admiralty have been instructed to aid French Marine as required. We do not know how many will be forced to capitulate, but we must share this loss together as best we can, and, above all, bear it without reproaches arising from inevitable confusion, stresses, and strains.

As soon as we have reorganised our evacuated troops, and prepared forces necessary to safeguard our life against threatened and perhaps imminent invasion, we shall build up a new B.E.F. from St. Nazaire. I am bringing Regulars from India and Palestine; Australians and Canadians are arriving soon. At present we are removing equipment south of Amiens beyond what is needed for five divisions. But this is only to get into order and meet impending shock, and we shall shortly send you new scheme for reinforcement of our troops in France. I send this in all comradeship. Do not hesitate to speak frankly to me.

*   *   *

On the 30th I held a meeting of the three Service Ministers and the Chiefs of Staff in the Admiralty War Room. We considered the events of the day on the Belgian coast. The total number of troops brought off had risen to 120,000, including only 6,000 French; 860 vessels of all kinds were at work. A message from Admiral Wake-Walker at Dunkirk said that, in spite of intense bombardment and air attack, 4,000 men had been embarked in the previous hour. He also thought that Dunkirk itself would probably be untenable by the next day. I emphasised the urgent need of getting off more French troops. To fail to do so might do irreparable harm to the relations between ourselves and our Ally. I also said that when the British strength was reduced to that of a corps we ought to tell Lord Gort to embark and return to England, leaving a Corps Commander in charge. The British Army would have to stick it out as long as possible so that the evacuation of the French could continue.

Knowing well the character of Lord Gort, I wrote out in my own hand the following order to him, which was sent officially by the War Office at 2 p.m. on the 30th:

Continue to defend the present perimeter to the utmost in order to cover maximum evacuation now proceeding well. Report every three hours through La Panne. If we can still communicate we shall send you an order to return to England with such officers as you may choose at the moment when we deem your command so reduced that it can be handed over to a Corps Commander. You should now nominate this Commander. If communications are broken you are to hand over and return as specified when your effective fighting force does not exceed the equivalent of three divisions. This is in accordance with correct military procedure, and no personal discretion is left you in the matter. On political grounds it would be a needless triumph to the enemy to capture you when only a small force remained under your orders. The Corps Commander chosen by you should be ordered to carry on the defence in conjunction with the French, and evacuation whether from Dunkirk or the beaches, but when in his judgment no further organised evacuation is possible and no further proportionate damage can be inflicted on the enemy he is authorised in consultation with the senior French Commander to capitulate formally to avoid useless slaughter.

It is possible that this last message influenced other great events and the fortunes of another valiant Commander. When I was at the White House at the end of December 1941 I learned from the President and Mr. Stimson of the approaching fate of General MacArthur and the American garrison at Corregidor. I thought it right to show them the way in which we had dealt with the position of a Commander-in-Chief whose force was reduced to a small fraction of his original command. The President and Mr. Stimson both read the telegram with profound attention, and I was struck by the impression it seemed to make upon them. A little later in the day Mr. Stimson came back and asked for a copy of it, which I immediately gave him. It may be (for I do not know) that this influenced them in the right decision which they took in ordering General MacArthur to hand over his command to one of his subordinate generals, and thus saved for all his future glorious services the great Commander who would otherwise have perished or passed the war as a Japanese captive. I should like to think this was true.

*　　*　　*

On the 30th members of Lord Gort's staff in conference with Admiral Ramsay at Dover informed him that daylight on June 1 was the latest time up to which the eastern perimeter might be expected to hold. Evacuation was therefore pressed on with the utmost urgency to ensure, so far as possible, that a British rearguard of no more than about four thousand men would then remain ashore. Later it was found that this number would be insufficient to defend the final covering positions, and it was decided to hold the British sector until midnight June 1–2, evacuation proceeding meanwhile on the basis of full equality between French and British forces.

Such was the situation when on the evening of May 31 Lord Gort in accordance with his orders handed over his command to Major-General Alexander and returned to England.

*　　*　　*

To avoid misunderstandings by keeping personal contact it was necessary for me to fly to Paris on May 31 for a meeting of the Supreme War Council. With me in the plane came Mr. Attlee and Generals Dill and Ismay. I also took General Spears, who had flown over on the 30th with the latest news from Paris. This brilliant officer and Member of Parliament was a friend of mine from the First Great War. Liaison officer between the left of the French and the right of the British Armies, he had taken me round the Vimy Ridge in 1916, and had made me friends with General Fayolle, who commanded the 33rd French Corps. Speaking French with a perfect accent and bearing five wound-stripes on his sleeve, he was a personality at this moment fitted to our anxious relations. When Frenchmen and Englishmen are in trouble together and arguments break out, the Frenchman is often voluble and vehement, and the Englishman unresponsive or even rude. But Spears could say things to the high French personnel with an ease and force which I have never seen equalled.

This time we did not go to the Quai d'Orsay, but to M. Reynaud's room at the War Office in the Rue Saint-Dominique. Attlee and I found Reynaud and Marshal Pétain opposite to us as the only French Ministers. This was the first appearance of Pétain, now Vice-President of the Council, at any of our meetings. He wore plain clothes. Our Ambassador, Dill, Ismay, and Spears were with us, and Weygand and Darlan, Captain de Margerie, head of Reynaud's private office, and M. Baudouin, Secretary of the French War Cabinet, represented the French.

The first question was the position in Norway. I said that the British Government was of the considered opinion that the Narvik area should be evacuated at once. Our troops there, the destroyers involved, and a hundred anti-aircraft guns were badly wanted elsewhere. We therefore proposed an evacuation beginning on June 2. The British Navy would transport and repatriate the French forces, the King of Norway, and any Norwegian troops who wished to come. Reynaud said that the French Government agreed with this policy. The destroyers would be urgently required in the Mediterranean in the event of war with Italy. The 16,000 men would be very valuable on the line of the Aisne and the Somme. This matter was therefore settled.

I then turned to Dunkirk. The French seemed to have no more idea of what was happening to the Northern Armies than we had about the main French front. When I told them that 165,000 men, of whom 15,000 were French, had been taken off they were astonished. They naturally drew attention to the marked British preponderance. I explained that this was due largely to the fact that there had been many British administrative units in the back area who had been able to embark before fighting troops could be spared from the front. Moreover, the French up to the present had had no orders to evacuate. One of the chief reasons why I had come to Paris was to make sure that the same orders were given to the French troops as to the British. The three British divisions now holding the centre would cover the evacuation of all the Allied forces. That, and the sea transport, would be the British contribution to offset the heavy Allied losses which must now be faced. His Majesty's Government had felt it necessary in the dire circumstances to order Lord Gort to take off fighting men and leave the wounded behind. If present hopes were confirmed, 200,000 able-bodied troops might be got away. This would be almost a miracle. Four days ago I would not have wagered on more than 50,000 as a maximum. I dwelt upon our terrible losses in equipment. Reynaud paid a handsome tribute to the work of the British Navy and Air Force, for which I thanked him. We then spoke at some length upon what could be done to rebuild the British forces in France.

Meanwhile Admiral Darlan had drafted a telegram to Admiral Abrial at Dunkirk:

(1) A bridgehead shall be held round Dunkirk with the divisions under your command and those under British command.

(2) As soon as you are convinced that no troops outside the bridgehead can make their way to the points of embarkation the troops holding the bridgehead shall withdraw and embark, *the British forces embarking first.*

I intervened at once to say that the British would not embark first, but that the evacuation should proceed on equal terms between the British and the French—"*Bras dessus bras dessous.*" The British would form the rearguard. This was agreed.

The conversation next turned to Italy. I expressed the British view that if Italy came in we should strike at her at once in the most effective manner. Many Italians were opposed to war, and all should be made to realise its severity. I proposed that we should strike by air-bombing at the north-western industrial triangle enclosed by the three cities of Milan, Turin and Genoa. Reynaud agreed that the Allies must strike at once; and Admiral Darlan said he had a plan ready for the naval and aerial bombardment of

Italy's oil supplies, largely stored along the coast between the frontier and Naples. The necessary technical discussions were arranged.

I then mentioned my desire that more Ministers of the Administration I had just formed should become acquainted with their French opposite numbers as soon as possible. For instance, I should like Mr. Bevin, the Minister of Labour and trade union leader, to visit Paris. Mr. Bevin was showing great energy, and under his leadership the British working class was now giving up holidays and privileges to a far greater extent than in the last war. Reynaud cordially assented.

After some talk about Tangier and the importance of keeping Spain out of the war, I spoke on the general outlook. The Allies, I said, must maintain an unflinching front against all their enemies. ... The United States had been roused by recent events, and, even if they did not enter the war, would soon be prepared to give us powerful aid. An invasion of England, if it took place, would have a still more profound effect on the United States. England did not fear invasion, and would resist it most fiercely in every village and hamlet. It was only after her essential need of troops had been met that the balance of her armed forces could be put at the disposal of her French ally. .... I was absolutely convinced we had only to carry on the fight to conquer. Even if one of us should be struck down, the other must not abandon the struggle. The British Government were prepared to wage war from the New World, if through some disaster England herself were laid waste. If Germany defeated either ally or both, she would give no mercy; we should be reduced to the status of vassals and slaves for ever. It would be better far that the civilisation of Western Europe with all its achievements should come to a tragic but splendid end than that the two great democracies should linger on, stripped of all that made life worth living.

Mr. Attlee then said that he entirely agreed with my view. "The British people now realise the danger with which they are faced, and know that in the event of a German victory everything they have built up will be destroyed. The Germans kill not only men, but ideas. Our people are resolved as never before in their history." Reynaud thanked us for what we had said. He was sure that the morale of the German people was not up to the level of the momentary triumph of their Army. If France could hold the Somme with the help of Britain and if American industry came in to make good the disparity in arms, then we could be sure of victory. He was most grateful, he said, for my renewed assurance that if one country went under the other would not abandon the struggle.

The formal meeting then ended.

After we rose from the table some of the principals talked together in the bay window in a somewhat different atmosphere. Chief among these was Marshal Pétain. Spears was with me, helping me out with my French and speaking himself. The young Frenchman, Captain de Margerie, had already spoken about fighting it out in Africa. But Marshal Pétain's attitude, detached and sombre, gave me the feeling that he would face a separate peace. The influence of his personality, his reputation, his serene acceptance of the march of adverse events, apart from any words he used, was almost overpowering to those under his spell. One of the Frenchmen, I cannot remember who, said in their polished way that a continuance of military reverses might in certain eventualities enforce a modification of foreign policy upon France. Here Spears rose to the occasion, and, addressing himself particularly to Marshal Pétain, said in perfect French: "I suppose you understand, M. le Maréchal, that that would mean blockade?" Someone else said: "That would perhaps be inevitable." But then Spears to Pétain's face: "That would not only mean blockade, but *bombardment* of all French ports in German hands." I was glad to have this said. I sang my usual song: we would fight on whatever happened or whoever fell out.

* * *

Again we had a night of petty raids, and in the morning I departed. Here was the information that awaited me on my return:

Prime Minister to General Weygand   1.VI.40
Crisis in evacuation now reached. Five fighter squadrons, acting almost continuously, is the most we can do, but six ships, several filled with troops, sunk by bombing this morning. Artillery fire menacing only practicable channel. Enemy closing in on reduced bridgehead. By trying to hold on till to-morrow we may lose all. By going to-night much may certainly be saved, though much will be lost. Nothing like numbers of effective French troops you mention believed in bridge-

head now, and we doubt whether such large numbers remain in area. Situation cannot be fully judged by Admiral Abrial in the fortress, nor by you, nor by us here. We have therefore ordered General Alexander, commanding British sector of bridgehead, to judge, in consultation with Admiral Abrial, whether to try to stay over to-morrow or not. Trust you will agree.

May 31 and June 1 saw the climax though not the end at Dunkirk. On these two days over 132,000 men were safely landed in England, nearly one-third of them having been brought from the beaches in small craft under fierce air attack and shell-fire. On June 1 from early dawn onward the enemy bombers made their greatest efforts, often timed when our own fighters had withdrawn to refuel. These attacks took heavy toll of the crowded shipping, which suffered almost as much as in all the previous week. On this single day our losses by air attack, by mines, E-boats, or other misadventure were thirty-one ships sunk and eleven damaged. On land the enemy increased their pressure on the bridgehead, doing their utmost to break through. They were held at bay by the desperate resistance of the Allied rear-guards.

The final phase was carried through with much skill and precision. For the first time it became possible to plan ahead instead of being forced to rely on hourly improvisations. At dawn on June 2 about four thousand British with seven anti-aircraft guns and twelve anti-tank guns remained on the outskirts of Dunkirk with the still considerable French forces holding the contracting perimeter. Evacuation was now possible only in darkness, and Admiral Ramsay determined to make a massed descent on the harbour that night with all his available resources. Besides tugs and small craft, forty-four ships were sent that even-ing from England, including eleven destroyers and fourteen mine-sweepers. Forty French and Belgian vessels also participated. Before midnight the British rearguard was embarked.

This was not however the end of the Dunkirk story. We had been prepared to carry considerably greater numbers of French that night than had offered themselves. The result was that when our ships, many of them still empty, had to withdraw at dawn, great numbers of French troops, many still in contact with the enemy, remained ashore. One more effort had to be made. Despite the exhaustion of ships' companies after so many days without rest or respite, the call was answered. On June 4 26,175 Frenchmen were landed in England, over twenty-one thousand of them in British ships. Unfortunately several thousands remained, who continued the fight in the contracting bridgehead until the morning of the 4th, when the enemy was in the outskirts of the town and they had come to an end of their powers. They had fought gallantly for many days to cover the evacuation of their British and French comrades. They were to spend the next years in captivity. Let us remember that but for the endurance of the Dunkirk rearguard the re-creation of an army in Britain for home defence and final victory would have been gravely prejudiced.

Finally, at 2.23 p.m. on June 4 the Admiralty, in agreement with the French, announced that Operation "Dynamo" was now completed.

BRITISH AND ALLIED TROOPS LANDED IN ENGLAND*

Date		From the Beaches	From Dunkirk Harbour	Total	Accumulated Total
May 27	..	Nil	7,669	7,669	7,669
28	..	5,930	11,874	17,804	25,473
29	..	13,752	33,558	47,310	72,783
30	..	29,512	24,311	53,823	126,606
31	..	22,942	45,072	68,014	194,620
June 1	..	17,348	47,081	64,429	259,049
2	..	6,695	19,561	26,256	285,305
3	..	1,870	24,876	26,746	312,051
4	..	622	25,553	26,175	338,226
GRAND TOTAL		98,671	239,555	338,226	

* * *

Parliament assembled on June 4, and it was my duty to lay the story fully before them both in public and later in secret session. The narrative requires only a few extracts from my speech, which is extant. It was imperative to explain not only to our own people but to the world that our resolve to fight on was based on serious

* These figures are taken from a final analysis of the Admiralty records. The War Office figure for the total number of men landed in England is 336,427.

grounds, and was no mere despairing effort. It was also right to lay bare my own reasons for confidence.

We must be very careful not to assign to this deliverance the attributes of a victory. Wars are not won by evacuations. But there was a victory inside this deliverance, which should be noted. It was gained by the Air Force. Many of our soldiers coming back have not seen the Air Force at work; they saw only the bombers which escaped its protective attack. They underrate its achievements. I have heard much talk of this; that is why I go out of my way to say this. I will tell you about it.

This was a great trial of strength between the British and German Air Forces. Can you conceive a greater objective for the Germans in the air than to make evacuation from these beaches impossible, and to sink all these ships which were displayed, almost to the extent of thousands? Could there have been an objective of greater military importance and significance for the whole purpose of the war than this? They tried hard, and they were beaten back; they were frustrated in their task. We got the Army away; and they have paid fourfold for any losses which they have inflicted. . . . All of our types and all our pilots have been vindicated as superior to what they have at present to face.

When we consider how much greater would be our advantage in defending the air above this Island against an overseas attack, I must say that I find in these facts a sure basis upon which practical and reassuring thoughts may rest. I will pay my tribute to these young airmen. The great French Army was very largely, for the time being, cast back and disturbed by the onrush of a few thousands of armoured vehicles. May it not also be that the cause of civilisation itself will be defended by the skill and devotion of a few thousand airmen?

We are told that Herr Hitler has a plan for invading the British Isles. This has often been thought of before. When Napoleon lay at Boulogne for a year with his flat-bottomed boats and his Grand Army he was told by someone: "There are bitter weeds in England." There are certainly a great many more of them since the British Expeditionary Force returned.

The whole question of Home Defence against invasion is, of course, powerfully affected by the fact that we have for the time being in this Island incomparably stronger military forces than we have ever had at any moment in this war or the last. But this will not continue. We shall not be content with a defensive war. We have our duty to our Ally. We have to reconstitute and build up the British Expeditionary Force once again, under its gallant Commander-in-Chief, Lord Gort. All this is in train; but in the interval we must put our defences in this Island into such a high state of organisation that the fewest possible numbers will be required to give effective security and that the largest possible potential of offensive effort may be realised. On this we are now engaged.

I ended in a passage which was to prove, as will be seen, a timely and important factor in United States decisions.

"Even though large tracts of Europe and many old and famous States have fallen or may fall into the grip of the Gestapo and all the odious apparatus of Nazi rule, we shall not flag or fail. We shall go on to the end. We shall fight in France, we shall fight in the seas and oceans, we shall fight with growing confidence and growing strength in the air; we shall defend our Island, whatever the cost may be. We shall fight on the beaches, we shall fight on the landing-grounds, we shall fight in the fields and in the streets, we shall fight in the hills; we shall never surrender; and even if, which I do not for a moment believe, this Island or a large part of it were subjugated and starving, then our Empire beyond the seas, armed and guarded by the British Fleet, would carry on the struggle, until, in God's good time, the New World, with all its power and might, steps forth to the rescue and the liberation of the Old."

CHAPTER VI

THE RUSH FOR THE SPOILS

Traditional British and Italian Friendship – Advantages to Italy and Mussolini of Neutrality – My Message to Mussolini on Becoming Prime Minister – His Hard Response – Reynaud's Visit to London of May 26 – France and Britain Invite President Roosevelt to Intervene – My Telegram Conveying the Cabinet Decision of May 28 – Preparations to Strike at Italy Should She Declare War – Italy and Yugoslavia – The Italian Declaration of War – The Attack on the Alpine Front Stopped by the French Army – Ciano's Letter to Me of December 23, 1943 – President Roosevelt's Denunciation of Italy – My Telegram to Him of June 11 – Anglo-Soviet Relations – Molotov's Congratulations upon German Victories – Sir Stafford Cripps Appointed Ambassador to Moscow – My Letter to Stalin of June 25, 1940 – The Soviet Share of the Spoil.

*T*HE friendship between the British and Italian peoples sprang from the days of Garibaldi and Cavour. Every stage in the liberation of Northern Italy from Austria and every step towards Italian unity and independence had commanded the sympathies of Victorian Liberalism. This had bred a warm and enduring response. The declaration in the original Treaty of Triple Alliance between Italy, Germany, and the Austro-Hungarian Empire stipulated that in no circumstances should Italy be drawn into war with Great Britain. British influence had powerfully contributed to the Italian accession to the Allied cause in the First World War. The rise of Mussolini and the establishment of Fascism as a counter to Bolshevism had in its early phases divided British opinion on party lines, but had not affected the broad foundations of goodwill between the peoples. We have seen that until Mussolini's designs against Abyssinia had raised grave issues he had ranged himself with Great Britain in oppo-

sition to Hitlerism and German ambitions. I have told in the previous volume the sad tale of how the Baldwin-Chamberlain
policy about Abyssinia brought us the worst of both worlds, how
we estranged the Italian dictator without breaking his power, and
how the League of Nations was injured without Abyssinia being
saved. We have also seen the earnest but futile efforts made by
Mr. Chamberlain, Sir Samuel Hoare, and Lord Halifax to win
back during the period of appeasement Mussolini's lost favour.
And finally there was the growth of Mussolini's conviction that
Britain's sun had set, and that Italy's future could, with German
help, be founded on the ruins of the British Empire. This had
been followed by the creation of the Berlin-Rome Axis, in
accordance with which Italy might well have been expected to
enter the war against Britain and France on its very first day.

It was certainly only common prudence for Mussolini to see
how the war would go before committing himself and his country
irrevocably. The process of waiting was by no means unprofit-
able. Italy was courted by both sides, and gained much consideration for her interests, many profitable contracts, and time to
improve her armaments. Thus the twilight months had passed.
It is an interesting speculation what the Italian fortunes would
have been if this policy had been maintained. The United States
with its large Italian vote might well have made it clear to Hitler
that an attempt to rally Italy to his side by force of arms would
raise the gravest issues. Peace, prosperity, and growing power
would have been the prize of a persistent neutrality. Once Hitler
was embroiled with Russia this happy state might have been
almost indefinitely prolonged, with ever-growing benefits, and
Mussolini might have stood forth in the peace or in the closing
year of the war as the wisest statesman the sunny peninsula and its
industrious and prolific people had known. This was a more
agreeable situation than that which in fact awaited him.

At the time when I was Chancellor of the Exchequer under Mr.
Baldwin in the years after 1924 I did what I could to preserve the
traditional friendship between Italy and Britain. I made a debt
settlement with Count Volpi which contrasted very favourably
with the arrangements made with France. I received the warmest
expressions of gratitude from the Duce, and with difficulty
escaped the highest decoration. Moreover, in the conflict between
Fascism and Bolshevism there was no doubt where my sym-

pathies and convictions lay. On the two occasions in 1927 when I met Mussolini our personal relations had been intimate and easy. I would never have encouraged Britain to make a breach with him about Abyssinia or roused the League of Nations against him unless we were prepared to go to war in the last extreme. He, like Hitler, understood and in a way respected my campaign for British rearmament, though he was very glad British public opinion did not support my view.

In the crisis we had now reached of the disastrous Battle of France it was clearly my duty as Prime Minister to do my utmost to keep Italy out of the conflict, and though I did not indulge in vain hopes I at once used what resources and influence I might possess. Six days after becoming head of the Government I wrote at the Cabinet's desire the appeal to Mussolini which, together with his answer, was published two years later in very different circumstances.

Prime Minister to Signor Mussolini 16.v.40

Now that I have taken up my office as Prime Minister and Minister of Defence I look back to our meetings in Rome and feel a desire to speak words of goodwill to you as Chief of the Italian nation across what seems to be a swiftly-widening gulf. Is it too late to stop a river of blood from flowing between the British and Italian peoples? We can no doubt inflict grievous injuries upon one another and maul each other cruelly, and darken the Mediterranean with our strife. If you so decree, it must be so; but I declare that I have never been the enemy of Italian greatness, nor ever at heart the foe of the Italian lawgiver. It is idle to predict the course of the great battles now raging in Europe, but I am sure that whatever may happen on the Continent England will go on to the end, even quite alone, as we have done before, and I believe with some assurance that we shall be aided in increasing measure by the United States, and, indeed, by all the Americas.

I beg you to believe that it is in no spirit of weakness or of fear that I make this solemn appeal, which will remain on record. Down the ages above all other calls comes the cry that the joint heirs of Latin and Christian civilisation must not be ranged against one another in mortal strife. Hearken to it, I beseech you in all honour and respect, before the dread signal is given. It will never be given by us.

The response was hard. It had at least the merit of candour.

Signor Mussolini to Prime Minister 18.v.40

I reply to the message which you have sent me in order to tell you that you are certainly aware of grave reasons of an historical and contingent character which have ranged our two countries in opposite camps. Without going back very far in time I remind you of the initiative taken in 1935 by your Government to organise at Geneva sanctions against Italy, engaged in securing for herself a small space in the African sun without causing the slightest injury to your interests and territories or those of others. I remind you also of the real and actual state of servitude in which Italy finds herself in her own sea. If it was to honour your signature that your Government declared war on Germany, you will understand that the same sense of honour and of respect for engagements assumed in the Italian-German Treaty guides Italian policy to-day and to-morrow in the face of any event whatsoever.

From this moment we could have no doubt of Mussolini's intention to enter the war at his most favourable opportunity. His resolve had in fact been made as soon as the defeat of the French armies was obvious. On May 13 he had told Ciano that he would declare war on France and Britain within a month. His official decision to declare war on any date suitable after June 5 was imparted to the Italian Chiefs of Staff on May 29. At Hitler's request the date was postponed to June 10.

* * *

On May 26, while the fate of the Northern Armies hung in the balance and no one could be sure that any would escape, Reynaud flew over to England to have a talk with us about this topic, which had not been absent from our minds. The Italian declaration of war must be expected at any moment. Thus France would burn upon another front, and a new foe would march hungrily upon her in the South. Could anything be done to buy off Mussolini? That was the question posed. I did not think there was the slightest chance, and every fact that the French Premier used as an argument for trying only made me surer there was no hope. However, Reynaud was under strong pressure at home, and we on our side wished to give full consideration to our Ally, whose one vital weapon, her Army, was breaking in her hand. M. Reynaud has published a full account of his visit, and especially of his conversations.* Lord Halifax, Mr. Chamberlain, Mr. Attlee, and Mr. Eden were also at our meetings. Although there was no need to marshal the grave facts, M. Reynaud dwelt not obscurely upon the possible French withdrawal from the war.

* Reynaud, *La France a sauvé l'Europe*, Vol. II, pp. 200 ff.

He himself would fight on, but there was always the possibility that he might soon be replaced by others of a different temper.

We had already on May 25 at the instance of the French Government made a joint request to President Roosevelt to intervene. In this message Britain and France authorised him to state that we understood Italy had territorial grievances against us in the Mediterranean, that we were disposed to consider at once any reasonable claims, that the Allies would admit Italy to the Peace Conference with a status equal to that of any belligerent, and that we would invite the President to see that any agreement reached now was carried out. The President acted accordingly; but his addresses were repulsed by the Italian dictator in the most abrupt manner. At our meeting with Reynaud we had already this answer before us. The French Premier now suggested more precise proposals. Obviously, if these were to remedy Italy's "state of servitude in her own sea", they must affect the status both of Gibraltar and Suez. France was prepared to make similar concessions about Tunis.

We were not able to show any favour to these ideas. This was not because it was wrong to examine them or because it did not seem worth while at this moment to pay a heavy price to keep Italy out of the war. My own feeling was that at the pitch in which our affairs lay we had nothing to offer which Mussolini could not take for himself or be given by Hitler if we were defeated. One cannot easily make a bargain at the last gasp. Once we started negotiating for the friendly mediation of the Duce we should destroy our power of fighting on. I found my colleagues very stiff and tough. All our minds ran much more on bombing Milan and Turin the moment Mussolini declared war, and seeing how he liked that. Reynaud, who did not at heart disagree, seemed convinced, or at least content. The most we could promise was to bring the matter before the Cabinet and send a definite answer the next day. Reynaud and I lunched alone together at the Admiralty. The following telegram, the greater part of which is my own wording, embodies the conclusions of the War Cabinet:

Prime Minister to M. Reynaud   28.v.40
   1. I have with my colleagues examined with the most careful and sympathetic attention the proposal for an approach by way of precise offer of concessions to Signor Mussolini that you have forwarded to

me to-day, fully realising the terrible situation with which we are both faced at this moment.

2. Since we last discussed this matter the new fact which has occurred, namely, the capitulation of the Belgian Army, has greatly changed our position for the worse, for it is evident that the chance of withdrawing the armies of Generals Blanchard and Gort from the Channel ports has become very problematical. The first effect of such a disaster must be to make it impossible at such a moment for Germany to put forward any terms likely to be acceptable, and neither we nor you would be prepared to give up our independence without fighting for it to the end.

3. In the formula prepared last Sunday by Lord Halifax it was suggested that if Signor Mussolini would co-operate with us in securing a settlement of all European questions which would safeguard our independence and form the basis of a just and durable peace for Europe we should be prepared to discuss his claims in the Mediterranean. You now propose to add certain specific offers, which I cannot suppose would have any chance of moving Signor Mussolini, and which once made could not be subsequently withdrawn, in order to induce him to undertake the *rôle* of mediator, which the formula discussed on Sunday contemplated.

4. I and my colleagues believe that Signor Mussolini has long had it in mind that he might eventually fill this *rôle*, no doubt counting upon substantial advantages for Italy in the process. But we are convinced that at this moment when Hitler is flushed with victory and certainly counts on early and complete collapse of Allied resistance it would be impossible for Signor Mussolini to put forward proposals for a conference with any success. I may remind you also that the President of the U.S.A. has received a wholly negative reply to the proposal which we jointly asked him to make, and that no response has been made to the approach which Lord Halifax made to the Italian Ambassador here last Saturday.

5. Therefore, without excluding the possibility of an approach to Signor Mussolini at some time, we cannot feel that this would be the right moment, and I am bound to add that in my opinion the effect on the morale of our people, which is now firm and resolute, would be extremely dangerous. You yourself can best judge what would be the effect in France.

6. You will ask, then, how is the situation to be improved? My reply is that by showing that after the loss of our two [Northern] armies and the support of our Belgian ally we still have stout hearts and confidence in ourselves we shall at once strengthen our hands in negotiations and draw the admiration and perhaps the material help of

the U.S.A. Moreover, we feel that as long as we stand together our undefeated Navy and our Air Force, which is daily destroying German fighters and bombers at a formidable rate, afford us the means of exercising in our common interest a continuous pressure upon Germany's internal life.

7. We have reason to believe that the Germans too are working to a time-table, and that their losses and the hardships imposed on them, together with the fear of our air raids, is undermining their courage. It would indeed be a tragedy if by too hasty an acceptance of defeat we threw away a chance that was almost within our grasp of securing an honourable issue from the struggle.

8. In my view, if we both stand out we may yet save ourselves from the fate of Denmark and Poland. Our success must depend first on our unity, then on our courage and endurance.

This did not prevent the French Government from making a few days later a direct offer of their own to Italy of territorial concessions, which Mussolini treated with disdain. "He was not interested," said Ciano to the French Ambassador on June 3, "in recovering any French territories by peaceful negotiation. He had decided to make war on France."* This was only what we had expected.

*　　*　　*

I now gave daily a series of directives to make sure that if we were subjected to this odious attack by Mussolini we should be able to strike back at once.

Prime Minister to General Ismay　　　　　　　　　　　　　　28.v.40

1. Pray bring the following before the C.O.S. Committee:
What measures have been taken, in the event of Italy's going to war, to attack Italian forces in Abyssinia, sending rifles and money to the Abyssinian insurgents, and generally to disturb that country?
I understand General Smuts has sent a Union brigade to East Africa. Is it there yet? When will it be? What other arrangements are made? What is the strength of the Khartoum garrison, including troops in the Blue Nile Province? This is the opportunity for the Abyssinians to liberate themselves, with Allied help.

2. If France is still our ally after an Italian declaration of war, it would appear extremely desirable that the combined Fleets, acting from opposite ends of the Mediterranean, should pursue an active offensive against Italy. It is important that at the outset collision should

* See Reynaud, Vol. II, p. 209.

take place both with the Italian Navy and Air Force, in order that we can see what their quality really is, and whether it has changed at all since the last war. The purely defensive strategy contemplated by Commander-in-Chief Mediterranean ought not to be accepted. Unless it is found that the fighting qualities of the Italians are high, it will be much better that the Fleet at Alexandria should sally forth and run some risks than that it should remain in a posture so markedly defensive. Risks must be run at this juncture in all theatres.

3. I presume that the Admiralty have a plan in the event of France becoming neutral.

Prime Minister to General Ismay (and others)   29.V.40

We must have eight battalions from Palestine home at the earliest moment. I regard the Mediterranean as closed to troopships. The choice is therefore between the Red Sea and the Persian Gulf. Let this alternative route [across the desert to the Gulf] be examined this afternoon, and Admiralty be consulted, and report to me on relative times and safety. The Australians can be left in Palestine for the moment, but the High Commissioner, like others, must conform to the supreme requirements of the State.

Admiralty should say whether it would be possible to pick these men up at the Cape in the big liners for extra speed.

Prime Minister to First Lord of the Admiralty   30.V.40

What measures have been taken to seize all Italian ships at the moment of war? How many are there in British ports, and what can be done about them on the seas or in foreign ports? Will you kindly pass this to the proper department immediately.

At the Supreme War Council in Paris on May 31, which has already been described, it was agreed that the Allies should undertake offensive operations against selected objectives in Italy at the earliest possible moment and that the French and British naval and air staffs should concert their plans. We had also agreed that in the event of Italian aggression against Greece, of which there were indications, we should make sure that Crete did not fall into enemy hands. I pursued the same theme in my minutes.

Prime Minister to Secretary of State for Air and Chief of
Air Staff   2.VI.40

It is of the utmost importance, in view of the [possible] raids on Lyons and Marseilles, that we should be able to strike back with our heavy bombers at Italy the moment she enters the war. I consider therefore that these squadrons should be flown to their aerodromes in

Southern France at the earliest moment when French permission can be obtained and when the servicing units are ready for their reception.

Pray let me know at our meeting to-night what you propose.

Prime Minister to S. of S. for Air and C.A.S.   6.VI.40

It is of the highest importance that we should strike at Italy the moment war breaks out, or an overbearing ultimatum is received. Please let me know the exact position of the servicing units which are on their way to the southern aerodromes in France.

An early Italian plan, favoured particularly by Ciano, had been that Italian action in Europe should be confined to the launching of an attack on Yugoslavia, thus consolidating Italy's power in Eastern Europe and strengthening her potential economic position. Mussolini himself was for a time won over to this idea. Graziani records that at the end of April the Duce told him: "We must bring Yugoslavia to her knees; we have need of raw materials, and it is in her mines that we must find them. In consequence my strategic directive is—defensive in the west (France) and offensive in the east (Yugoslavia). Prepare a study of the problem."* Graziani claims that he advised strongly against committing the Italian armies, short as they were of equipment, particularly of artillery, to a repetition of the Isonzo campaign of 1915. There were also political arguments against the Yugoslav plan. The Germans were anxious at this moment to avoid disturbing Eastern Europe. They feared it would provoke British action in the Balkans and might inadvertently tempt Russia to further activity in the East. I was not unaware of this aspect of Italian policy.

Prime Minister to Secretary of State for Foreign Affairs   6.VI.40

I have hitherto argued against going to war with Italy because she attacked [i.e., if she were to attack] Yugoslavia, and have wished to see whether it was a serious attack upon Yugoslavian independence or merely taking some naval bases in the Adriatic. However, this situation has changed. Italy is continually threatening to go to war with England and France, and not by "the back door". We are so near a break with Italy on grounds which have nothing to do with Yugoslavia that it would seem that our main aim might well be now to procure this Balkan mobilisation. Will you think this over?

*   *   *

* Graziani, *Ho Difeso la Patria*, p. 189

In spite of the extreme efforts made by the United States, of which Mr. Hull has given an impressive account in his memoirs,★ nothing could turn Mussolini from his course. Our preparations to meet the new assault and complication were well advanced when the moment came. On June 10 at 4.45 p.m. the Italian Minister for Foreign Affairs informed the British Ambassador that Italy would consider herself at war with the United Kingdom from midnight that day. A similar communication was made to the French Government. When Ciano delivered his note to the French Ambassador, M. François-Poncet remarked as he reached the door: "You too will find the Germans are hard masters." From his balcony in Rome Mussolini announced to well-organised crowds that Italy was at war with France and Britain. It was, as Ciano is said to have apologetically remarked later on, "a chance which comes only once in five thousand years." Such chances, though rare, are not necessarily good.

Forthwith the Italians attacked the French troops on the Alpine front and Great Britain reciprocally declared war on Italy. Five Italian ships detained at Gibraltar were seized, and orders were given to the Navy to intercept and bring into controlled ports all Italian vessels at sea. On the night of the 12th our bomber squadrons, after a long flight from England, which meant light loads, dropped their first bombs upon Turin and Milan. We looked forward however to a much heavier delivery as soon as we could use the French airfields at Marseilles.

It may be convenient at this point to dispose of the brief Franco-Italian campaign. The French could only muster three divisions, with fortress troops equivalent to three more, to meet invasion over the Alpine passes and along the Riviera coast by the western group of Italian armies. These comprised thirty-two divisions, under Prince Umberto. Moreover, strong German armour, rapidly descending the Rhone valley, soon began to traverse the French rear. Nevertheless the Italians were still confronted, and even pinned down, at every point on the new front by the French Alpine units, even after Paris had fallen and Lyons was in German hands. When on June 18 Hitler and Mussolini met at Munich the Duce had little cause to boast. A new Italian offensive was therefore launched on June 21. The French Alpine positions however

★ *The Memoirs of Cordell Hull*, Vol. I, Chap. 56.

17 The beach at Torquay in 1940.

18 A fast patrol launch on the Thames.
19 The Blitz of London: scenes of destruction around Saint Paul's Cathedral.

20 The intensive manufacture of shells in British factories.

21 The return of British war wounded from Flanders.

proved impregnable, and the major Italian effort towards Nice was halted in the outskirts of Mentone. But although the French Army on the south-eastern borders saved its honour, the German march to the south behind them made further fighting impossible, and the conclusion of the armistice with Germany was linked with a French request to Italy for the cessation of hostilities.

*   *   *

My account of this Italian tragedy may fittingly be closed here by the letter which the unlucky Ciano wrote me shortly before his execution at the orders of his father-in-law.

VERONA, December 23, 1943

Signor Churchill.

You will not be surprised that as I approach the hour of my death I should turn to you whom I profoundly admire as the champion of a crusade, though you did at one time make an unjust statement against me.

I was never Mussolini's accomplice in that crime against our country and humanity, that of fighting side by side with the Germans. Indeed the opposite is the truth, and if last August I vanished from Rome it was because the Germans had convinced me that my children were in imminent danger. After they had pledged themselves to take me to Spain, they deported me and my family, against my will, to Bavaria. Now, I have been nearly three months in the prisons of Verona, abandoned to the barbarous treatment of the S.S. My end is near, and I have been told that in a few days my death will be decided, which to me will be no more nor less [than] a release from this daily martyrdom. And I prefer death to witnessing the shame and irreparable damage of an Italy which has been under Hun domination.

The crime which I am now about to expiate is that of having witnessed and been disgusted by the cold, cruel, and cynical preparation for this war by Hitler and the Germans. I was the only foreigner to see at close quarters this loathsome clique of bandits preparing to plunge the world into a bloody war. Now, in accordance with gangster rule, they are planning to suppress a dangerous witness. But they have miscalculated, for already a long time ago I put a diary of mine and various documents in a safe place, which will prove, more than I myself could, the crimes committed by those people with whom later that tragic and vile puppet Mussolini associated himself through his vanity and disregard of moral values.

I have made arrangements that as soon as possible after my death these documents, of the existence of which Sir Percy Loraine was aware at the time of his Mission in Rome, should be put at the disposal of the Allied Press.

Perhaps what I am offering you to-day is but little, but that and my life are all I can offer to the cause of liberty and justice, in the triumph of which I fanatically believe.

This testimony of mine should be brought to light so that the world may know, may hate and may remember, and that those who will have to judge the future should not be ignorant of the fact that the misfortune of Italy was not the fault of her people, but due to the shameful behaviour of one man.

Yours sincerely,
G. CIANO

* * *

A speech from President Roosevelt had been announced for the night of the 10th. About midnight I listened to it with a group of officers in the Admiralty War Room, where I still worked. When he uttered the scathing words about Italy, "On this 10th day of June, 1940, the hand that held the dagger has struck it into the back of its neighbour," there was a deep growl of satisfaction. I wondered about the Italian vote in the approaching Presidential Election; but I knew that Roosevelt was a most experienced American party politician, although never afraid to run risks for the sake of his resolves. It was a magnificent speech, instinct with passion and carrying to us a message of hope. While the impression was strong upon me, and before going to bed, I expressed my gratitude.

Former Naval Person to President Roosevelt   **11.VI.40**
We all listened to you last night, and were fortified by the grand scope of your declaration. Your statement that the material aid of the United States will be given to the Allies in their struggle is a strong encouragement in a dark but not unhopeful hour. Everything must be done to keep France in the fight and to prevent any idea of the fall of Paris, should it occur, becoming the occasion of any kind of parley. The hope with which you inspire them may give them the strength to persevere. They should continue to defend every yard of their soil and use the full fighting force of their Army. Hitler, thus baffled of quick results, will turn upon us, and we are preparing ourselves to resist his fury and defend our Island. Having saved the B.E.F., we do not lack troops at home, and as soon as divisions can be equipped on the much higher scale needed for Continental service they will be dispatched to France.

Our intention is to have a strong army fighting in France for the campaign of 1941. I have already cabled you about aeroplanes, including flying-boats, which are so needful to us in the impending struggle for the life of Great Britain. But even more pressing is the need for destroyers. The Italian outrage makes it necessary for us to cope with a much larger number of submarines, which may come out into the Atlantic and perhaps be based on Spanish ports. To this the only counter is destroyers. Nothing is so important as for us to have the thirty or forty old destroyers you have already had reconditioned. We can fit them very rapidly with our Asdics, and they will bridge the gap of six months before our war-time new construction comes into play. We will return them or their equivalents to you, without fail, at six months' notice if at any time you need them. The next six months are vital. If while we have to guard the East Coast against invasion a new heavy German-Italian submarine attack is launched against our commerce the strain may be beyond our resources and the ocean traffic by which we live may be strangled. Not a day should be lost. I send you my heartfelt thanks and those of my colleagues for all you are doing and seeking to do for what we may now indeed call the Common Cause.

*　　*　　*

The rush for the spoils had begun. But Mussolini was not the only hungry animal seeking prey. To join the Jackal came the Bear.

I have recorded in the previous volume the course of Anglo-Soviet relations up till the outbreak of war, and the hostility, verging upon an actual breach with Britain and France, which arose during the Russian invasion of Finland. Germany and Russia now worked together as closely as their deep divergences of interest permitted. Hitler and Stalin had much in common as totalitarians, and their systems of government were akin. M. Molotov beamed on the German Ambassador, Count Schulenburg, on every important occasion, and was forward and fulsome in his approval of German policy and praise for Hitler's military measures. When the German assault had been made upon Norway he had said (April 9) that the Soviet Government understood the measures which were forced upon Germany. The English had certainly gone much too far. They had disregarded completely the rights of neutral nations. . . . *"We wish Germany complete success in her defensive measures."** Hitler had

_____

* *Nazi-Soviet Relations*, 1939-1941, p. 138

taken pains to inform Stalin on the morning of May 10 of the onslaught he had begun upon France and the neutral Low Countries. "I called on Molotov," wrote Schulenburg. "He appreciated the news, and added that he understood that Germany had to protect herself against Anglo-French attack. He had no doubt of our success."[*]

Although these expressions of their opinion were of course unknown till after the war, we were under no illusions about the Russian attitude. We none the less pursued a patient policy of trying to re-establish relations of a confidential character with Russia, trusting to the march of events and to their fundamental antagonisms to Germany. It was thought wise to use the abilities of Sir Stafford Cripps as Ambassador to Moscow. He willingly accepted this bleak and unpromising task. We did not at that time realise sufficiently that Soviet Communists hate extreme Left Wing politicians even more than they do Tories or Liberals. The nearer a man is to Communism in sentiment the more obnoxious he is to the Soviets unless he joins the party. The Soviet Government agreed to receive Cripps as Ambassador, and explained this step to their Nazi confederates. "The Soviet Union", wrote Schulenburg to Berlin on May 29, "is interested in obtaining rubber and tin from England in exchange for lumber. There is no reason for apprehension concerning Cripps's mission, since there is no reason to doubt the loyal attitude of the Soviet Union towards us, and since the unchanged direction of Soviet policy towards England precludes damage to Germany or vital German interests. There are no indications of any kind here for belief that the latest German successes cause alarm or fear of Germany in the Soviet Government."[†]

The collapse of France and the destruction of the French armies and of all counter-poise in the West ought to have produced some reaction in Stalin's mind, but nothing seemed to warn the Soviet leaders of the gravity of their own peril. On June 18, when the French defeat was total, Schulenburg reported: "Molotov summoned me this evening to his office and expressed the warmest congratulations of the Soviet Government on *the splendid success* of the German Armed Forces."[‡] This was almost

---

[*] *Nazi-Soviet Relations*, 1939-1941, p. 142
[†] *Ibid.*, p. 143
[‡] *Ibid.*, p. 154

exactly a year from the date when these same Armed Forces, taking the Soviet Government by complete surprise, fell upon Russia in cataracts of fire and steel. We now know that only four months later in 1940 Hitler definitely decided upon a war of extermination against the Soviets, and began the long, vast, stealthy movement of these much-congratulated German armies to the East. No recollection of their miscalculation and former conduct ever prevented the Soviet Government and its Communist agents and associates all over the world from screaming for a Second Front, in which Britain, whom they had consigned to ruin and servitude, was to play a leading part.

However, we comprehended the future more truly than these cold-blooded calculators, and understood their dangers and their interests better than they did themselves. I now addressed myself for the first time to Stalin.

Prime Minister to Monsieur Stalin   25.VI.40
    At this time, when the face of Europe is changing hourly, I should like to take the opportunity of your receiving His Majesty's new Ambassador to ask the latter to convey to you a message from myself.

    Geographically our two countries lie at the opposite extremities of Europe, and from the point of view of systems of government it may be said that they stand for widely differing systems of political thought. But I trust that these facts need not prevent the relations between our two countries in the international sphere from being harmonious and mutually beneficial.

    In the past—indeed in the recent past—our relations have, it must be acknowledged, been hampered by mutual suspicions; and last August the Soviet Government decided that the interests of the Soviet Union required that they should break off negotiations with us and enter into a close relation with Germany. Thus Germany became your friend almost at the same moment as she became our enemy.

    But since then a new factor has arisen which I venture to think makes it desirable that both our countries should re-establish our previous contact, so that if necessary we may be able to consult together as regards those affairs in Europe which must necessarily interest us both. At the present moment the problem before all Europe—our two countries included—is how the States and peoples of Europe are going to react towards the prospect of Germany establishing a hegemony over the continent.

    The fact that both our countries lie not in Europe but on her extremities puts them in a special position. We are better enabled than others less fortunately placed to resist Germany's hegemony, and, as you know, the British Government certainly intend to use their geographical position and their great resources to this end.

In fact, Great Britain's policy is concentrated on two objects—one, to save herself from German domination, which the Nazi Government wishes to impose, and the other, to free the rest of Europe from the domination which Germany is now in process of imposing on it.

The Soviet Union is alone in a position to judge whether Germany's present bid for the hegemony of Europe threatens the interests of the Soviet Union, and if so how best these interests can be safeguarded. But I have felt that the crisis through which Europe, and indeed the world, is passing is so grave as to warrant my laying before you frankly the position as it presents itself to the British Government. This, I hope, will ensure that in any discussion that the Soviet Government may have with Sir S. Cripps there should be no misunderstanding as to the policy of His Majesty's Government or of their readiness to discuss fully with the Soviet Government any of the vast problems created by Germany's present attempt to pursue in Europe a methodical process by successive stages of conquest and absorption.

There was of course no answer. I did not expect one. Sir Stafford Cripps reached Moscow safely, and even had an interview of a formal and frigid character with M. Stalin.

*　　*　　*

Meanwhile the Soviet Government was busy collecting its spoils. On June 14, the day Paris fell, Moscow had sent an ultimatum to Lithuania accusing her and the other Baltic States of military conspiracy against the U.S.S.R. and demanding radical changes of government and military concessions. On June 15 Red Army troops invaded the country, and the President, Smetona, fled into East Prussia. Latvia and Estonia were exposed to the same treatment. Pro-Soviet Governments must be set up forthwith and Soviet garrisons admitted into these small countries. Resistance was out of the question. The President of Latvia was deported to Russia, and Mr. Vyshinsky arrived to nominate a Provisional Government to manage new elections. In Estonia the pattern was identical. On June 19 Zhdanov arrived in Tallinn to install a similar *régime*. On August 3-6 the pretence of pro-Soviet friendly and democratic Governments was swept away, and the Kremlin annexed the Baltic States to the Soviet Union.

The Russian ultimatum to Roumania was delivered to the

Roumanian Minister in Moscow at 10 p.m. on June 26. The cession of Bessarabia and the northern part of the province of Bukovina was demanded, and an immediate reply requested by the following day. Germany, though annoyed by this precipitate action of Russia, which threatened her economic interests in Roumania, was bound by the terms of the German-Soviet pact of August 1939, which recognised the exclusive political interest of Russia in these areas of South-east Europe. The German Government therefore counselled Roumania to yield. On June 27 Roumanian troops were withdrawn from the two provinces concerned, and the territories passed into Russian hands. The armed forces of the Soviet Union were now firmly planted on the shores of the Baltic and at the mouths of the Danube.

CHAPTER VII

BACK TO FRANCE

June 4—June 12

High Morale of the Army – My First Thoughts and Directive, June 2, 1940 – The Lost Equipment – The President, General Marshall, and Mr. Stettinius – An Act of Faith – The Double Tensions of June – Reconstitution of the British Army – Its Fearful Lack of Modern Weapons – Decision to Send Our Only Two Well-armed Divisions to France – The Battle of France: Final Phase – Destruction of the 51st Highland Division, June 11–12 – "Auld Scotland Counts for Something Still" – My Fourth Visit to France: Briare – Weygand and Pétain – General Georges Summoned – My Discussion with Weygand – The French Prevent the Royal Air Force from Bombing Turin and Milan – The Germans Enter Paris – Renewed Conference Next Morning – Admiral Darlan's Promise – Farewell to G.Q.G. – Our Journey Home – My Report to the War Cabinet of the Conference.

WHEN it was known how many men had been rescued from Dunkirk, a sense of deliverance spread in the Island and throughout the Empire. There was a feeling of intense relief, melting almost into triumph. The safe homecoming of a quarter of a million men, the flower of our Army, was a milestone in our pilgrimage through years of defeat. The achievement of the Southern Railway and the Movements Branch of the War Office, of the staffs at the ports in the Thames Estuary, and above all at Dover, where over 200,000 men were handled and rapidly distributed throughout the country, is worthy of the highest praise. The troops returned with nothing but rifles and bayonets and a few hundred machine-guns, and were forthwith sent to their homes for seven days' leave. Their joy at being once again united with their families did not overcome a stern desire to engage the enemy at the earliest moment. Those who had actually fought the Germans in the field had the belief that, given a fair chance, they could beat them. Their morale was high, and they rejoined their regiments and batteries with alacrity.

All the Ministers and departmental officers, permanent or newly-chosen, acted with confidence and vigour night and day, and there are many tales to be told besides this one. Personally I felt uplifted, and my mind drew easily and freely from the knowledge I had gathered in my life. I was exhilarated by the salvation of the Army. I present, for what they are worth, the directives to the departments and submissions to the War Cabinet which I issued day by day. Ismay carried them to the Chiefs of Staff, and Bridges to the War Cabinet and the departments. Mistakes were corrected and gaps filled. Amendments and improvements were often made, but in the main, to the degree perhaps of 90 per cent., action was taken, and with a speed and effectiveness which no Dictatorship could rival.

Here were my first thoughts at the moment when it became certain that the Army had escaped.

Prime Minister to General Ismay   2.VI.40

Notes for C.O.S., etc., by the Minister of Defence.

The successful evacuation of the B.E.F. has revolutionised the Home Defence position. As soon as the B.E.F. units can be re-formed on a Home Defence basis we have a mass of trained troops in the country which would require a raid to be executed on a prohibitively large scale. Even 200,000 men would not be beyond our compass. The difficulties of a descent and its risks and losses increase with every addition to the first 10,000. We must at once take a new view of the situation. Certain questions must be considered, chiefly by the War Office, but also by the Joint Staffs:

1. What is the shortest time in which the B.E.F. can be given a new fighting value?

2. Upon what scheme would they be organised? Will it be for service at Home in the first instance and only secondarily dispatch to France? On the whole, I prefer this.

3. The B.E.F. in France must immediately be reconstituted, otherwise the French will not continue in the war. Even if Paris is lost, they must be adjured to continue a gigantic guerrilla. A scheme should be considered for a bridgehead and area of disembarkation in Brittany, where a large army can be developed. We must have plans worked

out which will show the French that there is a way through if they will only be steadfast.

4. As soon as the B.E.F. is reconstituted for Home Defence three divisions should be sent to join our two divisions south of the Somme, or wherever the French left may be by then. It is for consideration whether the Canadian Division should not go at once. Pray let me have a scheme.

5. Had we known a week ago what we now know about the Dunkirk evacuation, Narvik would have presented itself in a different light. Even now the question of maintaining a garrison there for some weeks on a self-contained basis should be reconsidered. I am deeply impressed with the vice and peril of chopping and changing. The letter of the Minister of Economic Warfare as well as the telegram of some days ago from the C.-in-C. must however receive one final weighing.

6. Ask Admiralty to supply a latest return of the state of the destroyer flotillas, showing what reinforcements have arrived or are expected within the month of June, and how many will come from repair.

7. It should now be possible to allow the eight Regular battalions in Palestine to be relieved by the eight native battalions from India *before* they are brought home, as brought home they must be, to constitute the cadres of the new B.E.F.

8. As soon as the Australians land, the big ships should be turned round and should carry eight or ten Territorial battalions to Bombay. They should bring back a second eight Regular battalions from India, and afterwards carry to India a second eight or ten Territorial battalions from England. It is for consideration how far the same principle should be applied to batteries in India.

9. Our losses in equipment must be expected to delay the fruition of our expansion of the B.E.F. from the twenty divisions formerly aimed at by Z* + 12 months to no more than fifteen divisions by Z + 18; but we must have a project to put before the French. The essence of this should be the armoured division, the 51st, the Canadians, and two Territorial divisions under Lord Gort by mid-July, and the augmenting of this force by six divisions formed from the twenty-four Regular battalions in conjunction with Territorials, a second Canadian division, an Australian division, and two Territorial divisions by Z + 18. Perhaps we may even be able to improve on this.

10. It is of the highest urgency to have at least half a dozen brigade groups formed from the Regulars of the B.E.F. for Home Defence.

11. What air co-operation is arranged to cover the final evacuation to-night? It ought to be possible to reduce the pressure on the rear-guard at this critical moment.

* "Z" means the beginning of the war, September 3, 1939

I close with a general observation. As I have personally felt less afraid of a German attempt at invasion than of the piercing of the French line on the Somme or Aisne and the fall of Paris, I have naturally believed the Germans would choose the latter. This probability is greatly increased by the fact that they will realise that the armed forces in Great Britain are now far stronger than they have ever been, and that their raiding parties would not have to meet half-trained formations, but the men whose mettle they have already tested, and from whom they have recoiled, not daring seriously to molest their departure. The next few days, before the B.E.F. or any substantial portion of it can be reorganised, must be considered as still critical.

* * *

There was of course a darker side to Dunkirk. We had lost the whole equipment of the Army to which all the first fruits of our factories had hitherto been given:

> 7,000 tons of ammunition.
> 90,000 rifles.
> 2,300 guns.
> 82,000 vehicles.
> 8,000 Bren guns.
> 400 anti-tank rifles.

Many months must elapse, even if the existing programmes were fulfilled without interruption by the enemy, before this loss could be repaired.

However, across the Atlantic in the United States strong emotions were already stirring in the breasts of its leading men. A precise and excellent account of these events is given by Mr. Stettinius,* the worthy son of my old Munitions colleague of the First World War, one of our truest friends. It was at once realised that the bulk of the British Army had got away only with the loss of all their equipment. As early as June 1 the President sent out orders to the War and Navy Departments to report what weapons they could spare for Britain and France. At the head of the American Army as Chief of Staff was General Marshall, not only a soldier of proved quality, but a man of commanding vision. He instantly directed his Chief of Ordnance and his Assistant Chief of Staff to survey the entire list of the American reserve ordnance and munitions stocks. In forty-eight hours the

---

* In *Lend-Lease—Weapon for Victory*, 1944.

answers were given, and on June 3 Marshall approved the lists. The first list comprised half a million .30 calibre rifles out of two million manufactured in 1917 and 1918 and stored in grease for more than twenty years. For these there were about 250 cartridges apiece. There were 900 *"soixante-quinze"* field guns, with a million rounds, 80,000 machine-guns, and various other items. In his excellent book Mr. Stettinius says: "Since every hour counted, it was decided that the Army should sell (for thirty-seven million dollars) everything on the list to one concern, which could in turn resell immediately to the British and French." The Chief of Ordnance, Major-General Wesson, was told to handle the matter, and immediately on June 3 all the American Army depots and arsenals started packing the material for shipment. By the end of the week more than six hundred heavily-loaded freight cars were rolling towards the Army docks at Raritan, New Jersey, up the river from Gravesend Bay. By June 11 a dozen British merchant ships moved into the bay and anchored, and loading from lighters began.

By these extraordinary measures the United States left themselves with the equipment for only 1,800,000 men, the minimum figure stipulated by the American Army's mobilisation plan. All this reads easily now, but at that time it was a supreme act of faith and leadership for the United States to deprive themselves of this very considerable mass of arms for the sake of a country which many deemed already beaten. They never had need to repent of it. As will presently be recounted, we ferried these precious weapons safely across the Atlantic during July, and they formed not only a material gain, but an important factor in all calculations made by friend or foe about invasion.

* * *

Mr. Cordell Hull has a passage in his memoirs* which is relevant at this point:

In response to Reynaud's almost pitiful pleas for backing, the President urged Mr. Churchill to send planes to France; but the Prime Minister refused. Bullitt [the United States Ambassador in Paris], outraged by this decision, communicated to the President and me on June 5 his fear that the British might be conserving their Air Force and Fleet so as to use them as bargaining points in negotiations with Hitler.

* *The Memoirs of Cordell Hull*, Vol. I, pp. 774-5.

The President and I, however, thought differently. France was finished, but we were convinced that Britain, under Churchill's indomitable leadership, intended to fight on. There would be no negotiations between London and Berlin. Only the day before Bullitt's telegram Churchill had made his magnificent speech in the House of Commons. . . .

The President and I believed Mr. Churchill meant what he said. Had we had any doubt of Britain's determination to keep on fighting, we would not have taken the steps we did to get material aid to her. There would have been no logic in sending arms to Britain if we had thought that before they arrived there Churchill's Government would surrender to Germany.

★   ★   ★

The month of June was particularly trying to all of us, because of the dual and opposite stresses to which in our naked condition we were subjected by our duty to France on the one hand and the need to create an effective army at home and to fortify the Island on the other. The double tension of antagonistic but vital needs was most severe. Nevertheless we followed a firm and steady policy without undue excitement. First priority continued to be given to sending whatever trained and equipped troops we had in order to reconstitute the B.E.F. in France. After that our efforts were devoted to the defence of the Island—first, by re-forming and re-equipping the Regular Army; secondly, by fortifying the likely landing-places; thirdly, by arming and organising the population, so far as was possible; and of course by bringing home whatever forces could be gathered from the Empire. At this time the most imminent dangers seemed to be the landing of comparatively small but highly mobile German tank forces which would rip us up and disorganise our defence, and also parachute descents. In close contact with the new Secretary of State for War, Anthony Eden, I busied myself on all this.

The following scheme was devised by the Secretary of State and the War Office for reconstituting the Army in accordance with the directives which had been issued. Seven mobile brigade groups were already in existence. The divisions returned from Dunkirk were reconstituted, re-equipped as fast as possible, and took up their stations. In time the seven brigade groups were absorbed into the re-formed divisions. There were available fourteen Territorial divisions of high-quality men who had been nine months ardently training under war conditions and were partly equipped. One of these, the 52nd, was already fit for service overseas. There was a second armoured division and four Army tank brigades in process of formation, but without tanks. There was the 1st Canadian Division, fully equipped.

It was not men that were lacking, but arms. Over 80,000 rifles were retrieved from the communications and bases south of the Seine, and by the middle of June every fighting man in the Regular forces had at least a personal weapon in his hand. We had very little field artillery, even for the Regular Army. Nearly all the new 25-pounders had been lost in France. There remained about five hundred 18-pounders, 4.5-inch and 6-inch howitzers. There were only 103 cruiser, 114 Infantry, and 252 light tanks. Fifty of the Infantry tanks were at home in a battalion of the Royal Tank Regiment, and the remainder were in training-schools. Never has a great nation been so naked before her foes.

* * *

From the beginning I kept in the closest contact with my old friends now at the head of the Governments of Canada and South Africa.

Prime Minister to Mr. Mackenzie King 5.VI.40

British situation vastly improved by miraculous evacuation of B.E.F., which gives us an army in the Island more than capable, when re-equipped, of coping with any invading force likely to be landed. Also evacuation was a main trial of strength between British and German Air Forces. Germans have been unable to prevent evacuation, though largely superior in numbers, and have suffered at least three times our loss. For technical reasons, British Air Force would have many more advantages in defending the air above the Island than in operating overseas. Principal remaining danger is of course air [craft] factories, but if our air defence is so strong that enemy can only come on dark nights precision will not be easy. I therefore feel solid confidence in British ability to continue the war, defend the Island and the Empire, and maintain the blockade.

I do not know whether it will be possible to keep France in the war or not. I hope they will, even at the worst, maintain a gigantic guerrilla. We are reconstituting the B.E.F. out of other units.

We must be careful not to let Americans view too complacently prospect of a British collapse, out of which they would get the British Fleet and the guardianship of the British Empire, minus Great Britain.

If United States were in the war and England [were] conquered locally, it would be natural that events should follow the above course. But if America continued neutral, and we were overpowered, I cannot tell what policy might be adopted by a pro-German administration such as would undoubtedly be set up.

Although President is our best friend, no practical help has [reached us] from the United States as yet. We have not expected them to send military aid, but they have not even sent any worthy contribution in destroyers or planes, or by a visit of a squadron of their Fleet to Southern Irish ports. Any pressure which you can apply in this direction would be invaluable.

We are most deeply grateful to you for all your help and for [the four Canadian] destroyers, which have already gone into action against a U-boat. Kindest regards.

Smuts, far off in South Africa and without the latest information upon the specialised problems of Insular Air Defence, naturally viewed the tragedy of France according to orthodox principles. "Concentrate everything at the decisive point." I had the advantage of knowing the facts, and of the detailed advice of Air Chief Marshal Dowding, head of Fighter Command. If Smuts and I had been together for half an hour and I could have put the data before him we should have agreed, as we always did on large military issues.

Prime Minister to General Smuts   9.VI.40
We are of course doing all we can both from the air and by sending divisions as fast as they can be equipped to France. It would be wrong to send the bulk of our fighters to this battle, and when it was lost, as is probable, be left with no means of carrying on the war. I think we have a harder, longer, and more hopeful duty to perform. Advantages of resisting German air attack in this Island, where we can concentrate very powerful fighter strength, and hope to knock out four or five hostiles to one of ours, are far superior to fighting in France, where we are inevitably outnumbered and rarely exceed two to one ratio of destruction, and where our aircraft are often destroyed at exposed aerodromes. This battle does not turn on the score or so of fighter squadrons we could transport with their plant in the next month. Even if by using them up we held the enemy, Hitler could immediately throw his whole [air] strength against our undefended Island and destroy our means of future production by daylight attack. The classical principles of war which you mention are in this case modified by the actual quantitative data. *I see only one sure way through now,*

to wit, that Hitler should attack this country, and in so doing break his air weapon. If this happens he will be left to face the winter with Europe writhing under his heel, and probably with the United States against him after the Presidential election is over.

Am most grateful to you for cable. Please always give me your counsel, my old and valiant friend.

*   *   *

Apart from our last twenty-five fighter squadrons, on which we were adamant, we regarded the duty of sending aid to the French Army as paramount. The movement of the 52nd Lowland Division to France, under previous orders, was due to begin on June 7. These orders were confirmed. The 3rd Division, under General Montgomery, was put first in equipment and assigned to France. The leading division of the Canadian Army, which had concentrated in England early in the year and was well armed, was directed, with the full assent of the Dominion Government, to Brest, to begin arriving there on June 11 for what might by this time already be deemed a forlorn hope. The two French light divisions evacuated from Norway were also sent home, together with all the French units and individuals we had carried away from Dunkirk.

That we should have sent our only two formed divisions, the 52nd Lowland Division and 1st Canadian Division, over to our failing French ally in this mortal crisis, when the whole fury of Germany must soon fall upon us, must be set to our credit against the very limited forces we had been able to put into France in the first eight months of war. Looking back on it, I wonder how, when we were resolved to continue the war to the death, and under the threat of invasion, and France was evidently falling, we had the nerve to strip ourselves of the remaining effective military formations we possessed. This was only possible because we understood the difficulties of the Channel crossing without the command of the sea or the air, or the necessary landing-craft.

*   *   *

We had still in France, behind the Somme, the 51st Highland Division, which had been withdrawn from the Maginot Line and was in good condition, and the 52nd Lowland Division, which was arriving in Normandy. There was also our 1st (and only) Armoured Division, less the tank battalion and the support group, which had been sent to Calais. This however had lost heavily in attempts to cross the Somme as part of Weygand's plan. By June 1 it was reduced to one-third of its strength, and was sent back across the Seine to refit. At the same time a composite force known as "Beauman Force" was scraped together from the bases and lines of communication in France. It consisted of nine improvised infantry battalions, armed mainly with rifles, and very few anti-tank weapons. It had neither transport nor signals.

The Tenth French Army, with this British contingent, tried to hold the line of the Somme. The 51st Division alone had a front of sixteen miles, and the rest of the army was equally strained. On June 4, with a French division and French tanks, they attacked the German bridgehead at Abbeville, but without success.

On June 5 the final phase of the Battle of France began. The French front consisted of the Second, Third, and Fourth Groups of Armies. The Second defended the Rhine front and the Maginot Line; the Fourth stood along the Aisne, and the Third from the Aisne to the mouth of the Somme. This Third Army Group comprised the Sixth, Seventh, and Tenth Armies; and all the British forces in France formed part of the Tenth Army. All this immense line, in which there stood at this moment nearly one and a half million men, or perhaps sixty-five divisions, was now to be assaulted by one hundred and twenty-four German divisions, also formed in three Army Groups, viz.: Coastal Sector, Bock; Central Sector, Rundstedt; Eastern Sector, Leeb. These attacked on June 5, June 9, and June 15 respectively. On the night of June 5 we learned that a German offensive had been launched that morning on a seventy-mile front from Amiens to the Laon–Soissons road. This was war on the largest scale.

We have seen how the German armour had been hobbled and held back in the Dunkirk battle, in order to save it for the final phase in France. All this armour now rolled forward upon the weak and improvised or quivering French front between Paris and the sea. It is here only possible to record the battle on the coastal flank, in which we played a part. On June 7 the Germans renewed their attack, and two armoured divisions drove towards Rouen so as to split the Tenth French Army. The left French IXth Corps, including the Highland Division, two French infantry divisions, and two cavalry divisions, or what was left of them,

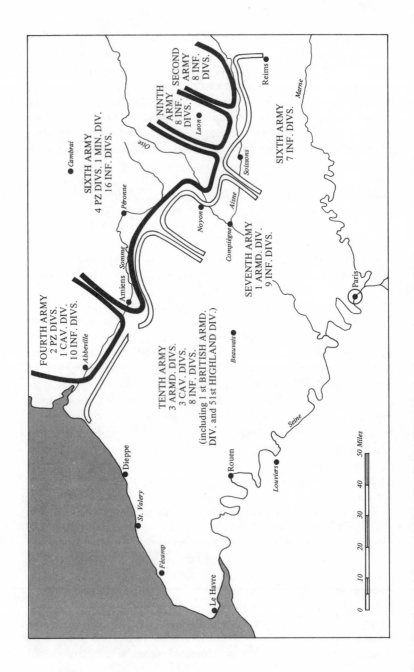

THE OPPOSING FORCES ON THE WESTERN FLANK,
5 JUNE 1940

THE GERMAN ADVANCE, 5-9 JUNE

were separated from the rest of the Tenth Army front. "Beauman Force", supported by thirty British tanks, now attempted to cover Rouen. On June 8 they were driven back to the Seine, and that night the Germans entered the city. The 51st Division, with the remnants of the French IXth Corps, was cut off in the Rouen–Dieppe *cul-de-sac*.

We had been intensely concerned lest this division should be driven back to the Havre peninsula and thus be separated from the main armies, and its commander, Major-General Fortune, had been told to fall back if necessary in the direction of Rouen. This movement was forbidden by the already disintegrating French command. Repeated urgent representations were made by us, but they were of no avail. A dogged refusal to face facts led to the ruin of the French IXth Corps and our 51st Division. On June 9, when Rouen was already in German hands, our men had but newly reached Dieppe, thirty-five miles to the north. Only then were orders received to withdraw to Havre. A force was sent back to cover the movement, but before the main bodies could move the Germans interposed. Striking from the east, they reached the sea, and the greater part of the 51st Division, with many of the French, was cut off. It was a case of gross mismanagement, for this very danger was visible a full three days before.

On the 10th, after sharp fighting, the division fell back, together with the French IXth Corps, to the perimeter of St. Valery, expecting to be evacuated by sea. Meanwhile all our other forces in the Havre peninsula were embarking speedily and safely. During the night of the 11th–12th fog prevented the ships from evacuating the troops from St. Valery. By morning on the 12th the Germans had reached the sea-cliffs to the south and the beach was under direct fire. White flags appeared in the town. The French corps capitulated at eight o'clock, and the remains of the Highland Division were forced to do so at 10.30 a.m. Only 1,350 British officers and men and 930 French escaped; 8,000 British and 4,000 French fell into the hands of the 7th Panzer Division, commanded by General Rommel. I was vexed that the French had not allowed our division to retire on Rouen in good time, but had kept it waiting till it could neither reach Havre nor retreat southward, and thus forced it to surrender with their own troops. The fate of the Highland Division was hard, but in after years not unavenged by those Scots who filled their places, re-created the division by merging it with the 9th Scottish, and marched across all the battlefields from Alamein to final victory beyond the Rhine.

Some lines* of Dr. Charles Murray's, written in the First World War, came into my mind, and it is fitting to print them here:

> Half-mast the castle banner droops,
>   The Laird's lament was played yestreen,
> An' mony a widowed cottar wife
>   Is greetin' at her shank aleen.
> In Freedom's cause, for ane that fa's,
>   We'll glean the glens an' send them three,
> To clip the reivin' eagle's claws
>   An' drook his feathers i' the sea.
>   For gallant loons, in brochs an' toons,
>   Are leavin' shop an' yaird an' mill,
>   A' keen to show baith friend an' foe
>   Auld Scotland counts for something still.

*   *   *

About eleven o'clock on the morning of June 11 there was a message from Reynaud, who had also cabled to the President. The French tragedy had moved and slid downward. For several days past I had pressed for a meeting of the Supreme Council. We could no longer meet in Paris. We were not told what were the conditions there. Certainly the German spearheads were very close. I had had some difficulty in obtaining a rendezvous, but this was no time to stand on ceremony. We must know what the French were going to do. Reynaud now told me that he could receive us at Briare, near Orleans. The seat of government was moving from Paris to Tours. Grand-Quartier-Général was near Briare. He specified the airfield to which I should come. Nothing loth, I ordered the Flamingo to be ready at Hendon after luncheon, and, having obtained the approval of my colleagues at the morning Cabinet, we started about two o'clock. Before leaving I cabled to the President.

Former Naval Person to President Roosevelt   11.VI.40
    The French have sent for me again, which means that crisis has arrived. Am just off. Anything you can say or do to help them now may make the difference.

---

* From *Hamewith and Other Poems*, by courtesy of Messrs. Constable & Co.

We are also worried about Ireland. An American squadron at Berehaven would do no end of good, I am sure.

*   *   *

This was my fourth journey to France; and since military conditions evidently predominated, I asked the Secretary of State for War, Mr. Eden, to come with me, as well as General Dill, now C.I.G.S., and of course Ismay. The German aircraft were now reaching far down into the Channel, and we had to make a still wider sweep. As before, the Flamingo had an escort of twelve Spitfires. After a couple of hours we alighted at a small landing-ground. There were a few Frenchmen about, and soon a colonel arrived in a motor-car. I displayed the smiling countenance and confident air which are thought suitable when things are very bad, but the Frenchman was dull and unresponsive. I realised immediately how very far things had fallen even since we were in Paris a week before. After an interval we were conducted to the château, where we found M. Reynaud, Marshal Pétain, General Weygand, the Air General Vuillemin, and some others, including the relatively junior General de Gaulle, who had just been appointed Under-Secretary for National Defence. Hard by on the railway was the Headquarters train, in which some of our party were accommodated. The château possessed but one telephone, in the lavatory. It was kept very busy, with long delays and endless shouted repetitions.

At seven o'clock we entered into conference. General Ismay kept a record. I merely reproduce my lasting impressions, which in no way disagree with it. There were no reproaches or recriminations. We were all up against brute facts. We British did not know where exactly the front line lay, and certainly there was anxiety about some dart by the German armour—even upon us. In effect, the discussion ran on the following lines: I urged the French Government to defend Paris. I emphasised the enormous absorbing power of the house-to-house defence of a great city upon an invading army. I recalled to Marshal Pétain the nights we had spent together in his train at Beauvais after the British Fifth Army disaster in 1918, and how he, as I put it, not mentioning Marshal Foch, had restored the situation. I also reminded him how Clemenceau had said: "I will fight in front of Paris, in Paris, and behind Paris." The Marshal replied very quietly and with dignity that in those days he had a mass of manœuvre of upwards of sixty divisions; now there was none. He mentioned that there were then sixty British divisions in the line. Making Paris into a ruin would not affect the final event.

Then General Weygand exposed the military position, so far as he knew it, in the fluid battle proceeding fifty or sixty miles away, and he paid a high tribute to the prowess of the French Army. He requested that every reinforcement should be sent—above all, that every British fighter air squadron should immediately be thrown into the battle. "Here," he said, "is the decisive point. Now is the decisive moment. It is therefore wrong to keep *any* squadrons back in England." But in accordance with the Cabinet decision, taken in the presence of Air Chief Marshal Dowding, whom I had brought specially to a Cabinet meeting, I replied: "This is not the decisive point and this is not the decisive moment. That moment will come when Hitler hurls his Luftwaffe against Great Britain. If we can keep command of the air, and if we can keep the seas open, as we certainly shall keep them open, we will win it all back for you."* Twenty-five fighter squadrons must be maintained at all costs for the defence of Britain and the Channel, and nothing would make us give up these. We intended to continue the war whatever happened, and we believed we could do so for an indefinite time, but to give up these squadrons would destroy our chance of life. At this stage I asked that General Georges, the Commander-in-Chief of the North-Western Front, who was in the neighbourhood, should be sent for, and this was accordingly done.

Presently General Georges arrived. After being apprised of what had passed, he confirmed the account of the French front which had been given by Weygand. I again urged my guerrilla plan. The German Army was not so strong as might appear at their points of impact. If all the French armies, every division and brigade, fought the troops on their front with the utmost vigour a general standstill might be achieved. I was answered by statements of the frightful conditions on the roads, crowded with refugees harried by unresisted machine-gun fire from the German aeroplanes, and of the wholesale flight of vast numbers of inhabitants and the increasing breakdown of the machinery of government and of military control. At one point General

* I am obliged to General Ismay for his recollection of these words.

Weygand mentioned that the French might have to ask for an armistice. Reynaud at once snapped at him: "That is a political affair." According to Ismay I said: "If it is thought best for France in her agony that her Army should capitulate, let there be no hesitation on our account, because whatever you may do we shall fight on for ever and ever and ever." When I said that the French Army, fighting on, wherever it might be, could hold or wear out a hundred German divisions, General Weygand replied: "Even if that were so, they would still have another hundred to invade and conquer you. What would you do then?" On this I said that I was not a military expert, but that my technical advisers were of the opinion that the best method of dealing with a German invasion of the Island of Britain was to drown as many as possible on the way over and knock the others on the head as they crawled ashore. Weygand answered with a sad smile: "At any rate I must admit you have a very good anti-tank obstacle." These were the last striking words I remember to have heard from him. In all this miserable discussion it must be borne in mind that I was haunted and undermined by the grief I felt that Britain, with her 48,000,000 population, had not been able to make a greater contribution to the land war against Germany, and that so far nine-tenths of the slaughter and ninety-nine-hundredths of the suffering had fallen upon France and upon France alone.

After another hour or so we got up and washed our hands while a meal was brought to the conference table. In this interval I talked to General Georges privately, and suggested first the continuance of fighting everywhere on the home front and a prolonged guerrilla in the mountainous regions, and secondly the move to Africa, which a week before I had regarded as "defeatist". My respected friend, who, although charged with much direct responsibility, had never had a free hand to lead the French armies, did not seem to think there was much hope in either of these.

I have written lightly of the happenings of these days, but here to all of us was real agony of mind and soul.

*   *   *

At about ten o'clock everyone took their places at the dinner. I sat on M. Reynaud's right and General de Gaulle was on my other side. There was soup, an omelette or something, coffee and light wine. Even at this point in our awful tribulation under the

German scourge we were quite friendly. But presently there was a jarring interlude. The reader will recall the importance I had attached to striking hard at Italy the moment she entered the war, and the arrangement that had been made with full French concurrence to move a force of British heavy bombers to the French airfields near Marseilles in order to attack Turin and Milan. All was now in readiness to strike. Scarcely had we sat down when Air Marshal Barratt, commanding the British Air Force in France, rang up Ismay on the telephone to say that the local authorities objected to the British bombers taking off, on the grounds that an attack on Italy would only bring reprisals upon the South of France, which the British were in no position to resist or prevent. Reynaud, Weygand, Eden, Dill, and I left the table, and, after some parleying, Reynaud agreed that orders should be sent to the French authorities concerned that the bombers were not to be stopped. But later that night Air Marshal Barratt reported that the French people near the airfields had dragged all kinds of country carts and lorries on to them, and that it had been impossible for the bombers to start on their mission.

Presently, when we left the dinner table and sat with some coffee and brandy, M. Reynaud told me that Marshal Pétain had informed him that it would be necessary for France to seek an armistice, and that he had written a paper upon the subject which he wished him to read. "He has not," said Reynaud, "handed it to me yet. He is still ashamed to do it." He ought also to have been ashamed to support even tacitly Weygand's demand for our last twenty-five squadrons of fighters, when he had made up his mind that all was lost and that France should give in. Thus we all went unhappily to bed in this disordered château or in the military train a few miles away. The Germans entered Paris on the 14th.

* * *

Early in the morning we resumed our conference. Air Marshal Barratt was present. Reynaud renewed his appeal for five more squadrons of fighters to be based in France, and General Weygand said that he was badly in need of day bombers to make up for his lack of troops. I gave them an assurance that the whole question of increased air support for France would be examined carefully and sympathetically by the War Cabinet immediately I got back to London; but I again emphasised that it would be a vital mistake to denude the United Kingdom of its essential Home defences.*

Towards the end of this short meeting I put the following specific questions:

(i) Will not the mass of Paris and its suburbs present an obstacle dividing and delaying the enemy as in 1914, or like Madrid?

(ii) May this not enable a counter-stroke to be organised with British and French forces across the Lower Seine?

(iii) If the period of co-ordinated war ends, will that not mean an almost equal dispersion of the enemy forces? Would not a war of columns and [attacks] upon the enemy communications be possible? Are the enemy resources sufficient to hold down all the countries at present conquered as well as a large part of France, while they are fighting the French Army and Great Britain?

(iv) Is it not possible thus to prolong the resistance until the United States come in?

General Weygand, while agreeing with the conception of the counter-stroke on the Lower Seine, said that he had inadequate forces to implement it. He added that, in his judgment, the Germans had got plenty to spare to hold down all the countries at present conquered, as well as a large part of France. Reynaud added that the Germans had raised fifty-five divisions and had built four thousand to five thousand heavy tanks since the outbreak of war. This was of course an immense exaggeration of what they had built.

In conclusion, I expressed in the most formal manner my hope that if there was any change in the situation the French Government would let the British Government know at once, in order that we might come over and see them at any convenient spot, before they took any final decisions which would govern their action in the second phase of the war.

We then took leave of Pétain, Weygand, and the staff of G.Q.G., and this was the last we saw of them. Finally I took

* In this connection it is interesting to note a statement made by General Gamelin to the Conseil Supérieure de l'Air on March 15, 1938. "In the event of Britain coming to our aid, it is reasonable to hope that she would agree to reinforce our bomber arm by using our air bases. On the other hand, it is quite unlikely [peu probable] that she would agree to send to France the fighter units that are responsible for the defence of her own territory."

Admiral Darlan apart and spoke to him alone. "Darlan, you must never let them get the French Fleet." He promised solemnly that he would never do so.

*　　*　　*

Lack of suitable petrol made it impossible for the twelve Spitfires to escort us. We had to choose between waiting till it cleared up or taking a chance in the Flamingo. We were assured that it would be cloudy all the way. It was urgently necessary to get back home. Accordingly we started alone, calling for an escort to meet us, if possible, over the Channel. As we approached the coast the skies cleared and presently became cloudless. Eight thousand feet below us on our right hand was Havre, burning. The smoke drifted away to the eastward. No new escort was to be seen. Presently I noticed some consultations going on with the captain, and immediately after we dived to a hundred feet or so above the calm sea, where aeroplanes are often invisible. What had happened? I learned later that they had seen two German aircraft below us firing at fishing-boats. We were lucky that their pilots did not look upwards. The new escort met us as we approached the English shore, and the faithful Flamingo alighted safely at Hendon.

*　　*　　*

At five o'clock that evening I reported to the War Cabinet the results of my mission.

I described the condition of the French armies as it had been reported to the conference by General Weygand. For six days they had been fighting night and day, and they were now almost wholly exhausted. The enemy attack, launched by a hundred and twenty divisions, with supporting armour, had fallen on forty French divisions, which had been out-manœuvred and out-matched at every point. The enemy's armoured forces had caused great disorganisation among the headquarters of the higher formations, which were unwieldy and, when on the move, unable to exercise control over the lower formations. The French armies were now on the last line on which they could attempt to offer an organised resistance. This line had already been penetrated in two or three places; and if it collapsed General Weygand would not be responsible for carrying on the struggle.

General Weygand evidently saw no prospect of the French

going on fighting, and Marshal Pétain had quite made up his mind that peace must be made. He believed that France was being systematically destroyed by the Germans, and that it was his duty to save the rest of the country from this fate. I mentioned his memorandum to this effect, which he had shown to Reynaud but had not left with him. "There can be no doubt," I said, "that Pétain is a dangerous man at this juncture: he was always a defeatist, even in the last war." On the other hand, M. Reynaud had seemed quite determined to fight on, and General de Gaulle, who had attended the conference with him, was in favour of carrying on a guerrilla warfare. He was young and energetic and had made a very favourable impression on me. I thought it probable that if the present line collapsed Reynaud would turn to him to take command. Admiral Darlan also had declared that he would never surrender the French Navy to the enemy: in the last resort, he had said, he would send it over to Canada; but in this he might be overruled by the French politicians.

It was clear that France was near the end of organised resistance, and a chapter in the war was now closing. The French might by some means continue the struggle. There might even be two French Governments, one which made peace, and one which organised resistance from the French colonies, carrying on the war at sea through the French Fleet and in France through guerrillas. It was too early yet to tell. Though for a period we might still have to send some support to France, we must now concentrate our main efforts on the defence of our Island.

CHAPTER VIII

HOME DEFENCE
June

Intense British Effort – Imminent Dangers – The Question of "Commandos" – Local Defence Volunteers Renamed "Home Guard" – Lack of Means of Attacking Enemy Tanks – Major Jefferis' Experimental Establishment – The Sticky Bomb – Help for de Gaulle's Free French – Arrangements for Repatriation of other French Troops – Care of French Wounded – Freeing British Troops for Intensive Training – The Press and Air Raids – Danger of German Use of Captured European Factories – Questions Arising in the Middle East and India – Question of Arming the Jewish Colonists in Palestine – Progress of Our Plan of Defence – The Great Anti-Tank Obstacle and Other Measures.

*T*HE reader of these pages in future years should realise how dense and baffling is the veil of the Unknown. Now in the full light of the after-time it is easy to see where we were ignorant or too much alarmed, where we were careless or clumsy. Twice in two months we had been taken completely by surprise. The overrunning of Norway and the break-through at Sedan, with all that followed from these, proved the deadly power of the German initiative. What else had they got ready—prepared and organised to the last inch? Would they suddenly pounce out of the blue with new weapons, perfect planning, and overwhelming force upon our almost totally unequipped and disarmed Island at any one of a dozen or score of possible landing-places? Or would they go to Ireland? He would have been a very foolish man who allowed his reasoning, however clean-cut and seemingly sure, to blot out any possibility against which provision could be made.

"Depend upon it," said Dr. Johnson, "when a man knows he is going to be hanged in a fortnight, it concentrates his mind wonderfully." I was always sure we should win, but nevertheless I was highly geared up by the situation, and very thankful to be able to make my views effective. June 6 seems to have been for me an active and not barren day. My minutes, dictated as I lay in bed in the morning and pondered on the dark horizon, show the variety of topics upon which it was necessary to give directions.

First I called upon the Minister of Supply (Mr. Herbert Morrison) for an account of the progress of various devices connected with our rockets and sensitive fuzes for use against aircraft, on which some progress had been made, and upon the Minister of Aircraft Production (Lord Beaverbrook) for weekly reports on the design and production of automatic bomb sights and low altitude R.D.F. (Radio Direction Finding) and A.I. (Air Interception). I did this to direct the attention of these two new Ministers with their vast departments to those topics, in which I had already long been especially interested. I asked the Admiralty to transfer at least fifty trained and half-trained pilots temporarily to Fighter Command. Fifty-five actually took part in the great air battle. I called for a plan to be prepared to strike at Italy by air raids on Turin and Milan, should she enter the war against us. I asked the War Office for plans for forming a Dutch Brigade in accordance with the desires of the exiled Netherlands Government, and pressed the Foreign Secretary for the recognition of the Belgian Government, apart from the prisoner King, as the sole constitutional Belgian authority, and for the encouragement of mobilisation in Yugoslavia as a counter to Italian threats. I asked that the aerodromes at Bardufosse and Skaarnlands, which we had constructed in the Narvik area and were about to abandon, should be made unusable for as long as possible by means of delayed-action bombs buried in them. I remembered how effectively the Germans had by this method delayed our use in 1918 of the railways when they finally retreated. Alas! we had no bombs of long-delay in any numbers. I was worried about the many ships lying in Malta harbour in various conditions of repair in view of impending Italian hostility. I wrote a long minute to the Minister of Supply about timber felling and production at home. This was one of the most important methods of reducing the tonnage of our imports. Besides, we should get no more timber from Norway for a long time to come. Many of these minutes will be found in Appendix A.

I longed for more Regular troops with which to rebuild and expand the Army. Wars are not won by heroic militias.

Prime Minister to Secretary of State for War   6.VI.40

1. It is more than a fortnight since I was told that eight battalions could leave India and arrive in this country in forty-two days from the order being given. The order was given. Now it is not till June 6 (*i.e.*, to-day) that the first eight battalions leave India on their voyage round the Cape, arriving only July 25.

2. The Australians are coming in the big ships, but they seem to have wasted a week at Capetown, and are now only proceeding at eighteen knots, instead of the twenty I was assured were possible. It is hoped they will be here about the 15th. Is this so? At any rate, whenever they arrive the big ships should be immediately filled with Territorials—the more the better—preferably twelve battalions, and sent off to India at full speed. As soon as they arrive in India they should embark another eight Regular battalions for this country, making the voyage again at full speed. They should then take another batch of Territorials to India. Future transferences can be discussed later. . . . All I am asking now is that the big ships should go to and fro at full speed.

3. I am very sorry indeed to find the virtual deadlock which local objections have imposed upon the battalions from Palestine. It is quite natural that General Wavell should look at the situation only from his own viewpoint. Here we have to think of building up a good Army in order to make up, as far as possible, for the lamentable failure to support the French by an adequate B.E.F. during the first year of the war. Do you realise that in the first year of the late war we brought forty-seven divisions into action, and that these were divisions of twelve battalions plus one Pioneer battalion, not nine as now? We are indeed the victims of a feeble and weary departmentalism.

4. Owing to the saving of the B.E.F., I have been willing to wait for the relief of the eight battalions from Palestine by eight native Indian battalions, provided these latter were sent at once; but you give me no time-table for this. I have not yet received any report on whether it is possible to send these British battalions and their Indian relief via Basra and the Persian Gulf.

Perhaps you would very kindly let me have this in the first instance.

5. I am prepared also to consider as an alternative, or an immediate step, the sending home [*i.e.*, to Britain] of the rest of the Australian

corps. Perhaps you will let me have a note on this, showing especially dates at which the moves can be made.

6. You must not think I am ignoring the position in the Middle East. On the contrary, it seems to me that we should draw upon India much more largely, and that a ceaseless stream of Indian units should be passing into Palestine and Egypt via Bombay and [by] Karachi across the desert route. India is doing nothing worth speaking of at the present time. In the last war not only did we have all the [British] Regular troops out [of India] in the first nine months (many more than are there now), but also an Indian Corps fought by Christmas in France. Our weakness, slowness, lack of grip and drive are very apparent on the background of what was done twenty-five years ago. I really think that you, Lloyd, and Amery ought to be able to lift our affairs in the East and Middle East out of the catalepsy by which they are smitten.

*　*　*

This was a time when all Britain worked and strove to the utmost limit and was united as never before. Men and women toiled at the lathes and machines in the factories till they fell exhausted on the floor and had to be dragged away and ordered home, while their places were occupied by newcomers ahead of time. The one desire of all the males and many women was to have a weapon. The Cabinet and Government were locked together by bonds the memory of which is still cherished by all. The sense of fear seemed entirely lacking in the people, and their representatives in Parliament were not unworthy of their mood. We had not suffered like France under the German flail. Nothing moves an Englishman so much as the threat of invasion, the reality unknown for a thousand years. Vast numbers of people were resolved to conquer or die. There was no need to rouse their spirit by oratory. They were glad to hear me express their sentiments and give them good reasons for what they meant to do, or try to do. The only possible divergence was from people who wished to do even more than was possible, and had the idea that frenzy might sharpen action.

Our decision to send our only two well-armed divisions back to France made it all the more necessary to take every possible measure to defend the Island against direct assault.

Prime Minister to General Ismay　　　　　　　　18.VI.40

I should like to be informed upon (1) the coastal watch and coastal batteries; (2) the gorging of the harbours and defended inlets (*i.e.*, the making of the landward defences); (3) the troops held in immediate support of the foregoing; (4) the mobile columns and brigade groups; (5) the General Reserve.

Someone should explain to me the state of these different forces, including the guns available in each area. I gave directions that the 8th Tank Regiment should be immediately equipped with Infantry and cruiser tanks until they have fifty-two new tanks, all well armoured and well gunned. What has been done with the output of this month and last month? Make sure it is not languishing in depots, but passes swiftly to troops. General Carr is responsible for this. Let him report.

What are the ideas of C.-in-C., H.F., about Storm Troops? We have always set our faces against this idea, but the Germans certainly gained in the last war by adopting it, and this time it has been a leading cause of their victory. There ought to be at least twenty thousand Storm Troops or "Leopards" [eventually called "Commandos"] drawn from existing units, ready to spring at the throat of any small landings or descents. These officers and men should be armed with the latest equipment, tommy guns, grenades, etc., and should be given great facilities in motor-cycles and armoured cars.

* * *

Mr. Eden's plan of raising Local Defence Volunteers, which he had proposed to the Cabinet on May 13, met with an immediate response in all parts of the country.

Prime Minister to Secretary of State for War   22.VI.40
Could I have a brief statement of the L.D.V. position, showing the progress achieved in raising and arming them, and whether they are designed for observation or for serious fighting? What is their relationship to the police, the Military Command, and the Regional Commissioners? From whom do they receive their orders, and to whom do they report? It would be a great comfort if this could be compressed on one or two sheets of paper.

I had always hankered for the name "Home Guard". I had indeed suggested it in October 1939.

Prime Minister to Secretary of State for War   26.VI.40
I don't think much of the name "Local Defence Volunteers" for your very large new force. The word "local" is uninspiring. Mr. Herbert Morrison suggested to me to-day the title "Civic Guard", but I think "Home Guard" would be better. Don't hesitate to change

on account of already having made armlets, etc., if it is thought the title of Home Guard would be more compulsive.

Prime Minister to Secretary of State for War 27.VI.40

I hope you liked my suggestion of changing the name "Local Defence Volunteers", which is associated with Local Government and Local Option, to "Home Guard". I found everybody liked this in my tour yesterday.

The change was accordingly made, and the mighty organisation, which presently approached one and a half million men and gradually acquired good weapons, rolled forward.

★   ★   ★

In these days my principal fear was of German tanks coming ashore. Since my mind was attracted to landing tanks on their coasts, I naturally thought they might have the same idea. We had hardly any anti-tank guns or ammunition, or even ordinary field artillery. The plight to which we were reduced in dealing with this danger may be measured from the following incident. I visited our beaches in St. Margaret's Bay, near Dover. The Brigadier informed me that he had only three anti-tank guns in his brigade, covering four or five miles of this highly-menaced coastline. He declared that he had only six rounds of ammunition for each gun, and he asked me with a slight air of challenge whether he was justified in letting his men fire one single round for practice in order that they might at least know how the weapon worked. I replied that we could not afford practice rounds, and that fire should be held for the last moment at the closest range.

This was therefore no time to proceed by ordinary channels in devising expedients. In order to secure quick action, free from departmental processes, upon any bright idea or gadget, I decided to keep under my own hand as Minister of Defence the experimental establishment formed by Major Jefferis at Whitchurch. While engaged upon the fluvial mines in 1939 I had had useful contacts with this brilliant officer, whose ingenious, inventive mind proved, as will be seen, fruitful during the whole war. Lindemann was in close touch with him and me. I used their brains and my power. Major Jefferis and others connected with him were at work upon a bomb which could be thrown at a tank, perhaps from a window, and would stick upon it. The impact of a very high explosive in actual contact with a steel plate is particularly effective. We had the picture in mind that devoted soldiers or civilians would run close up to the tank and even thrust the bomb upon it, though its explosion cost them their lives. There were undoubtedly many who would have done it. I thought also that the bomb fixed on a rod might be fired with a reduced charge from rifles.

Prime Minister to General Ismay   6.VI.40

It is of the utmost importance to find some projectile which can be fired from a rifle at a tank, like a rifle grenade, or from an anti-tank rifle, like a trench-mortar bomb. The "sticky" bomb seems to be useful for the first of these, but perhaps this is not so. Anyhow, concentrate attention upon finding something that can be fired from anti-tank rifles or from ordinary rifles.

I pressed the matter hard.

Prime Minister to General Ismay   16.VI.40

Who is responsible for making the "sticky" bomb? I am told that a great sloth is being shown in pressing this forward. Ask General Carr to report to-day upon the position, and to let me have on one sheet of paper the back history of the subject from the moment when the question was first raised.

The matter is to be pressed forward from day to day, and I wish to receive a report every three days.

Prime Minister to General Ismay   24.VI.40

I minuted some days ago about the "sticky" bombs. All preparations for manufacture should proceed in anticipation that the further trials will be successful. Let me have a time-table showing why it is that delay has crept into all the process, which is so urgent.

Prime Minister to General Ismay   24.VI.40

I understand that the trials were not entirely successful and the bomb failed to stick on tanks which were covered with dust and mud. No doubt some more sticky mixture can be devised and Major Jefferis should persevere.

Any chortling by officials who have been slothful in pushing this bomb over the fact that at present it has not succeeded will be viewed with great disfavour by me.

In the end the "sticky" bomb was accepted as one of our best emergency weapons. We never had to use it at home; but in

Syria, where equally primitive conditions prevailed, it proved its value.

*   *   *

We had evidently to do our utmost to form French forces which might aid General de Gaulle in keeping the true personification of France alive.

Prime Minister to First Lord of the Admiralty
and other Service Ministers   27.VI.40

1. The French naval personnel at Aintree Camp, numbering 13,600, equally with the 5,530 military at Trentham Park, the 1,900 at Arrow Park, and the details at Blackpool, are to be immediately repatriated to French territory, *i.e.*, Morocco, in French ships now in our hands.

2. They should be told we will take them to French Africa because all French metropolitan ports are in German hands, and that the French Government will arrange for their future movements.

3. If however any wish to remain here to fight against Germany, they must immediately make this clear. Care must be taken that no officer or man is sent back into French jurisdiction against his will. The shipping is to be ready to-morrow. The troops should move under their own officers, and carry their personal arms, but as little ammunition as possible. Some arrangements should be made for their pay. The French material on board ships from Narvik will be taken over by us with the ammunition from the *Lombardy* and other ships as against expenses to which we are put.

4. Great care is to be taken of the French wounded. All who can be moved without danger should be sent back direct to France if possible. The French Government should be asked where they wish them delivered, and if at French metropolitan ports, should arrange with the Germans for their safe entry; otherwise Casablanca. All dangerous cases must be dealt with here.

5. Apart from any volunteers in the above groups of personnel who may wish to stay, there must be many individuals who have made their way here, hoping to continue to fight. These also should be given the option of returning to France, or serving in the French units under General de Gaulle, who should be told of our decisions, and given reasonable facilities to collect his people. I have abandoned the hope that he could address the formed bodies, as their morale has deteriorated too fast.

*   *   *

My desire that our own Army should regain its poise and fighting quality was at first hampered because so many troops were being absorbed in fortifying their own localities or sectors of the coast.

Prime Minister to Secretary of State for War 25.VI.40

It is shocking that only fifty-seven thousand men [civilians] are being employed on all these [defence] works. Moreover, I fear that the troops are being used in large numbers on fortifications. At the present stage they should be drilling and training for at least eight hours a day, including one smart parade every morning. All the labour necessary should be found from civilian sources. I found it extremely difficult to see even a single battalion on parade in East Anglia during my visit. The fighting troops in the brigade groups should neither be used for guarding vulnerable points nor for making fortifications. Naturally a change like this cannot be made at once, but let me have your proposals for bringing it about as soon as possible.

*   *   *

Prime Minister to Minister of Information 26.VI.40

The Press and broadcast should be asked to handle air raids in a cool way and on a diminishing tone of public interest. The facts should be chronicled without undue prominence or headlines. The people should be accustomed to treat air raids as a matter of ordinary routine. Localities affected should not be mentioned with any precision. Photographs showing shattered houses should not be published unless there is something very peculiar about them, or to illustrate how well the Anderson shelters work. It must be clear that the vast majority of people are not at all affected by any single air raid, and would hardly sustain any evil impression if it were not thrust before them. Everyone should learn to take air raids and air-raid alarms as if they were no more than thunderstorms. Pray try to impress this upon the newspaper authorities, and persuade them to help. If there is difficulty in this, I would myself see the Newspaper Proprietors' Association, but I hope this will not be necessary. The Press should be complimented on their work so far in this matter.

Prime Minister to Secretary of State for War 27.VI.40

Enclosed [dates of troop convoys from India] make me anxious to know how you propose to use these eight fine Regular battalions. Obviously they will be a reinforcement for your shock troops. One would suppose they might make the infantry of two divisions, with five good Territorial battalions added to each division, total eighteen. Should they not also yield up a certain number of officers and N.C.O.s to stiffen the Territorial battalions so attached? You would thus have six brigades of infantry quite soon. Alas, I fear the artillery must lag behind, but not, I trust, for long.

*   *   *

As rumours grew of peace proposals and a message was sent to us from the Vatican through Berne I thought it right to send the following minute to the Foreign Secretary:

28.VI.40

I hope it will be made clear to the Nuncio that we do not desire to make any inquiries as to terms of peace with Hitler, and that all our agents are strictly forbidden to entertain any such suggestions.

But here is the record of a qualm:

Prime Minister to Professor Lindemann   29.VI.40

While we are hastening our preparations for air mastery, the Germans will be organising the whole industries of the captured countries for air production and other war production suitable [for use] against us. It is therefore a race. They will not be able to get the captured factories working immediately, and meanwhile we shall get round the invasion danger through the growth of our defences and Army strength. But what sort of relative outputs must be faced next year unless we are able to bomb the newly-acquired German plants? Germany also, being relieved from the need of keeping a gigantic army in constant contact with the French Army, must have spare capacity for the air and other methods of attacking us. Must we not expect this will be very great? How soon can it come into play? Hitherto I have been looking at the next three months because of the emergency, but what about 1941? It seems to me that only immense American supplies can be of use in turning the corner.

*   *   *

As the month of June ground itself out, the sense of potential invasion at any moment grew upon us all.

Prime Minister to General Ismay   30.VI.40

The Admiralty charts of tides and state of the moon, Humber, Thames Estuary, Beachy Head, should be studied with a view to ascertaining on which days conditions will be most favourable to a sea-borne landing. The Admiralty view is sought.

A landing or descent in Ireland was always a deep anxiety to the Chiefs of Staff. But our resources seemed to me too limited for serious troop movements.

Prime Minister to General Ismay   30.VI.40

It would be taking an undue risk to remove one of our only two thoroughly-equipped divisions out of Great Britain at this juncture. Moreover, it is doubtful whether the Irish situation will require the use of divisional formations complete with their technical vehicles as if for Continental war. The statement that it would take ten days to transport a division from this country to Ireland, even though every preparation can be made beforehand, is not satisfactory. Schemes should be prepared to enable two or three lightly-equipped brigades to move at short notice, and in not more than three days, into Northern Ireland. Duplicate transport should be sent on ahead. It would be a mistake to send any large force of artillery to Ireland. It is not at all likely that a naval descent will be effected there. Air-borne descents cannot carry much artillery. Finally, nothing that can happen in Ireland can be immediately decisive.

*   *   *

In bringing home the troops from Palestine I had difficulties with both my old friends, the Secretary of State for India, Mr. Amery, and the Secretary of State for the Colonies, Lord Lloyd, who was a convinced anti-Zionist and pro-Arab. I wished to arm the Jewish colonists. Mr. Amery at the India Office had a different view from mine about the part which India should play. I wanted Indian troops at once to come into Palestine and the Middle East, whereas the Viceroy and the India Office were naturally inclined to a long-term plan of creating a great Indian Army based upon Indian munitions factories.

*   *   *

Prime Minister to Secretary of State for India   22.VI.40

1. We have already very large masses of troops in India of which no use is being made for the general purposes of the war. The assistance of India this time is incomparably below that of 1914–18. . . . It seems to me very likely that the war will spread to the Middle East, and the climates of Iraq, Palestine, and Egypt are well suited to Indian troops. I recommend their organisation in brigade groups, each with a proportion of artillery on the new British model. I should hope that six or eight of these groups could be ready this winter. They should include some brigades of Gurkhas.

2. The process of liberating the Regular British battalions must continue, and I much regret that a fortnight's delay has become

inevitable in returning you the Territorial battalions in exchange. You should reassure the Viceroy that it is going forward.

*   *   *

Prime Minister to Secretary of State for the Colonies   28.VI.40
    The failure of the policy which you favour is proved by the very large numbers of sorely-needed troops you [we] have to keep in Palestine:

> 6 battalions of infantry,
> 9 regiments of Yeomanry,
> 8 battalions of Australian infantry,

the whole probably more than twenty thousand men. This is the price we have to pay for the anti-Jewish policy which has been persisted in for some years. Should the war go heavily into Egypt, all these troops will have to be withdrawn, and the position of the Jewish colonists will be one of the greatest danger. Indeed I am sure that we shall be told we cannot withdraw these troops, though they include some of our best, and are vitally needed elsewhere. If the Jews were properly armed, our forces would become available, and there would be no danger of the Jews attacking the Arabs, because they are entirely dependent upon us and upon our command of the seas. I think it is little less than a scandal that at a time when we are fighting for our lives these very large forces should be immobilised in support of a policy which commends itself only to a section of the Conservative Party.
    I had hoped you would take a broad view of the Palestine situation, and would make it an earnest objective to set the British garrison free. I could certainly not associate myself with such an answer as you have drawn up for me. I do not at all admit that Arab feeling in the Near East and India would be prejudiced in the manner you suggest. Now that we have the Turks in such a friendly relationship the position is much more secure.

*   *   *

For the first time in a hundred and twenty-five years a powerful enemy was now established across the narrow waters of the English Channel. Our re-formed Regular Army, and the larger but less well trained Territorials, had to be organised and deployed to create an elaborate system of defences, and to stand ready, if the invader came, to destroy him—for there could be no escape. It was for both sides "Kill or Cure". Already the Home Guard could be included in the general framework of defence. On June 25 General Ironside, Commander-in-Chief Home Forces, exposed his plans to the Chiefs of Staff. They were of course scrutinised with anxious care by the experts, and I examined them myself with no little attention. On the whole they stood approved. There were three main elements in this early outline of a great future plan: first, an entrenched "crust" on the probable invasion beaches of the coast, whose defenders should fight where they stood, supported by mobile reserves for immediate counter-attack; secondly, a line of anti-tank obstacles, manned by the Home Guard, running down the east centre of England and protecting London and the great industrial centres from inroads by armoured vehicles; thirdly, behind that line, the main reserves for major counter-offensive action.

Ceaseless additions and refinements to this first plan were effected as the weeks and months passed; but the general conception remained. All troops, if attacked, should stand firm, not in linear only but *in all-round defence*, whilst others moved rapidly to destroy the attackers, whether they came from sea or air. Men who had been cut off from immediate help would not have merely remained in position. Active measures were prepared to harass the enemy from behind; to interfere with his communications and to destroy material, as the Russians did with great results when the German tide flowed over their country a year later. Many people must have been bewildered by the innumerable activities all around them. They could understand the necessity for wiring and mining the beaches, the anti-tank obstacles at the defiles, the concrete pillboxes at the cross-roads, the intrusions into their houses to fill an attic with sandbags, on to their golf-courses or most fertile fields and gardens to burrow out some wide anti-tank ditch. All these inconveniences, and much more, they accepted in good part. But sometimes they must have wondered if there was a general scheme, or whether lesser individuals were not running amok in their energetic use of newly-granted powers of interference with the property of the citizen.

There was however a central plan, elaborate, co-ordinated, and all-embracing. As it grew it shaped itself thus: the overall Command was maintained at General Headquarters in London. All Great Britain and Northern Ireland were divided into seven Commands; these again into areas of Corps and Divisional Commands. Commands, Corps, and Divisions were each required to hold a proportion of their resources in mobile reserve, only the minimum being detailed to hold their own particular defences. Gradually there were built up in rear of the beaches zones of defence in each divisional area; behind these were similar "Corps Zones" and "Command Zones", the whole system amounting in depth to a hundred miles or more. And behind these was established the main anti-tank obstacle running across Southern England and northwards into Nottinghamshire. Above all was the final reserve directly under the Commander-in-Chief of the Home Forces. This it was our policy to keep as large and mobile as possible.

Within this general structure were many variations. Each of our ports on the east and south coasts was a special study. Direct frontal attack upon a defended port seemed an unlikely contingency, and all were made into strong points equally capable of defence from the landward or the seaward side. It astonishes me that when this principle of fortifying the gorges was so universally accepted and rigorously enforced by all military authorities at home no similar measures were adopted at Singapore by the succession of high officers employed there. But this is a later story. Obstacles were placed on many thousand square miles of Britain to impede the landing of air-borne troops. All our aerodromes, Radar stations, and fuel depots, of which even in the summer of 1940 there were three hundred and seventy-five, needed defence by special garrisons and by their own airmen. Many thousands of "vulnerable points", bridges, power-stations, depots, vital factories, and the like had to be guarded day and night from sabotage or sudden onset. Schemes were ready for the immediate demolition of resources helpful to the enemy if captured. The destruction of port facilities, the cratering of key roads, the paralysis of motor transport and of telephones and telegraph-stations, of rolling stock or permanent way, before they passed out of our control, were planned to the last detail. Yet despite all these wise and necessary precautions, in which the civilian departments gave unstinted help to the military, there was no question of a "scorched earth policy"; England was to be defended by its people, not destroyed.

CHAPTER IX

THE FRENCH AGONY

Telegram to the President – My Visit to Tours – Increasing Degeneration – M. Baudouin – The Great Mandel – Conversation with Reynaud – My Refusal to Release France from the Obligation of March 28, 1940 – Resolute Attitude of MM. Herriot and Jeanneney – "L'Homme du Destin" – French Government Decide to Move to Bordeaux – President Roosevelt to M. Reynaud, June 13 – My Telegram to the President – And to Reynaud – "Indissoluble Union of France and Britain" – Disappointing Telegram from the President – My Telegram to the President of June 14–15 – Great Battle of June 9 along the Aisne – Defeat of the French – Forlorn Resistance on the Maginot Line – Our Slender Contribution – General Brooke's New Command – Talk of a Bridgehead in Brittany – Brooke Declares the Military Situation Hopeless – I Agree – Our Troops Withdraw and Re-embark, June 16–18 – The Pétain Government Asks for an Armistice – A Second Dunkirk Evacuation – A Hundred and Thirty-six Thousand British and Twenty Thousand Poles Carried to Britain – The "Lancastria" Horror – My Message of June 16 to the Dominions Prime Ministers – My Hopes of the Air Battle over Britain.

FUTURE generations may deem it noteworthy that the supreme question of whether we should fight on alone never found a place upon the War Cabinet agenda. It was taken for granted and as a matter of course by these men of all parties in the State, and we were much too busy to waste time upon such unreal, academic issues. We were united also in viewing the new phase with good confidence. It was decided to tell the Dominions the whole facts. I was invited to send a message in the same sense to President Roosevelt, and also to sustain the determination of the French Government and assure them of our utmost support.

Former Naval Person to President Roosevelt 12.VI.40

I spent last night and this morning at the French G.Q.G., where the situation was explained to me in the gravest terms by Generals Weygand and Georges. You have no doubt received full particulars from Mr. Bullitt. The practical point is what will happen when and if the French front breaks, Paris is taken, and General Weygand reports formally to his Government that France can no longer continue what he calls "co-ordinated war". The aged Marshal Pétain, who was none too good in April and July 1918, is, I fear, ready to lend his name and prestige to a treaty of peace for France. Reynaud, on the other hand, is for fighting on, and he has a young General de Gaulle, who believes much can be done. Admiral Darlan declares he will send the French Fleet to Canada. It would be disastrous if the two big modern ships fell into bad hands. It seems to me that there must be many elements in France who will wish to continue the struggle either in France or in the French colonies, or in both. This therefore is the moment for you to strengthen Reynaud the utmost you can, and try to tip the balance in favour of the best and longest possible French resistance. I venture to put this point before you, although I know you must understand it as well as I do.

*   *   *

On June 13 I made my last visit to France for four years almost to a day. The French Government had now withdrawn to Tours, and tension had mounted steadily. I took Edward Halifax and General Ismay with me, and Max Beaverbrook volunteered to come too. In trouble he is always buoyant. This time the weather was cloudless, and we sailed over in the midst of our Spitfire squadron, making however a rather wider sweep to the southward than before. Arrived over Tours, we found the airport had been heavily bombed the night before, but we and all our escort landed smoothly in spite of the craters. Immediately one sensed the increasing degeneration of affairs. No one came to meet us or seemed to expect us. We borrowed a service car from the station commander and motored into the city, making for the Prefecture, where it was said the French Government had their headquarters. No one of consequence was there, but Reynaud was reported to be motoring in from the country, and Mandel was also to arrive soon.

It being already nearly two o'clock, I insisted upon luncheon, and after some parleyings we drove through streets crowded with refugees' cars, most of them with a mattress on top and crammed

22   A French 75 mm. gun.

23-24 The German advance in Northern France.

25 British Mark VI light tanks during the battle for France.
26 Street fighting in a northern French town.

27 The French rout.
28 Rouen burning.

with luggage. We found a café, which was closed, but after explanations we obtained a meal. During luncheon I was visited by M. Baudouin, whose influence had risen in these latter days. He began at once in his soft, silky manner about the hopelessness of the French resistance. If the United States would declare war on Germany it might be possible for France to continue. What did I think about this? I did not discuss the question further than to say that I hoped America would come in, and that we should certainly fight on. He afterwards, I was told, spread it about that I had agreed that France should surrender unless the United States came in.

We then returned to the Prefecture, where Mandel, Minister of the Interior, awaited us. This faithful former secretary of Clemenceau, and a bearer forward of his life's message, seemed in the best of spirits. He was energy and defiance personified. His luncheon, an attractive chicken, was uneaten on the tray before him. He was a ray of sunshine. He had a telephone in each hand, through which he was constantly giving orders and decisions. His ideas were simple: fight on to the end in France, in order to cover the largest possible movement into Africa. This was the last time I saw this valiant Frenchman. The restored French Republic rightly shot to death the hirelings who murdered him. His memory is honoured by his countrymen and their allies.

Presently M. Reynaud arrived. At first he seemed depressed. General Weygand had reported to him that the French armies were exhausted. The line was pierced in many places; refugees were pouring along all the roads through the country, and many of the troops were in disorder. The Generalissimo felt it was necessary to ask for an armistice while there were still enough French troops to keep order until peace could be made. Such was the military advice. He would send that day a further message to Mr. Roosevelt saying that the last hour had come and that the fate of the Allied cause lay in America's hand. Hence arose the alternative of armistice and peace.

M. Reynaud proceeded to say that the Council of Ministers had on the previous day instructed him to inquire what would be Britain's attitude should the worst come. He himself was well aware of the solemn pledge that no separate peace would be entered into by either ally. General Weygand and others pointed out that France had already sacrificed everything in the common cause. She had nothing left; but she had succeeded in greatly weakening the common foe. It would in those circumstances be a shock if Britain failed to concede that France was physically unable to carry on, if France was still expected to fight on and thus deliver up her people to the certainty of corruption and evil transformation at the hands of ruthless specialists in the art of bringing conquered peoples to heel. That then was the question which he had to put. Would Great Britain realise the hard facts with which France was faced?

The official British record reads as follows:

Mr. Churchill said that Great Britain realised how much France had suffered and was suffering. Her own turn would come, and she was ready. She grieved to find that her contribution to the land struggle was at present so small, owing to the reverses which had been met with as a result of applying an agreed strategy in the North. The British had not yet felt the German lash, but were aware of its force. They nevertheless had but one thought: to win the war and destroy Hitlerism. Everything was subordinate to that aim; no difficulties, no regrets, could stand in the way. He was well assured of British capacity for enduring and persisting, for striking back till the foe was beaten. They would therefore hope that France would carry on fighting south of Paris down to the sea, and if need be from North Africa. At all costs time must be gained. The period of waiting was not limitless: a pledge from the United States would make it quite short. The alternative course meant destruction for France quite as certainly. Hitler would abide by no pledges. If on the other hand France remained in the struggle, with her fine Navy, her great Empire, her Army still able to carry on guerrilla warfare on a gigantic scale, and if Germany failed to destroy England, which she must do or go under, if then Germany's might in the air was broken, then the whole hateful edifice of Nazidom would topple over. Given immediate help from America, perhaps even a declaration of war, victory was not so far off. At all events England would fight on. She had not and would not alter her resolve: no terms, no surrender. The alternatives for her were death or victory. That was his answer to M. Reynaud's question.

M. Reynaud replied that he had never doubted England's determination. He was however anxious to know how the British Government would react in a certain contingency. The French Government—the present one or another—might say: "We know you will carry on. We would also, if we saw any hope of a victory. But we see no sufficient hopes of an early victory. We cannot count on American help. *There is no light at the end of the tunnel.* We cannot abandon our people

to indefinite German domination. We must come to terms. We have
no choice. . . ." It was already too late to organise a redoubt in
Brittany. Nowhere would a genuine French Government have a hope
of escaping capture on French soil. . . . The question to Britain would
therefore take the form: "Will you acknowledge that France has given
her best, her youth and life-blood; that she can do no more; and that
she is entitled, having nothing further to contribute to the common
cause, to enter into a separate peace while maintaining the solidarity
implicit in the solemn agreement entered into three months previously?"

Mr. Churchill said that in no case would Britain waste time and
energy in reproaches and recriminations. That did not mean that she
would consent to action contrary to the recent agreement. The first
step ought to be M. Reynaud's further message putting the present
position squarely to President Roosevelt. Let them await the answer
before considering anything else. If England won the war France
would be restored in her dignity and in her greatness.

All the same I thought the issue raised at this point was so
serious that I asked to withdraw with my colleagues before
answering it. So Lords Halifax and Beaverbrook and the rest
of our party went out into a dripping but sunlit garden and
talked things over for half an hour. On our return I re-stated our
position. We could not agree to a separate peace however it
might come. Our war aim remained the total defeat of Hitler,
and we felt that we could still bring this about. We were therefore
not in a position to release France from her obligation. Whatever
happened, we would level no reproaches against France; but that
was a different matter from consenting to release her from her
pledge. I urged that the French should now send a new appeal to
President Roosevelt, which we would support from London.
M. Reynaud agreed to do this, and promised that the French
would hold on until the result of his final appeal was known.

Before leaving I made one particular request to M. Reynaud.
Over four hundred German pilots, the bulk of whom had been
shot down by the R.A.F., were prisoners in France. Having
regard to the situation, they should be handed over to our custody
M. Reynaud willingly gave this promise, but soon he had no
power to keep it. These German pilots all became available for
the Battle of Britain, and we had to shoot them down a second
time.

At the end of our talk M. Reynaud took us into the adjoining room, where MM. Herriot and Jeanneney, the Presidents of the Chamber and Senate respectively, were seated. Both these French patriots spoke with passionate emotion about fighting on to the death. As we went down the crowded passage into the courtyard I saw General de Gaulle standing stolid and expressionless at the doorway. Greeting him, I said in a low tone, in French: *"L'homme du destin."* He remained impassive. In the courtyard there must have been more than a hundred leading Frenchmen in frightful misery. Clemenceau's son was brought up to me. I wrung his hand. The Spitfires were already in the air, and I slept sound on our swift and uneventful journey home. This was wise, for there was a long way to go before bed-time.

* * *

After our departure from Tours at about half-past five M. Reynaud met his Cabinet again at Cangé. They were vexed that I and my colleagues had not come there to join them. We should have been very willing to do so, no matter how late we had to fly home. But we were never invited; nor did we know there was to be a French Cabinet meeting.

At Cangé the decision was taken to move the French Government to Bordeaux, and Reynaud sent off his telegram to Roosevelt with its desperate appeal for the entry on the scene at least of the American Fleet.

At 10.15 p.m. I made my new report to the Cabinet. My account was endorsed by my two companions. While we were still sitting Ambassador Kennedy arrived with President Roosevelt's reply to Reynaud's appeal of June 10.

President Roosevelt to M. Reynaud   13.VI.40
Your message of June 10 has moved me very deeply. As I have already stated to you and to Mr. Churchill, this Government is doing everything in its power to make available to the Allied Governments the material they so urgently require, and our efforts to do still more are being redoubled. This is so because of our faith in and our support of the ideals for which the Allies are fighting.

The magnificent resistance of the French and British Armies has profoundly impressed the American people.

I am, personally, particularly impressed by your declaration that France will continue to fight on behalf of Democracy, even if it means slow withdrawal, even to North Africa and the Atlantic. It is most important to remember that the French and British Fleets continue [in] mastery of the Atlantic and other oceans; also to remember that vital materials from the outside world are necessary to maintain all armies.

I am also greatly heartened by what Prime Minister Churchill said a few days ago about the continued resistance of the British Empire, and that determination would seem to apply equally to the great French Empire all over the world. Naval power in world affairs still carries the lessons of history, as Admiral Darlan well knows.

We all thought the President had gone a very long way. He had authorised Reynaud to publish his message of June 10, with all that that implied, and now he had sent this formidable answer. If, upon this, France decided to endure the further torture of the war, the United States would be deeply committed to enter it. At any rate, it contained two points which were tantamount to belligerence: first, a promise of all material aid, which implied active assistance; secondly, a call to go on fighting even if the Government were driven right out of France. I sent our thanks to the President immediately, and I also sought to commend the President's message to Reynaud in the most favourable terms. Perhaps these points were stressed unduly; but it was necessary to make the most of everything we had or could get.

Former Naval Person to President Roosevelt   13.VI.40
Ambassador Kennedy will have told you about the British meeting to-day with the French at Tours, of which I showed him our record. I cannot exaggerate its critical character. They were very nearly gone. Weygand had advocated an armistice while he still has enough troops to prevent France from lapsing into anarchy. Reynaud asked us whether, in view of the sacrifices and sufferings of France, we would release her from the obligation about not making a separate peace. Although the fact that we have unavoidably been out of this terrible battle weighed with us, I did not hesitate in the name of the British Government to refuse consent to an armistice or separate peace. I urged that this issue should not be discussed until a further appeal had been made by Reynaud to you and the United States, which I undertook to second. Agreement was reached on this, and a much better mood prevailed for the moment in Reynaud and his Ministers.

Reynaud felt strongly that it would be beyond his power to encourage his people to fight on without hope of ultimate victory, and that that hope could only be kindled by American intervention up to the extreme limit open to you. As he put it, they wanted to see light at the end of the tunnel.

While we were flying back here your magnificent message was sent, and Ambassador Kennedy brought it to me on my arrival. The British Cabinet were profoundly impressed, and desire me to express their gratitude for it, but, Mr. President, I must tell you that it seems to me absolutely vital that this message should be published to-morrow, June 14, in order that it may play the decisive part in turning the course of world history. It will, I am sure, decide the French to deny Hitler a patched-up peace with France. He needs this peace in order to destroy us and take a long step forward to world mastery. All the far-reaching plans, strategic, economic, political, and moral, which your message expounds may be still-born if the French cut out now. Therefore I urge that the message should be published now. We realise fully that the moment Hitler finds he cannot dictate a Nazi peace in Paris he will turn his fury on to us. We shall do our best to withstand it, and if we succeed wide new doors are open upon the future and all will come out even at the end of the day.

To M. Reynaud I sent this message:

13.VI.40

On returning here we received a copy of President Roosevelt's answer to your appeal of June 10. Cabinet is united in considering this magnificent document as decisive in favour of the continued resistance of France in accordance with your own declaration of June 10 about fighting before Paris, behind Paris, in a province, or, if necessary, in Africa or across the Atlantic. The promise of redoubled material aid is coupled with definite advice and exhortation to France to continue the struggle even under the grievous conditions which you mentioned. If France on this message of President Roosevelt's continues in the field and in the war, we feel that the United States is committed beyond recall to take the only remaining step, namely, becoming a belligerent in form as she already has constituted herself in fact. Constitution of United States makes it impossible, as you foresaw, for the President to declare war himself, but if you act on his reply now received we sincerely believe that this must inevitably follow. We are asking the President to allow publication of the message, but, even if he does not agree to this for a day or two, it is on the record and can afford the basis for your action. I do beg you and your colleagues, whose resolution we so much admired to-day, not to miss this sovereign opportunity of bringing about the world-wide oceanic and economic coalition which must be fatal to Nazi domination. We see before us a definite plan of campaign, and the light which you spoke of shines at the end of the tunnel.

Finally, in accordance with the Cabinet's wishes, I sent a formal message of good cheer to the French Government, in which the note of an indissoluble union between our two countries was struck for the first time.

Prime Minister to M. Reynaud   13.VI.40

In this solemn hour for the British and French nations and for the cause of Freedom and Democracy to which they have vowed themselves, His Majesty's Government desire to pay to the Government of the French Republic the tribute which is due to the heroic fortitude and constancy of the French armies in battle against enormous odds. Their effort is worthy of the most glorious traditions of France, and has inflicted deep and long-lasting injury upon the enemy's strength. Great Britain will continue to give the utmost aid in her power. We take this opportunity of proclaiming the indissoluble union of our two peoples and of our two Empires. We cannot measure the various forms of tribulation which will fall upon our peoples in the near future. We are sure that the ordeal by fire will only fuse them together into one unconquerable whole. We renew to the French Republic our pledge and resolve to continue the struggle at all costs in France, in this Island, upon the oceans and in the air, wherever it may lead us, using all our resources to the utmost limit and sharing together the burden of repairing the ravages of war. We shall never turn from the conflict until France stands safe and erect in all her grandeur, until the wronged and enslaved States and peoples have been liberated, and until civilisation is freed from the nightmare of Nazidom. That this day will dawn we are more sure than ever. It may dawn sooner than we now have the right to expect.

All these three messages were drafted by me before I went to bed after midnight on the 13th. They were written actually in the small hours of the 14th.

The next day arrived a telegram from the President explaining that he could not agree to the publication of his message to Reynaud. He himself, according to Mr. Kennedy, had wished to do so, but the State Department, while in full sympathy with him, saw the gravest dangers. The President thanked me for my account of the meeting at Tours and complimented the British and French Governments on the courage of their troops. He renewed the assurances about furnishing all possible material and supplies; but he then said he had told Ambassador Kennedy to inform me that his message of the 13th was in no sense intended to commit and did not commit the Government of the United States to military participation. There was no authority under the

American Constitution except Congress which could make any commitment of that nature. He bore particularly in mind the question of the French Fleet. Congress, at his desire, had appropriated fifty million dollars for the purpose of supplying food and clothing to civilian refugees in France. Finally he assured me that he appreciated the significance and weight of what I had set forth in my message.

This was a disappointing telegram.

Around our table we all fully understood the risks the President ran of being charged with exceeding his constitutional authority, and consequently of being defeated on this issue at the approaching election, on which our fate, and much more, depended. I was convinced that he would give up life itself, to say nothing of public office, for the cause of world freedom now in such awful peril. But what would have been the good of that? Across the Atlantic I could feel his suffering. In the White House the torment was of a different character from that of Bordeaux or London. But the degree of personal stress was not unequal.

In my reply I tried to arm the President with some arguments which he could use to others about the danger to the United States if Europe fell and Britain failed. This was no matter of sentiment, but of life and death.

Former Naval Person to President Roosevelt   14–15.VI.40

I am grateful to you for your telegram and I have reported its operative passages to Reynaud, to whom I had imparted a rather more sanguine view. He will, I am sure, be disappointed at non-publication. I understand all your difficulties with American public opinion and Congress, but events are moving downward at a pace where they will pass beyond the control of American public opinion when at last it is ripened. Have you considered what offers Hitler may choose to make to France? He may say: "Surrender the Fleet intact and I will leave you Alsace-Lorraine," or alternatively: "If you do not give me your ships I will destroy your towns." I am personally convinced that America will in the end go to all lengths, but this moment is supremely critical for France. A declaration that the United States will if necessary enter the war might save France. Failing that, in a few days French resistance may have crumpled and we shall be left alone.

Although the present Government and I personally would never fail to send the Fleet across the Atlantic if resistance was beaten down here, a point may be reached in the struggle where the present Ministers no longer have control of affairs and when very easy terms could be obtained for the British Island by their becoming a vassal state of the Hitler Empire. A pro-German Government would certainly be called into being to make peace, and might present to a shattered or a starving nation an almost irresistible case for entire submission to the Nazi will. The fate of the British Fleet, as I have already mentioned to you, would be decisive on the future of the United States, because if it were joined to the Fleets of Japan, France, and Italy and the great resources of German industry overwhelming sea-power would be in Hitler's hands. He might of course use it with a merciful moderation. On the other hand, he might not. This revolution in sea-power might happen very quickly, and certainly long before the United States would be able to prepare against it. If we go down you may have a United States of Europe under the Nazi command far more numerous, far stronger, far better armed than the New World.

I know well, Mr. President, that your eye will already have searched these depths, but I feel I have the right to place on record the vital manner in which American interests are at stake in our battle and that of France.

I am sending you through Ambassador Kennedy a paper on destroyer strength prepared by the Naval Staff for your information. If we have to keep, as we shall, the bulk of our destroyers on the East Coast to guard against invasion, how shall we be able to cope with a German-Italian attack on the food and trade by which we live? The sending of the thirty-five destroyers as I have already described will bridge the gap until our new construction comes in at the end of the year. Here is a definite practical and possibly decisive step which can be taken at once, and I urge most earnestly that you will weigh my words.

*　　*　　*

Meanwhile the situation on the French front went from bad to worse. The German operations north-west of Paris, in which our 51st Division had been lost, had brought the enemy, by June 9, to the lower reaches of the Seine and the Oise. On the southern banks the dispersed remnants of the Tenth and Seventh French Armies were hastily organising a defence; they had been riven asunder, and to close the gap the garrison of the capital, the so-called Armée de Paris, had been marched out and interposed.

Farther to the east, along the Aisne, the Sixth, Fourth, and Second Armies were in far better shape. They had had three weeks in which to establish themselves and to absorb such reinforcements as had been sent. During all the period of Dunkirk

and of the drive to Rouen they had been left comparatively
undisturbed, but their strength was small for the hundred miles
they had to hold, and the enemy had used the time to concentrate
against them a great mass of divisions to deliver the final blow.
On June 9 it fell. Despite a dogged resistance, for the French were
now fighting with great resolution, bridgeheads were established
south of the river from Soissons to Rethel, and in the next two
days these were expanded until the Marne was reached. German
Panzer divisions, which had played so decisive a part in the drive
down the coast, were brought across to join the new battle.
Eight of these, in two great thrusts, turned the French defeat
into a rout. The French armies, decimated and in confusion, were
quite unable to withstand this powerful assembly of superior
numbers, equipment, and technique. In four days, by June 16,
the enemy had reached Orleans and the Loire; while to the east
the other thrust had passed through Dijon and Besançon, almost
to the Swiss frontier.

West of Paris the remains of the Tenth Army, the equivalent
of no more than two divisions, had been pressed back south-
westwards from the Seine towards Alençon. The capital fell on
the 14th; its defending armies, the Seventh and the Armée de
Paris, were scattered; a great gap now separated the exiguous
French and British forces in the west from the rest and the remains
of the once proud Army of France.

And what of the Maginot Line, the shield of France, and its
defenders? Until June 14 no direct attack was made, and already
some of the active formations, leaving behind the garrison troops,
had started to join, if they could, the fast-withdrawing armies of
the centre. But it was too late. On that day the Maginot Line
was penetrated before Saarbrucken and across the Rhine by
Colmar; the retreating French were caught up in the battle and
unable to extricate themselves. Two days later the German penetration to Besançon had cut off their retreat. More than four
hundred thousand men were surrounded without hope of escape.
Many encircled garrisons held out desperately; they refused to
surrender until after the armistice, when French officers were
dispatched to give them the order. The last forts obeyed on
June 30, the commander protesting that his defences were still
intact at every point.

Thus the vast disorganised battle drew to its conclusion all along the French front. It remains only to recount the slender part which the British were able to play.

*　　*　　*

General Brooke had won distinction in the retreat to Dunkirk, and especially by his battle in the gap opened by the Belgian surrender. We had therefore chosen him to command the British troops which remained in France and all reinforcements until they should reach sufficient numbers to require the presence of Lord Gort as an Army Commander. Brooke had now arrived in France, and on the 14th he met Generals Weygand and Georges. Weygand stated that the French forces were no longer capable of organised resistance or concerted action. The French Army was broken into four groups, of which its Tenth Army was the westernmost. Weygand also told him that the Allied Governments had agreed that a bridgehead should be created in the Brittany peninsula, to be held jointly by the French and British troops on a line running roughly north and south through Rennes. He ordered him to deploy his forces on a defensive line running through this town. Brooke pointed out that this line of defence was 150 kilometres long and required at least fifteen divisions. He was told that the instructions he was receiving must be regarded as an order.

It is true that on June 11 at Briare Reynaud and I had agreed to try to draw a kind of "Torres Vedras line" across the foot of the Brittany peninsula. Everything however was dissolving at the same time, and the plan, for what it was worth, never reached the domain of action. In itself the idea was sound, but there were no facts to clothe it with reality. Once the main French armies were broken or destroyed, this bridgehead, precious though it was, could not have been held for long against concentrated German attack. But even a few weeks' resistance here would have maintained contact with Britain and enabled large French withdrawals to Africa from other parts of the immense front, now torn to shreds. If the battle in France was to continue, it could be only in the Brest peninsula and in wooded or mountainous regions like the Vosges. The alternative for the French was surrender. Let none, therefore, mock at the conception of a bridgehead in Brittany. The Allied armies under Eisenhower, then an unknown American colonel, bought it back for us later at a high price.

169

THE LAST STAND OF THE FRENCH ARMY,
JUNE 1940

General Brooke, after his talk with the French commanders, and having measured from his own headquarters a scene which was getting worse every hour, reported to the War Office and by telephone to Mr. Eden that the position was hopeless. All further reinforcements should be stopped, and the remainder of the British Expeditionary Force, now amounting to a hundred and fifty thousand men, should be re-embarked at once. On the night of June 14, as I was thought to be obdurate, he rang me up on a telephone line which by luck and effort was open, and pressed this view upon me. I could hear quite well, and after ten minutes I was convinced that he was right and we must go. Orders were given accordingly. He was released from French command. The back-loading of great quantities of stores, equipment, and men began. The leading elements of the Canadian Division which had landed got back into their ships, and the 52nd Division, which, apart from its 157th Brigade, had not yet been committed to action, retreated on Brest. No British troops operating under the Tenth French Army were withdrawn; but all else of ours took to the ships at Brest, Cherbourg, St. Malo, and St. Nazaire. On June 15 our troops were released from the orders of the Tenth French Army, and next day, when it carried out a further withdrawal to the south, they moved towards Cherbourg. The 157th Brigade, after heavy fighting, was extricated that night, and, retiring in their lorries, embarked during the night of the 17th-18th. On June 17 it was announced that the Pétain Government had asked for an armistice, ordering all French forces to cease fighting, without even communicating this information to our troops. General Brooke was consequently told to come away with all men he could embark and any equipment he could save.

We repeated now on a considerable scale, though with larger vessels, the Dunkirk evacuation. Over twenty thousand Polish troops who refused to capitulate cut their way to the sea and were carried by our ships to Britain. The Germans pursued our forces at all points. In the Cherbourg peninsula they were in contact with our rearguard ten miles south of the harbour on the morning of the 18th. The last ship left at 4 p.m., when the enemy, led by Rommel's 7th Panzer Division, were within three miles of the port. Very few of our men were taken prisoners.

In all there were evacuated from all French harbours 136,000 British troops and 310 guns; a total, with the Poles, of 156,000 men. This reflects great credit on General Brooke's embarkation staff, of whom the chief, General de Fonblanque, a British officer, died shortly afterwards as the result of his exertions.

At Brest and the western ports the evacuations were numerous. The German air attack on the transports was heavy. One frightful incident occurred on the 17th at St. Nazaire. The 20,000-ton liner *Lancastria*, with five thousand men on board, was bombed just as she was about to leave. Upwards of three thousand men perished. The rest were rescued under continued air attack by the devotion of the small craft. When this news came to me in the quiet Cabinet Room during the afternoon I forbade its publication, saying: "The newspapers have got quite enough disaster for to-day at least." I had intended to release the news a few days later, but events crowded upon us so black and so quickly that I forgot to lift the ban, and it was some time before the knowledge of this horror became public.

* * *

To lessen the shock of the impending French surrender, it was necessary at this time to send a message to the Dominions Prime Ministers showing them that our resolve to continue the struggle although alone was not based upon mere obstinacy or desperation, and to convince them by practical and technical reasons, of which they might well be unaware, of the real strength of our position. I therefore dictated the following statement on the afternoon of June 16, a day already filled with much business.

Prime Minister to the Prime Ministers of Canada, Australia, New Zealand, and South Africa   16.VI.40

[Some sentences of introduction particular to each.]

I do not regard the situation as having passed beyond our strength. It is by no means certain that the French will not fight on in Africa and at sea, but, whatever they do, Hitler will have to break us in this Island or lose the war. Our principal danger is his concentrated air attack by bombing, coupled with parachute and air-borne landings and attempts to run an invading force across the sea. This danger has faced us ever since the beginning of the war, and the French could never have saved us from it, as he could always switch on to us. Undoubtedly it is aggravated by the conquests Hitler has made upon the European coast close to our shores. Nevertheless, in principle the danger is the same. I do not see why we should not be able to meet it. The Navy has never pretended to prevent a raid of five or ten thousand men, but we do not see how a force of, say, eighty to a hundred thousand could be transported across the sea, and still less maintained, in the teeth of superior sea-power. As long as our Air Force is in being it provides a powerful aid to the Fleet in preventing sea-borne landings and will take a very heavy toll of air-borne landings.

Although we have suffered heavy losses by assisting the French and during the Dunkirk evacuation, we have managed to husband our air fighter strength in spite of poignant appeals from France to throw it improvidently into the great land battle, which it could not have turned decisively. I am happy to tell you that it is now as strong as it has ever been, and that the flow of machines is coming forward far more rapidly than ever before; in fact, pilots have now become the limiting factor at the moment. Our fighter aircraft have been wont to inflict a loss of two or two and a half to one even when fighting under the adverse conditions in France. During the evacuation of Dunkirk, which was a sort of No-man's Land, we inflicted a loss of three or four to one, and often saw German formations turn away from a quarter of their numbers of our planes. But all air authorities agree that the advantage in defending this country against an oversea air attack will be still greater, because, first, we shall know pretty well by our various devices where they are coming, and because our squadrons lie close enough together to enable us to concentrate against the attackers and provide enough to attack both the bombers and the protecting fighters at the same time. All their shot-down machines will be total losses; many of ours and our pilots will fight again. Therefore I do not think it by any means impossible that we may so maul them that they will find daylight attacks too expensive.

The major danger will be from night attack on our aircraft factories, but this, again, is far less accurate than daylight attack, and we have many plans for minimising its effect. Of course their numbers are much greater than ours, but not so much greater as to deprive us of a good and reasonable prospect of wearing them out after some weeks or even months of air struggle. Meanwhile of course our bomber force will be striking continually at their key points, especially oil refineries and air factories, and at their congested and centralised war industry in the Ruhr. We hope our people will stand up to this bombardment as well as the enemy. It will, on both sides, be on an unprecedented scale. All our information goes to show that the Germans have not liked what they have got so far.

It must be remembered that, now that the B.E.F. is home and largely rearmed or rearming, if not upon a Continental scale, at any rate good enough for Home defence, we have far stronger military forces in this Island than we have ever had in the late war or in this war.

GENERAL MAP WESTERN FRANCE
(CHERBOURG–BREST)

Therefore we hope that such numbers of the enemy as may be landed from the air or by sea-borne raid will be destroyed and be an example to those who try to follow. No doubt we must expect novel forms of attack and attempts to bring tanks across the sea. We are preparing ourselves to deal with these as far as we can foresee them. No one can predict or guarantee the course of a life-and-death struggle of this character, but we shall certainly enter upon it in good heart.

I have given you this full explanation to show you that there are solid reasons behind our resolve not to allow the fate of France, whatever it may be, to deter us from going on to the end. I personally believe that the spectacle of the fierce struggle and carnage in our Island will draw the United States into the war, and even if we should be beaten down through the superior numbers of the enemy's Air Force it will always be possible, as I indicated to the House of Commons in my last speech, to send our fleets across the oceans, where they will protect the Empire and enable it to continue the war and the blockade, I trust in conjunction with the United States, until the Hitler *régime* breaks under the strain. We shall let you know at every stage how you can help, being assured that you will do all in human power, as we, for our part, are entirely resolved to do.

I composed this in the Cabinet Room, and it was typed as I spoke. The door to the garden was wide open, and outside the sun shone warm and bright. Air Marshal Newall, the Chief of the Air Staff, sat on the terrace meanwhile, and when I had finished revising the draft I took it out to him in case there were any improvements or corrections to be made. He was evidently moved, and presently said he agreed with every word. I was comforted and fortified myself by putting my convictions upon record, and when I read the message over the final time before sending it off I felt a glow of sober confidence. This was certainly justified by what happened. All came true.

CHAPTER X

THE BORDEAUX ARMISTICE

The French Government Moves to Bordeaux – General Weygand's Attitude – Weygand and Reynaud – M. Chautemps' Insidious Proposal – The French Decision to Ask for Terms – British Insistence on the Safeguarding of the French Fleet – My Telegram to Reynaud of June 16 – A New Issue Arises – British Offer of Indissoluble Union with France – High Hopes of General de Gaulle that this would Strengthen M. Reynaud – M. Reynaud's Satisfaction – My Telegram of June 16 Suspended – Plan for Me to Visit Bordeaux by Cruiser with the Labour and Liberal Party Leaders Frustrated – Unfavourable Reception of the British Offer – Fall of the Reynaud Cabinet – Reynaud's Resignation – A Conversation with M. Monnet and General de Gaulle in Downing Street – Marshal Pétain Forms a French Government for an Armistice – My Message to Marshal Pétain and General Weygand, June 17 – My Broadcast of June 17 – General Spears Plans the Escape of General de Gaulle – Further Talk of Resistance in Africa – Mandel's Intentions – Admiral Darlan's Trap – Voyage of the "Massilia" – Mandel at Casablanca – Mr. Duff Cooper's Mission – Fate of the French Patriots – Jobbing Backwards – My Settled Conviction.

W E must now quit the field of military disaster for the convulsions in the French Cabinet and the personages who surrounded it at Bordeaux.

It is not easy to establish the exact sequence of events. The British War Cabinet sat almost continuously, and messages were sent off from time to time as decisions were taken. As they took two or three hours to transmit in cipher, and probably another hour to deliver, the telephone was freely used by the officials of the Foreign Office to convey the substance to our Ambassador, and he also used the telephone frequently in reply. Therefore there are overlaps and short-circuits which are confusing. Events were moving at such a speed on both sides of the Channel that it would be misleading to present the tale as if it were an orderly flow of argument and decision.

M. Reynaud reached the new seat of government from Tours during the evening of the 14th. He received the British Ambassador about nine o'clock. Sir Ronald Campbell informed him that His Majesty's Government intended to insist on the terms of the agreement of March 28, binding both parties not to make any terms with the enemy. He also offered to provide all the necessary shipping in the event of the French Government resolving to move to North Africa. Both these statements were in accordance with the Ambassador's current instructions.

On the morning of the 15th Reynaud again received the Ambassador, and told him that he had definitely decided to divide the Government in half and to establish a centre of authority beyond the sea. Such a policy would obviously carry with it the removal of the French Fleet to ports beyond German power. Later that morning President Roosevelt's reply to Reynaud's appeal of June 13 was received. Although I had made the best of it in my telegram to the French Premier, I knew it was bound to disappoint him. Material aid, if Congress approved, was offered; but there was no question of any American entry into the war. France had no reason to expect such a declaration at this moment, and the President had not either the power to give it himself or to obtain it from Congress. There had been no meetings of the Council of Ministers since that at Cangé, near Tours, on the evening of the 13th. The Ministers having now all reached Bordeaux, the Council was summoned for the afternoon.

* * *

General Weygand had been for some days convinced that all further resistance was vain. He therefore wished to force the French Government to ask for an armistice while the French Army still retained enough discipline and strength to maintain internal order on the morrow of defeat. He had a profound, lifelong dislike of the Parliamentary *régime* of the Third Republic. As an ardently religious Catholic, he saw in the ruin which had overwhelmed his country the chastisement of God for its abandonment of the Christian faith. He therefore used the power of his supreme military position far beyond the limits which his professional responsibilities, great as they were, justified or required. He confronted the Prime Minister with declarations that the French armies could fight no more, and that it was time to stop a horrible and useless massacre before general anarchy supervened.

Paul Reynaud, on the other hand, realised that the battle in France was over, but still hoped to carry on the war from Africa and the French Empire and with the French Fleet. None of the other States overrun by Hitler had withdrawn from the war. Physically in their own lands they were gripped, but from overseas their Governments had kept the flag flying and the national cause alive. Reynaud wished to follow their example, and with much more solid resources. He sought a solution on the lines of the Dutch capitulation. This, while it left the Army, whose chiefs had refused to fight any longer, free to lay down its arms wherever it was in contact with the enemy, nevertheless preserved to the State its sovereign right to continue the struggle by all the means in its power.

This issue was fought out between the Premier and the Generalissimo at a stormy interview before the Council meeting. Reynaud offered Weygand written authority from the Government to order the "Cease Fire". Weygand refused with indignation the suggestion of a military surrender. "He would never accept the casting of this shame upon the banners of the French Army." The Act of Surrender, which he deemed imperative, must be that of the Government and of the State, to which the army he commanded would dutifully conform. In so acting General Weygand, though a sincere and unselfish man, behaved wrongly. He asserted the right of a soldier to dominate the duly-constituted Government of the Republic, and thus to bring the whole resistance not only of France but of her Empire to an end contrary to the decision of his political and lawful chief.

Apart from these formalities and talk about the honour of the French Army there stood a practical point. An armistice formally entered into by the French Government would mean the end of the war for France. By negotiation part of the country might be left unoccupied and part of the Army free; whereas if the war were continued from overseas all who had not escaped from France would be controlled directly by the Germans, and millions of Frenchmen would be carried off to Germany as prisoners of war without the protection of any agreement. This was a substantial argument, but it belonged to the Government of the Republic and not to the Commander-in-Chief of the Army to decide upon it. Weygand's position that because the army under his orders would in his opinion fight no more the French Republic must give in and order its armed forces to obey an order which he was certainly willing to carry out finds no foundation in the law and practice of civilised States or in the professional honour of a soldier. In theory at least the Prime Minister had his remedy. He could have replied: "You are affronting the Constitution of the Republic. You are dismissed from this moment from your command. I will obtain the necessary sanction from the President."

Unfortunately M. Reynaud was not sufficiently sure of his position. Behind the presumptuous General loomed the illustrious Marshal Pétain, the centre of the band of defeatist Ministers whom Reynaud had so recently and so improvidently brought into the French Government and Council, and who were all resolved to stop the war. Behind these again crouched the sinister figure of Laval, who had installed himself at Bordeaux City Hall, surrounded by a clique of agitated Senators and Deputies. Laval's policy had the force and merit of simplicity. France must not only make peace with Germany; she must change sides, she must become the ally of the conqueror, and by her loyalty and services against the common foe across the Channel save her interests and her provinces and finish up on the victorious side. Evidently M. Reynaud, exhausted by the ordeals through which he had passed, had not the life or strength for so searching a personal ordeal, which would indeed have taxed the resources of an Oliver Cromwell or of a Clemenceau, of Stalin or of Hitler.

In the discussions on the afternoon of the 15th, at which the President of the Republic was present, Reynaud, having explained the situation to his colleagues, appealed to Marshal Pétain to persuade General Weygand to the Cabinet view. He could not have chosen a worse envoy. The Marshal left the room. There was an interval. After a while he returned with Weygand, whose position he now supported. At this serious juncture M. Chautemps, an important Minister, slid in an insidious proposal which wore the aspect of a compromise and was attractive to the waverers. He stated in the name of the Leftist elements of the Cabinet that Reynaud was right in affirming that an agreement with the enemy was impossible, but that it would be prudent to make a gesture which would unite France. They should ask the Germans what the conditions of armistice would be, remaining entirely free to reject them. It was not of course possible to embark on this slippery slope and stop. The mere announcement that the French Government were asking the Germans on what terms an armistice would be granted was sufficient in itself to destroy what remained of the morale of the French Army. How could the soldier be ordered to cast away his life in obdurate resistance after so fatal a signal had been given? However, combined with the demonstration which they had witnessed from Pétain and Weygand, the Chautemps suggestion had a deadly effect on the majority. It was agreed to ask His Majesty's Government how they would view such a step, informing them at the same time that in no circumstances would the surrender of the Fleet be allowed. Reynaud now rose from the table and declared his intention to resign. But the President of the Republic restrained him, and declared that if Reynaud went he would go too. When the confused discussion was resumed no clear distinction was drawn between declining to surrender the French Fleet to the Germans and putting it out of German power by sailing it to ports outside France. It was agreed that the British Government should be asked to consent to the inquiry about the German terms. The message was immediately dispatched.

*　　*　　*

The next morning Reynaud received the British Ambassador again, and was told that the British would accept the French request on the condition that the French Fleet was placed beyond German power—in fact, that it should be directed to British ports. These instructions had been telephoned to Campbell from London to save time. At eleven o'clock the distracted Council of Ministers met again, President Lebrun being present. The President of the Senate, M. Jeanneney, was brought in to endorse, both on his own behalf and on that of his colleague the President of the Chamber, M. Herriot, the proposal of the Premier to transfer the Government to North Africa. Up rose Marshal Pétain and read a letter, which it is believed had been written for him by another hand, resigning from the Cabinet. Having finished his speech, he prepared to leave the room. He was persuaded by the President of the Republic to remain on the condition that an answer would be given to him during the day. The Marshal had also complained of the delay in asking for an armistice. Reynaud replied that if one asked an ally to free one from an obligation it was customary to await the answer. The session then closed. After luncheon the Ambassador brought to Reynaud the textual answer of the British Government, of which he had already given the telephoned purport in his conversation of the morning.

*　　*　　*

In these days the War Cabinet were in a state of unusual emotion. The fall and the fate of France dominated their minds. Our own plight, and what we should have to face and face alone, seemed to take a second place. Grief for our ally in her agony, and desire to do anything in human power to aid her, was the prevailing mood. There was also the overpowering importance of making sure of the French Fleet. It was in this spirit that a proposal for "an indissoluble union" between France and Britain was conceived.

I was not the prime mover. I first heard of a definite plan at a luncheon at the Carlton Club on the 15th, at which were present Lord Halifax, M. Corbin, Sir Robert Vansittart, and one or two others. It was evident that there had been considerable discussion beforehand. On the 14th Vansittart and Desmond Morton had met M. Monnet and M. Pleven (members of the French Economic Mission in London), and been joined by General de Gaulle, who had flown over to make arrangements for shipping to carry the French Government and as many French troops as possible to Africa. These gentlemen had evolved the outline of a declaration for a Franco-British Union with the object, apart from its general merits, of giving M. Reynaud some new fact of a vivid and stimulating nature with which to carry a majority of his Cabinet into the move to Africa and the continuance of the war. My first reaction was unfavourable. I asked a number of questions of a critical character, and was by no means convinced. However, at the end of our long Cabinet that afternoon the subject was raised. I was somewhat surprised to see the staid, stolid, experienced politicians of all parties engage themselves so passionately in an immense design whose implications and consequences were not in any way thought out. I did not resist, but yielded easily to these generous surges which carried our resolves to a very high level of unselfish and undaunted action.

When the War Cabinet met the next morning we first addressed ourselves to the answer to be given to M. Reynaud's request sent the night before the formal release of France from her obligations under the Anglo-French Agreement. The Cabinet authorised the following reply, which at their request I went into the next room and drafted myself. It was dispatched from London at 12.35 p.m. on the 16th. It endorsed and repeated in a formal manner the telephoned instructions sent to Campbell early in the morning.

Foreign Office to Sir R. Campbell
Please give M. Reynaud the following message, which has been approved by the Cabinet:

Mr. Churchill to M. Reynaud   16 June, 1940, 12.35 p.m.
Our agreement forbidding separate negotiations, whether for armistice or peace, was made with the French Republic, and not with any particular French Administration or statesman. It therefore involves the honour of France. Nevertheless, *provided, but only provided, that the French Fleet is sailed forthwith for British harbours pending negotiations,* His Majesty's Government give their full consent to an inquiry by the French Government to ascertain the terms of an armistice for France. His Majesty's Government, being resolved to continue the war, wholly exclude themselves from all part in the above-mentioned inquiry concerning an armistice.

Early in the afternoon a second message in similar terms was sent by the Foreign Office to Sir Ronald Campbell (June 16, 3.10 p.m.).

Both messages were stiff, and embodied the main purpose of the War Cabinet at their morning meeting.

Foreign Office to Sir R. Campbell
You should inform M. Reynaud as follows:
We expect to be consulted as soon as any armistice terms are received. This is necessary not merely in virtue of treaty forbidding separate peace or armistice, but also in view of vital consequences of any armistice to ourselves, having regard especially to the fact that British troops are fighting with French Army. You should impress on

French Government that in stipulating for removal of French Fleet to British ports we have in mind French interests as well as our own, and are convinced that it will strengthen the hands of the French Government in any armistice discussions if they can show that the French Navy is out of reach of the German forces. As regards the French Air Force, we assume that every effort will be made to fly it to North Africa, unless indeed the French Government would prefer to send it to this country.

We count on the French Government doing all they can both before and during any armistice discussions to extricate the Polish, Belgian, and Czech troops at present in France, and to send them to North Africa. Arrangements are being made to receive Polish and Belgian Governments in this country.

*   *   *

We reassembled at 3 p.m. that same afternoon. I recalled to the Cabinet that at the conclusion of our meeting the day before there had been some discussion on a proposal for the issue of some further declaration of closer union between France and Great Britain. I had seen General de Gaulle in the morning, and he had impressed on me that some dramatic move was essential to give M. Reynaud the support which he needed to keep his Government in the war, and suggested that a proclamation of the indissoluble union of the French and British peoples would serve the purpose. Both General de Gaulle and M. Corbin had been concerned at the sharpness of the decision reached by the War Cabinet that morning, and embodied in the telegrams already dispatched. I had heard that a new declaration had been drafted for consideration, and that General de Gaulle had telephoned to M. Reynaud. As a result it had seemed advisable to suspend action for the moment. A telegram had therefore been sent to Sir Ronald Campbell instructing him to suspend delivery accordingly.

The Foreign Secretary then said that after our morning meeting he had seen Sir Robert Vansittart, whom he had previously asked to draft some dramatic announcement which might strengthen M. Reynaud's hand. Vansittart had been in consultation with General de Gaulle, M. Monnet, M. Pleven, and Major Morton. Between them they had drafted a proclamation. General de Gaulle had impressed upon them the need for publishing the document as quickly as possible, and wished to take the draft back with him to France that night. De Gaulle had also suggested that I should go to meet M. Reynaud next day.

The draft statement was passed round, and everyone read it with deep attention. All the difficulties were immediately apparent, but in the end a Declaration of Union seemed to command general assent. I stated that my first instinct had been against the idea, but that in this crisis we must not let ourselves be accused of lack of imagination. Some dramatic announcement was clearly necessary to keep the French going. The proposal could not be lightly turned aside, and I was encouraged at finding so great a body of opinion in the War Cabinet favourable to it.

At 3.55 p.m. we were told that the French Council of Ministers would meet at 5 p.m. to decide whether further resistance was possible. Secondly, General de Gaulle had been informed by M. Reynaud on the telephone that if a favourable answer on the proposed proclamation of unity was received by 5 p.m. M. Reynaud felt he could hold the position. On this the War Cabinet approved the final draft proclamation of an Anglo-French Union, and authorised its dispatch to M. Reynaud by the hand of General de Gaulle. This was telephoned to M. Reynaud forthwith. The War Cabinet further invited me, Mr. Attlee, and Sir Archibald Sinclair, representing the three British parties, to meet M. Reynaud at the earliest moment to discuss the draft proclamation and related questions.

Here is the final draft:

DECLARATION OF UNION

At this most fateful moment in the history of the modern world the Governments of the United Kingdom and the French Republic make this declaration of indissoluble union and unyielding resolution in their common defence of justice and freedom against subjection to a system which reduces mankind to a life of robots and slaves.

The two Governments declare that France and Great Britain shall no longer be two nations, but one Franco-British Union.

The constitution of the Union will provide for joint organs of defence, foreign, financial, and economic policies.

Every citizen of France will enjoy immediately citizenship of Great Britain; every British subject will become a citizen of France.

Both countries will share responsibility for the repair of the devastation of war, wherever it occurs in their territories, and the resources of both shall be equally, and as one, applied to that purpose.

During the war there shall be a single War Cabinet, and all the forces of Britain and France, whether on land, sea, or in the air, will be placed under its direction. It will govern from wherever it best can. The two Parliaments will be formally associated. The nations of the British Empire are already forming new armies. France will keep her available forces in the field, on the sea, and in the air. The Union appeals to the United States to fortify the economic resources of the Allies, and to bring her powerful material aid to the common cause.

The Union will concentrate its whole energy against the power of the enemy, no matter where the battle may be.

And thus we shall conquer.

Of all this Parliament was informed in due course. But the issue by then had ceased to count.

I did not, as has been seen, draft the statement myself. It was composed around the table, and I made my contribution to it. I then took it into the next room, where de Gaulle was waiting with Vansittart, Desmond Morton, and M. Corbin. The General read it with an air of unwonted enthusiasm; and, as soon as contact with Bordeaux could be obtained, began to telephone it to M. Reynaud. He hoped with us that this solemn pledge of union and brotherhood between the two nations and Empires would give the struggling French Premier the means to carry his Government to Africa with all possible forces and order the French Navy to sail for harbours outside impending German control.

*   *   *

We must now pass to the other end of the wire. The British Ambassador delivered the two messages in answer to the French request to be released from their obligation of March 28. According to his account, M. Reynaud, who was in a dejected mood, did not take them well. He at once remarked that the withdrawal of the French Mediterranean Fleet to British ports would invite the immediate seizure of Tunis by Italy, and also create difficulties for the British Fleet. He had got no further than this when my message, telephoned by General de Gaulle, came through. "It acted," said the Ambassador, "like a tonic." Reynaud said that for a document like that he would fight to the last. In came at that moment M. Mandel and M. Marin. They obviously were equally relieved. M. Reynaud then left "with a light step" to read the document to the President of the Republic. He believed that, armed with this immense guarantee, he would be able to carry his Council with him on the policy of retiring to Africa and waging war. My telegram instructing the Ambassador to delay the presentation of the two stiff messages, or anyhow to suspend action upon them, arrived immediately after the Premier had gone. A messenger was therefore sent after him to say that the two earlier messages should be considered as "cancelled". "Suspended" would have been a better word. The War Cabinet had not altered its position in any respect. We felt however that it would be better to give the "Declaration of Union" its full chance under the most favourable conditions. If the French Council of Ministers were rallied by it, the greater would carry the less, and the removal of the Fleet from German power would follow automatically. If our offer did not find favour our rights and claims would revive in their full force. We could not tell what was going on inside the French Government, nor know that this was the last time we should ever be able to deal with M. Reynaud.

I had spoken to him on the telephone some time this day proposing that I should come out immediately to see him. In view of the uncertainty about what was happening or about to happen at Bordeaux, my colleagues in the War Cabinet wished me to go in a cruiser, and a rendezvous was duly arranged for the next day off the Brittany coast. I ought to have flown. But even so it would have been too late.

The following was sent from the Foreign Office:

To Sir R. Campbell, Bordeaux   June 16, 6.45 p.m.
The P.M., accompanied by the Lord Privy Seal, Secretary of State for Air, and three Chiefs of Staff and certain others, arrives at Concarneau at twelve noon to-morrow, the 17th, in a cruiser for a meeting with M. Reynaud. General de Gaulle has been informed of the above and has expressed the view that time and rendezvous would be convenient. We suggest the meeting be held on board as arousing less attention. H.M.S. *Berkeley* has been warned to be at the disposal of M. Reynaud and party if desired.

And also from the Foreign Secretary by telephone at 8 p.m., June 16:

Following is reason why you have been asked to suspend action on my last two telegrams.

After consultation with General de Gaulle, P.M. has decided to meet M. Reynaud to-morrow in Brittany to make a further attempt to dissuade the French Government from asking for an armistice. For this purpose, on the advice of General de Gaulle, he will offer to M. Reynaud to join in issuing forthwith a declaration announcing immediate constitution of closest Anglo-French Union in all spheres in order to carry on the war. Text of draft declaration as authorised by H.M.G. is contained in my immediately following telegram. You should read this text to M. Reynaud at once.

An outline of this proposed declaration has already been telephoned by General de Gaulle to M. Reynaud, who has replied that such a declaration by the two Governments would make all the difference to the decision of the French Government. General is returning to-night with copy.

Our War Cabinet sat until six o'clock on the 16th, and thereafter I set out on my mission. I took with me the Leaders of the Labour and Liberal Parties, the three Chiefs of Staff, and various important officers and officials. A special train was waiting at Waterloo. We could reach Southampton in two hours, and a night of steaming at thirty knots in the cruiser would bring us to the rendezvous by noon on the 17th. We had taken our seats in the train. My wife had come to see me off. There was an odd delay in starting. Evidently some hitch had occurred. Presently my private secretary arrived from Downing Street breathless with the following message from Campbell at Bordeaux:

Ministerial crisis has opened. . . . Hope to have news by midnight. Meanwhile meeting arranged for to-morrow impossible.

On this I returned to Downing Street with a heavy heart.

* * *

The final scene in the Reynaud Cabinet was as follows.

The hopes which M. Reynaud had founded upon the Declaration of Union were soon dispelled. Rarely has so generous a proposal encountered such a hostile reception. The Premier read the document twice to the Council. He declared himself strongly for it, and added that he was arranging a meeting with me for the next day to discuss the details. But the agitated Ministers, some famous, some nobodies, torn by division and under the terrible hammer of defeat, were staggered. Some, we are told, had heard about it by a tapping of telephones. These were the defeatists. Most were wholly unprepared to receive such far-reaching themes. The overwhelming feeling of the Council was to reject the whole plan. Surprise and mistrust dominated the majority, and even the most friendly and resolute were baffled. The Council had met expecting to receive the answer to the French request, on which they had all agreed, that Britain should release France from her obligations of March 28, in order that the French might ask the Germans what their terms of armistice would be. It is possible, even probable, that if our formal answer had been laid before them the majority would have accepted our primary condition about sending their Fleet to Britain, or at least would have made some other suitable proposal and thus have freed them to open negotiations with the enemy, while reserving to themselves a final option of retirement to Africa if the German conditions were too severe. But now there was a classic example of "Order, counter-order, disorder".

Paul Reynaud was quite unable to overcome the unfavourable impression which the proposal of Anglo-French Union created. The defeatist section, led by Marshal Pétain, refused even to examine it. Violent charges were made. It was "a last-minute plan", "a surprise", "a scheme to put France in tutelage, or to carry off her colonial empire". It relegated France, so they said, to the position of a Dominion. Others complained that not even equality of status was offered to the French, because Frenchmen were to receive only the citizenship of the British Empire instead of that of Great Britain, while the British were to be citizens of France. This suggestion is contradicted by the text.

Beyond these came other arguments. Weygand had convinced Pétain without much difficulty that England was lost. High French military authorities had advised: "In three weeks England will have her neck wrung like a chicken." To make a union with Great Britain was, according to Pétain, "fusion with a corpse". Ybarnegaray, who had been so stout in the previous war, exclaimed: "Better be a Nazi province. At least we know what that means." Senator Reibel, a personal friend of General Weygand's, declared that this scheme meant complete destruction for France, and anyhow definite subordination to England. In vain did Reynaud reply: "I prefer to collaborate with my allies rather than with my enemies." And

Mandel: "Would you rather be a German district than a British Dominion?" All was in vain.

We are assured that Reynaud's statement of our proposal was never put to a vote in the Council. It collapsed of itself. This was a personal and fatal reverse for the struggling Premier which marked the end of his influence and authority upon the Council. All further discussion turned upon the armistice and asking the Germans what terms they would give, and in this M. Chautemps was cool and steadfast. Our two telegrams about the Fleet were never presented to the Council. The demand that it should be sailed to British ports as a prelude to the negotiations with the Germans was never considered by the Reynaud Cabinet, which was now in complete decomposition. At about eight o'clock Reynaud, utterly exhausted by the physical and mental strain to which he had for so many days been subjected, sent his resignation to the President, and advised him to send for Marshal Pétain. This action must be judged precipitate. He still seems to have cherished the hope that he could keep his rendezvous with me the next day, and spoke of this to General Spears. "To-morrow there will be another Government, and you will no longer speak for anyone," said Spears.

According to Campbell (sent by telephone, June 16):

M. Reynaud, who had been so heartened this afternoon by P.M.'s magnificent message, told us later that forces in favour of ascertaining terms of armistice had become too strong for him. He had read the message twice to Council of Ministers and explained its import and the hope which it held out for the future. It had been of no avail.

We worked on him for half an hour, encouraging him to try to get rid of the evil influences among his colleagues. After seeing M. Mandel for a moment we then called for second time to-day on the President of Senate, M. Jeanneney, whose views (like those of President of Chamber) are sound, in hope of his being able to influence President of Republic to insist on M. Reynaud forming new Government.

We begged him to make it very clear to President that offer contained in P.M.'s message would not be extended to a Government which entered into negotiation with enemy.

An hour or so later M. Reynaud informed us that he was beaten and had handed in his resignation. Combination of Marshal Pétain and General Weygand (who were living in another world and imagined they could sit round a green table discussing armistice terms in the old manner) had proved too much for weak members of Government, on whom they worked by waving the spectre of revolution.

*　　*　　*

On the afternoon of June 16 M. Monnet and General de Gaulle visited me in the Cabinet Room. The General in his capacity of Under-Secretary of State for National Defence had just ordered the French ship *Pasteur*, which was carrying weapons to Bordeaux from America, to proceed instead to a British port. Monnet was very active upon a plan to transfer all French contracts for munitions in America to Britain if France made a separate peace. He evidently expected this, and wished to save as much as possible from what seemed to him to be the wreck of the world. His whole attitude in this respect was most helpful. Then he turned to our sending all our remaining fighter air squadrons to share in the final battle in France, which was of course already over. I told him that there was no possibility of this being done. Even at this stage he used the usual arguments—"the decisive battle", "now or never", "if France falls all falls", and so forth. But I could not do anything to oblige him in this field. My two French visitors then got up and moved towards the door, Monnet leading. As they reached it, de Gaulle, who had hitherto scarcely uttered a single word, turned back, and, taking two or three paces towards me, said in English: "I think you are quite right." Under an impassive, unperturbable demeanour he seemed to me to have a remarkable capacity for feeling pain. I preserved the impression, in contact with this very tall, phlegmatic man: "Here is the Constable of France." He returned that afternoon in a British aeroplane, which I had placed at his disposal, to Bordeaux. But not for long.

*　　*　　*

Forthwith Marshal Pétain formed a French Government with the main purpose of seeking an immediate armistice from Germany. Late on the night of June 16 the defeatist group of which he was the head was already so shaped and knit together that the process did not take long. M. Chautemps ("to ask for terms is not necessarily to accept them") was Vice-President of the Council. General Weygand, whose view was that all was over, held the Ministry of National Defence. Admiral Darlan was Minister of Marine, and M. Baudouin Minister for Foreign Affairs.

The only hitch apparently arose over M. Laval. The Marshal's first thought had been to offer him the post of Minister of Justice. Laval brushed this aside with disdain. He demanded the Ministry of Foreign Affairs, from which position alone he conceived it possible to carry out his plan of reversing the alliances of France, finishing up England, and joining as a minor partner the New Nazi Europe. Marshal Pétain surrendered at once to the vehemence of this formidable personality. M. Baudouin, who had already undertaken the Foreign Office, for which he knew himself to be utterly inadequate, was quite ready to give it up. But when he mentioned the fact to M. Charles-Roux, Permanent Under-Secretary to the Ministry of Foreign Affairs, the latter was indignant. He enlisted the support of Weygand. When Weygand entered the room and addressed the illustrious Marshal, Laval became so furious that both the military chiefs were overwhelmed. The permanent official however refused point-blank to serve under Laval. Confronted with this, the Marshal again subsided, and after a violent scene Laval departed in wrath and dudgeon.

This was a critical moment. When, four months later, on October 28, Laval eventually became Foreign Minister there was a new consciousness of military values. British resistance to Germany was by then a factor. Apparently the Island could not be entirely discounted. Anyhow, its neck had not been "wrung like a chicken's in three weeks". This was a new fact; and a fact at which the whole French nation rejoiced.

*   *   *

Our telegram of the 16th had made our assent to inquiries about an armistice conditional upon the sailing of the French Fleet to British harbours. It had already been presented formally to Marshal Pétain. The War Cabinet approved, at my suggestion, a further message emphasising the point. But we were talking to the void.

On the 17th also I sent a personal message to Marshal Pétain and General Weygand, of which copies were to be furnished by our Ambassador to the French President and Admiral Darlan:

I wish to repeat to you my profound conviction that the illustrious Marshal Pétain and the famous General Weygand, our comrades in two great wars against the Germans, will not injure their ally by delivering over to the enemy the fine French Fleet. Such an act would scarify their names for a thousand years of history. Yet this result may easily come by frittering away these few precious hours when the Fleet can be sailed to safety in British or American ports, carrying with it the hope of the future and the honour of France.

In order that these appeals might not lack personal reinforcement on the spot, we sent the First Sea Lord, who believed himself to be in intimate personal and professional touch with Admiral Darlan, the First Lord, Mr. A. V. Alexander, and Lord Lloyd, Secretary of State for the Colonies, so long known as a friend of France. All these three laboured to make what contacts they could with the new Ministers during the 19th. They received many solemn assurances that the Fleet would never be allowed to fall into German hands. But no more French warships moved beyond the reach of the swiftly approaching German power.

* * *

At the desire of the Cabinet I had broadcast the following statement on the evening of June 17:

The news from France is very bad, and I grieve for the gallant French people who have fallen into this terrible misfortune. Nothing will alter our feelings towards them or our faith that the genius of France will rise again. What has happened in France makes no difference to our actions and purpose. We have become the sole champions now in arms to defend the world cause. We shall do our best to be worthy of this high honour. We shall defend our Island home, and with the British Empire we shall fight on unconquerable until the curse of Hitler is lifted from the brows of mankind. We are sure that in the end all will come right.

* * *

On the morning of the 17th I mentioned to my colleagues in the Cabinet a telephone conversation which I had had during the night with General Spears, who said he did not think he could perform any useful service in the new structure at Bordeaux. He spoke with some anxiety about the safety of General de Gaulle. Spears had apparently been warned that as things were shaping it might be well for de Gaulle to leave France. I readily assented to a good plan being made for this. So that very morning—the 17th—de Gaulle went to his office in Bordeaux, made a number of engagements for the afternoon, as a blind, and then drove to the airfield with his friend Spears to see him off. They shook hands and said good-bye, and as the plane began to move de Gaulle stepped in and slammed the door. The machine soared off into the air, while the French police and officials gaped. De Gaulle carried with him, in this small aeroplane, the honour of France.

That same evening he made his memorable broadcast to the French people. One passage should be quoted here:

France is not alone. She has a vast Empire behind her. She can unite with the British Empire, which holds the seas, and is continuing the struggle. She can utilise to the full, as England is doing, the vast industrial resources of the United States.

Other Frenchmen who wished to fight on were not so fortunate. When the Pétain Government was formed the plan of going to Africa to set up a centre of power outside German control was still open. It was discussed at a meeting of the Pétain Cabinet on June 18. The same evening President Lebrun, Pétain, and the Presidents of the Senate and the Chamber met together. There seems to have been general agreement at least to send a representative body to North Africa. Even the Marshal was not hostile. He himself intended to stay, but saw no reason why Chautemps, Vice-President of the Council, should not go and act in his name. When rumours of an impending exodus ran round agitated Bordeaux Weygand was hostile. Such a move, he thought, would wreck the "honourable" armistice negotiations which had already been begun by way of Madrid, on French initiative, on June 17. Laval was deeply alarmed. He feared that the setting up of an effective resistance administration outside France would frustrate the policy on which he was resolved. He set to work on the clusters of Deputies and Senators crowded into Bordeaux.

Darlan, as Minister of Marine, took a different view. To pack off all the principal critics of his conduct in a ship seemed at the moment to him a most convenient solution of many difficulties. Once aboard, all those who went would be in his power, and there would be plenty of time for the Government to settle what to do. With the approval of the new Cabinet, he offered passages on the armed auxiliary cruiser *Massilia* to all political figures of influence who wished to go to Africa. The ship was to sail from the mouth of the Gironde on the 20th. Many however who had planned to go to Africa, including Jeanneney and Herriot, suspected a trap, and preferred to travel overland through Spain. The final party, apart from refugees, consisted of twenty-four Deputies and one Senator, and included Mandel, Campinchi, and Daladier, who had all been actively pressing for the move to Africa. On the afternoon of the 21st the *Massilia* sailed. On the 23rd the ship's radio announced that the Pétain Government had accepted and signed the armistice with Germany. Campinchi immediately tried to persuade the captain to set his course for England, but this officer no doubt had his instructions and met his former political chief of two days before with a bleak refusal. The unlucky band of patriots passed anxious hours, till on the evening of June 24 the *Massilia* anchored at Casablanca.

Mandel now acted with his usual decision. He had with Daladier drafted a proclamation setting up a resistance administration in North Africa with himself as Premier. He went on shore, and, after calling on the British Consul, established himself at the Hôtel Excelsior. He then attempted to send his proclamation out through the Havas Agency. When General Noguès read its text he was disturbed. He intercepted the message, and it was telegraphed not to the world but to Darlan and Pétain. They had now made up their minds to have no alternative and potentially rival Government outside German power. Mandel was arrested at his hotel and brought before the local court, but the magistrate, afterwards dismissed by Vichy, declared there was no case against him and set him free. He was however, by the orders of Governor-General Noguès, re-arrested and put back on the *Massilia*, which henceforth was detained in the harbour under strict control without its passengers having any communication with the shore.

Without of course knowing any of the facts here set forth, I was already concerned about the fate of Frenchmen who wished to fight on.

Prime Minister to General Ismay   24.VI.40

It seems most important to establish now before the trap closes an organisation for enabling French officers and soldiers, as well as important technicians, who wish to fight, to make their way to various ports. A sort of "underground railway" as in the olden days of slavery should be established and a Scarlet Pimpernel organisation set up. I have no doubt there will be a steady flow of determined men, and we need all we can get for the defence of the French colonies. The Admiralty and Air Force must co-operate. General de Gaulle and his Committee would of course be the operative authority.

At our meeting of the War Cabinet late at night on June 25 we heard among other things that a ship with a large number of prominent French politicians on board had passed Rabat. We decided to establish contact with them at once. Mr. Duff Cooper, the Minister of Information, accompanied by Lord Gort, started for Rabat at dawn in a Sunderland flying-boat. They found the town in mourning. Flags were flying at half-mast, church bells were tolling, and a solemn service was taking place in the cathedral to bewail the defeat of France. All their attempts to get in touch with Mandel were prevented. The Deputy-Governor, named Morice, declared not only on the telephone, but in a personal interview which Duff Cooper demanded, that he had no choice but to obey the orders of his superiors. "If General Noguès tells me to shoot myself I will gladly obey. Unfortunately, the orders he has given me are more cruel." The former French Ministers and Deputies were in fact to be treated as escaped prisoners. Our mission had no choice but to return the way they came. A few days later (July 1) I gave instructions to the Admiralty to try to cut out the *Massilia* and rescue those on board. No plan could however be made, and for nearly three weeks she lay under the batteries of Casablanca, after which the whole party were brought back to France and disposed of as the Vichy Government thought convenient to themselves and agreeable to their German masters. Mandel began his long and painful internment which ended in his murder by German orders at the end of 1944. Thus perished the hope of setting up a strong representative French Government, either in Africa or in London.

* * *

Although vain, the process of trying to imagine what would have happened if some important event or decision had been different is often tempting and sometimes instructive. The manner of the fall of France was decided on June 16 by a dozen chances, each measured by a hair's-breadth. If Paul Reynaud had survived the 16th I should have been with him at noon on the 17th, accompanied by the most powerful delegation that has ever left our shores, armed with plenary powers in the name of the British nation. Certainly we should have confronted Pétain, Weygand, Chautemps, and the rest with our blunt proposition: "No release from the obligation of March 28 unless the French Fleet is sailed to British ports. On the other hand, we offer an indissoluble Anglo-French Union. Go to Africa and let us fight it out together." Surely we should have been aided by the President of the Republic, by the Presidents of the two French Chambers, and by all that resolute band who gathered behind Reynaud, Mandel, and de Gaulle. It seems to me probable that we should have uplifted and converted the defeatists round the table, or left them in a minority or even under arrest.

But let us pursue this ghostly speculation further. The French Government would have retired to North Africa. The Anglo-French Super-State or Working Committee, to which it would probably in practice have reduced itself, would have faced Hitler. The British and French Fleets from their harbours would have enjoyed complete mastery of the Mediterranean, and free passage through it for all troops and supplies. Whatever British air force could be spared from the defence of Britain, and what was left of the French Air Force, nourished by American production and based on the French North African airfields, would soon have become an offensive factor of the first importance. Malta, instead of being for so long a care and peril, would at once have taken its place as our most active naval base. Italy could have been attacked with heavy bombing from Africa far easier than from England. Her communications with the Italian armies in Libya and Tripolitania would have been effectively severed. Using no more fighter aircraft than we actually employed in the defence of Egypt and sending to the Mediterranean theatre no more troops than we actually sent, or held ready to send, we might well, with the remains of the French Army, have transferred the war from the East to the Central Mediterranean, and during 1941 the entire North African shore might have been cleared of Italian forces.

France would never have ceased to be one of the principal belligerent allies, and would have been spared the fearful schism which rent and still rends her people. Her homeland no doubt would have lain prostrate under the German rule, but that was only what actually happened after the Anglo-American descent in November 1942. Now that the whole story is before us no one can doubt that the armistice did not spare France a pang.

It is still more shadowy to guess what Hitler would have done. Would he have forced his way through Spain, with or without Spanish agreement, and, after assaulting and perhaps capturing Gibraltar, have invaded Tangier and Morocco? This was an area which deeply concerned the United States, and was ever prominent in President Roosevelt's mind. How could Hitler have made this major attack through Spain on Africa and yet have fought the Battle of Britain? He would have had to choose. If he chose Africa we, with the command of the sea and the French bases, could have moved both troops and air forces into Morocco and Algeria quicker than he, and in greater strength. We should certainly have welcomed in the autumn and winter of 1940 a vehement campaign in or from a friendly French North-West Africa.

Surveying the whole scene in the after-light, it seems unlikely that Hitler's main decision and the major events of the war, namely the Battle of Britain and the German surge to the East, would have been changed by the retirement of the French Government to North Africa. After the fall of Paris, when Hitler danced his jig of joy, he naturally dealt with very large propositions. Once France was prostrate he must if possible conquer or destroy Great Britain. His only other choice was Russia. A major operation through Spain into North-West Africa would have prejudiced both these tremendous adventures, or at least have prevented his attack on the Balkans. I have no doubt that it would have been better for all the Allies if the French Government had gone to North Africa; and that this would have remained true whether Hitler followed them and us thither or not.

One day when I was convalescing at Marrakesh in January 1944 General Georges came to luncheon. In the course of casual conversation I aired the fancy that perhaps the French Government's failure to go to Africa in June 1940 had all turned out for the best. At the Pétain trial in August 1945 the General thought it right to state this in evidence. I make no complaint, but my retrospective speculation on this occasion does not represent my considered opinion either during the war or now.

CHAPTER XI

ADMIRAL DARLAN AND THE
FRENCH FLEET. ORAN

Would Britain Surrender? – My Speech of June 18 – "Their Finest Hour" – Admiral Darlan's Opportunity – His Final Letter to Me – Armistice, Article 8 – A Dire Decision – Operation "Catapult": Zero Day, July 3 – Our Terms to the French – The Tragedy of Oran – My Report to Parliament, July 4 – World Impression on Elimination of French Navy.

AFTER the collapse of France the question which arose in the minds of all our friends and foes was: "Will Britain surrender too?" So far as public statements count in the teeth of events, I had in the name of His Majesty's Government repeatedly declared our resolve to fight on alone. After Dunkirk on June 4 I had used the expression "if necessary for years, *if necessary alone*". This was not inserted without design, and the French Ambassador in London had been instructed the next day to inquire what I actually meant. He was told "exactly what was said". I could remind the House of my remark when I addressed it on June 18, the morrow of the Bordeaux collapse. I then gave "some indication of the solid practical grounds on which we based our inflexible resolve to continue the war". I was able to assure Parliament that our professional advisers of the three Services were confident that there were good and reasonable hopes of ultimate victory. I told them that I had received from all the four Dominions Prime Ministers messages in which they endorsed our decision to fight on and declared themselves ready to share our fortunes. "In casting up this dread balance-sheet and contemplating our dangers with a disillusioned eye I see great reasons for vigilance and exertion, but none whatever for panic or fear." I added: "During the first four years of the last war the Allies experienced nothing but disaster and disappointment. . . . We repeatedly asked ourselves the question 'How are we going to win?' and no one was ever able to answer it with much precision, until at the end, quite suddenly, quite unexpectedly, our terrible foe collapsed before us, and we were so glutted with victory that in our folly we threw it away.

"However matters may go in France or with the French Government or other French Governments, we in this Island and in the British Empire will never lose our sense of comradeship with the French people. . . . If final victory rewards our toils they shall share the gains—aye, and freedom shall be restored to all. We abate nothing of our just demands; not one jot or tittle do we recede. . . . Czechs, Poles, Norwegians, Dutch, Belgians, have joined their causes to our own. All these shall be restored." I ended:

"What General Weygand called the Battle of France is over. I expect that the Battle of Britain is about to begin. Upon this battle depends the survival of Christian civilisation. Upon it depends our own British life, and the long continuity of our institutions and our Empire. The whole fury and might of the enemy must very soon be turned on us. Hitler knows that he will have to break us in this Island or lose the war. If we can stand up to him, all Europe may be free and the life of the world may move forward into broad, sunlit uplands. But if we fail, then the whole world, including the United States, including all that we have known and cared for, will sink into the abyss of a new Dark Age, made more sinister, and perhaps more protracted, by the lights of perverted science. Let us therefore brace ourselves to our duties, and so bear ourselves that, if the British Empire and its Commonwealth last for a thousand years, men will still say: 'This was their finest hour.' "

All these often-quoted words were made good in the hour of victory. But now they were only words. Foreigners who do not understand the temper of the British race all over the globe when its blood is up might have supposed that they were only a bold front, set up as a good prelude for peace negotiations. Hitler's need to finish the war in the West was obvious. He was in a position to offer the most tempting terms. To those who like myself had studied his moves it did not seem impossible that he would consent to leave Britain and her Empire and Fleet intact and make a peace which would have secured him that free hand in the East of which Ribbentrop had talked to me in 1937, and which was his heart's main desire. So far we had not done him much harm. We had indeed only added our own defeat to his triumph over France. Can one wonder that astute calculators in many countries, ignorant as they mostly were of the problems of overseas invasion, and of the quality of our Air Force, and who dwelt under the overwhelming impression of German might and terror, were not convinced? Not every Government called into being by Democracy or by Despotism, and not every nation, while quite alone, and as it seemed abandoned, would have courted the horrors of invasion and disdained a fair chance of peace for which many plausible excuses could be presented. Rhetoric was no guarantee. Another administration might come into being. "The war-mongers have had their chance and failed." America had stood aloof. No one was under any obligation to Soviet Russia. Why should not Britain join the spectators who in Japan and in the United States, in Sweden, and in Spain, might watch with detached interest, or even relish, a mutually destructive struggle between the Nazi and Communist Empires? Future generations will find it hard to believe that the issues I have summarised here were never thought worth a place upon the Cabinet agenda, or even mentioned in our most private conclaves. Doubts could be swept away only by deeds. The deeds were to come.

* * *

Meanwhile I telegraphed to Lord Lothian, who, at the desire of the United States naval authorities, had asked anxiously whether ammunition for the British Fleet and material for its repair ought not to be sent from England across the Atlantic:

22.VI.40

There is no warrant for such precautions at the present time.

I also sent the following telegrams to my Dominions friends.

To Mr. Mackenzie King:

24.VI.40

If you will read again my telegram of June 5 you will see that there is no question of trying to make a bargain with the United States about their entry into the war and our dispatch of the Fleet across the Atlantic should the Mother Country be defeated. On the contrary, I doubt very much the wisdom of dwelling upon the last contingency at the present time. I have good confidence in our ability to defend this Island, and I see no reason to make preparation for or give any countenance to the transfer of the British Fleet. I shall myself never enter into any peace negotiations with Hitler, but obviously I cannot bind a future Government, which, if we were deserted by the United States and beaten down here, might very easily be a kind of Quisling affair ready to accept German overlordship and protection. It would be a help if you would impress this danger upon the President, as I have done in my telegrams to him.

All good wishes, and we are very glad your grand Canadian Division is with us in our fight for Britain.

To Smuts I cabled again:

27.VI.40

Obviously, we have first to repulse any attack on Great Britain by invasion, and show ourselves able to maintain our development of air-power. This can only be settled by trial. *If Hitler fails to beat us here he will probably recoil eastwards. Indeed, he may do this even without trying invasion*, to find employment for his Army, and take the edge off the winter strain upon him.

I do not expect the winter strain will prove decisive, but to try to hold all Europe down in a starving condition with only Gestapo and military occupation *and no large theme appealing to the masses* is not an arrangement which can last long.

Development of our air-power, particularly in regions unaffected by bombing, should cause him ever-increasing difficulties, possibly decisive difficulties, in Germany, no matter what successes he has in Europe *or Asia*.

Our large Army now being created for Home Defence is being formed on the principle of attack, *and opportunity for large-scale offensive amphibious operations may come in 1940 and 1941.* We are still working on the 55-division basis here, but as our munitions supply expands and Empire resources are mobilised larger numbers may be possible. After all, we are now at last on interior lines. Hitler has vast hungry areas to defend, and we have the command of the seas. Choice of objectives in Western Europe is therefore wide.

I send you these personal notes in order to keep in closest contact with your thoughts, which ever weigh with me.

It was with good confidence that we entered upon the supreme test.

29 A German outpost in Ile-de-France.

30 The enemy at the gates of Paris.

31 A parade of German amphibious vehicles along the Champs-Elysées.

32 A German soldier standing guard on the Place de la Concorde.

Prime Minister to Lord Lothian (Washington) 28.VI.40

No doubt I shall make some broadcast presently, but I don't think words count for much now. Too much attention should not be paid to eddies of United States opinion. Only force of events can govern them. Up till April they were so sure the Allies would win that they did not think help necessary. Now they are so sure we shall lose that they do not think it possible. I feel good confidence we can repel invasion and keep alive in the air. Anyhow, we are going to try. Never cease to impress on President and others that if this country were successfully invaded and largely occupied after heavy fighting some Quisling Government would be formed to make peace on the basis of our becoming a German Protectorate. In this case the British Fleet would be the solid contribution with which this Peace Government would buy terms. Feeling in England against United States would be similar to French bitterness against us now. We have really not had any help worth speaking of from the United States so far. [The rifles and field-guns did not arrive till the end of July. The destroyers had been refused.] We know President is our best friend, but it is no use trying to dance attendance upon Republican and Democratic Conventions. What really matters is whether Hitler is master of Britain in three months or not. I think not. But this is a matter which cannot be argued beforehand. Your mood should be bland and phlegmatic. No one is down-hearted here.

* * *

In the closing days at Bordeaux Admiral Darlan became very important. My contacts with him had been few and formal. I respected him for the work he had done in re-creating the French Navy, which after ten years of his professional control was more efficient than at any time since the French Revolution. When in December 1939 he had visited England we gave him an official dinner at the Admiralty. In response to the toast, he began by reminding us that his great-grandfather had been killed at the Battle of Trafalgar. I therefore thought of him as one of those good Frenchmen who hate England. Our Anglo-French naval discussions in January had also shown how very jealous the Admiral was of his professional position in relation to whoever was the political Minister of Marine. This had become a positive obsession, and, I believe, played a definite part in his action.

For the rest, Darlan had been present at most of the conferences which I have described, and as the end of the French resistance approached he had repeatedly assured me that whatever happened the French Fleet should never fall into German hands. Now at Bordeaux came the fateful moment in the career of this ambitious, self-seeking, and capable Admiral. His authority over the Fleet was for all practical purposes absolute. He had only to order the ships to British, American, or French colonial harbours—some had already started—to be obeyed. In the morning of June 17, after the fall of M. Reynaud's Cabinet, he declared to General Georges that he was resolved to give the order. The next day Georges met him in the afternoon and asked him what had happened. Darlan replied that he had changed his mind. When asked why, he answered simply: "I am now Minister of Marine." This did not mean that he had changed his mind in order to become Minister of Marine, but that being Minister of Marine he had a different point of view.

How vain are human calculations of self-interest! Rarely has there been a more convincing example. Admiral Darlan had but to sail in any one of his ships to any port outside France to become the master of all French interests beyond German control. He would not have come, like General de Gaulle, with only an unconquerable heart and a few kindred spirits. He would have carried with him outside the German reach the fourth Navy in the world, whose officers and men were personally devoted to him. Acting thus, Darlan would have become the chief of the French Resistance with a mighty weapon in his hand. British and American dockyards and arsenals would have been at his disposal for the maintenance of his fleet. The French gold reserve in the United States would have assured him, once recognised, of ample resources. The whole French Empire would have rallied to him. Nothing could have prevented him from being the Liberator of France. The fame and power which he so ardently desired were in his grasp. Instead, he went forward through two years of worrying and ignominious office to a violent death, a dishonoured grave, and a name long to be execrated by the French Navy and the nation he had hitherto served so well.

*   *   *

There is a final note which should be struck at this point. In a letter which Darlan wrote to me on December 4, 1942, just three weeks before his assassination, he vehemently claimed that he had kept his word. As this letter states his case and should be on record, I print it here. It cannot be disputed that no French ship was ever manned by the Germans or used against us by them in the war. This was not entirely due to Admiral Darlan's measures; but he had certainly built up in the minds of the officers and men of the French Navy that at all costs their ships should be destroyed before being seized by the Germans, whom he disliked as much as he did the English.

Admiral Darlan to Mr. Churchill*

Dear Mr. Prime Minister,   ALGIERS, December 4, 1942

On June 12, 1940, at Briare, at the headquarters of General Weygand, you took me aside and said to me: "Darlan, I hope you will never surrender the Fleet." I answered you: "There is no question of doing so; it would be contrary to our naval traditions and honour." The First Lord of the Admiralty, Alexander, and the First Sea Lord, Pound, received the same reply on June 17, 1940, at Bordeaux, as did Lord Lloyd. If I did not consent to authorise the French Fleet to proceed to British ports, it was because I knew that such a decision would bring about the total occupation of Metropolitan France as well as North Africa.

I admit having been overcome by a great bitterness and a great resentment against England as the result of the painful events which touched me as a sailor; furthermore it seemed to me that you did not believe my word. One day Lord Halifax sent me word by M. Dupuy that in England my word was not doubted, but that it was believed that I should not be able to keep it. The voluntary destruction of the Fleet at Toulon has just proved that I was right, because even though I no longer commanded, the Fleet executed the orders which I had given and maintained, contrary to the wishes of the Laval Government. On the orders of my chief, the Marshal, I was obliged, from January 1941 to April 1942, to adopt a policy which would prevent France and its Empire from being occupied and crushed by the Axis Powers. This policy was by the force of events opposed to yours. What else could I do? At that time you were not able to help us, and any gesture towards you would have led to the most disastrous consequences for my country. If we had not assumed the obligation to defend the Empire by our own forces (I always refused German aid, even in Syria) the Axis would have come to Africa and our own Army would have been discarded; the First British Army undoubtedly would not be before Tunis to-day with French troops at its side to combat the Germans and Italians.

When the Allied Forces landed in Africa on November 8 I at first executed the orders I had received. Then as soon as this became

* Translated.

impossible I ordered the cessation of the fighting in order to avoid unnecessary bloodshed and a fight which was contrary to the intimate sentiments of those engaged. Disavowed by Vichy and not wishing to resume the fight, I placed myself at the disposition of the American military authorities, only in that way being able to remain faithful to my oath. On November 11 I learned of the violation of the Armistice Convention by the Germans, the occupation of France, and the solemn protest of the Marshal. I then considered that I could resume my liberty of action, and that, remaining faithful to the person of the Marshal, I could follow that road which was most favourable to the welfare of the French Empire, that of the fight against the Axis Supported by the high authorities of French Africa and by public opinion, and acting as the eventual substitute of the Chief of State I formed the High Commissariat in Africa and ordered the French forces to fight at the side of the Allies. Since then French West Africa has recognised my authority. I should never have been able to accomplish this result if I had not acted under the ægis of the Marshal and if I were simply represented as a dissident. I have the conviction that all Frenchmen who now fight against Germany each in his own manner will finally achieve a general reconciliation, but I believe that for the moment they must continue their separate action. There is a certain resentment, notably in French West Africa, which is too active for me to obtain more, as you know. I follow my *rôle* without attacking anyone; I ask for reciprocity. For the moment the only thing that counts is to defeat the Axis; the French people when liberated will later choose their political *régime* and their leaders.

I thank you, Mr. Prime Minister, for having associated yourself with President Roosevelt in declaring that, like the United States, Great Britain wishes the integral re-establishment of French sovereignty as it existed in 1939. When my country has recovered its integrity and its liberty my only ambition will be to retire with the sentimen· of having served it well.

Please accept, Mr. Prime Minister, the assurances of my highe consideration. FRANÇOIS DARLAN, Admiral of the Fleet

*   *   *

Those of us who were responsible at the summit in London understood the physical structure of our Island strength and were sure of the spirit of the nation. The confidence with which we faced the immediate future was not founded, as was commonly supposed abroad, upon audacious bluff or rhetorical appeal, but upon a sober consciousness and calculation of practical facts When I spoke in the House of Commons I founded myself upon realities which I and others had carefully studied—some for many years. I will presently analyse in detail the Invasion problem as I and my expert advisers saw it in these memorable days. But first of all there was one step to take. It was obvious, and it was dire.

The addition of the French Navy to the German and Italian Fleets, with the menace of Japan measureless upon the horizon, confronted Great Britain with mortal dangers and gravely affected the safety of the United States. Article 8 of the Armistice prescribed that the French Fleet, except that part left free for safeguarding French colonial interests, "shall be collected in ports to be specified and there demobilised and disarmed under German or Italian control". It was therefore clear that the French war vessels would pass into that control while fully armed. It was true that in the same article the German Government solemnly declared that they had no intention of using them for their own purposes during the war. But who in his senses would trust the word of Hitler after his shameful record and the facts of the hour? Furthermore, the article excepted from this assurance "those units necessary for coast surveillance and mine-sweeping". The interpretation of this lay with the Germans. Finally, the Armistice could at any time be voided on any pretext of non-observance. There was in fact no security for us at all. At all costs, at all risks, in one way or another, we must make sure that the Navy of France did not fall into wrong hands, and then perhaps bring us and others to ruin.

The War Cabinet never hesitated. Those Ministers who, the week before, had given their whole hearts to France and offered common nationhood resolved that all necessary measures should be taken. This was a hateful decision, the most unnatural and painful in which I have ever been concerned. It recalled the episode of the seizure by the Royal Navy of the Danish fleet at Copenhagen in 1807; but now the French had been only yesterday our dear Allies, and our sympathy for the misery of France was sincere. On the other hand, the life of the State and the salvation of our cause were at stake. It was Greek tragedy. But no act was ever more necessary for the life of Britain and for all that depended upon it. I thought of Danton in 1793: "The coalesced Kings threaten us, and we hurl at their feet as a gage of battle the head of a King." The whole event was in this order of ideas.

*   *   *

The French Navy was disposed in the following manner: Two battleships, four light cruisers (or *contre-torpilleurs*), some submarines, including a very large one, the *Surcouf*, eight destroyers, and about two hundred smaller but valuable mine-sweeping and anti-submarine craft lay for the most part at Portsmouth and Plymouth. These were in our power. At Alexandria there were a French battleship, four French cruisers, three of them modern 8-inch-gun cruisers, and a number of smaller ships. These were covered by a strong British battle squadron. At Oran, at the other end of the Mediterranean, and at its adjacent military port of Mers-el-Kebir, were two of the finest vessels of the French fleet, the *Dunkerque* and the *Strasbourg*, modern battle-cruisers much superior to the *Scharnhorst* and *Gneisenau*, and built for the express purpose of being superior to them. These vessels in German hands on our trade routes would have been most disagreeable. With them were two French battleships, several light cruisers, and a number of destroyers, submarines, and other vessels. At Algiers were seven cruisers, of which four were 8-inch armed, and at Martinique an aircraft-carrier and two light cruisers. At Casablanca lay the *Jean Bart*, newly arrived from St. Nazaire, but without her guns. This was one of the key ships in the computation of world naval strength. She was unfinished, and could not be finished at Casablanca. She must not go elsewhere. The *Richelieu*, which was far nearer completion, had reached Dakar. She could steam, and her 15-inch guns could fire. There were many other French ships of minor importance in various ports. Finally, at Toulon a number of warships were beyond our reach. Operation "Catapult" comprised the simultaneous seizure, control, or effective disablement or destruction of all the accessible French Fleet.

Prime Minister to General Ismay   1.VII.40

1. The Admiralty are retaining *Nelson* and her four destroyers in home waters, and Operation "Catapult" should go forward, aiming at daybreak the 3rd.

2. During the night of 2nd–3rd all necessary measures should be taken at Portsmouth and Plymouth, at Alexandria, and if possible at Martinique, on the same lines as "Catapult". The reactions to these measures at Dakar and Casablanca must be considered, and every precaution taken to prevent the escape of valuable units.

On account of the pressure of events, I added also:

The Admiralty should endeavour to raise the flotillas in the narrow seas to a strength of forty destroyers, with additional cruiser support. An effort should be made to reach this strength during the next two or three days and hold it for the following fortnight, when the position can be reviewed. The losses in the Western Approaches must be accepted meanwhile. I should like also a daily return of the numbers of craft on patrol or available between Portsmouth and the Tyne.

* * *

In the early morning of July 3 all the French vessels at Portsmouth and Plymouth were taken under British control. The action was sudden and necessarily a surprise. Overwhelming force was employed, and the whole transaction showed how easily the Germans could have taken possession of any French warships lying in ports which they controlled. In Britain the transfer, except in the *Surcouf*, was amicable, and the crews came willingly ashore. In the *Surcouf* two gallant British officers and a leading seaman were killed,* and another seaman wounded. One French seaman also was killed, but many hundreds volunteered to join us. The *Surcouf*, after rendering distinguished service, perished on February 19, 1942, with all her gallant French crew.

* * *

The deadly stroke was in the Western Mediterranean. Here, at Gibraltar, Vice-Admiral Somerville with "Force H", consisting of the battle-cruiser *Hood*, the battleships *Valiant* and *Resolution*, the aircraft-carrier *Ark Royal*, two cruisers, and eleven destroyers, received orders sent from the Admiralty at 2.25 a.m. on July 1:

Be prepared for "Catapult" July 3.

Among Somerville's officers was Captain Holland, a gallant and distinguished officer, lately Naval Attaché in Paris and with keen French sympathies, who was influential. In the early afternoon of July 1 the Vice-Admiral telegraphed:

After talk with Holland and others Vice-Admiral "Force H" is impressed with their view that the use of force should be avoided at all costs. Holland considers offensive action on our part would alienate all French wherever they are.

To this the Admiralty replied at 6.20 p.m.:

Firm intention of H.M.G. that if French will not accept any of your alternatives they are to be destroyed.

* Commander D. V. Sprague, R.N., Lieutenant P. M. K. Griffiths, R.N., and Leading Seaman A. Webb, R.N.

Shortly after midnight (1.08 a.m., July 2) Admiral Somerville was sent the following carefully conceived text of the communication to be made to the French admiral:

His Majesty's Government have sent me to inform you as follows:

They agreed to the French Government approaching the German Government only on the condition that before an armistice was concluded the French Fleet should be sent to British ports to prevent it falling into the hands of the enemy. The Council of Ministers declared on 18th June that before capitulation on land the French Fleet would join up with the British Navy or sink itself.*

While the present French Government may consider that the terms of their armistices with Germany and Italy are reconcilable with these undertakings, H.M. Government find it impossible from our previous experiences to believe that Germany and Italy will not at any moment which suits them seize French warships and use them against Britain and her allies. The Italian armistice prescribes that French ships should return to metropolitan ports, and under the armistice France is required to yield up units for coast defence and minesweeping.

It is impossible for us, your comrades up to now, to allow your fine ships to fall into the power of the German or Italian enemy. We are determined to fight on to the end, and if we win, as we think we shall, we shall never forget that France was our Ally, that our interests are the same as hers, and that our common enemy is Germany. Should we conquer, we solemnly declare that we shall restore the greatness and territory of France. For this purpose, we must make sure that the best ships of the French Navy are not used against us by the common foe. In these circumstances His Majesty's Government have instructed me to demand that the French Fleet now at Mers-el-Kebir and Oran shall act in accordance with one of the following alternatives:

(a) Sail with us and continue to fight for victory against the Germans and Italians.

(b) Sail with reduced crews under our control to a British port. The reduced crews will be repatriated at the earliest moment.

If either of these courses is adopted by you, we will restore your ships to France at the conclusion of the war, or pay full compensation if they are damaged meanwhile.

(c) Alternatively, if you feel bound to stipulate that your ships should not be used against the Germans or Italians unless these break

---

* Misunderstanding was caused by this paragraph. As late as June 14 Admiral Darlan had favoured the idea of sending the French Fleet to British ports in certain eventualities, but by June 18 he had become Minister of Marine. Thereafter the new French Government under Marshal Pétain would not give the specific assurance demanded by the British. The second sentence in this paragraph therefore no longer represented the position of the French Government. In the crisis this last-minute change was not appreciated by the Admiralty officials concerned.

the Armistice, then sail them with us with reduced crews to some French port in the West Indies—Martinique, for instance—where they can be demilitarised to our satisfaction, or perhaps be entrusted to the United States and remain safe until the end of the war, the crews being repatriated.

If you refuse these fair offers, I must, with profound regret, require you to sink your ships within six hours.

Finally, failing the above, I have the orders of His Majesty's Government to use whatever force may be necessary to prevent your ships from falling into German or Italian hands.

In the evening of the 2nd I requested the Admiralty to send the Vice-Admiral the following message (dispatched 10.55 p.m.):

You are charged with one of the most disagreeable and difficult tasks that a British Admiral has ever been faced with, but we have complete confidence in you and rely on you to carry it out relentlessly.

The Admiral sailed at daylight and was off Oran at about nine-thirty. He sent Captain Holland himself in a destroyer to wait upon the French Admiral Gensoul. After being refused an interview Holland sent by messengers the document already quoted. Admiral Gensoul replied in writing, that in no case would the French warships be allowed to fall intact into German and Italian hands, and that force would be met with force.

All day negotiations continued. At 4.15 p.m. Captain Holland was at last permitted to board the *Dunkerque*, but the ensuing meeting with the French Admiral was frigid. Admiral Gensoul had meanwhile sent two messages to the French Admiralty, and at 3 p.m. the French Council of Ministers had met to consider the British terms. General Weygand was present at this meeting, and what transpired has now been recorded by his biographer. From this it seems that the third alternative, namely, the removal of the French Fleet to the West Indies, was never mentioned. He states, "... It would appear that Admiral Darlan, whether deliberately or not, or whether he was aware of them or not, I do not know, *did not in fact inform us of all the details of the matter at the time*. It now appears that the terms of the British ultimatum were less crude than we were led to believe, and suggested a third and far more acceptable alternative, namely, the departure of the Fleet for West Indian waters."[*] No explanation of this omission, if it were an omission, has so far been seen.

* *The Rôle of General Weygand*, by Jacques Weygand.

The distress of the British Admiral and his principal officers was evident to us from the signals which had passed. Nothing but the most direct orders compelled them to open fire on those who had been so lately their comrades. At the Admiralty also there was manifest emotion. But there was no weakening in the resolve of the War Cabinet. I sat all the afternoon in the Cabinet Room in frequent contact with my principal colleagues and the First Lord and First Sea Lord. A final signal was dispatched at 6.26 p.m.:

French ships must comply with our terms or sink themselves or be sunk by you before dark.

But the action had already begun. At 5.54 p.m. Admiral Somerville opened fire upon this powerful French fleet, which was also protected by its shore batteries. At 6.0 p.m. he reported that he was heavily engaged. The bombardment lasted for some ten minutes. The battleship *Bretagne* was blown up. The *Dunkerque* ran aground. The battleship *Provence* was beached. The *Strasbourg* escaped, and, though attacked by torpedo aircraft from the *Ark Royal*, reached Toulon, as did also the cruisers from Algiers.

At Alexandria, after protracted negotiations with Admiral Cunningham, the French Admiral Godefroy agreed to discharge his oil fuel, to remove important parts of his gun-mechanisms, and to repatriate some of his crews. At Dakar on July 8 an attack was made on the battleship *Richelieu* by the aircraft-carrier *Hermes*, and most gallantly by a motor-boat. The *Richelieu* was hit by an air torpedo and seriously damaged. The French aircraft-carrier and two light cruisers in the French West Indies were immobilised after long-drawn-out discussions under an agreement with the United States.

On July 4 I reported at length to the House of Commons what we had done. Although the battle-cruiser *Strasbourg* had escaped from Oran and the effective disablement of the *Richelieu* had not then been reported, the measures we had taken had removed the French Navy from major German calculations. I spoke for an hour or more that afternoon, and gave a detailed account of all these sombre events as they were known to me. I have nothing to add to the account which I then gave to Parliament and to the world. I thought it better, for the sake of proportion, to end upon a note which placed this mournful episode in true relation with the plight in which we stood. I therefore read to the House the admonition which I had, with Cabinet approval, circulated through the inner circles of the governing machine the day before.

On what may be the eve of an attempted invasion or battle for our native land, the Prime Minister desires to impress upon all persons holding responsible positions in the Government, in the Fighting Services, or in the Civil departments their duty to maintain a spirit of alert and confident energy. While every precaution must be taken that time and means afford, there are no grounds for supposing that more German troops can be landed in this country, either from the air or across the sea, than can be destroyed or captured by the strong forces at present under arms. The Royal Air Force is in excellent order and at the highest strength yet attained. The German Navy was never so weak nor the British Army at home so strong as now. The Prime Minister expects all His Majesty's servants in high places to set an example of steadiness and resolution. They should check and rebuke the expression of loose and ill-digested opinions in their circles, or by their subordinates. They should not hesitate to report, or if necessary remove, any persons, officers, or officials who are found to be consciously exercising a disturbing or depressing influence, and whose talk is calculated to spread alarm and despondency. Thus alone will they be worthy of the fighting men who, in the air, on the sea, and on land, have already met the enemy without any sense of being outmatched in martial qualities.

The House was very silent during the recital, but at the end there occurred a scene unique in my own experience. Everybody seemed to stand up all around, cheering, for what seemed a long time. Up till this moment the Conservative Party had treated me with some reserve, and it was from the Labour benches that I received the warmest welcome when I entered the House or rose on serious occasions. But now all joined in solemn stentorian accord.

The elimination of the French Navy as an important factor almost at a single stroke by violent action produced a profound impression in every country. Here was this Britain which so many had counted down and out, which strangers had supposed to be quivering on the brink of surrender to the mighty power arrayed against her, striking ruthlessly at her dearest friends of yesterday and securing for a while to herself the undisputed command of the sea. It was made plain that the British War Cabinet feared nothing and would stop at nothing. This was true.

* * *

The Pétain Government had moved to Vichy on July 1, and proceeded to set itself up as the Government of Unoccupied France. On receiving the news of Oran they ordered retaliation by air upon Gibraltar, and a few bombs were dropped upon the harbour from their African stations. On July 5 they formally broke off relations with Great Britain. On July 11 President Lebrun gave place to Marshal Pétain, who was installed as Chief of the State by an enormous majority of 569 against 80, with 17 abstentions and many absentees.

The genius of France enabled her people to comprehend the whole significance of Oran, and in her agony to draw new hope and strength from this additional bitter pang. General de Gaulle, whom I did not consult beforehand, was magnificent in his demeanour, and France liberated and restored has ratified his conduct. I am indebted to M. Teitgen, a prominent member of the Resistance Movement, afterwards French Minister of Defence, for a tale which should be told. In a village near Toulon dwelt two peasant families, each of whom had lost their sailor son by British fire at Oran. A funeral service was arranged to which all their neighbours sought to go. Both families requested that the Union Jack should lie upon the coffins side by side with the Tricolour, and their wishes were respectfully observed. In this we may see how the comprehending spirit of simple folk touches the sublime.

* * *

Immense relief spread through the high Government circles in the United States. The Atlantic Ocean seemed to regain its sheltering power, and a long vista of time opened out for the necessary preparations for the safety of the great Republic. Henceforth there was no more talk about Britain giving in. The only question was, would she be invaded and conquered? That was the issue which was now to be put to the proof.

CHAPTER XII

THE APPARATUS OF COUNTER-ATTACK

1940

My Own Reactions after Dunkirk – Minute to General Ismay of June 4 – A Retrogression – My Old Plans of July 1917 – An Early Idea of Tank Landing-craft – The Germ of the "Mulberry" Harbours of 1944 – Directive to General Ismay on Counter-attack – "Commandos" – Tank Landing-craft and Parachutists – My Minute of July 7, 1940, Calling for Beach Landing-craft for Six or Seven Hundred Tanks – Minute of August 5, 1940, on Programme of Armoured Divisions – Overseas Transportation for Two Divisions at a Time – Creation of the Combined Operations Command – Appointment of Sir Roger Keyes – The Joint Planning Committee is Placed Directly Under the Minister of Defence – Progress of the Landing-craft Construction in 1940 and 1941 – My Telegram to the President of July 25, 1941 – My Consistent Purpose to Land Armour on Beaches.

MY first reaction to the "Miracle of Dunkirk" had been to turn it to proper use by mounting a counter-offensive. When so much was uncertain, the need to recover the initiative glared forth. June 4 was much occupied for me by the need to prepare and deliver the long and serious speech to the House of Commons of which some account has been given, but as soon as this was over I made haste to strike the note which I thought should rule our minds and inspire our actions at this moment.

Prime Minister to General Ismay   4.VI.40

    We are greatly concerned—and it is certainly wise to be so—with the dangers of the Germans landing in England in spite of our possessing the command of the seas and having very strong defence by fighters in the air. Every creek, every beach, every harbour has become to us a source of anxiety. Besides this the parachutists may sweep over and take Liverpool or Ireland, and so forth. All this mood is very good if it engenders energy. But if it is so easy for the Germans to invade us, in spite of sea-power, some may feel inclined to ask the question, why should it be thought impossible for us to do anything of the same kind to them? The completely defensive habit of mind which has ruined the French must not be allowed to ruin all our initiative. It is of the highest consequence to keep the largest numbers of German forces all along the coasts of the countries they have conquered, and we should immediately set to work to organise raiding forces on these coasts where the populations are friendly. Such forces might be composed of self-contained, thoroughly-equipped units of say one thousand up to not more than ten thousand when combined. Surprise would be ensured by the fact that the destination would be concealed until the last moment. What we have seen at Dunkirk shows how quickly troops can be moved off (and I suppose on to) selected points if need be. How wonderful it would be if the Germans could be made to wonder where they were going to be struck next, instead of forcing us to try to wall in the Island and roof it over! An effort must be made to shake off the mental and moral prostration to the will and initiative of the enemy from which we suffer.

    Ismay conveyed this to the Chiefs of Staff, and in principle it received their cordial approval and was reflected in many of the decisions which we took. Out of it gradually sprang a policy. My thought was at this time firmly fixed on tank warfare, not merely defensive but offensive. This required the construction of large numbers of tank-landing vessels, which henceforward became one of my constant cares. As all this was destined to become of major importance in the future I must now make a retrogression into a subject which had long ago lain in my mind and was now revived.

*   *   *

    I had always been fascinated by amphibious warfare, and the idea of using tanks to run ashore from specially-constructed landing-craft on beaches where they were not expected had long been in my mind. Ten days before I joined Mr. Lloyd George's

Government as Minister of Munitions on July 17, 1917, I had prepared, without expert assistance, a scheme for the capture of the two Frisian islands Borkum and Sylt. The object was to secure an overseas base for flotillas and cruisers and for such air forces as were available in those days, in order to force the naval fighting, in which we had a great numerical superiority, and by re-establishing close blockade relieve the pressure of the U-boat war, then at its height, against our Atlantic supply-line and the movement of the American armies to France. Mr. Lloyd George was impressed with the plan, and had it specially printed for the Admiralty and the War Cabinet.

It contained the following paragraph, 22c, which has never yet seen the light of day:

The landing of the troops upon the island [of Borkum or Sylt] under cover of the guns of the Fleet [should be] aided by gas and smoke from torpedo-proof transports by means of *bullet-proof lighters*. Approximately one hundred should be provided for landing a division. In addition a number—say fifty—*tank-landing lighters should be provided, each carrying a tank or tanks* [and] fitted for wire-cutting in its bow. By means of a drawbridge or shelving bow [the tanks] would land under [their] own power, and prevent the infantry from being held up by wire when attacking the gorges of the forts and batteries. This is a new feature, and removes one of the very great previous difficulties, namely, the rapid landing of [our] field artillery to cut wire.

And further, paragraph 27:

There is always the danger of the enemy getting wind of our intentions and reinforcing his garrisons with good troops beforehand, at any rate so far as Borkum, about which he must always be very sensitive, is concerned. On the other hand, *the landing could be effected under the shields of lighters, proof against machine-gun bullets,* and too numerous to be seriously affected by heavy gunfire [*i.e.*, the fire of heavy guns]; *and tanks employed in even larger numbers than are here suggested, especially the quick-moving tank and lighter varieties,* would operate in an area where no preparations could have been made to receive them. These may be thought new and important favourable considerations.

*   *   *

In this paper also I had an alternative plan for making an artificial island in the shallow waters of Horn Reef (to the northward).

Para. 30. One of the methods suggested for investigation is as follows: *A number of flat-bottomed barges or caissons, made not of steel, but of concrete,* should be prepared in the Humber, at Harwich, and in the Wash, the Medway, and the Thames. These structures would be adapted to the depths in which they were to be sunk, according to a general plan. They would float when empty of water, and thus could be towed across to the site of the artificial island. On arrival at the buoys marking the island sea-cocks would be opened, and they would settle down on the bottom. They could subsequently be gradually filled with sand, as opportunity served, by suction dredgers. These structures would range in size from 50′ × 40′ × 20′ to 120′ × 80′ × 40′. *By this means a torpedo- and weather-proof harbour, like an atoll, would be created in the open sea, with regular pens for the destroyers and submarines, and alighting-platforms for aeroplanes.*

This project, if feasible, is capable of great elaboration, and it might be applied in various places. Concrete vessels can perhaps be made to carry a complete heavy gun turret, and these, on the admission of water to their outer chambers, would sit on the sea floor, like the Solent forts, at the desired points. Other sinkable structures could be made to contain store-rooms, oil-tanks, or living-chambers. It is not possible, without an expert inquiry, to do more here than indicate the possibilities, which embrace nothing less than the creation, transportation in pieces, assemblement and posing of an artificial island and destroyer base.

31. Such a scheme, if found mechanically sound, avoids the need of employing troops and all the risks of storming a fortified island. *It could be applied as a surprise, for although the construction of these concrete vessels would probably be known in Germany, the natural conclusion would be that they were intended for an attempt to block up the river-mouths, which indeed is an idea not to be excluded.* Thus, until the island or system of breakwaters actually began to grow the enemy would not penetrate the design.

A year's preparation would however be required.

For nearly a quarter of a century this paper had slumbered in the archives of the Committee of Imperial Defence. I did not print it in *The World Crisis*, of which it was to have been a chapter, for reasons of space, and because it was never put into effect. This was fortunate, because the ideas expressed were in this war more than ever vital; and the Germans certainly read my war books with attention. Indeed a staff study of the writings of any one in my position would be a matter of normal routine. The underlying conceptions of this old paper were deeply imprinted in my mind, and in the new emergency formed the foundation of action which, after a long interval, found memorable expression in the vast fleet of tank-landing craft of 1943 and in the "Mulberry" harbours of 1944.

* * *

On this same not unfertile 6th of June, 1940, flushed with the sense of deliverance and the power to plan ahead, I began a long series of minutes in which the design and construction of tank-landing craft was ordered and steadily pressed.

Prime Minister to General Ismay   6.VI.40

Further to my minute of yesterday [dated June 4] about offensive action: when the Australians arrive it is a question whether they should not be organised in detachments of 250, equipped with grenades, trench-mortars, tommy-guns, armoured vehicles, and the like, capable of acting against an attack in this country, but also capable of landing on the friendly coasts now held by the enemy. We have got to get out of our minds the idea that the Channel ports and all the country between them are enemy territory. What arrangements are being made for good agents in Denmark, Holland, Belgium, and along the French coast? Enterprises must be prepared, with specially-trained troops of the hunter class, who can develop a reign of terror down these coasts, first of all on the "butcher and bolt" policy; but later on, or perhaps as soon as we are organised, we could surprise Calais or Boulogne, kill and capture the Hun garrison, and hold the place until all the preparations to reduce it by siege or heavy storm have been made, and then away. The passive resistance war, in which we have acquitted ourselves so well, must come to an end. I look to the Joint Chiefs of the Staff to propose me measures for a vigorous, enterprising and ceaseless offensive against the whole German-occupied coastline. *Tanks and A.F.V.s [Armoured Fighting Vehicles] must be made in flat-bottomed boats, out of which they can crawl ashore,* do a deep raid inland, cutting a vital communication, and then back, leaving a trail of German corpses behind them. It is probable that when the best troops go on to the attack of Paris only the ordinary German troops of the line will be left. The lives of these must be made an intense torment. The following measures should be taken:

1. *Proposals for organising the Striking Companies.*
2. *Proposals for transporting and landing tanks on the beach,* observing that we are supposed to have the command of the sea, while the enemy have not.

3. A proper system of espionage and intelligence along the whole coasts.

4. Deployment of parachute troops on a scale equal to five thousand.

5. Half a dozen of our 15-inch guns should be lined up [*i.e.*, with inner tubes] immediately to fire fifty or sixty miles, and should be mounted either on railway mountings or on steel and concrete platforms, so as to break up the fire of the German guns that will certainly in less than four months be firing across the Channel.

Action in many directions followed accordingly. The "Striking Companies" emerged under the name of "Commandos", ten of which were now raised from the Regular Army and the Royal Marines. The nucleus of this organisation had begun to take shape in the Norwegian campaign. An account will be given in its proper place of the cross-Channel heavy guns. I regret however that I allowed the scale I had proposed for British parachute troops to be reduced from five thousand to five hundred.

* * *

I recurred at intervals to the building of landing-craft, on which my mind constantly dwelt both as a peril to us and in the future as a project against the enemy. Development of small assault craft had been started before the outbreak of war, and a few had been employed at Narvik. Most of these had been lost either there or at Dunkirk. Now we required not only the small craft which could be lifted in the troop-carrying ships, but sea-going vessels capable themselves of transporting tanks and guns to the assault and landing them on to the beaches.

Prime Minister to Minister of Supply   7.VII.40

What is being done about designing and planning vessels to transport tanks across the sea for a British attack on enemy countries? This might well be remitted as a study to Mr. Hopkins, former Chief Constructor of the Navy, who must have leisure now that Cultivator No. 6* is out of fashion. These must be able to move six or seven hundred vehicles in one voyage and land them on the beach, or, alternatively, take them off the beaches, as well, of course, as landing them on quays—if it be possible to combine the two.

Prime Minister to General Ismay   5.VIII.40

I asked the other day for a forecast of the development of the armoured divisions which will be required in 1941—namely, five by

* A trench-cutting machine for attacking fortified lines.

the end of March and one additional every month until a total of ten is reached at the end of August 1941; and also for the composition of each division in armoured and ancillary vehicles of all kinds.

Pray let me know how far the War Office plans have proceeded, and whether the number of tanks ordered corresponds with a programme of these dimensions.

Let me further have a report on the progress of the means of transportation overseas, which should be adequate to the movement at one moment of two armoured divisions. Who is doing this—Admiralty or Ministry of Supply? I suggested that Mr. Hopkins might have some spare time available.

Prime Minister to General Ismay   9.VIII.40
Get me a further report about the designs and types of vessels to transport armoured vehicles by sea and land on [to] beaches.

In July I created a separate Combined Operations Command under the Chiefs of Staff for the study and exercise of this form of warfare, and Admiral of the Fleet Sir Roger Keyes became its chief. His close personal contact with me and with the Defence Office served to overcome any departmental difficulties arising from this unusual appointment.

Prime Minister to General Ismay and Sir Edward Bridges 17.VII.40
I have appointed Admiral of the Fleet Sir Roger Keyes as Director of Combined Operations. He should take over the duties and resources now assigned to General Bourne. General Bourne should be informed that, owing to the larger scope now to be given to these operations, it is essential to have an officer of higher rank in charge, and that the change in no way reflects upon him or those associated with him. Evidently he will have to co-operate effectively. I formed a high opinion of this officer's work as Adjutant-General Royal Marines, and in any case the Royal Marines must play a leading part in this organisation.

Pending any further arrangements, Sir Roger Keyes will form contact with the Service departments through General Ismay as representing the Minister of Defence.

* * *

I have already explained how smoothly the office of Minister of Defence came into being and grew in authority. At the end of August I took the only formal step which I ever found necessary. Hitherto the Joint Planning Committee had worked under the Chiefs of Staff and looked to them as their immediate and official superiors. I felt it necessary to have this important though up till now not very effective body under my personal control. Therefore I asked the War Cabinet to give approval to this definite change in our war machine. This was readily accorded me by all my colleagues, and I gave the following instructions:

Prime Minister to General Ismay and Sir Edward Bridges   24.VIII.40

1. The Joint Planning Committee will from Monday next work directly under the orders of the Minister of Defence and will become a part of the Minister of Defence's office—formerly the C.I.D. Secretariat. Accommodation will be found for them at Richmond Terrace. They will retain their present positions in and contacts with the three Service departments. They will work out the details of such plans as are communicated to them by the Minister of Defence. They may initiate plans of their own after reference to General Ismay. They will, of course, be at the service of the Chiefs of Staff Committee for the elaboration of any matters sent to them.

2. All plans produced by the Joint Planning Committee or elaborated by them under instructions as above will be referred to the Chiefs of Staff Committee for their observations.

3. Thereafter should doubts and differences exist, or in important cases, all plans will be reviewed by the Defence Committee of the War Cabinet, which will consist of the Prime Minister, the Lord Privy Seal, and Lord Beaverbrook, and the three Service Ministers; the three Chiefs of Staff, with General Ismay, being in attendance.

4. The Prime Minister assumes the responsibility of keeping the War Cabinet informed of what is in hand; but the relation of the Chiefs of Staff to the War Cabinet is unaltered.

The Chiefs of Staff accepted this change without serious demur. Sir John Dill, however, wrote a minute to the Secretary of State for War on which I was able to reassure him.

Prime Minister to Secretary of State for War   31.VIII.40

There is no question of the Joint Planning Committee "submitting military advice" to me. They are merely to work out plans in accordance with directions which I shall give. The advice as to whether these plans or any variants of them should be adopted will rest as at present with the Chiefs of Staff. It is quite clear that the Chiefs of Staff also have their collective responsibility for advising the Cabinet as well as the Prime Minister or Minister of Defence. It has not been thought necessary to make any alteration in their constitutional position. Moreover, I propose to work with and through them as heretofore.

I have found it necessary to have direct access to and control of the Joint Planning Staffs because after a year of war I cannot recall a single plan initiated by the existing machinery. I feel sure that I can count upon you and the other two Service Ministers to help me in giving a vigorous and positive direction to the conduct of the war, and in overcoming the dead weight of inertia and delay which has so far led us to being forestalled on every occasion by the enemy.

It will of course be necessary from time to time to increase the number of the Joint Planning Staffs.

In practice the new procedure worked in an easy and agreeable manner, and I cannot recall any difficulties which arose.

*   *   *

Henceforth intense energy was imparted to the development of all types of landing-craft, and a special department was formed in the Admiralty to deal with these matters. By October 1940 the trials of the first Landing-Craft Tank (L.C.T.) were in progress. Only about thirty of these were built, as they proved too small. An improved design followed, many of which were built in sections for more convenient transport by sea to the Middle East, where they began to arrive in the summer of 1941. These proved their worth, and as we gained experience the capabilities of later editions of these strange craft steadily improved. The Admiralty were greatly concerned at the inroads which this new form of specialised production might make into the resources of the shipbuilding industry. Fortunately it proved that the building of L.C.T. could be delegated to constructional engineering firms not engaged in shipbuilding, and thus the labour and plant of the larger shipyards need not be disturbed. This rendered possible the large-scale programme which we contemplated, but also placed a limit on the size of the craft.

The L.C.T. was suitable for cross-Channel raiding operations or for more extended work in the Mediterranean, but not for long voyages in the open sea. The need arose for a larger, more seaworthy vessel which besides transporting tanks and other vehicles on ocean voyages could also land them over beaches like the L.C.T. I gave directions for the design of such a vessel, which was first called an "Atlantic L.C.T.", but was soon re-named

"Landing Ship Tank" (L.S.T.). The building of these inevitably impinged on the resources of our hard-pressed shipyards. Thus, of the first design, nicknamed in the Admiralty the "Winette", only three were built; others were ordered in the United States and Canada, but were superseded by a later design. Meanwhile we converted three shallow-draft tankers to serve the same purpose, and these too rendered useful service later on.

By the end of 1940 we had a sound conception of the physical expression of amphibious warfare. The production of specialised craft and equipment of many kinds was gathering momentum, and the necessary formations to handle all this new material were being developed and trained under the Combined Operations Command. Special training centres for this purpose were established both at home and in the Middle East. All these ideas and their practical manifestation we presented to our American friends as they took shape. The results grew steadily across the years of struggle, and thus in good time they formed the apparatus which eventually played an indispensable part in our greatest plans and deeds. Our work in this field in these earlier years had such a profound effect on the future of the war that I must anticipate events by recording some of the material progress which we made later.

In the summer of 1941 the Chiefs of Staff pointed out that the programme of landing-craft construction was related only to small-scale operations and that our ultimate return to the Continent would demand a much greater effort than we could then afford. By this time the Admiralty had prepared a new design of the landing ship tank, and this was taken to the United States, where the details were jointly worked out. In February 1942 this vessel was put into production in America on a massive scale. It became the L.S.T.(2), which figured so prominently in all our later operations, making perhaps the greatest single contribution to the solution of the stubborn problem of landing heavy vehicles over beaches. Ultimately over a thousand of these were built.

Meanwhile the production of small craft of many types for use in a Continental assault was making steady progress on both sides of the Atlantic. All these required transport to the scene of action in the ships carrying the assaulting troops. Thus an immense conversion programme was initiated to fit British and American troopships to carry these craft as well as great quantities of other specialised equipment. These ships became known as Landing Ships Infantry (L.S.I.). Some were commissioned into the Royal Navy; others preserved their mercantile status, and their masters and crews served them with distinction in all our offensive operations. Such ships could ill be spared from the convoys carrying the endless stream of reinforcements to the Middle East and elsewhere, yet this sacrifice had to be made. Many other ancillary types of ship for use in the assault also came into being at this time. In 1940 and 1941 our efforts in this field were limited by the demands of the U-boat struggle. Not more than seven thousand men could be spared for landing-craft production up to the end of 1940, nor was this number greatly exceeded in the following year. However, by 1944 no less than seventy thousand men in Britain alone were dedicated to this stupendous task, besides much larger numbers in the United States.

*　　*　　*

As all our work in this sphere had a powerful bearing on the future of the war, I print at this point a telegram which I sent to the President in 1941:

25.VII.41

We have been considering here our war plans, not only for the fighting of 1942, but also for 1943. After providing for the security of essential bases, it is necessary to plan on the largest scale the forces needed for victory. In broad outline we must aim first at intensifying the blockade and propaganda. Then we must subject Germany and Italy to a ceaseless and ever-growing air bombardment. These measures may themselves produce an internal convulsion or collapse. *But plans ought also to be made for coming to the aid of the conquered populations by landing armies of liberation when opportunity is ripe. For this purpose it will be necessary not only to have great numbers of tanks, but also of vessels capable of carrying them and landing them direct on to beaches.* It ought not to be difficult for you to make the necessary adaptation in some of the vast numbers of merchant vessels you are building so as to fit them for tank-landing ships.

And a little later:

Prime Minister to First Sea Lord　　　　　　　　　　8.IX.41

My idea was not that the President should build Winettes as such, apart from any already arranged for, but that, out of the great number of merchant vessels being constructed in the United States for 1942, he would fit out a certain number with brows and side-ports to enable tanks to be landed from them on beaches, or into tank landing-craft which would take them to the beaches.

Please help me to explain this point to him, showing what kind of alteration would be required in the American merchant ships now projected.

In view of the many accounts which are extant and multiplying of my supposed aversion from any kind of large-scale opposed-landing, such as took place in Normandy in 1944, it may be convenient if I make it clear that from the very beginning I provided a great deal of the impulse and authority for creating the immense apparatus and armada for the landing of armour on beaches, without which it is now universally recognised that all such major operations would have been impossible. I shall unfold this theme step by step in these volumes by means of documents written by me at the time, which show a true and consistent purpose on my part in harmony with the physical facts, and a close correspondence with what was actually done.

CHAPTER XIII

AT BAY
July 1940

Can Britain Survive? - Anxiety in the United States - Resolute Demeanour of the British Nation - The Relief of Simplicity - Hitler's "Peace Offer", July 19 - Our Response - German Diplomatic Approaches Rejected - The King of Sweden's Démarche - I Visit the Threatened Coasts - General Montgomery and the 3rd Division at Brighton - The Importance of Buses - General Brooke Succeeds Ironside in Command of the Home Army - My Contacts with General Brooke - Some Directives and Minutes of July - The Defence of London - Conditions in the Threatened Coastal Zones - Statistics on the Growth and Equipment of the Army - Lindemann's Diagrams - The Canadian Second Division Retrieved from Iceland - Need to Prevent Enemy Concentration of Shipping in the Channel - Arrival of the American Rifles - Special Precautions - The French "Seventy-fives" - The Growth of the German Channel Batteries - Our Counter-measures - My Visit to Admiral Ramsay at Dover - Progress of Our Batteries Coaxed and Urged - The Monitor "Erebus"-The Defence of the Kentish Promontory - British Heavy-Gun Concentration, September - Our Rising Strength - An Ordeal Averted.

IN these summer days of 1940 after the fall of France we were all alone. None of the British Dominions or India or the Colonies could send decisive aid, or send what they had in time. The victorious, enormous German armies, thoroughly equipped and with large reserves of captured weapons and arsenals behind them, were gathering for the final stroke. Italy, with numerous and imposing forces, had declared war upon us, and eagerly sought our destruction in the Mediterranean and in Egypt. In the Far East Japan glared inscrutably, and pointedly requested the closing of the Burma Road against supplies for China. Soviet

Russia was bound to Nazi Germany by her pact, and lent important aid to Hitler in raw materials. Spain, which had already occupied the International Zone of Tangier, might turn against us at any moment and demand Gibraltar, or invite the Germans to help her attack it, or mount batteries to hamper passage through the Straits. The France of Pétain and Bordeaux, soon moved to Vichy, might any day be forced to declare war upon us. What was left at Toulon of the French Fleet seemed to be in German power. Certainly we had no lack of foes.

After Oran it became clear to all countries that the British Government and nation were resolved to fight on to the last. But even if there were no moral weakness in Britain, how could the appalling physical facts be overcome? Our armies at home were known to be almost unarmed except for rifles. There were in fact hardly five hundred field-guns of any sort and hardly two hundred medium or heavy tanks in the whole country. Months must pass before our factories could make good even the munitions lost at Dunkirk. Can one wonder that the world at large was convinced that our hour of doom had struck?

Deep alarm spread through the United States, and indeed through all the surviving free countries. Americans gravely asked themselves whether it was right to cast away any of their own severely-limited resources to indulge a generous though hopeless sentiment. Ought they not to strain every nerve and nurse every weapon to remedy their own unpreparedness? It needed a very sure judgment to rise above these cogent, matter-of-fact arguments. The gratitude of the British nation is due to the noble President and his great officers and high advisers for never, even in the advent of the Third Term Presidential Election, losing their confidence in our fortunes or our will.

The buoyant and imperturbable temper of Britain, which I had the honour to express, may well have turned the scale. Here was this people, who in the years before the war had gone to the extreme bounds of pacifism and improvidence, who had indulged in the sport of party politics, and who, though so weakly armed, had advanced light-heartedly into the centre of European affairs, now confronted with the reckoning alike of their virtuous impulses and neglectful arrangements. They were not even dismayed. They defied the conquerors of Europe. They seemed willing to have their Island reduced to a shambles rather than give in. This would make a fine page in history. But there were other tales of this kind. Athens had been conquered by Sparta. The Carthaginians made a forlorn resistance to Rome. Not seldom in the annals of the past—and how much more often in tragedies never recorded or long-forgotten—had brave, proud, easy-going states, and even entire races, been wiped out, so that only their name or even no mention of them remains.

Few British and very few foreigners understood the peculiar technical advantages of our insular position; nor was it generally known how even in the irresolute years before the war the essentials of sea and latterly air defence had been maintained. It was nearly a thousand years since Britain had seen the fires of a foreign camp on English soil. At the summit of British resistance everyone remained calm, content to set their lives upon the cast. That this was our mood was gradually recognised by friends and foes throughout the whole world. What was there behind the mood? That could be settled only by brute force.

*   *   *

There was also another aspect. One of our greatest dangers during June lay in having our last reserves drawn away from us into a wasting, futile French resistance in France, and the strength of our air forces gradually worn down by their flights or transference to the Continent. If Hitler had been gifted with supernatural wisdom he would have slowed down the attack on the French front, making perhaps a pause of three or four weeks after Dunkirk on the line of the Seine, and meanwhile developing his preparations to invade England. Thus he would have had a deadly option, and could have tortured us with the hooks of either deserting France in her agony or squandering the last resources for our future existence. The more we urged the French to fight on, the greater was our obligation to aid them, and the more difficult it would have become to make any preparations for defence in England, and above all to keep in reserve the twenty-five squadrons of fighter aircraft on which all depended. On this point we should never have given way, but the refusal would have been bitterly resented by our struggling Ally, and would have poisoned all our relations. It was even with an actual sense of relief that some of our high commanders addressed themselves to our new and grimly simplified problem. As the commissionaire at one of the Service clubs in London said to a rather downcast member: "Anyhow, sir, we're in the Final, and it's to be played on the Home Ground."

*　　*　　*

The strength of our position was not, even at this date, under-rated by the German High Command. Ciano tells how, when he visited Hitler in Berlin on July 7, 1940, he had a long conversation with General von Keitel. Keitel, like Hitler, spoke to him about the attack on England. He repeated that up to the present nothing definite had been decided. He regarded the landing as possible, but considered it an "extremely difficult operation, which must be approached with the utmost caution, in view of the fact that the intelligence available on the military preparedness of the island and on the coastal defences is meagre and not very reliable".* What would appear to be easy and also essential was a major air attack upon the airfields, factories, and the principal communication centres in Great Britain. It was necessary however to bear in mind that the British Air Force was extremely efficient. Keitel calculated that the British had about fifteen hundred machines ready for defence and counter-attack. He admitted that recently the offensive action of the British Air Force had been greatly intensified. Bombing missions were carried out with noteworthy accuracy, and the groups of aircraft which appeared numbered up to eighty machines at a time. There was however in England a great shortage of pilots, and those who were now attacking the German cities could not be replaced by the new pilots, who were completely untrained. Keitel also insisted upon the necessity of striking at Gibraltar in order to disrupt the British imperial system. Neither Keitel nor Hitler made any reference to the duration of the war. Only Himmler said incidentally that the war ought to be finished by the beginning of October.

Such was Ciano's report. He also offered Hitler, at "the earnest wish of the Duce", an army of ten divisions and an air component of thirty squadrons to take part in the invasion. The army was politely declined. Some of the air squadrons came, but, as will be presently related, fared ill.

*　　*　　*

* Ciano, *Diplomatic Papers*, p. 378.

33 A depth-charge explodes as a British destroyer attacks a U-Boat.

34 A German submarine prepares to attack.
35 A German vessel on fire after an attack by the R.A.F.

36 The first photo of an attack on a convoy in the English Channel, 14th July, 1940.
37 The ''Home Fleet'' patrolling the North Sea.

38 A British freighter escorted by a warship.

On July 19 Hitler delivered his triumphant speech in the Reichstag, in which, after predicting that I would shortly take refuge in Canada, he made what has been called his Peace Offer. The operative sentences were:

In this hour I feel it to be my duty before my own conscience to appeal once more to reason and common sense in Great Britain as much as elsewhere. I consider myself in a position to make this appeal, since I am not a vanquished foe begging favours, but the victor, speaking in the name of reason. I can see no reason why this war need go on. I am grieved to think of the sacrifices it must claim. . . . Possibly Mr. Churchill will brush aside this statement of mine by saying it is merely born of fear and doubt of final victory. In that case I shall have relieved my conscience in regard to the things to come.

This gesture was accompanied during the following days by diplomatic representations through Sweden, the United States, and at the Vatican. Naturally Hitler would be very glad, after having subjugated Europe to his will, to bring the war to an end by procuring British acceptance of what he had done. It was in fact an offer not of peace but of readiness to accept the surrender by Britain of all she had entered the war to maintain. As the German Chargé d'Affaires in Washington had attempted some communication with our Ambassador there, I sent the following telegram:

20.VII.40

I do not know whether Lord Halifax is in town to-day, but Lord Lothian should be told on no account to make any reply to the German Chargé d'Affaires' message.

My first thought, however, was a solemn, formal debate in both Houses of Parliament. I therefore wrote at the same time to Mr. Chamberlain and Mr. Attlee.

20.VII.40

It might be worth while meeting Hitler's speech by resolutions in both Houses. These resolutions should be proposed by private Peers and Members. On the other hand, the occasion will add to our burdens. What do you say?

My colleagues thought that this would be making too much of the matter, upon which we were all of one mind. It was decided instead that the Foreign Secretary should dismiss Hitler's gesture in a broadcast. On the night of the 22nd he "brushed aside" Hitler's "summons to capitulate to his will". He contrasted Hitler's picture of Europe with the picture of the Europe for which we were fighting, and declared that "we shall not stop fighting until Freedom is secure". In fact however the rejection of any idea of a parley had already been given in the British Press and by the B.B.C., without any prompting from His Majesty's Government, as soon as Hitler's speech was heard over the radio.

Ciano, in his account of another meeting with Hitler on July 20, observes:

The reaction of the English Press to yesterday's speech has been such as to allow of no prospect of an understanding. Hitler is therefore preparing to strike the military blow at England. He stresses that Germany's strategic position, as well as her sphere of influence and of economic control, are such as to have already greatly weakened the possibilities of resistance by Great Britain, which will collapse under the first blows. The air attack already began some days ago, and is continually growing in intensity. The reaction of the anti-aircraft defences and of the British fighters is not seriously hindering the German air attack. The decisive offensive operation is now being studied, since the fullest preparations have been made.*

Ciano also records in his diaries that "Late in the evening of the 19th, when the first cold British reaction to the speech arrived, a sense of ill-concealed disappointment spread among the Germans." Hitler "would like an understanding with Great Britain. He knows that war with the British will be hard and bloody, and knows also that people everywhere are averse from bloodshed". Mussolini, on the other hand, "fears that the English may find in Hitler's much too cunning speech a pretext to begin negotiations". "That", remarks Ciano, "would be sad for Mussolini, because now more than ever he wants war."† He need not have fretted himself. He was not to be denied all the war he wanted.

There was no doubt continuous German diplomatic activity behind the scenes, and when on August 3 the King of Sweden thought fit to address us on the subject I suggested to the Foreign Secretary the following reply, which formed the basis of the official answer:

* Ciano, *Diplomatic Papers*, p. 381.
† *Ciano's Diaries*, pp. 277–8.

(*Begins.*) On October 12, 1939, His Majesty's Government defined at length their position towards German peace offers in maturely considered statements to Parliament. Since then a number of new hideous crimes have been committed by Nazi Germany against the smaller States upon her borders. Norway has been overrun, and is now occupied by a German invading army. Denmark has been seized and pillaged. Belgium and Holland, after all their efforts to placate Herr Hitler, and in spite of all the assurances given to them by the German Government that their neutrality would be respected, have been conquered and subjugated. In Holland particularly acts of long-prepared treachery and brutality culminated in the massacre of Rotterdam, where many thousands of Dutchmen were slaughtered and an important part of the city destroyed.

These horrible events have darkened the pages of European history with an indelible stain. His Majesty's Government see in them not the slightest cause to recede in any way from their principles and resolves as set forth in October 1939. On the contrary, their intention to prosecute the war against Germany by every means in their power until Hitlerism is finally broken and the world relieved from the curse which a wicked man has brought upon it has been strengthened to such a point that they would rather all perish in the common ruin than fail or falter in their duty. They firmly believe however that with the help of God they will not lack the means to discharge their task. This task may be long; but it will always be possible for Germany to ask for an armistice, as she did in 1918, or to publish her proposals for peace. Before however any such requests or proposals could even be considered it would be necessary that effective guarantees by deeds, not words, should be forthcoming from Germany which would ensure the restoration of the free and independent life of Czechoslovakia, Poland, Norway, Denmark, Holland, Belgium, and above all France, as well as the effectual security of Great Britain and the British Empire in a general peace. (*Ends.*)

I added:

The ideas set forth in the Foreign Office memo. appear to me to err in trying to be too clever, and to enter into refinements of policy unsuited to the tragic simplicity and grandeur of the times and the issues at stake. At this moment, when we have had no sort of success, the slightest opening will be misjudged. Indeed, a firm reply of the kind I have outlined is the only chance of extorting from Germany any offers which are not fantastic.

On the same day I issued the following statement to the Press:

3.VIII.40

The Prime Minister wishes it to be known that the possibility of German attempts at invasion has by no means passed away. The fact that the Germans are now putting about rumours that they do not intend an invasion should be regarded with a double dose of the suspicion which attaches to all their utterances. Our sense of growing strength and preparedness must not lead to the slightest relaxation of vigilance or moral alertness.

* * *

At the end of June the Chiefs of Staff through General Ismay had suggested to me at the Cabinet that I should visit the threatened sectors of the east and south coasts. Accordingly I devoted a day or two every week to this agreeable task, sleeping when necessary in my train, where I had every facility for carrying on my regular work and was in constant contact with Whitehall. I inspected the Tyne and the Humber and many possible landing-places. The Canadian Division, soon to be reinforced to a corps by the division sent to Iceland, did an exercise for me in Kent. I examined the landward defences of Harwich and Dover. One of my earliest visits was to the 3rd Division, commanded by General Montgomery, an officer whom I had not met before. My wife came with me. The 3rd Division was stationed near Brighton. It had been given the highest priority in re-equipment, and had been about to sail for France when the French resistance ended. General Montgomery's headquarters were near Steyning, and he showed me a small exercise of which the central feature was a flanking movement of Bren-gun carriers, of which he could at that moment muster only seven or eight. After this we drove together along the coast through Shoreham and Hove till we came to the familiar Brighton front, of which I had so many schoolboy memories. We dined in the Royal Albion Hotel, which stands opposite the end of the pier. The hotel was entirely empty, a great deal of evacuation having taken place; but there were still a number of people airing themselves on the beaches or the parade. I was amused to see a platoon of the Grenadier Guards making a sandbag machine-gun post in one of the kiosks of the pier, like those where in my childhood I had often admired the antics of the performing fleas. It was lovely weather. I had very good talks with the General, and enjoyed my outing thoroughly. However:

(Action this Day)
Prime Minister to Secretary of State for War   3.VII.40

I was disturbed to find the 3rd Division spread along thirty miles of coast, instead of being, as I had imagined, held back concentrated in reserve, ready to move against any serious head of invasion. But much more astonishing was the fact that the infantry of this division, which is otherwise fully mobile, are not provided with the buses necessary to move them to the point of action.* This provision of buses, waiting always ready and close at hand, is essential to all mobile units, and to none more than the 3rd Division while spread about the coast.

I heard the same complaint from Portsmouth that the troops there had not got their transport ready and close at hand. Considering the great masses of transport, both buses and lorries, which there are in this country, and the large numbers of drivers brought back from the B.E.F., it should be possible to remedy these deficiencies at once. I hope, at any rate, that the G.O.C. 3rd Division will be told to-day to take up, as he would like to do, the large number of buses which are even now plying for pleasure traffic up and down the sea front at Brighton.

*　*　*

In mid-July the Secretary of State for War recommended that General Brooke should replace General Ironside in command of our Home Forces. On July 19, in the course of my continuous inspection of the invasion sectors, I visited the Southern Command. Some sort of tactical exercise was presented to me in which no fewer than twelve tanks(!) were able to participate. All the afternoon I drove with General Brooke, who commanded this front. His record stood high. Not only had he fought the decisive flank-battle near Ypres during the retirement to Dunkirk, but he had acquitted himself with singular firmness and dexterity, in circumstances of unimaginable difficulty and confusion, when in command of the new forces we had sent to France during the first three weeks of June. I also had a personal link with Alan Brooke through his two gallant brothers—the friends of my early military life.†

---

* This was an old device which I had used for the Marine Brigade of the Royal Naval Division when we landed on the French coast in September 1914. We took fifty of them from the London streets, and the Admiralty carried them across in a night.

† His brother Victor was a subaltern in the 9th Lancers when I joined the 4th Hussars, and I formed a warm friendship with him in 1895 and 1896. His horse reared up and fell over backwards, breaking his pelvis, and he was sorely stricken for the rest of his life. However, he continued to be able to serve and ride, and perished gloriously from sheer

These connections and memories did not decide my opinion on the grave matters of selection; but they formed a personal foundation upon which my unbroken war-time association with Alan Brooke was maintained and ripened. We were four hours together in the motor-car on this July afternoon, 1940, and we seemed to be in agreement on the methods of Home Defence. After the necessary consultations with others, I approved the Secretary of State for War's proposal to place Brooke in command of the Home Forces in succession to General Ironside. Ironside accepted his retirement with the soldierly dignity which on all occasions characterised his actions.

During the invasion menace for a year and a half Brooke organised and commanded the Home Forces, and thereafter when he had become C.I.G.S. we continued together for three and a half years until victory was won. I shall presently narrate the benefits which I derived from his advice in the decisive changes of command in Egypt and the Middle East in August 1942, and also the heavy disappointment which I had to inflict upon him about the command of the cross-Channel invasion Operation "Overlord" in 1944. His long tenure as chairman of the Chiefs of Staff Committee during the greater part of the war and his work as C.I.G.S. enabled him to render services of the highest order, not only to the British Empire, but also to the Allied Cause. These volumes will record occasional differences between us, but also an overwhelming measure of agreement, and will witness to a friendship which I cherish.

*　　*　　*

Meanwhile we all faced in ever-increasing detail and tenacity the possibility of Invasion. Some of my minutes illustrate this process.

exhaustion whilst acting as liaison officer with the French Cavalry Corps in the retreat from Mons in 1914.

General Brooke had another brother, Ronnie. He was older than Victor and several years older than me. In the years 1895-98 he was thought to be a rising star in the British Army. Not only did he serve with distinction in all the campaigns which occurred, but he shone at the Staff College among his contemporaries. In the Boer War he was Adjutant of the South African Light Horse, and I for some months during the relief of Ladysmith was Assistant Adjutant, the regiment having six squadrons. Together we went through the fighting at Spion Kop, Vaal Krantz, and the Tugela. I learned much about tactics from him. Together we galloped into Ladysmith on the night of its liberation. Later on, in 1903, although I was only a youthful Member of Parliament, I was able to help him to the Somaliland campaign, in which he added to his high reputation. He was stricken down by arthritis at an early age, and could only command a reserve brigade at home during the First World War. Our friendship continued till his premature death in 1930.

AT BAY

(Action this Day)
Prime Minister to Secretary of State for Air and C.A.S. 3.VII.40
   I hear from every side of the need for throwing your main emphasis on bombing the ships and barges in all the ports under German control.

Prime Minister to General Ismay 2.VII.40
   See the letter [on the defence of London] from Mr. Wedgwood, M.P., which is interesting and characteristic. What is the position about London? I have a very clear view that we should fight every inch of it, and that it would *devour* quite a large invading army.

Prime Minister to Mr. Wedgwood 5.VII.40
   Many thanks for your letters. I am hoping to get a great many more rifles very soon, and to continue the process of arming the Home Guard (L.D.V.). You may rest assured that we should fight every street of London and its suburbs. It would *devour* an invading army, assuming one ever got so far. We hope however to drown the bulk of them in the salt sea.

   It is curious that the German army commander charged with the invasion plan used this same word "devour" about London, and determined to avoid it.

Prime Minister to General Ismay 4.VII.40
   What is being done to encourage and assist the people living in threatened sea-ports to make suitable shelters for themselves in which they could remain during an invasion? Active measures must be taken forthwith. Officers or representatives of the local authority should go round explaining to families that if they decide not to leave in accordance with our general advice, they should remain in the cellars, and arrangements should be made to prop up the building over-head. They should be assisted in this both with advice and materials. Their gas-masks should be inspected. All this must be put actively in operation from to-day. The process will stimulate voluntary evacua-tion, and at the same time make reasonable provision for those who remain.

Prime Minister to General Ismay 5.VII.40
   Clear instructions should now be issued about the people living in the threatened coastal zones: (1) They should be encouraged as much as possible to depart voluntarily, both by the pressure of a potential compulsory order hanging over them, and also by local (not national) propaganda through their Regional Commissioners or local bodies. Those who wish to stay, or can find nowhere to go on their own, should be told that if invasion impact occurs in their town or village on the coast they will not be able to leave till the battle is over. They

should therefore be encouraged and helped to put their cellars in order so that they have fairly safe places to go to. They should be supplied with whatever form of Anderson shelter is now available (I hear there are new forms not involving steel). Only those who are trustworthy should be allowed to stay. All doubtful elements should be removed.

Pray have precise proposals formulated upon these lines for my approval.

Prime Minister to Professor Lindemann   7.VII.40
  (Copy to General Ismay)

I want my "S" Branch to make a chart of all the thirty divisions, showing their progress towards complete equipment. Each division would be represented by a square divided into sections: officers and men, rifles, Bren guns, Bren-gun carriers, anti-tank rifles, anti-tank guns, field artillery, medium ditto (if any), transport sufficient to secure mobility of all three brigades simultaneously, etc. As and when a proportion of these subsidiary squares is completed a chart can be painted red. I should like to see this chart every week. A similar diagram can be prepared for the Home Guard. In this case it is only necessary to show rifles and uniforms.

Prime Minister to Secretary of State for War   7.VII.40

You shared my astonishment yesterday at the statement made to us by General McNaughton that the whole of the 2nd Canadian Division was destined for Iceland. It would surely be a very great mistake to allow these fine troops to be employed in so distant a theatre. Apparently the first three battalions have already gone there. No one was told anything about this. We require two Canadian divisions to work as a corps as soon as possible.

I am well aware of the arguments about training, etc., but they did not convince me. We ought to have another thorough re-examination of this point. Surely it should be possible to send second-line Territorial troops to Iceland, where they should fortify themselves at the key points, and then to have, say, one very high-class battalion of the "Gubbins" type in order to strike at any landing. I should be most grateful if you would deal with this.

Prime Minister to First Lord and First Sea Lord   7.VII.40

1. I cannot understand how we can tolerate the movement at sea along the French coast of any vessels without attacking them. It is not sufficient surely to use the air only. Destroyers should be sent under air escort. Are we really to resign ourselves to the Germans building up a large armada under our noses in the Channel, and conducting vessels through the Straits of Dover with impunity? This is the

beginning of a new and very dangerous threat which must be countered.

2. I should be glad of a report not only on the points mentioned above, but also on the state of our minefield there, and how it is to be improved. Is it true the mines have become defective after ten months? If so, several new rows should be laid. Why should not an effort be made to lay a minefield by night in the French passage, and lie in wait for any craft sent to sweep a channel through it? We really must not be put off from asserting our sea-power by the fact that the Germans are holding the French coast. If German guns open upon us a heavy ship should be sent to bombard them under proper air protection.

*　　*　　*

During this month of July American weapons in considerable quantities were safely brought across the Atlantic. This seemed to me so vital that I issued reiterated injunctions for care in their transportation and reception.

Prime Minister to Secretary of State for War　　　　　　　　　7.VII.40

I have asked the Admiralty to make very special arrangements for bringing in your rifle convoys. They are sending four destroyers far out to meet them, and all should arrive during the 9th. You can ascertain the hour from the Admiralty. I was so glad to hear that you were making all preparations for the unloading, reception, and distribution of these rifles. At least 100,000 ought to reach the troops that very night, or in the small hours of the following morning. Special trains should be used to distribute them and the ammunition according to a plan worked out beforehand exactly, and directed from the landing-port by some high officer thoroughly acquainted with it. It would seem likely that you would emphasise early distribution to the coastal districts, so that all the Home Guard in the danger areas should be the first served. Perhaps you would be good enough to let me know beforehand what you decide.

Prime Minister to General Ismay　　　　　　　　　　　　　　8.VII.40

Have any steps been taken to load the later portions of American ammunition, rifles, and guns upon faster ships than was the case last time? What are the ships in which the latest consignments are being packed, and what are their speeds? Will you kindly ascertain this from the Admiralty.

Prime Minister to First Lord　　　　　　　　　　　　　　27.VII.40

The great consignments of rifles and guns, together with their ammunition, which are now approaching this country are entirely on a different level from anything else we have transported across the ocean except the Canadian Division itself. Do not forget that 200,000 rifles mean 200,000 men, as the men are waiting for the rifles. The convoys approaching on July 31 are unique, and a special effort should be made to ensure their safe arrival. The loss of these rifles and field-guns would be a disaster of the first order.

When the ships from America approached our shores with their priceless arms special trains were waiting in all the ports to receive their cargoes. The Home Guard in every county, in every town, in every village, sat up all through the night to receive them. Men and women worked night and day making them fit for use. By the end of July we were an armed nation, so far as parachute or air-borne landings were concerned. We had become a "hornets' nest". Anyhow, if we had to go down fighting (which I did not anticipate) a lot of our men and some women had weapons in their hands. The arrival of the first instalment of the half-million .300 rifles for the Home Guard (albeit with only about fifty cartridges apiece, of which we dared only issue ten, and no factories yet set in motion) enabled us to transfer three hundred thousand .303 British-type rifles to the rapidly-expanding formations of the Regular Army.

At the "seventy-fives", with their thousand rounds apiece, some fastidious experts presently turned their noses up. There were no limbers and no immediate means of procuring more ammunition. Mixed calibres complicate operations. But I would have none of this, and during all 1940 and 1941 these nine hundred "seventy-fives" were a great addition to our military strength for Home Defence. Arrangements were devised and men were drilled to run them up on planks into lorries for movement. When you are fighting for existence any cannon is better than no cannon at all, and the French "seventy-five", although out-dated by the British 25-pounder and the German field-gun howitzer, was still a splendid weapon.

*   *   *

We had watched with attention the growth of the German heavy batteries along the Channel coast during August and September. By far the strongest concentration of this artillery was around Calais and Cape Gris-Nez, with the apparent purpose not only of forbidding the Straits to our warships but also of commanding the shortest route across them. We now know

STATE OF READINESS
INFANTRY DIVISIONS 13th July 1940

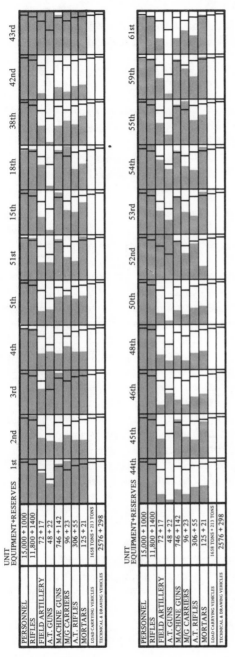

UNIT	EQUIPMENT + RESERVES
PERSONNEL	15,000 + 1000
RIFLES	11,800 + 1400
FIELD ARTILLERY	72 + 17
A.T. GUNS	48 + 22
MACHINE GUNS	746 + 142
M/G CARRIERS	96 + 23
A.T. RIFLES	306 + 55
MORTARS	125 + 21
LOAD-CARRYING VEHICLES	1658 TONS + 213 TONS
TECHNICAL & DRAWING VEHICLES	2576 + 298

1st 2nd 3rd 4th 5th 15th 18th 38th 42nd 43rd

UNIT	EQUIPMENT + RESERVES
PERSONNEL	15,000 + 1000
RIFLES	11,800 + 1400
FIELD ARTILLERY	72 + 17
A.T. GUNS	48 + 22
MACHINE GUNS	746 + 142
M/G CARRIERS	96 + 23
A.T. RIFLES	306 + 55
MORTARS	125 + 21
LOAD-CARRYING VEHICLES	1658 TONS + 213 TONS
TECHNICAL & DRAWING VEHICLES	2576 + 298

44th 45th 46th 50th 51st 52nd 53rd 54th 55th 59th 61st

UNIT EQUIPMENT + RESERVES   1st LONDON   2nd LONDON   1.CANADIAN   AUSTRALIAN N.Z.E.F.

UNIT	EQUIPMENT + RESERVES
PERSONNEL	15,000 + 1000
RIFLES	11,800 + 1400
FIELD ARTILLERY	72 + 17
A.T. GUNS	48 + 22
MACHINE GUNS	746 + 142
M/G CARRIERS	96 + 23
A.T. RIFLES	306 + 55
MORTARS	125 + 21
LOAD-CARRYING VEHICLES	1658 TONS + 213 TONS
TECHNICAL & DRAWING VEHICLES	2576 + 298

UNIT EQUIPMENT

RESERVES

Levels on 13th July 1940

that by the middle of September the following batteries were already mounted and ready for use in this region alone:

(a) Siegfried battery, south of Gris-Nez, with four 38-cm. guns.
(b) Friedrich-August battery, north of Boulogne, with three 30.5-cm. guns.
(c) Grosser Kurfuerst battery, at Gris-Nez, with four 28-cm. guns.
(d) Prinz Heinrich battery, between Calais and Blanc-Nez, with two 28-cm. guns.
(e) Oldenburg battery, east of Calais, with two 24-cm. guns.
(f) M.1, M.2, M.3, M.4 batteries, in the sector of Gris-Nez—Calais, with a total of fourteen 17-cm. guns.

Besides this no fewer than thirty-five heavy and medium batteries of the German Army, as well as seven batteries of captured guns, were sited along the French coast for defensive purposes by the end of August.

The orders which I had given in June for arming the Dover promontory with guns that could fire across the Channel had borne fruit, though not on the same scale. I took a personal interest in the whole of this business. I visited Dover several times in these anxious summer months. In the Citadel of the Castle large underground galleries and chambers had been cut in the chalk, and there was a wide balcony from which on clear days the shores of France, now in the hands of the enemy, could be seen. Admiral Ramsay, who commanded, was a friend of mine. He was the son of a colonel of the 4th Hussars under whom I had served in my youth, and I had often seen him as a child on the Barrack Square at Aldershot. When three years before the war he had resigned his position as Chief of Staff to the Home Fleet through a difference with its Commander-in-Chief, it was to me that he had come to seek advice. I had long talks with him, and together with the Dover Fortress Commander visited our rapidly-improving defences.

I carefully studied there and at home the Intelligence reports, which almost daily showed the progress of the German batteries. The series of minutes which I dictated about the Dover guns during August show my very great desire to break up some of the heaviest battery sites before their guns could reply. I certainly thought this ought to have been done in August, as we had at least three of the very heaviest guns capable of firing across the

Channel. Later on the Germans became too strong for us to court a duel.

Prime Minister to General Ismay   3.VIII.40

1. The 14-inch gun I ordered to be mounted at Dover should be ready in ample time to deal with this new German battery. It certainly should not fire until all the guns are in position. The plan for the shoot may however now be made, and I should like to know what arrangements for spotting aircraft, protected by fighters in strength, will be prepared for that joyous occasion. Also, when the two guns, 13.5's on railway mountings, will be ready, and whether they can reach the target mentioned. Several other camouflaged guns should be put up at various points, with arrangements to make suitable flashes, smoke and dust. Let me know what arrangements can be devised. I presume work on the railway extensions for the 13.5's is already in hand. Please report.

2. The movement of the German warships southward to Kiel creates a somewhat different situation from that dealt with in C.-in-C. Home Fleet's appreciation asked for some time ago about an invasion across the narrow waters supported by heavy ships. The Admiralty should be asked whether C.-in-C.'s attention should not be drawn to the altered dispositions of the enemy, in case he has anything further to say.

Prime Minister to First Lord   8.VIII.40

I am impressed by the speed and efficiency with which the emplacement for the 14-inch gun at Dover has been prepared and the gun itself mounted. Will you tell all those who have helped in this achievement how much I appreciate the sterling effort they have made.

The enemy batteries first opened fire on August 22, engaging a convoy without effect and later firing on Dover. They were replied to by one of our 14-inch guns which was now in action. Thenceforward there were artillery duels at irregular intervals. Dover was engaged six times in September, the heaviest day being September 9, when over one hundred and fifty shells were fired. Very little damage was done to convoys.

Prime Minister to First Lord and First Sea Lord   25.VIII.40

I shall be much obliged if you will make proposals for a shoot by *Erebus** against the German batteries at Gris-Nez. I was very glad to

---

* H.M.S. *Erebus* was a monitor of the first war mounting two 15-inch guns. After being refitted she went to Scapa for target practice in August. Delay arose in her working up practices through defects and bad weather and she did not reach Dover until late in September. It was therefore not until the night of September 29–30 that she carried out a bombardment of Calais.

hear you thought this practicable. It is most desirable. There is no reason why it should wait for the railway guns, though of course if they were ready they could follow on with the 14-inch at daybreak. We ought to smash these batteries. I hope we have not got to wait for the next moon for *Erebus*, and I shall be glad to know what are the moon conditions which you deem favourable.

Prime Minister to General Ismay and C.O.S. Committee   27.VIII.40

It would not seem unreasonable that the enemy should attempt gradually to master the Dover promontory and command the Channel at its narrowest point. This would be a natural preliminary to invasion. It would give occasion for continued fighting with our Air Force in the hope of exhausting them by numbers. It would tend to drive our warships from all the Channel bases. The concentration of many batteries on the French coast must be expected. What are we doing in defence of the Dover promontory by heavy artillery? Ten weeks ago I asked for heavy guns. One has been mounted. Two railway guns are expected. Now we are told these will be very inaccurate on account of super-charging. We ought to have a good many more heavy guns lined up inside to smaller calibre with stiffer rifling and a range of at least fifty miles, and firing at twenty-five or thirty miles would then become more accurate. I do not understand why I have not yet received proposals on this subject. We must insist upon maintaining superior artillery positions on the Dover promontory, no matter what form of attack they are exposed to. We have to fight for the command of the Straits by artillery, to destroy the enemy's batteries, and to multiply and fortify our own.

I have sent on other papers a request for a surprise attack by *Erebus*, which should be able to destroy the batteries at Gris-Nez. She has an armoured deck against air bombing. What is being done about this? When is she going into action? The Air Ministry should of course co-operate. The operation would take an offensive turn. We should require spotting aircraft by day. It may be that the first squadrons of Hurricanes fitted with Merlin 20 would be the best for this. If *Erebus* is attacked from the air she should be strongly defended, and action sought with the enemy Air Force.

Pray let me have your plans.

Prime Minister to General Ismay, for C.O.S. Committee   30.VIII.40

Further to my previous minute on defence of the Kentish promontory, we must expect that very powerful batteries in great numbers will be rapidly brought into being on the French coast. It would be a natural thought for the Germans to try to dominate the Straits by artillery. At present we are ahead of them with our 14-inch and two

STATE OF READINESS

(UNIT EQUIPMENT ONLY: EXCLUDING RESERVES) 7th Sept. 1940 (Personnel 31st Aug. 1940)

INFANTRY DIVISIONS

In excess of Establishment

Levels on 13th July 1940

13.5 railway guns. The Admiral at Dover should be furnished in addition, as soon as possible, with a large number of the most modern 6-inch or 8-inch guns. I understand the Admiralty is considering taking guns from [H.M.S.] *Newcastle* or *Glasgow*, which are under long repair. A record evolution should be made of getting one or two of these turrets mounted. Report to me about this and dates. There is a 9.2 Army experimental gun and mounting, and surely we have some 12-inch on railway mountings. If our ships cannot use the Straits the enemy must not be able to. Even if guns cannot fire on to the French shore they are none the less very valuable.

Some of our heavy artillery—the 18-inch howitzer and the 9.2's—should be planted in positions whence they could deny the ports and landings to the enemy, and, as C.I.G.S. mentioned, support the counter-attack which would be launched against any attempted bridgehead. Much of this mass of artillery I saved from the last war has done nothing, and has been under reconditioning for a whole year.

Let me have a good programme for using it to support counter-strokes and deny landings, both north and south of the Thames. Farther north I have seen already some very good heavy batteries.

I should like also to be informed of the real [actual] lines of defence drawn up between Dover and London and Harwich and London. Now that the coast is finished there is no reason why we should not develop these lines, which in no way detract from the principle of vehement counter-attack.

But the most urgent matter is one or two modern 6-inch to shoot all German craft up to 35,000 yards.

I am also endeavouring to obtain from United States at least a pair of their 16-inch coast defence weapons. These fire 45,000 yards, throwing a ton and a quarter, without being super-charged. They should therefore be very accurate. General Strong, United States Army, mentioned this to me as a promising line. He thought, without committing his Government, that the United States Army might be prepared to take a couple of these guns and their carriages away from some of their twin batteries.

Let me know all details about these guns. It ought to be possible to make the concrete foundation in three months, and I expect it would take as long to get these guns over here. There are very few ships that can carry them on their decks.

Prime Minister to General Ismay and First Sea Lord   31.VIII.40

It becomes particularly urgent to attack the batteries on the French shore. Yesterday's photographs show guns being actually hoisted up into position, and it will be wise to fire on them before they are able to reply. There are quite enough guns in position already. I trust therefore *Erebus* will not be delayed, as every day our task will become harder.

It seems most necessary to damage and delay the development of the hostile batteries in view of the fact that we are so far behindhand with our own.

At the beginning of September our heavy gun strength towards the sea was:

Pre-War Coast Defence

9.2-inch	two
6-inch	six

Recent Additions

14-inch (Naval)	one
9.2-inch	two (railway mountings)
6-inch (Naval)	two
4-inch (Naval)	two

These were soon to be further reinforced by two 13.5-inch guns from the old battleship *Iron Duke*, which were being erected on railway mountings, and a battery of four 5.5-inch guns from H.M.S. *Hood*. Many of these additional guns were manned by the Royal Navy and Royal Marines.

Although still inferior in numbers to the enemy we thus had a powerful fire concentration.

In addition, one of the 18-inch howitzers I had saved after the first war and twelve 12-inch howitzers were installed for engaging enemy landings. All these were mobile and would have brought a terrible fire on any landing area.

* * *

As the months of July and August passed without any disaster we settled ourselves down with increasing assurance that we could make a long and hard fight. Our gains of strength were borne in upon us from day to day. The entire population laboured to the last limit of its strength, and felt rewarded when they fell asleep after their toil or vigil by a growing sense that we should have time and that we should win. All the beaches now bristled with defences of various kinds. The whole country was organised in defensive localities. The factories poured out their weapons. By the end of August we had over two hundred and fifty new tanks! The fruits of the American "Act of Faith" had been gathered. The whole trained professional British Army and its Territorial comrades drilled and exercised from morn till night, and longed to meet the foe. The Home Guard overtopped the million mark, and when rifles were lacking grasped lustily the shotgun, the sporting rifle, the private pistol, or, when there was no firearm, the pike and the club. No Fifth Column existed in Britain, though a few spies were carefully rounded up and examined. What few Communists there were lay low. Everyone else gave all they had to give.

When Ribbentrop visited Rome in September he said to Ciano: "The English territorial defence is non-existent. A single German division will suffice to bring about a complete collapse." This merely shows his ignorance. I have often wondered however what would have happened if two hundred thousand German storm troops had actually established themselves ashore. The massacre would have been on both sides grim and great. There would have been neither mercy nor quarter. They would have used Terror, and we were prepared to go all lengths. I intended to use the slogan "You can always take one with you". I even calculated that the horrors of such a scene would in the last resort turn the scale in the United States. But none of these emotions was put to the proof. Far out on the grey waters of the North Sea and the Channel coursed and patrolled the faithful, eager flotillas peering through the night. High in the air soared the fighter pilots, or waited serene at a moment's notice around their excellent machines. This was a time when it was equally good to live or die.

CHAPTER XIV

THE INVASION PROBLEM

Former Studies of Invasion - The New Air-Power - My Statement to Parliament of June 18 - The First Rumours - My Note of June 28 - My Minute on "Invasion" of July 10 - Importance of Mobile Reserves - Two Thousand Miles of British Coastline - The First Sea Lord's Memorandum - Distribution of Potential Attack - I Double His Estimate for Safety - My Minute of August 5, 1940 - My Suggested Distribution of Our Army - Coincidence of Chiefs of Staff View - Our Emphasis on East Coast - The Germans Choose the South Coast - We Turn Our Front - Change in Our Dispositions between August and September - Persisting Dangers from Across the North Sea - Tension in July and August.

AFTER Dunkirk, and still more when three weeks later the French Government capitulated, the questions whether Hitler would, or secondly could, invade and conquer our Island rose, as we have seen, in all British minds. I was no novice at this problem. As First Lord I had for three years before the First Great War taken part in all the discussions of the Committee of Imperial Defence upon the point. On behalf of the Admiralty I had always argued that at least two divisions out of our Expeditionary Force of six should be kept at home until the Territorial Army and other war-time forces became militarily effective. As Admiral "Tug" Wilson put it: "The Navy cannot play international football without a goalkeeper." However, when at the outbreak of that war we found ourselves with the Navy fully mobilised, the Grand Fleet safe beyond hostile ken at sea, all surprises, treacheries, and accidents left behind us, we felt ourselves able at the Admiralty to be better than our word. At the extraordinary meeting of Ministers and high military

authorities which Mr. Asquith summoned to the Cabinet Room
on August 5, 1914, I declared formally, with the full agreement of
the First Sea Lord (Prince Louis of Battenberg), that the Navy
would guarantee the protection of the Island against invasion
or serious raid even if all the Regular troops were immediately
sent to the great battle impending in France. So far as we were
concerned, the whole Army could go. In the course of the first
six weeks all the six divisions went.

Sea-power, when properly understood, is a wonderful thing.
The passage of an army across salt water in the face of superior
fleets and flotillas is an almost impossible feat. Steam had added
enormously to the power of the Navy to defend Great Britain.
In Napoleon's day the same wind which would carry his flat-
bottomed boats across the Channel from Boulogne would drive
away our blockading squadrons. But everything that had happened since then had magnified the power of the superior navy
to destroy the invaders in transit. Every complication which
modern apparatus had added to armies made their voyage more
cumbrous and perilous, and the difficulties of their maintenance
when landed probably insuperable. At that former crisis in our
Island fortunes we possessed superior and, as it proved, ample sea-
power. The enemy was unable to gain a major sea battle against
us. He could not face our cruiser forces. In flotillas and light craft
we outnumbered him tenfold. Against this must be set the incal-
culable chances of weather, particularly fog. But even if this
were adverse and a descent were effected at one or more points
the problem of maintaining a hostile line of communications and
of nourishing any lodgments remained unsolved. Such was the
position in the First Great War.

But now there was the air. What effect had this sovereign
development produced upon the invasion problem? Evidently
if the enemy could dominate the narrow seas, on both sides of the
Straits of Dover, by superior air-power, the losses of our flotillas
would be very heavy and might eventually be fatal. No one
would wish, except on a supreme occasion, to bring heavy
battleships or large cruisers into waters commanded by the
German bombers. We did not in fact station any capital ships
south of the Forth or east of Plymouth. But from Harwich, the
Nore, Dover, Portsmouth, and Portland we maintained a tireless,
vigilant patrol of light fighting vessels which steadily increased in

number. By September they exceeded eight hundred, which only a hostile air-power could destroy, and then only by degrees.

But who had the power in the air? In the Battle of France we had fought the Germans against odds of two and three to one and inflicted losses in similar proportions. Over Dunkirk, where we had to maintain continuous patrol to cover the escape of the Army, we had fought at four or five to one with success and profit. Over our own waters and exposed coasts and counties Air Chief Marshal Dowding contemplated profitable fighting at seven or eight to one. The strength of the German Air Force at this time, taken as a whole, so far as we knew—and we were well informed —apart from particular concentrations, was about three to one. Although these were heavy odds at which to fight the brave and efficient German foe, I rested upon the conclusion that in our own air, over our own country and its waters, we could beat the German Air Force. And if this were true our naval power would continue to rule the seas and oceans, and would destroy all enemies who set their course towards us.

There was of course a third potential factor. Had the Germans with their renowned thoroughness and foresight secretly prepared a vast armada of special landing-craft, which needed no harbours or quays, but could land tanks, cannon, and motor vehicles anywhere on the beaches, and which thereafter could supply the landed troops? As has been shown, such ideas had risen in my mind long ago in 1917, and were now being actually developed as the result of my directions. We had however no reason to believe that anything of this kind existed in Germany, though it is always best when counting the cost not to exclude the worst. It took us four years of intense effort and experiment and immense material aid from the United States to provide such equipment on a scale equal to the Normandy landing. Much less would have sufficed the Germans at this moment. But they had only a few Siebel ferries.

Thus the invasion of England in the summer and autumn of 1940 required from Germany local naval superiority and air superiority and immense special fleets and landing-craft. But it was we who had the naval superiority; it was we who conquered the mastery in the air; and finally we believed, as we now know rightly, that they had not built or conceived any special craft. These were the foundations of my thought about invasion in 1940, from which I gave from day to day the instructions and directives which these chapters contain.

* * *

I laid the broad outlines plainly before Parliament on June 18:

The Navy has never pretended to be able to prevent raids by bodies of five or ten thousand men flung suddenly across and thrown ashore at several points on the coast some dark night or foggy morning. The efficacy of sea-power, especially under modern conditions, depends upon the invading force being of large size. It has to be of large size, in view of our military strength, to be of any use. If it is of large size, then the Navy have something they can find and meet and, as it were, bite on. Now we must remember that even five divisions, however lightly equipped, would require 200 to 250 ships, and with modern air reconnaissance and photography it would not be easy to collect such an armada, marshal it, and conduct it across the sea without any powerful naval forces to escort it; and there would be very great possibilities, to put it mildly, that this armada would be intercepted long before it reached the coast, and all the men drowned in the sea, or, at the worst, blown to pieces with their equipment while trying to land.

* * *

As early as the end of June some reports indicated that the enemy's plans might include the Channel, and I immediately called for inquiry.

Prime Minister to General Ismay   27.VI.40

It seems difficult to believe that any large force of transports could be brought to the Channel ports without our being aware of it, or that any system of mining would prevent our sweepers from clearing a way for attack on such transports on passage. However, it would be well if the Chiefs of Staff gave their attention to this rumour.

Anyhow, the possibility of a cross-Channel invasion, improbable though it was at that time, had to be most closely examined. I was not entirely satisfied with the military dispositions. It was imperative that the Army should know the exact task assigned to it, and above all should not fritter away strength in a sedentary dispersion along the threatened coasts or exhaust the national resources by manning unduly all the coasts. Therefore I wrote:

Prime Minister to General Ismay   28.VI.40

NOTE BY THE PRIME MINISTER TO C.O.S. COMMITTEE

1. See papers by Vice-Chiefs of Staff and further papers by C.O.S. Committee.

2. It is prudent to block off likely sections of the beaches with a good defence and to make secure all creeks and harbours on the east coast. The south coast is less immediately dangerous. No serious invasion is possible without a harbour with its quays, etc. No one can tell, should the Navy fail, on what part of the east coast the impact will fall. Perhaps there will be several lodgments. Once these are made all troops employed on other parts of the coastal crust will be as useless as those in the Maginot Line. Although fighting on the beaches is favourable to the defence, this advantage cannot be purchased by trying to guard all the beaches. The process must be selective. But if time permits defended sectors may be widened and improved.

3. Every effort should be made to man coast defences with sedentary troops, well sprinkled with experienced late-war officers. The safety of the country depends [however] on having a large number (now only nine, but should soon be fifteen) of "Leopard" brigade groups which can be directed swiftly, *i.e.*, within four hours, to the points of lodgment. Difficulties of landing on beaches are serious, even when the invader has reached them; but difficulties of nourishing a lodgment when exposed to heavy attack by land, air, and sea are far greater. All therefore depends on rapid, resolute engagement of any landed forces which may slip through the sea control. This should not be beyond our means provided the field troops are not consumed in beach defences, and are kept in a high condition of mobility, crouched and ready to spring.

4. In the unhappy event of the enemy capturing a port, larger formations with artillery will be necessary. There should be four or five good divisions held in general reserve to deal with such an improbable misfortune. The scale of lodgment to be anticipated should be not more than ten thousand men landed at three points simultaneously—say thirty thousand in all; the scale of air attack not more than fifteen thousand landed simultaneously at two or three points in all. The enemy will not have strength to repeat such descents often. It is very doubtful whether air-borne troops can be landed in force by night; by day they should be an easy prey [to our Air Force].

5. The tank story is somewhat different, and it is right to minimise by local cannon and obstacles the landing-places of tanks. The Admiralty should report upon the size, character, and speed of potential tank-carrying barges or floats, whether they will be self-propelled or towed and by what craft. As they can hardly go above seven miles

251

an hour they should be detected in summer-time after they have started, and even in fog or haze the R.D.F. stations should give warning while they are still several hours from land. The destroyers issuing from the sally-ports must strike at these with gusto. The arrangement of stops and blocks held by local sedentary forces should be steadily developed, and anti-tank squads formed. Our own tank reserve must engage the surviving invader tanks, and no doubt it is held in a position which allows swift railing [transport by rail] to the attacked area.

6. Parachutists, Fifth-Columnists, and enemy motor-cyclists who may penetrate or appear in disguise in unexpected places must be left to the Home Guard, reinforced by special squads. Much thought must be given to the [enemy] trick of wearing British uniform.

7. In general I find myself in agreement with the Commander-in-Chief's plan, but all possible field troops must be saved from the beaches and gathered into the "Leopard" brigades and other immediate mobile supports. Emphasis should be laid upon the main reserve. The battle will be won or lost, not on the beaches, but by the mobile brigades and the main reserve. Until the Air Force is worn down by prolonged air fighting and destruction of aircraft supply the power of the Navy remains decisive against any serious invasion.

8. The above observations apply only to the immediate summer months. We must be much better equipped and stronger before the autumn.

In July there was growing talk and anxiety on the subject both inside the British Government and at large. In spite of ceaseless reconnaissance and all the advantages of air photography, no evidence had yet reached us of large assemblies of transport in the Baltic or in the Rhine or Scheldt harbours, and we were sure that no movement either of shipping or self-propelled barges through the Straits into the Channel had taken place. Nevertheless preparation to resist invasion was the supreme task before us all, and intense thought was devoted to it throughout our war circle and Home Command.

INVASION

NOTE BY THE PRIME MINISTER

Prime Minister to C.-in-C. Home Forces, C.I.G.S., and
General Ismay   10.VII.40

1. I find it very difficult to visualise the kind of invasion all along the coast by troops carried in small craft, and even in boats. I have not seen any serious evidence of large masses of this class of craft being

assembled, and, except in very narrow waters, it would be a most hazardous and even suicidal operation to commit a large army to the accidents of the sea in the teeth of our very numerous armed patrolling forces. The Admiralty have over a thousand armed patrolling vessels, of which two or three hundred are always at sea, the whole being well manned by competent seafaring men. A surprise crossing should be impossible, and in the broader parts of the North Sea the invaders should be an easy prey, as part of their voyage would be made by daylight. Behind these patrolling craft are the flotillas of destroyers, of which forty destroyers are now disposed between the Humber and Portsmouth, the bulk being in the narrowest waters. The greater part of these are at sea every night, and rest in the day. They would therefore probably encounter the enemy vessels in transit during the night, but also could reach any landing-point or points on the front mentioned in two or three hours. They could immediately break up the landing-craft, interrupt the landing, and fire upon the landed troops, who, however lightly equipped, would have to have some proportion of ammunition and equipment carried on to the beaches from their boats. The flotillas would however need strong air support from our fighter aircraft during their intervention from dawn onwards. The provision of the air fighter escort for our destroyers after daybreak is essential to their most powerful intervention on the beaches.

2. You should see the Commander-in-Chief's (Home Fleet) reply to the question put to him by the desire of the Cabinet, *i.e.*, what happens if the enemy cover the passage of their invading army with their heavy warships? The answer is that, as far as we know at present, they have no heavy ships not under long repair, except those at Trondheim,* which are closely watched by our very largely superior forces. When the *Nelson* and *Barham* are worked up after refit in a few days' time (the 13th and 16th), it would be easily possible to make two forces of British heavy ships, either of which would be sufficiently strong; thus the danger of a northern outbreak could be contained, and at the same time a dart to the south by the Trondheim ships could be rapidly countered. Moreover, the cruisers in the Thames and Humber are themselves strong enough, with the flotillas, to attack effectively any light cruisers with which the enemy could cover an invasion. I feel therefore that it will be very difficult for the enemy to place large well-equipped bodies of troops on the east coast of England, whether in formed bodies or flung piecemeal on the beaches as they get across. Even greater difficulties would attend expeditions in larger vessels seeking to break out to the northward. It may further be added that at

---

* Actually the *Scharnhorst* and *Gneisenau*, which had been at Trondheim, had both been torpedoed and were out of action.

present there are no signs of any assemblies of ships or small craft sufficient to cause anxiety, except perhaps in Baltic ports. Frequent reconnaissance by the air and the constant watching by our submarines should give timely warning, and our minefields are an additional obstruction.

3. Even more unlikely is it that the south coast would be attacked. We know that no great mass of shipping exists in the French ports, and that the numbers of small boats there are not great. The Dover barrage is being replenished and extended to the French shore. This measure is of the utmost consequence, and the Admiralty are being asked to press it forward constantly and rapidly. *They do not think that any important vessels, warships or transports, have come through the Straits of Dover.* Therefore I find it difficult to believe that the south coast is in serious danger at the present time. Of course a small raid might be made upon Ireland from Brest. But this also would be dangerous to the raiders while at sea.

4. The main danger is from the Dutch and German harbours, which bear principally upon the coast from Dover to the Wash. As the nights lengthen this danger zone will extend northwards, but then, again, the weather becomes adverse and the "fishing-boat invasion" far more difficult. Moreover, with cloud the enemy air support may be lacking at the moment of his impact.

5. I hope therefore, relying on the above reasoning, which should be checked with the Admiralty, that you will be able *to bring an ever larger proportion of your formed divisions back from the coast into support or reserve, so that their training may proceed in the highest forms of offensive warfare and counter-attack,* and that the coast, as it becomes fortified, will be increasingly confided to troops other than those of the formed divisions, and also to the Home Guard. I am sure you will be in agreement with this view in principle, and the only question open would be the speed of the transformation. Here too I hope we shall be agreed that the utmost speed shall rule.

6. Air-borne attack is not dealt with in this note. It does not alter its conclusions.

★   ★   ★

It will be noted that my advisers and I deemed the east coast more likely to be attacked during July and August than the south coast. There was in fact no chance of either assault during these two months. As will presently be described, the German plan was to invade across the Channel with medium ships (4,000 to 5,000 tons) and small craft, and we now know that they never had any hope or intention of moving an army from the Baltic and North Sea ports in large transports; still less did they make any plans for an invasion from the Biscay ports. This does not mean that in choosing the south coast as their target they were thinking rightly and we wrongly. The east coast invasion was by far the more formidable if the enemy had had the means to attempt it. There could of course be no south coast invasion unless or until the necessary shipping had passed southwards through the Straits of Dover and had been assembled in the French Channel ports. Of this, during July, there was no sign.

We had none the less to prepare against all variants, and yet at the same time avoid the dispersion of our mobile forces, and to gather reserves. This nice and difficult problem could only be solved in relation to the news and events from week to week. The British coastline, indented with innumerable inlets, is over two thousand miles in circumference, without including Ireland. The only way of defending so vast a perimeter, any part or parts of which may be simultaneously or successively attacked, is by lines of observation and resistance around the coast or frontiers with the object of delaying an enemy, and meanwhile creating the largest possible reserves of highly-trained mobile troops so disposed as to be able to reach any point assailed in the shortest time for strong counter-attack. When in the last phases of the war Hitler found himself encircled and confronted with a similar problem he made, as we shall see, the gravest possible mistakes in handling it. He had created a spider's web of communications, *but he forgot the spider.* With the example of the unsound French dispositions for which such a fatal penalty had just been exacted fresh in our memories, we did not forget the "mass of manœuvre"; and I ceaselessly inculcated this policy to the utmost extent that our growing resources would allow.

The views in my paper of July 10 were in general harmony with Admiralty thought, and two days later Admiral Pound sent me a full and careful statement which he and the Naval Staff had drawn up in pursuance of it. Naturally and properly, the dangers we had to meet were forcefully stated.

But in summing up Admiral Pound said: *"It appears probable that a total of some hundred thousand men might reach these shores without being intercepted by naval forces* . . . but the maintenance of their line of supply, unless the German Air Force had overcome both our Air Force and our Navy, seems practically impossible.

... If the enemy undertook this operation he would do so in the hope that he could make a quick rush on London, living on the country as he went, and force the Government to capitulate." The First Sea Lord divided the hundred-thousand maximum figure both as to enemy ports of departure and the possible impact on our coasts as in the following table:

South coast from Bay of Biscay ports	20,000
South coast from Channel ports	5,000
East coast from Dutch and Belgian ports	12,000
East coast from German ports	50,000
Shetlands, Iceland, and coast of Scotland from Norwegian ports	10,000
	97,000

I was content with this estimate. As the enemy could not bring heavy weapons with them, and would speedily have the supply lines of any lodgments cut, the invading strength seemed even in July to be well within the capacity of our rapidly-improving Army. I remitted the two documents to the Staffs and Home Command.

MINUTE BY THE PRIME MINISTER   15.VII.40

The Chiefs of Staff and Home Defence should consider these papers. The First Sea Lord's memorandum may be taken as a working basis, and although I personally believe that the Admiralty will in fact be better than their word, and that the invaders' losses in transit would further reduce the scale of attack, yet the preparations of the land forces should be such as to make assurance doubly sure. *Indeed, for the land forces the scale of attack might well be doubled, namely, 200,000 men distributed as suggested [i.e., in the proportion suggested] by the First Sea Lord.* Our Home Army is already at a strength when it should be able to deal with such an invasion, and its strength is rapidly increasing.

I should be very glad if our plans to meet invasion on shore could be reviewed on this basis, so that the Cabinet may be informed of any modifications. It should be borne in mind that although the heaviest attack would seem likely to fall in the north, *yet the sovereign importance of London and the narrowness of the seas in this quarter make the south the theatre where the greatest precautions must be taken.*

There was general acceptance of this basis, and for the next few weeks we proceeded upon it. Upon the action to be taken

39 Hitler and his generals in July 1940. From left to right: Keitel, von Rundstedt,
   von Bock, Goering, von Brauchitsch, Ritter von Leeb, List, von Kluge, von
   Witsleben, von Reichenau.
40 The armistice is signed the 22nd June, 1940 at Compiègne.

41 De Gaulle broadcasting from London his famous appeal to the French people, 18th June, 1940.

42 Churchill broadcasting over the B.B.C.: "I have nothing to offer but blood, sweat and tears."

43 The Reynaud government of June 6th, 1940 (at the extreme right, General de Gaulle).
44 The first Pétain government: at Pétain's right Pierre Laval and at his left General Weygand.

by our main Fleet in the narrow waters precise orders were issued with which I was in full agreement. On July 20, after considerable discussion with Admiral Forbes, the Commander-in-Chief, the following decisions were promulgated by the Admiralty:

(i) Their Lordships do not expect our heavy ships to go south to break up an expedition landing on our coast in the absence of any reports indicating the presence of enemy heavy ships.
(ii) If enemy heavy ships support an expedition, accepting the risks involved in an approach to our coast in the southern part of the North Sea, then it is essential that our heavy ships should move south against them, also accepting risks.

In order to reach more definite conclusions about the varying probabilities and scales of attack on our extended coastline, so as to avoid undue spreading of our forces, I sent the Chiefs of Staff a further minute early in August.

DEFENCE AGAINST INVASION

MINUTE BY THE PRIME MINISTER AND MINISTER OF DEFENCE

5.VIII.40

Bearing in mind the immense cost in war energy and the disadvantages of attempting to defend the whole coast of Great Britain, and the dangers of being unduly committed to systems of passive defence, I should be glad if the following notes could be considered:

1. Our first line of defence against invasion must be as ever the enemy's ports. Air reconnaissance, submarine watching, and other means of obtaining information should be followed by resolute attacks with all our forces available and suitable upon any concentrations of enemy shipping.

2. Our second line of defence is the vigilant patrolling of the sea to intercept any invading expedition, and to destroy it in transit.

3. Our third line is the counter-attack upon the enemy when he makes any landfall, and particularly while he is engaged in the act of landing. This attack, which has long been ready from the sea, must be reinforced by air action; and both sea and air attacks must be continued so that it becomes impossible for the invader to nourish his lodgments.

4. The land defences and the Home Army are maintained primarily for the purpose of making the enemy come in such large numbers as to afford a proper target to the sea and air forces above mentioned, and

to make hostile preparations and movements noticeable to air and other forms of reconnaissance.

5. However, should the enemy succeed in landing at various points, he should be made to suffer as much as possible by local resistance on the beaches, combined with the aforesaid attack from the sea and the air. This forces him to use up his ammunition, and confines him to a limited area. The defence of any part of the coast must be measured, not by the forces on the coast, but by the number of hours within which strong counter-attacks by mobile troops can be brought to bear upon the landing-places. Such attacks should be hurled with the utmost speed and fury upon the enemy at his weakest moment, which is not, as is sometimes suggested, when actually getting out of his boats, but when sprawled upon the shore with his communications cut and his supplies running short. It ought to be possible to concentrate ten thousand men fully equipped within six hours, and twenty thousand men within twelve hours, upon any point where a serious lodgment has been effected. The withholding of the reserves until the full gravity of the attack is known is a nice problem for the Home Command.

6. It must be admitted that the task of the Navy and Air Force in preventing invasion becomes more difficult in the Narrow Seas, namely, from the Wash to Dover. This sector of the coast front is also nearest to the supreme enemy objective, London. The sector from Dover to Land's End is far less menaced, because the Navy and Air Force must make sure that no mass of shipping, still less protecting warships, can be passed into the French Channel ports. At present the scale of attack on this wide front is estimated by the Admiralty at no more than five thousand men.* Doubling this for greater security, it should be possible to make good arrangements for speedy counter-attack in superior numbers, and at the same time to achieve large economies of force on this southern sector, in which the beach troops should be at their minimum and the mobile reserves at their maximum. These mobile reserves must be available to move to the south-eastern sectors at short notice. *Evidently this situation can be judged only from week to week.*

7. When we come to the west coast of Britain, a new set of conditions rules. The enemy must commit himself to the broad seas, and there will be plenty of time, if his approach is detected, to attack him with cruisers and flotillas. The Admiralty dispositions should conform to this need. The enemy has at present no warships to escort him. Should we, for instance, care to send twelve thousand men unescorted in merchant ships to land on the Norwegian coast, or in the Skagerrak

* Here I omitted to mention the 20,000 which might come from the distant Biscay ports; but, as will be seen, my proposed disposition of our forces guarded against this potential but, as we now know, non-existent danger.

and Kattegat, in face of superior sea-power and air-power? It would be thought madness.

8. However, to make assurance triply sure, the Admiralty should pursue their plan of laying a strong minefield from Cornwall to Ireland, covering the Bristol Channel and the Irish Sea from southward attack. This minefield is all the more necessary now that by the adoption of the northabout route for commerce we have transferred a large part of our patrolling craft from the [South-] Western Approaches, which have become permanently more empty and unwatched.

9. The establishment of this minefield will simplify and mitigate all questions of local defence north of its point of contact with Cornwall. We must consider this sector from Cornwall to the Mull of Kintyre as the least vulnerable to sea-borne invasion. Here the works of defence should be confined to guarding by a few guns or land torpedo-tubes the principal harbours, and giving a moderate scale of protection to their gorges.* It is not admissible to lavish our limited resources upon this sector.

10. North of the Mull of Kintyre to Scapa Flow, the Shetlands, and the Faroes, all lies in the orbit of the main Fleet. The voyage of an expedition from the Norwegian coast would be very hazardous, and its arrival anywhere right round to Cromarty Firth would not raise immediately decisive issues. The enemy, who is now crouched, would then be sprawled. His advance would lie in difficult and sparsely-inhabited country. He could be contained until sufficient forces were brought to bear, and his communications immediately cut from the sea. This would make his position all the more difficult, as the distances to any important objective are much longer and he would require con-siderable wheeled transport. It would be impossible to fortify all landing-points in this sector, and it would be a waste of energy to attempt to do so. A much longer period may be allowed for counter-attack than in the south-east, opposite London.

11. From Cromarty Firth to the Wash is the second most important sector, ranking next after the Wash to Dover. Here however all the harbours and inlets are defended, both from the sea and from the rear, and it should be possible to counter-attack in superior force within twenty-four hours. The Tyne must be regarded as the second major objective after London, for here (and to a lesser extent at the Tees) grievous damage could be done by an invader or large-scale raider in a short time. On the other hand, the sea and air conditions are more favourable to us than to the southward.

12. The combined Staffs should endeavour to assign to all these sectors their relative scales of vulnerability and defence, both in the

---

* *I.e.*, their approaches from the rear.

number of men employed in the local defence of beaches and of harbours, and also in the number of days or hours within which heavy counter-attacks should be possible. As an indication of these relative scales of attack and defence, I set down for consideration the following:

Cromarty Firth to Wash inclusive*	3
Wash to Dover promontory	5
Dover promontory to Land's End, and round to start of minefield	$1\frac{1}{2}$
Start of minefield to the Mull of Kintyre	$\frac{1}{4}$
Mull of Kintyre northabout to Cromarty Firth	$\frac{1}{2}$

The Chiefs of Staff Committee, after another review of all our information, replied to this paper by a report from Colonel Hollis, who acted as their secretary.

DEFENCE AGAINST INVASION

Prime Minister 13.VIII.40

1. The Chiefs of Staff have examined, in consultation with the Commander-in-Chief Home Forces, your minute [of August 5], and find themselves in complete agreement with the principles enunciated in paragraphs 1 to 5.

2. The Commander-in-Chief assures us that the paramount importance of immediate counter-attack upon the enemy, should he obtain a temporary footing on these shores, has been impressed on all ranks, and that it is his policy to bring back divisions into reserve as soon as they are adequately trained and equipped for offensive operations.

3. The Chiefs of Staff also agree with your assessment of the relative scales of vulnerability to sea-borne attack of the various sectors of the coast. Indeed, it is remarkable how closely the present distribution of Home Defence divisions corresponds with your figures in paragraph 12. This is worked out as follows:

4. Your theoretical scales of defence are:

Cromarty Firth to Wash	3
Wash to Dover	5
Dover to North Cornwall	$1\frac{1}{2}$
North Cornwall to Mull of Kintyre	$\frac{1}{4}$
Mull of Kintyre to Cromarty Firth	$\frac{1}{2}$
Total	$10\frac{1}{4}$

* These are, of course, *proportions*, not divisional formations.

5. A force of ten divisions, if distributed in the above proportions, would give three divisions on Sector Forth–Wash, five divisions on Sector Wash–Dover, and so on. There are in fact twenty-six divisions in this Island, and, if your figures are multiplied by 2.6 and compared with actual distribution of these twenty-six divisions, the following picture results:

Sector	Distribution in accordance with Prime Minister's assessment of vulnerability	Actual distribution of divisions
Cromarty–Wash	$7\frac{1}{2}$	$8\frac{1}{2}$
Wash–Dover	$12\frac{1}{2}$	7–10
Dover–North Cornwall	$4\frac{1}{4}$	5–8
North Cornwall–Mull of Kintyre	$\frac{1}{2}$	2
Mull of Kintyre–Cromarty ..	$1\frac{1}{4}$	$\frac{1}{2}$

6. The similarity between the two sets of figures is even closer than appears at first sight, by reason of the fact that the reserve divisions located immediately north and north-west of London are available for deployment in either the Sector Wash–Dover or the Sector Dover–Portsmouth, and therefore the number of "available" divisions for these two sectors is variable. A total of fifteen divisions is available on the combined sectors against your suggested requirements of sixteen and three-quarters.

7. The Chiefs of Staff point out that your figures are based on scales of sea-borne attack, whereas the actual distribution takes into account the threat from air-borne attack as well. Thus although we may seem at present to be slightly over-insured along the south coast, the reason for this is that our defences there can be brought under the enemy fighter "umbrella" and can be subjected to assault across the Channel at comparatively short range.

* * *

Even while these documents were being considered and printed the situation had begun to change in a decisive manner. Our excellent Intelligence confirmed that the operation "Sea Lion" had been definitely ordered by Hitler and was in active preparation. It seemed certain that the man was going to try. Moreover, the front to be attacked was altogether different from *or additional to* the east coast, on which the Chiefs of Staff, the Admiralty and I, in full agreement, still laid the major emphasis.

But thereafter came a rapid transformation. A large number of self-propelled barges and motor-boats began to pass by night through the Straits of Dover, creeping along the French coast and gradually assembling in all the French Channel ports from Calais to Brest. Our daily photographs showed this movement with precision. It had not been found possible to re-lay our minefields close to the French shore. We immediately began to attack the vessels in transit with our small craft, and Bomber Command was concentrated upon the new set of invasion ports now opening upon us. At the same time a great deal of information came to hand about the assembly of a German Army or Armies of Invasion along this stretch of the hostile coast, of movement on the railways, and of large concentrations in the Pas de Calais and Normandy. Later on two mountain divisions with mules, evidently meant to scale the Folkestone cliffs, were reported near Boulogne. Meanwhile large numbers of powerful long-range batteries all along the French Channel coast came into existence.

In response to the new menace we began to shift our weight from one leg to the other and to improve all our facilities for moving our increasingly large mobile reserves towards the southern front. About the end of the first week of August General Brooke, now Commander-in-Chief Home Forces, pointed out that the threat of invasion was developing on the south coast as much as on the east. All the time our forces were increasing in numbers, efficiency, mobility, and equipment.

* * *

The change in our dispositions between August and September was as follows:

	AUGUST	SEPTEMBER
Wash–Thames	7 divisions	4 divisions plus 1 armoured brigade
South Coast	5 divisions	9 divisions plus 2 armoured brigades
Reserve for either sector	3 divisions	3 divisions plus 2 armoured divisions, plus 1 division (equivalent) London District
Total available South Coast	8 divisions	13 divisions plus 3 armoured divisions

Thus in the last half of September we were able to bring into action on the south coast front, including Dover, sixteen divisions of high quality, of which three were armoured divisions or their equivalent in brigades, all of which were additional to the local coastal defence and could come into action with great speed against any invasion landing. This provided us with a punch or series of punches which General Brooke was well poised to deliver as might be required; and no one more capable.

* * *

All this while we could not feel any assurance that the inlets and river-mouths from Calais to Terschelling and Heligoland, with all that swarm of islands off the Dutch and German coasts (the "Riddle of the Sands" of the previous war), might not conceal other large hostile forces with small or moderate-sized ships. An attack from Harwich right round to Portsmouth, Portland, or even Plymouth, centring upon the Kent promontory, seemed to impend. We had nothing but negative evidence that a third wave of invasion harmonised with the others might not be launched from the Baltic through the Skaggerak in large ships. This was indeed essential to a German success, because in no other way could heavy weapons reach the landed armies or large depots of supply be established in and around store-ships stranded near the east coast beaches.

We now entered upon a period of extreme tension and vigilance. We had of course all this time to maintain heavy forces north of the Wash, right up to Cromarty; and arrangements were perfected to draw from these should the assault declare itself decidedly in the south. The abundant intricate railway system of the Island and our continued mastery of our home air would have enabled us to move with certainty another four or five divisions to reinforce the southern defence if it were necessary on the fourth, fifth, and sixth days after the enemy's full effort had been exposed.

A very careful study was made of the moon and the tides. We thought that the enemy would like to cross by night and land at dawn; and we now know the German Army Command felt like this too. They would also be glad of a half-moonlight on the way over, so as to keep their order and make their true landfall. Measuring it all with precision, the Admiralty thought the most favourable conditions for the enemy would arise between the 15th and 30th of September. Here also we now find that we were in agreement with our foes. We had little doubt of our ability to destroy anything that got ashore on the Dover promontory or on the sector of coast from Dover to Portsmouth, or even Portland. As all our thoughts at the summit moved together in harmonious and detailed agreement, one could not help liking the picture which presented itself with growing definition. Here perhaps was the chance of striking a blow at the mighty enemy which would resound throughout the world. One could not help being inwardly excited alike by the atmosphere and the evidence of Hitler's intention which streamed in upon us. There were indeed some who on purely technical grounds, and for the sake of the effect the total defeat and destruction of his expedition would have on the general war, were quite content to see him try.

In July and August we had asserted air mastery over Great Britain, and were especially powerful and dominant over the Home Counties of the south-east. The Canadian Army Corps stood most conveniently posted between London and Dover. Their bayonets were sharp and their hearts were high. Proud would they have been to strike the decisive blow for Britain and Freedom. Similar passions burned in all breasts. Vast intricate systems of fortifications, defended localities, anti-tank obstacles, block-houses, pill-boxes, and the like laced the whole area. The coastline bristled with defences and batteries, and at the cost of heavier losses through reduced escorts in the Atlantic, and also by new construction coming into commission, the flotillas grew substantially in numbers and quality. We had brought the battleship *Revenge*, and the old target-ship and dummy-battle-ship *Centurion*, and a cruiser to Plymouth. The Home Fleet was at its maximum strength and could operate without much risk to the Humber and even to the Wash. In all respects therefore we were fully prepared.

Finally, we were already not far from the equinoctial gales customary in October. Evidently September was the month for Hitler to strike if he dared, and the tides and the moon-phase were favourable in the middle of that month.

* * *

There was some talk in Parliament after the danger had passed away of the "invasion scare". Certainly those who knew most were the least scared. Apart from mastery of the air and command of the sea, we had as large (if not so well equipped) an army, fresh and ardent, as that which Germany assembled in Normandy four years later to oppose our return to the Continent. In that case, although we landed a million men in the first month, with vast apparatus, and with every other condition favourable, the battle was long and severe, and nearly three months were required to enlarge the area originally seized and break out into the open field. But these were values only to be tested and known in the future.

* * *

It is time to go over to the other camp and set forth the enemy's preparations and plans as we now know them.

CHAPTER XV

OPERATION "SEA LION"

Plan of the German Admiralty – Their Conditions Met by the Conquest of France and the Low Countries – Heads of the Services' Meeting with the Fuehrer of July 21 – Hitler Comprehends the Difficulties but Gives the Order – Controversy between the German Navy and Army Staffs – Raeder and Halder at Variance – The Compromise Plan Agreed – Further Misgivings of the German Admiralty – Both German Navy and Army Chiefs Cast the Burden on Goering and the Air – Goering Accepts – Hitler Postpones D-Day – British Counteractivities – The "Cromwell" Order of September 7 – A Healthy Tonic – German Ignorance of Amphibious Warfare – Service Disunion – The Germans Stake All on the Air Battle.

SOON after war broke out on September 3, 1939, the German Admiralty, as we have learned from their captured archives, began their Staff study of the invasion of Britain. Unlike us, they had no doubt that the only way was across the narrow waters of the English Channel. They never considered any other alternative. If we had known this it would have been an important relief. An invasion across the Channel came upon our best-defended coast, the old sea front against France, where all the ports were fortified and our main flotilla bases and in later times most of our airfields and air-control stations for the defence of London were established. There was no part of the Island where we could come into action more quickly or in such great strength with all three Services. Admiral Raeder was anxious not to be found wanting should the demand to invade Britain be made upon the German Navy. At the same time he asked for a lot of conditions. The first of these was the entire control of the French, Belgian, and Dutch coasts, harbours, and river-mouths. Therefore the project slumbered during the Twilight War.

Suddenly all these conditions were surprisingly fulfilled, and it must have been with some misgivings but also satisfaction that on the morrow of Dunkirk and the French surrender he could present himself to the Fuehrer with a plan. On May 21 and again on June 20 he spoke to Hitler on the subject, not with a view to proposing an invasion, but in order to make sure that if it were ordered the planning in detail should not be rushed. Hitler was sceptical, saying that "he fully appreciated the exceptional difficulties of such an undertaking". He also nursed the hope that England would sue for peace. It was not until the last week in June that the Supreme Headquarters turned to this idea, nor till July 2 that the first directive was issued for planning the invasion of Britain as a possible event. "The Fuehrer has decided that under certain conditions—the most important of which is achieving air superiority—a landing in England may take place." On July 16 Hitler issued his directive: "Since England in spite of her militarily hopeless position shows no sign of coming to terms, I have decided to prepare a landing operation against England, and if necessary to carry it out. . . . The preparations for the entire operation must be completed by mid-August." Active measures in every direction were already in progress.

* * *

The German Navy plan, of which it is clear I had received an inkling in June, was essentially mechanical. Under the cover of heavy-gun batteries firing from Gris-Nez towards Dover, and a very strong artillery protection along the French coast in the Straits, they proposed to make a narrow corridor across the Channel on the shortest convenient line and to wall this in by minefields on either side, with outlying U-boat protection. Through this the Army was to be ferried over and supplied in a large number of successive waves. There the Navy stopped, and on this the German Army chiefs were left to address themselves to the problem.

Considering that we could, with our overwhelming naval superiority, tear these minefields to pieces with small craft under superior air-power and also destroy the dozen or score of U-boats concentrated to protect them, this was at the outset a bleak proposition. Nevertheless, after the fall of France anyone could see that the only hope of avoiding a long war, with all that it might entail, was to bring Britain to her knees. The German Navy itself had been, as we have recorded, knocked about in a most serious manner in the fighting off Norway; and in their crippled condition they could not offer more than minor support to the Army. Still, they had their plan, and no one could say that they had been caught unawares by good fortune.

The German Army Command had from the first regarded the invasion of England with considerable qualms. They had made no plans or preparations for it; and there had been no training. As the weeks of prodigious, delirious victory succeeded one another they were emboldened. The responsibility for the safe crossing was not departmentally theirs, and, once landed in strength, they felt that the task was within their power. Indeed, already in August Admiral Raeder felt it necessary to draw their attention to the dangers of the passage, during which perhaps the whole of the Army forces employed might be lost. Once the responsibility for putting the Army across was definitely thrust upon the Navy, the German Admiralty became consistently pessimistic.

On July 21 the heads of the three Services met the Fuehrer. He informed them that the decisive stage of the war had already been reached, but that England had not yet recognised it and still hoped for a turn of fate. He spoke of the support of England by the United States and of a possible change in German political relations with Soviet Russia. The execution of "Sea Lion", he said, must be regarded as the most effective means of bringing about a rapid conclusion of the war. After his long talks with Admiral Raeder, Hitler had begun to realise what the crossing of the Channel, with its tides and currents, and all the mysteries of the sea, involved. He described "Sea Lion" as "an exceptionally bold and daring undertaking". "Even if the way is short, this is not just a river crossing, but the crossing of a sea which is dominated by the enemy. This is not a case of a single-crossing operation, as in Norway; operational surprise cannot be expected; a defensively-prepared *and utterly determined enemy* faces us and dominates the sea area which we must use. For the Army operation forty divisions will be required. The most difficult part will be the material reinforcements and stores. We cannot count on supplies of any kind being available to us in England." The prerequisites were complete mastery of the air, the operational use

of powerful artillery in the Dover straits, and protection by
minefields. "The time of year," he said, "is an important factor,
since the weather in the North Sea and in the Channel during the
second half of September is very bad, and the fogs begin in the
middle of October. The main operation must therefore be completed by September 15, for after that date co-operation between
the Luftwaffe and the heavy weapons becomes too unreliable.
But as air co-operation is decisive it must be regarded as the
principal factor in fixing the date."

A vehement controversy, conducted with no little asperity,
arose in the German Staffs about the width of the front and the
number of points to be attacked. The Army demanded a series
of landings along the whole English southern coast from Dover to
Lyme Regis, west of Portland. They also desired an ancillary
landing north of Dover at Ramsgate. The German Naval Staff
now stated that the most suitable area for the safe crossing of the
English Channel was between the North Foreland and the western
end of the Isle of Wight. On this the Army Staff developed a
plan for a landing of 100,000 men, followed almost immediately
by 160,000 more at various points from Dover westward to
Lyme Bay. Colonel-General Halder, Chief of the Army Staff,
declared that it was necessary to land at least four divisions in the
Brighton area. He also required landings in the area Deal-
Ramsgate; at least thirteen divisions must be deployed, as far as
possible simultaneously, at points along the whole front. In
addition, the Luftwaffe demanded shipping to transport fifty-two
A.A. batteries with the first wave.

The Chief of the Naval Staff however made it clear that
nothing like so large or rapid a movement was possible. He
could not physically undertake to escort a landing fleet across the
whole width of the area mentioned. All he had meant was that
within these limits the Army should pick the best place. The
Navy had not enough strength, even with air supremacy, to
protect more than one passage at a time, and they thought the
narrowest parts of the Straits of Dover the least difficult. To carry
the whole of the 160,000 men of the second wave and their
equipment in a single operation would require two million tons
of shipping. Even if this fantastic requirement could have been
met, such quantities of shipping could not have been accommodated in the area of embarkation. Only the first échelons

could be thrown across for the formation of narrow bridgeheads, and at least two days would be needed to land the second échelons of these divisions, to say nothing of the second six divisions which were thought indispensable. He further pointed out that a broad-front landing would mean three to five and a half hours' difference in the times of high water at the various points selected. Either therefore unfavourable tide conditions must be accepted at some places, or simultaneous landings renounced. This objection must have been very difficult to answer.

Much valuable time had been consumed in these exchanges of memoranda. It was not until August 7 that the first verbal discussion took place between General Halder and the Chief of the Naval Staff. At this meeting Halder said: "I utterly reject the Navy's proposals. From the Army view-point I regard it as complete suicide. I might just as well put the troops that have been landed straight through the sausage-machine." The Naval Chief of Staff rejoined that he must equally reject the landing on a broad front, as that would lead only to a sacrifice of the troops on the passage over. In the end a compromise decision was given by Hitler which satisfied neither the Army nor the Navy. A Supreme Command Directive, issued on August 27, decided that "the Army operations must allow for the facts regarding available shipping space and security of the crossing and disembarkation". All landings in the Deal–Ramsgate area were abandoned, but the front was extended from Folkestone to Bognor. Thus it was nearly the end of August before even this measure of agreement was reached; and of course everything was subject to victory being gained in the air battle, which had now been raging for six weeks.

On the basis of the frontage at last fixed the final plan was made. The military command was entrusted to Rundstedt, but shortage of shipping reduced his force to thirteen divisions with twelve in reserve. The Sixteenth Army, from ports between Rotterdam and Boulogne, were to land in the neighbourhood of Hythe, Rye, Hastings, and Eastbourne, the Ninth Army, from ports between Boulogne and Havre, attacking between Brighton and Worthing. Dover was to be captured from the landward side; then both armies would advance to the covering line of Canterbury-Ashford-Mayfield-Arundel. In all, eleven divisions were to be landed in the first waves. A week after the landing it was hoped, optimistically, to advance yet farther, to Gravesend,

Reigate, Petersfield, Portsmouth. In reserve lay the Sixth Army, with divisions ready to reinforce, or, if circumstances allowed, to extend the frontage of attack to Weymouth. It would have been easy to increase these three armies, once the bridgeheads were gained, "because", says General Halder, "no military forces were facing the Germans on the Continent". There was indeed no lack of fierce and well-armed troops, but they required shipping and safe conveyance.

On the Naval Staff fell the heaviest initial task. Germany had about 1,200,000 tons of seagoing shipping available to meet all her needs. To embark the invasion force would require more than half this amount, and would involve great economic disturbance. By the beginning of September the Naval Staff were able to report that the following had been requisitioned:

> 168 transports (of 700,000 tons)
> 1,910 barges
> 419 tugs and trawlers
> 1,600 motor-boats

All this Armada had to be manned, and brought to the assembly ports by sea and canal. Meanwhile since early July we had made a succession of attacks on the shipping in Wilhelmshaven, Kiel, Cuxhaven, Bremen, and Emden; and raids were made on small craft and barges in French ports and Belgian canals. When on September 1 the great southward flow of invasion shipping began it was watched, reported, and violently assailed by the Royal Air Force along the whole front from Antwerp to Havre. The German Naval Staff recorded: "The enemy's continuous fighting defence off the coast, his concentration of bombers on the 'Sea Lion' embarkation ports, and his coastal reconnaissance activities indicate that he is now expecting an immediate landing."

And again: "The English bombers however and the mine-laying forces of the British Air Force . . . are still at full operational strength, and it must be confirmed that the activity of the British forces has undoubtedly been successful even if no decisive hindrance has yet been caused to German transport movement."

Yet, despite delays and damage, the German Navy completed the first part of its task. The 10 per cent. margin for accidents and losses it had provided was fully expended. What survived however did not fall short of the minimum it had planned to have for the first stage.

Both Navy and Army now cast their burden on the German Air Force. All this plan of the corridor, with its balustrades of minefields to be laid and maintained under the German Air Force canopy against the overwhelming superiority of the British flotillas and small craft, depended upon the defeat of the British Air Force and the complete mastery of the air by Germany over the Channel and South-East England, and not only over the crossing but over the landing-points. Both the older services passed the buck to Reichsmarschall Goering.

Goering was by no means unwilling to accept this responsibility, because he believed that the German Air Force, with its large numerical superiority, would, after some weeks of hard fighting, beat down the British air defence, destroy their airfields in Kent and Sussex, and establish a complete domination of the Channel. But apart from this he felt assured that the bombing of England, and particularly of London, would reduce the decadent, peace-loving British to a condition in which they would sue for peace, more especially if the threat of invasion grew steadily upon their horizon. The German Admiralty were by no means convinced; indeed their misgivings were profound. They considered "Sea Lion" should be launched only in the last resort, and in July they had recommended the postponement of the operation till the spring of 1941, unless *the unrestricted air attack and the unlimited U-boat warfare* should "cause the enemy to negotiate with the Fuehrer on his own terms". But Feldmarschall Keitel and General Jodl were glad to find the Air Supreme Commander so confident.

These were great days for Nazi Germany. Hitler had danced his jig of joy before enforcing the humiliation of the French Armistice at Compiègne. The German Army marched triumphantly through the Arc de Triomphe and down the Champs Elysées. What was there they could not do? Why hesitate to play out a winning hand? Thus each of the three services involved in the operation "Sea Lion" worked upon the hopeful factors in their own theme and left the ugly side to their companions.

As the days passed doubts and delays appeared and multiplied. Hitler's order of July 16 had laid down that all preparations were to be completed by the middle of August. All three services

SKETCH MAP OF GERMAN INVASION PLAN

saw that this was impossible. And at the end of July Hitler accepted September 15 as the earliest D-Day, reserving his decision for action until the results of the projected intensified air battle could be known.

On August 30 the Naval Staff reported that owing to British counter-action against the invasion fleet preparations could not be completed by September 15. At their request D-Day was postponed to September 21, with a proviso of ten days' previous warning. This meant that the preliminary order had to be issued on September 11. On September 10 the Naval Staff again reported their various difficulties from the weather, which is always tiresome, and from British counter-bombing. They pointed out that although the necessary naval preparations could in fact be completed by the 21st, the stipulated operational condition of undisputed air superiority over the Channel had not been achieved. On the 11th therefore Hitler postponed the preliminary order by three days, thus setting back the earliest D-Day to the 24th; on the 14th he further put it off.

* * *

On the 14th Admiral Raeder expressed the view that:

(a) The present air situation does not provide conditions for carrying out the operation, as the risk is still too great.

(b) If the "Sea Lion" operation fails, this will mean a great gain in prestige for the British; and the powerful effect of our attacks will thus be annulled.

(c) Air attacks on England, particularly on London, must continue without interruption. If the weather is favourable an intensification of the attacks is to be aimed at, without regard to "Sea Lion". The attacks must have a decisive outcome.

(d) "Sea Lion" however must not yet be cancelled, as the anxiety of the British must be kept up; if cancellation became known to the outside world, this would be a great relief to the British.

On the 17th the postponement became indefinite, and for good reason, in their view as in ours. Raeder continues:

(i) The preparations for a landing on the Channel coast are extensively known to the enemy, who is increasingly taking counter-measures. Symptoms are, for example, operational use of his aircraft for attacks and reconnaissances over the German operational harbours, frequent appearance of destroyers off the south coast of England, in the Straits of Dover and on the Franco-Belgian coast, stationing of his patrol vessels off the north coast of France, Churchill's last speech, etc.

(ii) The main units of the Home Fleet are being held in readiness to repel the landing, though the majority of the units are still in western bases.

(iii) Already a large number of destroyers (over thirty) have been located by air reconnaissance in the southern and south-eastern harbours.

(iv) All available information indicates that the enemy's naval forces are solely occupied with this theatre of operations.

* * *

During August the corpses of about forty German soldiers were washed up at scattered points along the coast between the Isle of Wight and Cornwall. The Germans had been practising embarkations in the barges along the French coast. Some of these barges put out to sea in order to escape British bombing and were sunk, either by bombing or bad weather. This was the source of a widespread rumour that the Germans had attempted an invasion and had suffered very heavy losses either by drowning or by being burnt in patches of sea covered with flaming oil. We took no steps to contradict such tales, which spread freely through the occupied countries in a wildly exaggerated form and gave much encouragement to the oppressed populations. In Brussels, for instance, a shop exhibited men's bathing-suits marked "For Channel swimming".

On September 7 the information before us showed that the westerly and southerly movement of barges and small ships to ports between Ostend and Havre was in progress, and as these assembly harbours were under heavy British air attack it was not likely the ships would be brought to them until shortly before the actual attempt. The striking strength of the German Air Force between Amsterdam and Brest had been increased by the transfer of one hundred and sixty bomber aircraft from Norway; and short-range dive-bomber units were observed on the forward airfields in the Pas de Calais area. Four Germans captured a few days earlier after landing from a rowing-boat on the south-east coast had confessed to being spies, and said that they were to be ready at any time during the next fortnight to report the movement of British reserve formations in the area Ipswich-London-Reading-Oxford. Moon and tide conditions between the 8th and

10th of September were favourable for invasion on the south-east coast. On this the Chiefs of Staff concluded that the possibility of invasion had become imminent and that the defence forces should stand by at immediate notice.

There was however at that time no machinery at General Headquarters, Home Forces, by which the existing eight hours' notice for readiness could be brought to "readiness for immediate action" by intermediate stages. The code-word "Cromwell", which meant "invasion imminent", was therefore issued by Home Forces at 8 p.m., September 7, to the Eastern and Southern Commands, implying action stations for the forward coastal divisions. It was also sent to all formations in the London area and to the IVth and VIIth Corps in G.H.Q. Reserve. It was repeated for information to all other commands in the United Kingdom. On this, in some parts of the country, the Home Guard commanders, acting on their own initiative, called out the Home Guard by ringing the church bells. This led to rumours of enemy parachutist landings, and also that German E-boats were approaching the coast. Neither I nor the Chiefs of Staff were aware that the decisive code-word "Cromwell" had been used, and the next morning instructions were given to devise intermediate stages by which vigilance could be increased on future occasions without declaring an invasion imminent. Even on receipt of the code-word "Cromwell" the Home Guard were not to be called out except for special tasks; and also church bells were to be rung only by order of a Home Guard who had himself seen as many as twenty-five parachutists landing, and not because other bells had been heard or for any other reason. As may be imagined, this incident caused a great deal of talk and stir, but no mention of it was made in the newspapers or in Parliament. It served as a useful tonic and rehearsal for all concerned.

* * *

Having traced the German invasion preparations steadily mounting to a climax, we have seen how the early mood of triumph changed gradually to one of doubt and finally to complete loss of confidence in the outcome. Confidence was in fact already destroyed in 1940, and, despite the revival of the project in 1941, it never again held the imagination of the German leaders as it had done in the halcyon days following the fall of France.

During the fateful months of July and August we see the Naval Commander, Raeder, endeavouring to teach his military and air colleagues about the grave difficulties attending large-scale amphibious war. He realised his own weakness and the lack of time for adequate preparation, and sought to impose limits on the grandiose plans advanced by Halder for landing immense forces simultaneously over a wide front. Meanwhile Goering with soaring ambition was determined to achieve spectacular victory with his Air Force alone and was disinclined to play the humbler *rôle* of working to a combined plan for the systematic reduction of opposing sea and air forces in the invasion area.

It is apparent from the records that the German High Command were very far from being a co-ordinated team working together with a common purpose and with a proper understanding of each other's capabilities and limitations. Each wished to be the brightest star in the firmament. Friction was apparent from the outset, and so long as Halder could thrust responsibility on to Raeder he did little to bring his own plans into line with practical possibilities. Intervention by the Fuehrer was necessary, but seems to have done little to improve the relations between the services. In Germany the prestige of the Army was paramount and the military leaders regarded their naval colleagues with some condescension. It is impossible to resist the conclusion that the German Army was reluctant to place itself in the hands of its sister service in a major operation. When questioned after the war about these plans, General Jodl impatiently remarked, "Our arrangements were much the same as those of Julius Cæsar". Here speaks the authentic German soldier in relation to the sea affair, having little conception of the problems involved in landing and deploying large military forces on a defended coast exposed to all the hazards of the sea.

In Britain, whatever our shortcomings, we understood the sea affair very thoroughly. For centuries it has been in our blood, and its traditions stir not only our sailors but the whole race. It was this above all things which enabled us to regard the menace of invasion with a steady gaze. The system of control of operations by the three Chiefs of Staff concerted under a Minister of Defence produced a standard of team-work, mutual understanding, and ready co-operation unrivalled in the past. When in course of time our opportunity came to undertake great invasions from the sea it was upon a foundation of solid achievement in preparation for the task and with a full understanding of the technical needs of such vast and hazardous undertakings. Had the Germans possessed in 1940 well-trained amphibious forces equipped with all the apparatus of modern amphibious war their task would still have been a forlorn hope in the face of our sea- and air-power. In fact they had neither the tools nor the training.

* * *

We have seen how our many anxieties and self-questionings led to a steady increase in the confidence with which from the beginning we had viewed the invasion project. On the other hand, the more the German High Command and the Fuehrer looked at the venture the less they liked it. We could not of course know each other's moods and valuations; but with every week from the middle of July to the middle of September the unknown identity of views upon the problem between the German and British Admiralties, between the German Supreme Command and the British Chiefs of Staff, and also between the Fuehrer and the author of this book, became more definitely pronounced. If we could have agreed equally well about other matters there need have been no war. It was of course common ground between us that all depended upon the battle in the air. The question was how this would end between the combatants; and in addition the Germans wondered whether the British people would stand up to the air bombardment, the effect of which in these days was greatly exaggerated, or whether they would crumple and force His Majesty's Government to capitulate. About this Reichsmarschall Goering had high hopes, and we had no fears.

APPENDIX

PRIME MINISTER'S PERSONAL MINUTES AND TELEGRAMS

MAY-AUGUST 1940

MAY

Prime Minister to General Ismay, for those concerned   18.V.40

The proximity fuze and the necessary rocket projectors have hitherto been treated as important protection for ships, but even larger numbers will be needed, even some perhaps more urgently, for the protection of aircraft factories and other exceptionally important points. What is being done about this? Let proposals be made to-morrow for setting up the necessary manufacture. Are any modifications in the design of the projectors necessary? The Director of Naval Ordnance can go on with the ship side of the business, but be careful no hold-up takes place in the supply for the vulnerable points ashore. Report to-morrow night what organisation or measures are required to procure this production.

Prime Minister to Secretary of State for the Colonies   23.V.40

I am in full agreement with the answer you propose to Wedgwood's* Questions, and I do not want Jewish forces raised to serve outside Palestine. The main and almost the sole aim in Palestine at the present time is to liberate the eleven battalions of excellent Regular troops who are now tethered there. For this purpose the Jews should be armed in their own defence, and properly organised as speedily as possible. We can always prevent them from attacking the Arabs by our sea-power, which cuts them off from the outer world, and by other friendly influences. On the other hand, we cannot leave them unarmed when our troops leave, as leave they must at a very early date.

Prime Minister to Minister of Aircraft Production   24.V.40

I should be much obliged if you would have a talk with Lindemann, so as to get at some agreed figures upon aircraft outputs, both recent and prospective. I have for a long time been convinced that the Air Ministry do not make enough of the deliveries with which they are

* Hon. Josiah Wedgwood, M.P.

supplied, and Lindemann is obtaining for me returns of all aircraft in their hands, so that one can see what use is made of them.

It is of the highest importance that all aircraft in storage and reserve should not only be made available for service, but that these should be organised in squadrons with their pilots. Now that the war is coming so close, the object must be to prepare the largest number of aircraft, even, as you said, training and civil aircraft, to carry bombs to enemy aerodromes on the Dutch, Belgian, and French coasts. I must get a full view of the figures, both of delivery and employment, and this can be kept up to date weekly.

Prime Minister to Professor Lindemann   24.V.40

Let me have on one sheet of paper a statement about the tanks. How many have we got with the Army? How many of each kind are being made each month? How many are there with the manufacturers? What are the forecasts? What are the plans for heavier tanks?

NOTE.—The present form of warfare, and the proof that tanks can overrun fortifications, will affect the plans for the "Cultivator", and it seems very likely that only a reduced number will be required.

Prime Minister to Sir Edward Bridges   24.V.40

I am sure there are far too many Committees of one kind and another which Ministers have to attend, and which do not yield a sufficient result. These should be reduced by suppression or amalgamation. Secondly, an effort should be made to reduce the returns with which the Cabinet is oppressed to a smaller compass and smaller number. Pray let proposals be made by the Cabinet Office staff for effecting these simplifications.

Prime Minister to Secretary of State for Air   27.V.40

In your communiqué to-day you distinguish in several cases between enemy aircraft "put out of action" or "destroyed". Is there any real difference between the two, or is it simply to avoid tautology? If so, this is not in accordance with the best authorities on English. Sense should not be sacrificed to sound.

Will you also report to-day whether you would like the weather to be clear or cloudy for the operations on the Belgian coast.

Prime Minister to General Ismay and C.I.G.S.   29.V.40

The change which has come over the war affects decisively the usefulness of "Cultivator No. 6". It may play its part in various operations, defensive and offensive, but it can no longer be considered the only method of breaking a fortified line. I suggest that the Minister of Supply should to-day be instructed to reduce the scheme by one-half. Probably in a few days it will be to one-quarter. The spare available capacity could be turned over to tanks. If the Germans can make tanks in nine months, surely we can do so. Let me have your general proposals for the priority construction of an additional thousand tanks capable of engaging the improved enemy pattern likely to be working in 1941.

There should also be formed, if it does not already exist, an Anti-tank Committee to study and devise all methods of attacking the latest German tanks. Pray let me have suggested list of names.

JUNE

Prime Minister to Sir Edward Bridges   3.VI.40

Has anything been done about shipping twenty thousand internees to Newfoundland or St. Helena? Is this one of the matters that the Lord President has in hand? If so would you please ask him about it. I should like to get them on the high seas as soon as possible, but I suppose considerable arrangements have to be made at the other end. Is it all going forward?

Prime Minister to Secretary of State for Air   3.VI.40

The Cabinet were distressed to hear from you that you were now running short of pilots for fighters, and that they had now become the limiting factor.

This is the first time that this particular admission of failure has been made by the Air Ministry. We know that immense masses of aircraft are devoted to the making of pilots, far beyond the proportion adopted by the Germans. We heard some months ago of many thousands of pilots for whom the Air Ministry declared they had no machines, and who consequently had to be "re-mustered": as many as seven thousand were mentioned, all of whom had done many more hours of flying than those done by German pilots now frequently captured. How then therefore is this new shortage to be explained?

Lord Beaverbrook has made a surprising improvement in the supply and repair of aeroplanes, and in clearing up the muddle and scandal of the aircraft production branch. I greatly hope that you will be able to do as much on the personnel side, for it will indeed be lamentable if we have machines standing idle for want of pilots to fly them.

Prime Minister to Professor Lindemann   3.VI.40

You are not presenting me as I should like every few days, or every week, with a short, clear statement of the falling off or improvement in munitions production. I am not able to form a clear view unless you do this.

Prime Minister to Professor Lindemann   3.VI.40

See attached paper [Production Programmes: Memorandum by Chiefs of Staff], which seems to contain a lot of loose thinking. Evidently we must "pull forward" everything that can be made effective in the next five months, and accept the consequent retardation of later production, but there is no reason whatever to alter, so far as I can see, the existing approved schemes for a three years' war. Indeed, they will be more necessary than ever if France drops out.

Pray let me have your views.

Prime Minister to Professor Lindemann   7.VI.40
(Secret.)

I am much grieved to hear of the further delay in the proximity fuze.

Considering the enormous importance of this, and the directions I have given that all possible pressure should be put behind it, it would surely have been right to have two or three firms simultaneously making the experimental pattern, so that if one failed the other could go on.

Please report to me what has been done.

You have not given me yet either a full statement of the production which is already ordered in rockets for the proximity fuze and in rockets for the ordinary fuze before we get the P.F.

It is of the utmost importance that you should go forward with the stabilising bomb-sight, as we must knock out their aircraft factories at the same rate that they affect ours. If you will gather together (*a*) all the people interested in the P.F. and (*b*) all those interested in the stabilised bomb-sight I will next week receive their reports and urge them on.

Prime Minister to Minister of Aircraft Production   11.VI.40

It was decided on December 22 at a conference on bomb-sight design that urgent action should be taken to convert 2,600 A.B.s, Mark II, into stabilised high-altitude bomb-sights, over 90 per cent. of the drawings then being completed. Please let me know exactly what followed. How is it that only one bomb-sight was converted? I should be very glad if you would look at the files and ascertain who was responsible for stifling action.

Prime Minister to Secretary of State for Air and C.A.S.   11.VI.40

This report* is most interesting, and I shall be glad if you will arrange to use the squadron you mentioned yesterday for the purpose of infecting the reaches mentioned, where the traffic is reported to be

---

* On the "Royal Marine" Operation. See Book II.

so heavy. We do not need to ask the French permission for this, but only for the continuous streaming of the naval fluvials. This I am doing. Meanwhile you should act as soon as you can on the lower reaches. Kindly report what you will do.

Prime Minister to Secretary of State for the Colonies   16.VI.40

Have you considered the advisability of raising a West Indies Regiment? It might have three battalions, strongly officered by British officers, and be representative of most of the islands; to be available for Imperial service; to give an outlet for the loyalty of the natives, and bring money into these poor islands.

At present we are short of weapons, but these will come along.

Prime Minister to First Lord of the Admiralty   17.VI.40

I am content with your proposed disposition of the heavy ships in the West, namely, *Repulse* and *Renown* to maintain the blockade at Scapa; *Rodney, Nelson,* and *Valiant* at Rosyth to cover the Island; *Hood* and *Ark Royal* to join *Resolution* at Gibraltar, to watch over the fate of the French Fleet.

It is of the utmost importance that the fleet at Alexandria should remain to cover Egypt from an Italian invasion, which would otherwise destroy prematurely all our position in the East. This fleet is well placed to sustain our interests in Turkey, to guard Egypt and the Canal, and can, if the situation changes, either fight its way westward or go through the Canal to guard the Empire or come round the Cape on to our trade routes.

The position of the Eastern fleet must be constantly watched, and can be reviewed when we know what happens to the French Fleet and whether Spain declares war or not.

Even if Spain declares war it does not follow that we should quit the Eastern Mediterranean. If we have to quit Gibraltar we must immediately take the Canaries, which will serve as a very good base to control the western entrance to the Mediterranean.

Prime Minister to Minister of Home Security   20.VI.40

I understand that it was settled last Saturday that your department was to take on the executive control of smoke as a means of hiding factories and similar industrial targets. I should be glad to know whom you have put in charge of this work, which I regard as of the highest importance, and what progress he has made.

Prime Minister to Admiralty   23.VI.40

I do not think it would be a good thing to keep *Hood* and *Ark Royal* lolling about in Gibraltar harbour, where they might be bombed at any time from the shore.

Surely when they have fuelled they should go to sea, and come back only unexpectedly and for short visits.

What is being done?

Prime Minister to General Ismay   24.VI.40

Has any news been received of the German prisoner pilots in France, whose return to this country was solemnly promised by Monsieur Reynaud?

Prime Minister to Secretary of State for Foreign Affairs   24.VI.40

It does not seem to be necessary to address the President again upon the subject of destroyers to-day or to-morrow. Evidently he will be influenced by what happens to the French Fleet, about which I am hopeful. I am doubtful about opening Staff talks at the present time. I think they would turn almost entirely from the American side upon the transfer of the British Fleet to transatlantic bases. Any discussion of this is bound to weaken confidence here at the moment when all must brace themselves for the supreme struggle. I will send the President another personal telegram about destroyers and flying-boats a little later on.

Prime Minister to Secretary of State for the Colonies   25.VI.40

The cruel penalties imposed by your predecessor upon the Jews in Palestine for arming have made it necessary to tie up needless forces for their protection. Pray let me know exactly what weapons and organisation the Jews have for self-defence.

Prime Minister to Minister of Supply   25.VI.40

Thank you for your letter of June 22 about increasing the import of steel from the United States. I understand that owing to the transfer of the French contracts to us our volume of purchases for the coming month has more than doubled and that we are now buying at the rate of about six hundred thousand tons a month. This is satisfactory, and we should certainly get as much from the United States as we can while we can.

Prime Minister to Secretary of State for Foreign Affairs   26.VI.40

I am sure we shall gain nothing by offering to "discuss" Gibraltar at the end of the war. Spaniards will know that, if we win, discussions would not be fruitful; and if we lose they would not be necessary. I do not believe mere verbiage of this kind will affect the Spanish decision.

Prime Minister to General Ismay   28.VI.40

Although our policy about the French Navy is clear, I should like to have an appreciation by the Admiralty of the consequences which are likely to follow—namely, a hostile attitude by France, and the seizure by Germany and Italy of any part of the French Navy which we cannot secure. I should like to have this on Sunday next.

Prime Minister to General Ismay   28.VI.40

This is a very unsatisfactory figure [of civilian labour*]. When I mentioned fifty-seven thousand the other day in the Cabinet I was assured that they represented a very small part of what were actually employed and that a hundred thousand was nearer the mark, and that many more were coming in before the end of the week. Now, instead, we have a figure of only forty thousand. Pray let me have a full explanation of this.

It is very wrong that fighting troops should be kept from their training because of the neglect to employ civilian labour.

The question must be brought up at the Cabinet on Monday.

Prime Minister to Home Secretary   28.VI.40

Let me see a list of prominent persons you have arrested.

Prime Minister to Professor Lindemann   29.VI.40

If we could have large supplies of multiple projectors and rockets directed by Radar irrespective of cloud or darkness, and also could have the proximity fuze working effectively by day and to a lesser extent in moonlight or starlight, the defence against air attack would become decisive. This combination is therefore the supreme immediate aim. We are not far from it in every respect, yet it seems to baffle us. Assemble your ideas and facts so that I may give extreme priority and impulse to this business.

Prime Minister to Professor Lindemann   29.VI.40

It seems to me that the blockade is largely ruined, in which case the sole decisive weapon in our hands would be overwhelming air attack upon Germany.

We should gain great relief in the immediate future from not having to maintain an army in France or sending supplies of beef, coal, etc., to France. Let me know about this.

How has the question of beef supplies been affected? We are freed from the obligation to supply the French Army with beef. There is really no reason why our Army at home should have rations far exceeding the heavy munitions workers'. The complications about frozen meat and fresh meat ought also to be affected by what has happened, although I am not sure which way.

---

* Labour for defence works. My former minute, dated 25.VI.40, is recorded in Book I, Chapter VIII, page 151.

JULY

Prime Minister to General Ismay   2.VII.40

If it be true that a few hundred German troops have been landed on Jersey or Guernsey by troop-carriers, plans should be studied to land secretly by night on the islands and kill or capture the invaders. This is exactly one of the exploits for which the Commandos would be suited. There ought to be no difficulty in getting all the necessary information from the inhabitants and from those evacuated. The only possible reinforcements which could reach the enemy during the fighting would be by aircraft-carriers, and here would be a good opportunity for the Air Force fighting machines. Pray let me have a plan.

Prime Minister to Secretary of State for Foreign Affairs   3.VII.40

I could not reconcile myself to leaving a large number of influential Frenchmen who are the adherents of the Pétain Government free to run an active and effective propaganda in our Service circles and in French circles in this country, against the whole policy of aiding General de Gaulle, to which we are publicly and earnestly committed. The attempt to set up a French Government in Morocco and to obtain control of the *Jean Bart* and other vessels, and to open up a campaign in Morocco, with a base on the Atlantic, is, in my opinion, vital. It was most cordially adopted by the Cabinet in principle, and, apart from technical details, I should find very great difficulty in becoming a party to its abandonment, and to our consequent relegation to the negative defensive, which has so long proved ruinous to our interests.

(Action this Day)
Prime Minister to V.C.N.S. and A.C.N.S.   5.VII.40

Could you let me know on one sheet of paper what arrangements you are making about the Channel convoys now that the Germans are all along the French coast? The attacks on the convoy yesterday, both from the air and by E-boats, were very serious, and I should like to be assured this morning that the situation is in hand and that the Air is contributing effectively.

Prime Minister to First Lord of the Admiralty, Secretary
of State for War, and Secretary of State for Air   5.VII.40
(Sir E. Bridges to implement)

It has been represented to me that our colleagues not in the War Cabinet but above the "line" are depressed at not knowing more of what is going forward in the military sphere. It would be advantageous if each of the Service Ministers could in rotation have a talk with them, answer questions, and explain the general position. If a weekly meeting were instituted, this would mean that each Service Minister would meet them every three weeks. I trust this would not be too heavy a burden upon you. Nothing must ever be said to anybody about future operations; these must always be kept in the most narrow circles; but explanations of the past and expositions of the present offer a wide field. On the assumption that the above is agreeable to you, I am giving directions through Sir Edward Bridges.

Prime Minister to Colonel Jacob   6.VII.40

Obtain a most careful report to-day from the Joint Intelligence Staff of any further indication of enemy preparations for raid or invasion. Let me have this to-night.

Prime Minister to Minister of Aircraft Production   8.VII.40

In the fierce light of the present emergency the fighter is the need, and the output of fighters must be the prime consideration till we have broken the enemy's attack. But when I look round to see how we can win the war I see that there is only one sure path. We have no Continental army which can defeat the German military power. The blockade is broken and Hitler has Asia and probably Africa to draw from. Should he be repulsed here or not try invasion, he will recoil eastward, and we have nothing to stop him. But there is one thing that will bring him back and bring him down, and that is an absolutely devastating, exterminating attack by very heavy bombers from this country upon the Nazi homeland. We must be able to overwhelm them by this means, without which I do not see a way through. We cannot accept any lower aim than air mastery. When can it be obtained?

Prime Minister to Secretary of State for Air   11.VII.40

Generally speaking, the losses in the bomber force seem unduly heavy, and the Bremen raid, from which only one out of six returned, is most grievous. At the present time a very heavy price may be paid (a) for information by reconnaissance of the conditions in the German ports and German-controlled ports and river-mouths; (b) for the bombing of barges or assemblies of ships thus detected. Apart from this, the long-range bombing of Germany should be conducted with a desire to save the machines and personnel as much as possible while keeping up a steady attack. It is most important to build up the numbers of the bomber force, which are very low at the present time.

Prime Minister to Home Secretary   11.VII.40

You should, I think, prepare a Bill vacating the seat of any Member of Parliament who continues during the present war outside the jurisdiction for more than six months without the leave of the Secretary of State.

Prime Minister to General Ismay   12.VII.40

What is being done to reproduce and install the small circular pill-boxes which can be sunk in the centre of aerodromes, and rise by means of a compressed-air bottle to two or three feet elevation, like a small turret commanding the aerodrome? I saw these for the first time when I visited Langley Aerodrome last week. This appears to afford an admirable means of anti-parachute defence, and it should surely be widely adopted. Let me have a plan.

Prime Minister to Secretary of State for War   12.VII.40

Now is the time to popularise your administration with the troops by giving to all regiments and units the little badges and distinctions they like so much. I saw the London Irish with their green and peacock-blue hackles. We can easily afford the expense of bronze badges, the weight of which is insignificant in metal. All regimental distinctions should be encouraged. The French Army made a great speciality of additional unofficial regimental badges, which they presented to people. I liked this idea, and I am sure it would amuse the troops, who will have to face a long vigil. I am delighted at the action you have taken about bands, but when are we going to hear them playing about the streets? Even quite small parade marches are highly beneficial, especially in towns like Liverpool and Glasgow; in fact, wherever there are troops and leisure for it there should be an attempt at military display.

Prime Minister to General Ismay, for C.O.S. Committee   12.VII.40

1. The contacts we have had with the Italians encourage the development of a more aggressive campaign against the Italian homeland by bombardment both from air and sea. It also seems most desirable that the Fleet should be able to use Malta more freely. A plan should be prepared to reinforce the air defences of Malta in the strongest manner with A.A. guns of various types and with aeroplanes. Malta was also the place where it was thought the aerial mine barrage from the "Egg-layer" would be useful. Finally, there are the P.E. fuzes,* which will be coming along at the end of August, which should give very good daylight results. If we could get a stronger air force there we might obtain considerable immunity from annoyance by retaliation.

2. Let a plan for the speediest anti-aircraft reinforcement of Malta be prepared forthwith, and let me have it in three days, with estimates

* This was the photo-electric fuze, and, although not very successful, was the fore-runner of the later proximity fuze.

in time. It should be possible to inform Malta to prepare emplacements for the guns before they are sent out.

Prime Minister to General Ismay   12.VII.40

Will you bring the following to the notice of the Chiefs of Staff:

It is the settled policy of His Majesty's Government to make good strong French contingents for land, sea, and air service, to encourage these men to volunteer to fight on with us, to look after them well, to indulge their sentiments about the French flag, etc., and to have them as representatives of a France which is continuing the war. It is the duty of the Chiefs of Staff to carry this policy out effectively.

The same principle also applies to Poles, Dutch, Czech, and Belgian contingents in this country, as well as to the Foreign Legion of anti-Nazi Germany. Mere questions of administrative inconvenience must not be allowed to stand in the way of this policy of the State. It is most necessary to give to the war which Great Britain is waging single-handed the broad, international character which will add greatly to our strength and prestige.

I hope I may receive assurances that this policy is being whole-heartedly pursued. I found the conditions at Olympia very bad, and there is no doubt that the French soldiers were discouraged by some officers from volunteering. An opportunity of assisting the French would be to make a great success of their function of July 14, when they are going to lay a wreath on the Foch statue.

Prime Minister to General Ismay   13.VII.40

Draw Admiralty attention to the importance of all these ships, especially *Western Prince*. What is her speed? It would be a disaster if we lost these fifty thousand rifles. Draw attention also to the immense consequence of the convoy which is leaving New York between July 8 and 12. When will these various convoys be in the danger zone? When will they arrive? Let me have a report on the measures to be taken.

Prime Minister to Sir Edward Bridges   13.VII.40

I am receiving from various sources suggestions that there should be another day of prayer and humiliation.

Will you find out privately what is thought about this by the Archbishop.

Prime Minister to General Ismay   14.VII.40

It seems to me very important that everybody should be made to look to their gas-masks now. I expect a great many of them require overhauling, and it may well be Hitler has some gas designs upon us.

Will you consider how the necessary overhauls can be set on foot. Action should be taken at once.

Prime Minister to General Ismay, for V.C.A.S. 15.VII.40

I am in full agreement with your proposal for bombing during the present moon-phase. I do not understand however why we have not been able to obtain results in the Kiel Canal. Nothing could be more important than this, as it prevents any movement of prepared shipping and barges from the Baltic for invasion purposes. I heard that you had dropped a number of bombs into this area, but that they did no good. Let me know what you have done about it in the past. How many raids, how many bombs, what kind of bombs, and what is the explanation that the canal still works? Can you make any plans for bettering results in the future? This is surely a matter of the very highest importance, and now is the time when it counts most.

Prime Minister to General Ismay 15.VII.40

Make sure that overhead cover against bombing attack is provided for the 14-inch gun. A structure of steel girders should be put up to carry sandbag cover similar to that over the 6-inch guns which are mounted along the coast. All should be camouflaged. You will be told that it will be necessary to change the guns after a hundred and twenty rounds. In that case the structure will have to be taken to pieces and put up again after the gun is changed. There should be no difficulty in this.

Prime Minister to General Ismay 17.VII.40

Press the War Office continually to develop the Foreign Legion, either by Pioneer Battalions or otherwise. Let me have weekly reports.

Prime Minister to Home Secretary 18.VII.40

I certainly do not propose to send a message by the senior child to Mr. Mackenzie King, or by the junior child either. If I sent any message by anyone, it would be that I entirely deprecate any stampede from this country at the present time.*

(Action this Day.)
Prime Minister to Home Secretary 19.VII.40

I have noticed lately very many sentences imposed for indiscretion by magistrates' and other courts throughout the country in their execution of recent legislation and regulation. All these cases should be reviewed by the Home Office, and His Majesty moved to remit the

* This refers to the Government-sponsored scheme for the evacuation of children to Canada and the U.S.A. The scheme was abandoned after the sinking of the *City of Benares* by a U-boat on September 17, 1940.

sentence where there was no malice or serious injury to the State. By selecting some of those cases which have recently figured in the public eye, and announcing remission publicly, you would give the necessary guidance without which it is difficult for local courts to assess the lead and purpose of Parliament.

Prime Minister to First Lord and First Sea Lord   20.VII.40

I have drawn attention to this danger before. I do not think *Hood* should be left lying in Gibraltar harbour at the mercy of a surprise bombardment by heavy howitzers. Both she and *Ark Royal* should go to sea for a cruise, with or without *Valiant* and *Resolution*, as may be thought fit. They could return to fuel or to carry out any operations, provided the Spanish situation has not further deteriorated. Pray let me have your proposals.

Prime Minister to Foreign Secretary   20.VII.40

Don't you think we might go very slow on all this general and equitable, fair and honourable peace business between China and Japan? Chiang does not want it; none of the pro-Chinese want it; and so far from helping us round the Burma Road difficulty, it will only make it worse. I am sure that it is not in our interest that the Japanese should be relieved of their preoccupation. Would it not be a good thing to give it a miss for a month or so, and see what happens?

Prime Minister to Secretary of State for War   20.VII.40

You may care to see this letter from Colonel Wedgwood on "London Defence". The only scale of attack which it seems to me need be contemplated for the centre of Government is, say, five hundred parachutists or Fifth Columnists. What is the present plan, and what is the scale against which it is being provided?

You might do something for Jos. He is a grand-hearted man.

Prime Minister to Minister without Portfolio   20.VII.40

I am rather doubtful, from information which has reached me, whether our home timber resources are being adequately developed.

This, of course, is primarily a matter for the Minister of Supply, who I know has made certain departmental adjustments recently with this particular end in view.

Prime Minister to General Ismay   21.VII.40

Let me have a statement showing the scheme of defence for the Central Government, Whitehall, etc. What was the scale of attack prescribed, and who was responsible for taking the measures? What was the reason for attempting to put an anti-tank obstacle across St. James's Park? Who ordered this? When was it counter-ordered?

Prime Minister to General Ismay   23.VII.40

I am told that the refuelling of fighter aeroplanes could be much
more rapidly achieved if there were more tankers on the aerodromes,
and considering that an attack by air would make every minute gained
in returning the fighters to the air most precious, I should be glad if
measures were taken at once to double or greatly increase the fuelling
facilities.

Prime Minister to Secretary of State for War   23.VII.40

I do not seem to have had any answer from you to my query about
whether the 2nd Canadian Division and all it stands for is being frittered
away in Iceland.

Prime Minister to Secretary of State for War   23.VII.40

1. It is of course urgent and indispensable that every effort should
be made to obtain secretly the best possible information about the
German forces in the various countries overrun, and to establish
intimate contacts with local people, and to plant agents. This, I hope,
is being done on the largest scale, as opportunity serves, by the new
organisation under M.E.W. [Ministry of Economic Warfare]. None
of this partakes of the nature of military operations.

2. It would be most unwise to disturb the coasts of any of these
countries by the kind of silly fiascos which were perpetrated at
Boulogne and Guernsey. The idea of working all these coasts up
against us by pin-prick raids and fulsome communiqués is one to be
strictly avoided.

3. Sir Roger Keyes is now studying the whole subject of medium
raids—*i.e.*, by not less than five nor more than ten thousand men. Two
or three of these might be brought off on the French coast during the
winter. As soon as the invasion danger recedes or is resolved, and Sir
R. K.'s paper-work is done, we will consult together and set the Staffs
to work upon detailed preparations. After these medium raids have
had their chance there will be no objection to stirring up the French
coast by minor forays.

4. During the spring and summer of 1941 large armoured irruptions
must be contemplated. The material for these is however so far
ahead of us that only very general study of their possibilities is now
necessary, and no directions need be given to the Staff upon them until
the end of August.

Prime Minister to General Ismay, for Chiefs of Staff   24.VII.40

Apart from the Anti-Nazi Germans, who can begin by being
pioneers, rifles and ammunition should be issued to all foreign corps.
Whether this should be from British Service rifles now in the posses-

sion of the Home Guard, but in process of being replaced by American rifles, or whether the foreign corps* should be armed with American rifles direct, has no doubt been considered. On the whole I am inclined to the former solution. It is most urgent to rearm the Poles and the French, as we may need them for foreign service in the near future. The armament of these foreign corps ranks *after* the armament of British troops so far as rifles are concerned, but they have priority over the Home Guard. They ought to have a small proportion of Bren guns, etc., even at the expense of our own men. What is being done to furnish them with artillery? Surely some of the 75's can be made to serve the purpose. The Polish unit should be ripened as much as possible. Pray let me have a weekly report of numbers and weapons.

(Action this Day)
Prime Minister to First Lord, First Sea Lord, and
V.C.N.S.   25.VII.40

I cannot help feeling that there is more in the plan of laying mines behind an invader's landing than the Naval Staff felt when I mentioned the matter three weeks ago. In the interval I sent a reminder asking that it should be further considered.

If an invader lands during the night or morning, the flotillas will attack him in rear during the day, and these flotillas will be heavily bombarded from the air, as part of the air battles which will be going on. If however when night falls a curtain or fender of mines can be laid close inshore, so as to cut off the landing-place from reinforcements of any kind, these mines, once laid, will not have to be guarded from air attack, and consequently will relieve the flotilla from the need of coming back on the second day, thus avoiding losses from the air and air protection. At any rate, I think it improvident not to provide for the option whether to seal off the hostile landing by attack of flotillas or mines. There may be several landings, and you may want to leave one sealed off with mines in order to attack another. Of course all the above would apply still more if the landing had got hold of a port instead of merely a beach.

Pray let this matter have further attention, and also say what craft

* French ..	..	..	..	2,000
Poles ..	..	..	..	14,000
Dutch ..	..	..	..	1,000
Czechs ..	..	..	..	4,000
Norwegians ..	..	..	1,000
Belgians	..	..	..	500
Anti-Nazi Germans ..		..		3,000
				25,500

are available for the purpose, or how soon they can be provided or adapted.

Prime Minister to V.C.N.S.   25.VII.40

Let me have a report on how far the German, Dutch, and Belgian harbours have been sealed up by mines or obstructions.

Prime Minister to Foreign Secretary   26.VII.40

I saw Mr. Quo yesterday, at his request, and explained to him frankly the position about the Burma Road. I told him verbally of the message I sent through the Foreign Office to Chiang Kai-shek. He was naturally anxious to extort some promise from me about what would happen when the three months had expired. I said it all depended upon what the situation was then, and that I could make no forecast. I assured him we should put no pressure on General Chiang to consent to terms or negotiations against his will and policy. Mr. Quo seemed fairly satisfied, though rueful.

Prime Minister to Chancellor of the Exchequer   28.VII.40

Now that the Roumanian Government are helping themselves to the property of British subjects, ought we not to show the Roumanians that we shall use their frozen fund to compensate our people? I understand that about six weeks ago you blocked Roumanian assets in London. We have been treated odiously by these people.

AUGUST

(Action this Day)
Prime Minister to First Lord and First Sea Lord   1.VIII.40

In view of the threatening attitude of Japan, it is vitally important to know about *Bismarck* and *Tirpitz*. Pray let me have your latest information. It seems to me that a great effort will have to be made by the Air Force to disable these ships, as their apparition in the next few months would be most dangerous.

Assuming Japan goes to war with us, or forces us into war, I suppose you would send *Hood*, three 8-inch-gun cruisers, two *Ramillies*, and twelve long-radius destroyers to Singapore.

Let me have the legends [*i.e.*, construction details] of the completed Japanese battle-cruisers.

(Action this Day)
Prime Minister to First Lord and First Sea Lord   2.VIII.40

I pray that we may never have to make this widespread distribution, but I am in full accord with the principles on which the Admiralty would propose to meet the strain. I should have thought that *Hood* would be a greater deterrent than *Renown*. Please let me have a report of the possibility of air attack on *Bismarck* and *Tirpitz*. This seems to me to be one of the most vital steps to take. Apart from this, there is no need to make any new dispositions at the present time on account of Japanese war-risk.

I was much concerned to hear of the sinking of the three tankers off Tory Island. I should like to see you move some destroyers from the East Coast thither. We had better wait, however, until the August moon-phase is over. During this time also the American guns and rifles will be distributed to the troops.

(Action this Day)
Prime Minister to General Ismay   2.VIII.40
1. Next week one of my principal tasks must be going through this scheme of the Air Ministry for increasing the pilots and for the training of pilots. Lord Beaverbrook should be asked for his views beforehand.
2. Let me have a report on the plans for lectures on tactical subjects for the troops in the autumn.
3. What has been done about the collection of scrap of all kinds? Let me have a short report on one page covering the progress made this year.
4. When at the Admiralty I took a special interest in the work of the Salvage Department, and held a meeting there four months ago. A naval officer, Captain Dewar, was then in charge. Let me have a report on what has happened to salvage since that day.
5. I am also expecting this week to reach a settlement about the functions of the A.R.P. and police in the case of invasion. The Lord Privy Seal was dealing with this in the first instance. At the same time we must consider allowing transfers from A.R.P. to the Home Guard, and their being made available for fighting purposes. To what extent has the payment of the A.R.P. personnel been discontinued or restricted? It ought to be continually restricted.
6. Let me have a report on the progress and future construction of the tank divisions. There should be five armoured divisions by March 31 [1941], and two more by the end of May. Let me know how far the present prospects of men and material allow of this. Let me know also what are the latest ideas for the structure and organisation of an armoured division. This should be prepared on one sheet of paper, showing all the principal elements and accessories.

Prime Minister to General Ismay   2.VIII.40
It is very important to get on with the uniforms for the Home Guard. Let me have a forecast of deliveries.

(*Action this Day*)
Prime Minister to First Lord   2.VIII.40

My objection was to anything in the nature of sinking at sight or
sinking without due provision for the safety of the crews. Provided
this is excluded, there can be no reason against sinking a captured ship
if, owing to air attack or other military reasons, it is impossible to
bring her into port as a prize. The disadvantages of sinking a ship and
losing valuable tonnage are obvious, and I do not see why in nineteen
cases out of twenty the Admiralty cannot put a prize crew on board
and send the ship in, in the ordinary way. I see no objection to the
action taken in the *Hermione* case,* which falls entirely within the
general principles set forth above.

Prime Minister to Sir Edward Bridges   2.VIII.40

The whole question of holidays and reduced hours should be considered by the Cabinet at an early date. It is far too soon to assume
that the danger has passed. It is a great mistake to tell the workpeople
that they are tired. On the other hand, certain easements are indispensable. Please communicate with Mr. Bevin, Lord Beaverbrook, and the
Minister of Supply, so that their views may be in readiness for Cabinet
conversation. I should also like to know what is being done about
holidays for the Civil Service and for Ministers, and persons in high
Service positions. Something will have to be done about this, but we
must be very careful not to be caught while in an August mood.

Prime Minister to Lord Privy Seal and Home Secretary   3.VIII.40

The attached memorandum by Lord Mottistone on duties of police
in the event of invasion raises a very difficult question, and one that
must be speedily settled. We cannot surely make ourselves responsible
for a system where the police will prevent the people from resisting the
enemy and will lay down their arms and become the enemy's servant
in any invaded area. I confess I do not see my way quite clearly to the
amendments required in the regulations. In principle however it
would seem that the police should withdraw from any invaded area
with the last of His Majesty's troops. This would also apply to the
A.R.P. and the fire brigades, etc. Their services will be used in other
districts. Perhaps on invasion being declared the police, A.R.P., fire
brigades, etc., should automatically become a part of the military
forces.

* The *Hermione* was a small Greek steamer which was intercepted by our cruisers in the
Ægean on July 28, 1940, while carrying a military cargo for Italy. Our ships were
attacked by aircraft when making the interception. The *Hermione* was therefore sunk, and
her crew left in boats near the land.

Prime Minister to General Ismay   3.VIII.40

All secret service reports about affairs in France or other captive countries are to be shown to Major Morton, who is responsible for keeping me informed. Make sure this instruction is obeyed.

Prime Minister to Secretary of State for War   3.VIII.40

It seems quite possible that a portion of General de Gaulle's forces will be used in the near future. It therefore becomes of the utmost consequence and urgency to complete the equipment of his three battalions, company of tanks, headquarters, etc. Evidently action is being taken already, but I shall be much obliged if you will accelerate this action by every means in your power, and also if you will let me know in what way the situation has improved since Major Morton's minute of yesterday.

Prime Minister to Sir Edward Bridges, and others concerned   3.VIII.40

1. I think the circular about work in the factories and holidays for whole establishments should, whatever the agreement of the Production Council, be brought before the Cabinet on Tuesday by the Minister of Labour. We must give holidays without creating a holiday atmosphere. It would therefore seem desirable to announce only that "such local arrangements as are possible are being made for staggered holidays", or something like that.

2. I approve Sir Horace Wilson's letter to departments. It arose out of my instructions to him.

3. I shall be very glad if you will adjust the holidays of Ministers, and make sure that the Services arrange for similar relief in case of high military officers at the centre of government.

Prime Minister to Sir Edward Bridges   4.VIII.40

I circulate to my colleagues the enclosed report on the first use of the U.P. weapon with the wire curtain at Dover. This appears to be of high importance, and may well inaugurate a decisive change in the relations of ground and air, particularly in respect of ships and ports exposed to dive-bombing attack.

Prime Minister to Professor Lindemann   4.VIII.40

What are you doing to focus the discussions on food, shipping, and agricultural policy for the second twelve months of the war? I thought it looked like 18,000,000 tons of shipping [for food], plough up 1,500,000 more acres, and instruct the Food Department to submit a plan both for increasing rations and building up further food reserves. This should be possible on the above basis.

Prime Minister to Secretary of State for Air and C.A.S.   4.VIII.40

The danger of Japanese hostility makes it all the more important that the German capital ships should be put out of action. I understand that the Air Force intends to make heavy attacks on these ships as soon as there is sufficient moon. *Scharnhorst* and the *Gneisenau*, both in floating docks at Kiel, the *Bismarck* at Hamburg, and the *Tirpitz* at Wilhelmshaven, are all targets of supreme consequence. Even a few months' delay in *Bismarck* will affect the whole balance of sea-power to a serious degree. I shall be glad to hear from you.

Prime Minister to General Ismay   5.VIII.40

I am not satisfied with the volume or quality of information received from the unoccupied area of France. We seem to be as much cut off from these territories as from Germany. I do not wish such reports as are received to be sifted and digested by the various Intelligence authorities. For the present Major Morton will inspect them for me and submit what he considers of major interest. He is to see everything and submit *authentic documents for me in their original form.*

Further, I await proposals for improving and extending our information about France and for keeping a continued flow of agents moving to and fro. For this purpose naval facilities can, if necessary, be invoked. So far as the Vichy Government is concerned, it is not creditable that we have so little information. To what extent are American, Swiss, and Spanish agents being used?

Prime Minister to General Ismay   5.VIII.40

What orders are extant for the future production of U.P. Multiple Projectors in groups of twenties, tens, fives, and also single projectors?

What amount of ammunition—

         (*a*) of the ordinary rocket,
         (*b*) of the aerial mine,
         (*c*) of the P.E. fuze,
         (*d*) of the radio fuze,

is on order? What are the forecasts of deliveries in the next six months in all cases?

Presently the P.E. fuze will probably supersede the aerial mine for use in multiple projectors mounted on H.M. ships. This will entail an alteration of the projector tubes. The Admiralty should be asked to study this betimes, so that the new tubes can be fitted on the existing mountings of H.M. ships with the least possible delay from the moment that this change appears desirable.

The Admiralty should also be asked to report whether any progress has been made on firing short aerial mines from ships' guns.

I wish to refresh my memory with what happened about this before I left the Admiralty.

Prime Minister to Minister of Mines   6.VIII.40
I saw it stated that you were piling up large reserves of coal during the summer for use during the winter. I should be glad to know how far this very wise precaution has advanced. We were very short and anxious in January last, and I hope you are taking precautions.

Prime Minister to Secretary of State for War   7.VIII.40
Please let me know what is being done to train men in the use of the sticky bomb, which is now beginning to come through in quantity.

Prime Minister to General Ismay   9.VIII.40
Ask for a statement of the Ministry of Supply importation programme under various heads. Professor Lindemann should be consulted about these heads. Let me see them.

The programme for the second year of the war has not yet been presented to me in a coherent form.

*Prime Minister to Secretary of State for War and
C.I.G.S.*   9.VIII.40
I was much concerned to find that the 1st Division, which has an exceptionally high proportion of equipment, and includes a Brigade of Guards, should be dispersed along the beaches, instead of being held in reserve for counter-attack. What is the number of divisions which are now free and out of the line, and what is the argument for keeping divisions with a high equipment of guns, etc., on the beaches?

Prime Minister to Lord Beaverbrook   9.VIII.40
If it came to a choice between hampering air production or tank production, I would sacrifice the tank, but I do not think this is the case, as the points of overlap are not numerous and ought to be adjustable. I gathered from you that you thought you could arrange with the Minister of Supply.

Prime Minister to Minister of Information   9.VIII.40
It is important to keep General de Gaulle active in French on the broadcast, and to relay by every possible means our French propaganda to Africa. I am told the Belgians will help from the Congo.

Have we any means of repeating to the West African stations the agreement made between us and de Gaulle?

Prime Minister to General Ismay   10.VIII.40
Let me have a weekly return of the deliveries to troops of the

American 75's and the .300 rifles to Home Guard, with consequent liberation by them of Lee-Metfords. Begin at once.

Prime Minister to General Ismay, for C.O.S. Committee 10.VIII.40

The Prime Minister would be glad to have a report from the C.O.S. Committee, after conference with the C.-in-C. Home Forces, upon the small arms ammunition position on the beaches and with the Reserves.

Prime Minister to Minister of Mines 11.VIII.40

I felt sure you would take advantage of the breakdown of the export market to increase our stocks all over the country. I hope you will press on with this, especially as regards our essential gas, water, and electricity works. I note that the gas and electricity supplies are about 20 per cent. up. We cannot go wrong in piling up such well-distributed stocks, which are sure to be used sooner or later.

I am sending a note to the Minister of Transport to call his attention to the position of the railways.

The tremendous upset in your plans due to the collapse of France and the loss of three-quarters of our export markets must have put a great strain on your department. It must be very difficult after all your efforts to increase production to explain the sudden slump, but I have no doubt the men will understand. Indeed, what you tell me about the fortitude of the Kent miners is an encouraging sign of the spirit which I believe informs all the working men in the country.

Prime Minister to Minister of Information 11.VIII.40

In view of certain activities we are planning for General de Gaulle, it is of the highest importance that the broadcasting of French news in North and West Africa should be carried to the highest point. Please make sure that the B.B.C. conform to this requirement, and let me have a report on Monday to the effect that all is satisfactorily arranged.

I cannot emphasise too strongly that you have full authority to make the B.B.C. obey.

(Action this Day)
Prime Minister to Minister of Transport 11.VIII.40

I should be grateful for a full report on the steps taken by your department to deal with the difficulties which may arise from the bombing and closing of ports.

One-quarter of our imports, it seems, normally comes in through the Port of London, and one-fifth through the Mersey, with a tenth each through Southampton, the Bristol Channel, and the Humber.

We must envisage these entrances being wholly or partially closed, either one at a time or even several at a time, but I have no doubt you have worked out plans to take account of the various contingencies.

In view of our large accretions of shipping it may well be that port facilities and roadway facilities may be a more stringent bottleneck than shortage of tonnage, so that the preparations you make to meet the various possible eventualities may be of the greatest importance.

Prime Minister to Sir Edward Bridges 12.VIII.40

How does the position now stand about a Timber Controller under the Ministry of Supply?

Ask for a short summary from the Ministry of Supply of the present timber position and policy.

Prime Minister to Lord Privy Seal and
Captain Margesson 12.VIII.40

It would probably be convenient for me to make a general statement on the war, covering the first year and also the first quarter of the new Government, before the House rises. This would be expected, and I suppose Tuesday, the 20th, would be the best day. This should, of course, be in public session. Perhaps you will let me know what you wish. An announcement could be made in good time this week.

It would save me a lot of trouble if a record could be taken at the time, so that the speech could be repeated over the wireless in the evening, or such parts of it as are of general interest. Can this be arranged without a Resolution? If not, could a Resolution be passed this week? I do not think the House would object.

Prime Minister to Home Secretary 12.VIII.40

The drafts [about instructions to police in case of invasion] submitted do not correspond with my view of the recent Cabinet decision. We do not contemplate or encourage fighting by persons not in the armed forces, but we do not forbid it. The police, and as soon as possible the A.R.P. services, are to be divided into combatant and non-combatant, armed and unarmed. The armed will co-operate actively in fighting with the Home Guard and Regulars in their neighbourhood, and will withdraw with them if necessary; the unarmed will actively assist in the "stay put" policy for civilians. Should they fall into an area effectively occupied by the enemy, they may surrender and submit with the rest of the inhabitants, but must not in those circumstances give any aid to the enemy in maintaining order, or in any other way. They may assist the civil population as far as possible.

Prime Minister to Minister of Transport   13.VIII.40

I should be glad to know what stocks of coal are now held by the railways, and how they compare with those normally held. With the stoppage of our export trade to Europe there should be a great surplus just now, and no doubt you are taking advantage of this to fill up every available dump so that we shall have a well-distributed stock for the railways in case of any interruptions, or even in case of another very hard winter. Negotiations about price should not be allowed to hold up the process of re-stocking. If necessary, some form of arbitration will have to be employed to make sure that the prices paid are fair.

Prime Minister to Secretary of State for War   13.VIII.40

If, owing to lack of equipment and other facilities, it is necessary to limit the numbers of the active Home Guard, would it not be possible to recruit a Home Guard Reserve, members of which would for the time being be provided with no weapons and no uniform other than arm-bands? Their only duties would be to attend such courses of instruction as could be organised locally in the use of simple weapons like the "Molotov cocktail", and to report for orders in the event of invasion.

Unless some such step is taken, those who are refused enlistment will be bewildered and disappointed, and one of the primary objects of the Home Guard, which was to provide for the people as a whole an opportunity of helping to defend their homes, will be lost. I am anxious to avoid the disappointment and frustration which the stoppage of recruiting for the Home Guard is likely to cause to many people.

Please let me know what you think of this proposal.

Prime Minister to General Ismay   19.VIII.40

Is it true that Admiral [John] Cunningham says that the only suitable day for "Menace" [Dakar] is September 12, and that if this day is missed owing to storm no other days will be open till the 27th or 28th, when tide and moon will again be satisfactory? All this raises most grave questions. The Admiral cannot take up a position that only in ideal conditions of tide and moon can the operation be begun. It has got to be begun as soon as possible, as long as conditions are practicable, even though they be not the best. People have to fight in war on all sorts of days, and under all sorts of conditions. It will be a great misfortune if there is any delay beyond the 8th. Pray report to me on this to-day.

Prime Minister to General Ismay   21.VIII.40

I am not convinced by these arguments about flame-throwers. The question is one to be settled relatively to other forms of war effort.

The prospects of invasion are rapidly receding. The likelihood in an invasion of a column of troops marching up the very defile in which these installations have been laid on appears remote. The idea of setting up a Petroleum Warfare Executive is a needless multiplication of our apparatus. I have no doubt whatever that the method would be very effective if ever the occasion arose, but will it arise, and in this case would it be at the point expected? Troops do not march along roads without having first cleared their way by small parties and guarded their flanks on each side of defiles.

Prime Minister to First Lord   22.VIII.40

I await your proposals about the resumption of the capital ship programme, which was approved by the late Cabinet on my initiative. This cannot be settled apart from the general demand upon steel and labour, but in principle I favour its resumption.

I hope opportunity will now be taken to repair the disastrous neglect to convert the *Royal Sovereign* class into properly armoured and bulged bombarding vessels with heavy deck armour. These will be needed next year for the attack on Italy. It is lamentable that we have not got them now. They should certainly take precedence over the resumption of battleship construction.

Prime Minister to General Ismay   24.VIII.40

Report to me on the position of Major Jefferis. By whom is he employed? Whom is he under? I regard this officer as a singularly capable and forceful man, who should be brought forward to a higher position. He ought certainly to be promoted Lieutenant-Colonel, as it will give him more authority.

Prime Minister to C.A.S. and V.C.A.S.   24.VIII.40

It is of high importance to increase both the number of squadrons and the number of aircraft and crews immediately available. After a year of war we have only operationally fit about 1,750, of which again only three-quarters are immediately available. You cannot rest satisfied with this, which is less than the number we were supposed to have available before the war.

Prime Minister to Minister of Transport   25.VIII.40

I have read with interest your memorandum on Port Clearance.

I note that the Minister of Shipping doubts whether the country could be supplied through the West Coast ports on the scale you envisage. I should be glad to have your views on this.

Does not the widespread dislocation caused by the cold spell last winter raise some doubts as to the ready adaptability of the railway system in case of sudden emergency?

No doubt arrangements have been made for the importation of oil, which is not included in the food or supply programme. It appears that over two-fifths of our oil imports come through London and Southampton in peace-time. Our stocks are high, but if road transport had to be used more fully to relieve the railways our consumption would of course increase.

I presume that you have discussed their import programmes with the Ministers of Food and of Supply, so that alternative schemes will be ready in case of great diversions.

Prime Minister to Secretary of State for War   25.VIII.40

I have been following with much interest the growth and development of the new guerrilla formations of the Home Guard known as "Auxiliary Units".

From what I hear these units are being organised with thoroughness and imagination, and should, in the event of invasion, prove a useful addition to the regular forces.

Perhaps you will keep me informed of progress.

Prime Minister to First Lord and First Sea Lord   25.VIII.40

The enclosed returns show losses of over forty thousand tons reported in a single day. I regard this matter as so serious as to require special consideration by the War Cabinet. Will you therefore have prepared a statement showing the recent losses, their cause, the measures which have been taken by the Admiralty to cope with the danger, any further measures which you feel it necessary to propose, and whether there is any way in which the War Cabinet can assist the Admiralty.

I should be glad if you would make this report to the War Cabinet on Thursday next.

(Action this Day)
Prime Minister to General Ismay   25.VIII.40

Address the War Office forthwith upon the situation disclosed at Slough. Point out the danger of this large concentration of vehicles; the desirability of dispersing and concealing the vehicles. Ask that a plan should be examined for de-centralising this depot as far as possible. We should also make sure that no sediment or surplus accumulates in the depot. It would be a great pity if a thousand valuable vehicles were ruined by an air attack.

Prime Minister to Secretary of State for Air   25.VIII.40

I visited Kenley [Air Station] on Thursday, saw the gunner in question, and had a rocket fired off. Moreover, it was the Admiralty Committee over which I presided early in the year which produced the idea of using these distress rockets. I am therefore well acquainted with the subject. The Air Ministry, not for the first time, spread itself into very large demands, and, using its priority, barged in heavily into other forms of not less important production. I agree that P.A.C.* rockets may be a good interim defence against low-flying attack, but they have to take their place in the general scheme. I thought myself about five thousand a month would be sufficient, but I am willing to agree to one thousand five hundred a week, or six thousand a month. This figure could be somewhat extended if the wire-recovery projects you mention were further developed and proved an effective economy.

(Action this Day)
Prime Minister to Secretary of State for War   25.VIII.40
War Office have accepted from the War Cabinet the responsibility for dealing with delayed-action bombs. This may become a feature of the enemy attack. A number were thrown last night into the City, causing obstruction. They may even try them on Whitehall! It seems to me that energetic effort should be made to provide sufficient squads to deal with this form of attack in the large centres. The squads must be highly mobile, so as not to waste men and material. They must move in motor-lorries quickly from one point to another. I presume a careful system of reporting all unexploded bombs and the time at which they fell is in operation, and that this information will be sent immediately to the delayed-action section of Home Defence, which has no doubt already been established, and also the various local branches. The service, which is highly dangerous, must be considered particularly honourable, and rewards should follow its successful discharge.

I should be very glad to see your plans for the new section, together with numbers, and it will also be interesting to have a short account of the work done up to date and the methods employed. I presume you are in touch with all the scientific authorities you need.

On the other hand, I am asking the Air Ministry for information as to their reciprocating this process on the enemy.

(General Ismay to see.)

Prime Minister to Secretary of State for Air   25.VIII.40
I cannot feel you are justified in maintaining the present scale of communication squadrons when we are fighting so heavily. The sole end should surely be to increase the reserve and operational strength of our fighting squadrons and to meet the problem of trainer aircraft. Surely your dominant idea should be "Strength for battle". Every-

---

* The letters stand for "Parachute and Cable". The P.A.C. rocket was one form of the U.P. weapon. A description of the latter is given in a minute dated January 13, 1940. See Book II, p. 302.

thing should be keyed on to this, and administrative convenience or local vested interests must be made to give way. In your place I should comb and re-comb. I have been shocked to see the enormous numbers at Hendon, and I would far rather give up flying on inspections altogether for members of the Government than that this should be made a reason for keeping these forces out of the fight.

I should have thought that Hendon could provide at least two good squadrons of fighter or bomber aircraft of the reserve category, and that they should have the machines issued to them and practise on them as occasion serves. Then they could be thrown in when an emergency came.

Ought you not every day to call in question in your own mind every non-military aspect of the Air Force? The tendency of every Station Commander is naturally to keep as much in his hands as possible. The Admirals do exactly the same. Even when you have had a thorough search, if you look around a few weeks later you will see more fat has been gathered.

I hope you will feel able to give some consideration to these views of your old friend.

Prime Minister to First Lord and First Sea Lord   27.VIII.40

Will you kindly send the following to Admiral Cunningham, Commander-in-Chief Mediterranean:

Following from Prime Minister, Minister of Defence:

Main object of directive was to safeguard Alexandria. Only a limited number of troops can be maintained Mersa Matruh, as G.O.C. Middle East will inform you. Every effort is to be made to defend this position. If however it and intermediate positions are forced or turned, it will be necessary to hold the line from Alexandria southwards along the cultivated area [of the Delta]. Air attack on the Fleet at Alexandria is not necessarily less effective from a hundred and twenty miles distance than from twenty miles, since aeroplanes often fly at three hundred miles per hour and have ample endurance. In practice it is usually thought better to hold aerodromes a little back of the actual fighting line. They do not move forward concurrently with the fronts of armies. Everyone here understands the grievous consequence of the fall of Alexandria, and that it would probably entail the Fleet leaving the Mediterranean. If however you have any helpful suggestion to make for the more effective defence of Mersa Matruh or of any positions in advance of it I should be obliged if you would tell me.

Prime Minister to General Ismay, for Joint Planning Staff   28.VIII.40

Now that the long nights are approaching the question of the blackout must be reviewed. I am in favour of a policy not of *black-out* but of *blackable-out*. For this purpose a considerable system of auxiliary electric street-lighting must be worked out. The whole of the centre of London, now lighted by incandescent gas, must be given priority. The best methods in the centres of other great cities must also be studied and local schemes must be examined. Thus the lights can be switched down and up and finally out on an air-raid warning being given. The lights themselves should not be of a too brilliant character. The subdued lighting of shop windows must also be studied with a view to extending the facilities given last Christmas on a permanent basis. Where factories are allowed to continue working at night in spite of the black-out there can be no objection to extending blackable-out lighting to the surrounding districts, thus tending to make the target less defined. Consideration should also be given to decoy lighting and baffle lighting in open spaces at suitable distances from vulnerable points.

Prime Minister to Secretary of State for Air, C.A.S.,
and General Ismay 29.VIII.40

I was much concerned on visiting Manston Aerodrome yesterday to find that although more than four clear days have passed since it was last raided the greater part of the craters on the landing ground remained unfilled and the aerodrome was barely serviceable. When you remember what the Germans did at the Stavanger aerodrome and the enormous rapidity with which craters were filled I must protest emphatically against this feeble method of repairing damage. Altogether there were one hundred and fifty people available to work, including those that could be provided from the Air Force personnel. These were doing their best. No effective appliances were available, and the whole process appeared disproportionate to the value of maintaining this fighting vantage ground.

All craters should be filled in within twenty-four hours at most, and every case where a crater is unfilled for a longer period should be reported to higher authorities. In order to secure this better service it will be necessary to form some crater-filling companies. You might begin with, say, two of two hundred and fifty each for the South of England, which is under this intensive attack. These companies should be equipped with all helpful appliances and be highly mobile, so that in a few hours they can be at work on any site which has been cratered. Meanwhile, at every aerodrome in the attack area, and later elsewhere, there must be accumulated by local contractors stocks of gravel, rubble, and other appropriate materials sufficient to fill without replenishment at least one hundred craters. Thus the mobile air-field repair companies would arrive to find all the material all ready on the spot.

I saw some time ago that the Germans filled in the shell holes by some process of having the gravel in wooden frameworks. The

V.C.N.S. drew my attention to it during the Norwegian operation, and he could perhaps put you on to the telegram referred to.

In what department of the Air Ministry does this process now fall?

After the craters had been refilled camouflage effort might be made to pretend they had not been, but this is a refinement.

Prime Minister to General Ismay
(For all departments concerned, including Service Dept.,
Home Security, M.A.P., and Supply)   30.VIII.40

We must expect that many windows will be broken in the bombing raids, and during the winter glass may become scarce, with serious resultant damage to buildings if not replaced.

The utmost economy is to be practised in the use of glass. Where windows are broken they should, if possible, be boarded up, except for one or two panes. We cannot afford the full-sized windows in glass. All glass not needed for hot-houses should be stored if the hot-houses are empty. I saw at Manston a large hot-house with a great quantity of glass; enough was broken to make it useless, and I directed that the rest should be carefully stored.

What is the condition of glass supply? It would seem necessary to press the manufacturers.

Government buildings should all be fitted with emergency windows, containing only one or two glass panes, which, when the existing framework is blown in, can be substituted. Let me have a full report on the position.

Prime Minister to General Ismay   31.VIII.40

If French India wish for trade they should be made to signify association with General de Gaulle. Otherwise no trade! This is not a matter upon which to be easy-going. Secretary of State for India to be informed.

The accession of any French possessions now is of importance.

Prime Minister to General Ismay   31.VIII.40

I have not approved of any further cruiser tanks being dispatched to the Middle East beyond those which have already gone. Although in principle it is desirable to complete the dispatch of a full armoured division, further movements from this country can only be decided in relation to situation of home forces. No decision of this importance must be taken without reference to me, and in this case I should have to consult the Cabinet.

Prime Minister to Minister of Supply   31.VIII.40

I am very glad to know that the chemical warfare stocks are piling up in this country. Let me know what the total now amounts to. The necessary containers should be brought level with supply. Do these stocks keep? Press on.

INDEX

Abbeville, 42, 53; Germans take, 64, 70; abortive attack on, 131

Abrial, Admiral, 98, 101

Abyssinia, Italian designs on, 105-6

Aden, 40

Admiralty, assembles small vessels for evacuation of Army, 52-3; department of, for landing-craft, 221-2; minute to, 285; and P.E. fuzes for ships, 300

Aerial mines, U.P., 300; for Malta, 290

Africa, Darlan and French, 204; French broadcasts to, 301-2. *See also* North Africa

Air attack, on *Bismarck* and *Tirpitz*, 296-7, 300; defence against, 307. *See also* Air raid(s)

Air-borne troops, danger from, 127, 146, 172; protection against, 156; in Channel Islands, 288

Aircraft, British need for, 23, 50, 117; factories, German attack on, 79, 128, 173; priority for production of, 301; factories, protection of, 281; making full use of, 281-2, 307-8

Aircraft Production, Ministry of, Beaverbrook and, 12; results achieved by, 283

Airfields, R.A.F., German attacks on, 272; damage done to, 309; anti-parachute defence of, 290; tankers on, 294; repairs to, 309-10

Air Ministry, and supply of aircraft, 281-3; and P.A.C. rockets, 307

Air-power, in relation to invasion problem, 248-9, 267-9, 272-4, 278; deciding factor, 289

Air raid(s), British losses by. 5; on Germany, 7, 173, 228, 287, 289, 292; on England, 49, 78-9, 228, 230; on Paris, 59, 100; on Dunkirk and beaches, 89, 91-2, 101-2; on Italy, preparations for, 98-9, 112-13; on Italy, 114, 139; reports of, in Press and on the wireless, 151; on troop transports off France, 172; on London—*see under* London; closing of ports by, 302-3

Aisne, river, 167

Albert Canal, 11, 26, 30, 31-2, 35

Alexander, Rt. Hon. A. V., First Lord of Admiralty, 13; minutes to, 150, 236-7,

285, 288, 295-6, 298, 305-6, 308; in Bordeaux, 191, 211

Alexander, Field-Marshal the Hon. Sir Harold (Viscount, of Tunis), 4, 68; at Dunkirk, 96, 101

Alexandria, British fleet at, 112, 285, 308; French fleet at, 206-7, 210

Algiers, French fleet at, 206, 210

Aliens, in Britain, 50

Amery, Rt. Hon. L. S., Secretary of State for India and Burma, 13, 146; and use of Indian troops, 153

Amiens, 42, 53, 57-9, 63

Ammunition, distribution of, for Home Defence, 301-2

Amphibious warfare, planning for, 214-223; Germans unprepared for, 278

Anderson, Rt. Hon. Sir John, Home Secretary and Minister of Home Security, 13; minutes to, 285, 287, 289, 292, 298, 303

Anderson shelters, 236

Anti-aircraft, British need for equipment, 23; rockets, 144

Anti-Nazi Germans, 291-2, 294-5

Anti-tank defences, 148, 155-6; devices, 148-50; Committee, 283

Antwerp, retreat to defences of, 36, 39

Arabs, and arming of Jews, 154

Ardennes, German attack through, 28, 34-35, 66; thought impassable, 30, 33-4, 66

Ark Royal H.M.S., at Oran, 208, 210; at Gibraltar, 285, 293

Armoured divisions, British, 128; in France, 130, 131; development of, 218-219; transport for, 219. *See also* Tanks

Arnold, General Henry H. (U.S.A.), 20

A.R.P. services—*see* Civil Defence Service

Arras, 42, 53, 57-8, 63, 69; defence of, 48; British attack at, 60-2, 74; loss of, 62, 67, 72

Arundel, 270

Asdics, 117

Ashford, 270

Asquith, Rt. Hon. H.H. (Earl of Oxford and Asquith), 248

Atlantic Ocean, U-boats destroyed in, 5, 7; shipping losses in, 8; mastery of, 163, 212; convoys of arms brought over, 237-8

Attlee, Rt. Hon. Clement R., Deputy Leader of Commons, 9; in National Coalition Government, 11; Lord Privy Seal, 13; on Defence Committee, 18, 220; presents Defence of Realm Bill, 57; at Supreme War Council in Paris, 97-7, 99; and Hitler's Peace Offer, 229; minutes to, 298, 303; mentioned, 108, 183

Australia, informed of British position, 172

Australian forces, arrival of, 40, 50, 124, 145; in Palestine, 112; suggested employment for, 217

Baldwin, Rt. Hon. Stanley (Earl Baldwin of Bewdley), 106

Balkans, Italy and, 113. See also Greece, Roumania, etc.

Baltic Sea, possibility of invasion from, 254, 263, 292

Baltic States, annexed by Russia, 120

Bapaume, 58

Bardufosse aerodrome, 144

Barham, H.M.S., 253

Barratt, Air Chief Marshal Sir A. S., 139

Battleships, resumption of construction programme, 305

Baudouin, Paul, 97, 159, 190

B.B.C., reporting of air raids by, 151; rejection of Peace Offer announced by, 230; French broadcasts of, 301-2

"Beauman Force", 131, 134

Beaverbrook, Lord, Minister of Aircraft Production, 12, 14, 144, 283; visits France with Churchill, 158, 161; on Defence Committee, 220; minutes to, 281, 284, 289, 301; mentioned, 298

Belgian Army, 26, 28-30, 57; driven back, 35, 36, 74; withdrawal of, 52, 55, 58; no direction received by, 61; broken front of, 67, 73-7; possibility of capitulation of, 76, 78; scheme to evacuate, 80; surrender of, 80-1, 83-4, 110

Belgian troops in France 182; Government in Britain, 182; contingent in Britain, 291, 295 n.; help from Congo, 301

Belgium, resistance by, 11; neutrality of prevents joint planning, 26, 31-2; invasion of, 27, 30, 31; Allied advance into, 30-2, 35, 66; Government of,

continues to fight, 81, 84; recognition of Government of, 144; agents in, 217; occupation of, 231; possible invasion from, 263

Berehaven, 136

Bergues, 77, 86, 91

Berkeley, H.M.S., 185

Bessarabia, ceded to Russia, 121

Besson, General, 28

Bevin, Rt. Hon. Ernest, Minister of Labour, 12-13, 99; mentioned, 298

Billotte, General, in the Battle of France, 26, 28-9, 60; shortcomings of, 48, 51, 67; death of, 55, 58

Birmingham, aircraft industries in, 79

Biscay, possible invasion from ports of, 258 n.

Bismarck, the, value of air attack on, 296-7, 300

Black-out, Churchill suggests modifications in, 308-9

Blanchard, General, 60-2; arranges withdrawal to coast, 76; opposed to evacuation, 81-2

Blockade, of France, 100; of Germany, weakening of, 289

Bock, General von, 27-8, 131

Bognor, 270

Bomb sights, automatic, 144; stabilised, 284

Bombs, delayed-action, 144, 306; "sticky", 149-50, 300

Bordeaux, French Government at, 162, 179-92, 201-2; Laval in, 178; de Gaulle escapes from, 191-2

Borkum, scheme to capture (1917), 215

Boulogne, 53, 294; Germans in, 64; defence and evacuation of, 70, 74; gun-battery near, 241; invasion troops near, 262

Bourne, General Sir A. G. B., 219

Brauchitsch, General von, 68-9

Bremen, attacks on shipping in, 271; raid on, 289

Brest, evacuation from, 171-2; invasion troops in, 254, 262

Bretagne, the, 210

Briare, Supreme War Council at, 135, 169, 203

Bridges, Sir Edward, 17-18, 123; minutes to, 17, 219-20, 282-3, 288, 291, 298-9, 303

Brighton, 232-3, 269, 270

Bristol Channel, 302

British Army, fighting forces of, throughout war, 5-6; for Home Defence, 103,

123-5, 173, 246, 252-3, 254, 256-8; reconstruction of, after Dunkirk, 127-8; Highland Division of, in France, 130, 131, 134-5; employed on defence works, 151; arms for, 236-8, 301-2; distribution of, 259-62; regimental distinctions for, 290; band-playing in, 290. *See also* Armoured Division; British Expeditionary Force; Commandos; Territorial Army.

British Empire, contribution of, to war effort, 4-8; determination to fight on in, 163; Fleet to protect, 174

British Expeditionary Force, deployment of, 25-6, 30; frontier defences of, 32, 60, 74; numerical weakness of, 32; repulses attacks, 39, 84; ordered to withdraw, 40, 51-2, 62; dangers facing, 45, 55-6; withdraws to coast, 48, 52-3, 56, 67-78, 80-6; preparations to evacuate, 52-3, 76-7, 80; lost equipment of, 56, 67, 124-5, 128, 226; ordered to attack, 58; put on half-rations, 60; in fighting round Arras, 60-2; flank exposed by Belgian surrender, 75-6, 84; evacuation of, 88 *et seq.*; building of new, 94-5, 103, 117, 123-4, 127-30; in England, 122-3, 173; remnants of, in France, 130, 132, 169, 181; final evacuation of, 171-2. *See also* British Army

Brittany, bridgehead in, 123, 161, 169; Churchill and Reynaud propose to meet in, 185-6

Brooke, Field-Marshal Sir Alan (Viscount Alanbrooke), C.I.G.S., 19, 234; with B.E.F., 68, 84-5, 169; evacuates troops, 171, 233; in command of Home Defence, 233-4, 262-3; Churchill's association with, 233-4; minutes to, 252

Brooke, Ronnie, 234 *n.*

Brooke, Victor, 233 *n.*

Brown, Rt. Hon. Ernest, Secretary of State for Scotland, 14

Bukovina, Russia and, 121

Bulge, Battle of the, 43 *n.*, 44-6

Bullitt, William C., and the French plea for British air support, 126; mentioned, 158

Burma Road, closing of, 225, 293

Calais, evacuation from, planned, 53; German threat to, 64, 80; defence of, 70-3; British tanks in, 71-2, 131; gun-batteries near, 238, 240; bombardment of, 241 *n.*; invasion troops in, 262

Caldecote, Viscount, Dominions Secretary and Leader of Lords, 14

Cambrai, 57-8, 62, 74

Campbell, Rt. Hon. Sir Ronald, Ambassador to France, 176, 179, 181-2, 184-6; supports Reynaud, 188

Campinchi, César, 193

Canada, promise to send French Fleet to, 142, 158; tank landing-craft built in, 222; evacuation of children to, 292 *n.*

Canadian Forces, in Dunkirk, 71; for France, 124, 128, 130, 171; in Home Defence, 232, 264; in Iceland, 236, 294

Canary Islands, plan to seize, 284

Cangé, French Cabinet meet at, 162, 176

Canterbury, 270

Cape route, shipping deflected to, 40, 112

Carr, Lt.-General L., 147, 149

Carvin, 76

Casablanca, *Massilia* at, 193-4; *Jean Bart* at, 206; mentioned, 150

"Catapult", Operation, 206-10

Centurion, H.M.S., 264

Chamberlain, Rt. Hon. Neville, in National Coalition Government, 9-10; Lord President, 13; Churchill's letters to, 10, 48; on Defence Committee, 18; presents Defence of Realm Bill, 57; Italian policy of, 106; at the talks in London with M. Reynaud, 108; and Hitler's Peace Offer, 229

Channel ports of France, plans to raid, 217; invasion forces at, 250, 255, 258, 262

Charles-Roux, François, 190

Chautemps, Camille, suggests asking conditions of armistice, 178-9, 188; Vice-President of Council, 189, 192

Chemical warfare, precautions against use of, 291-2; stocks for, 310-11

Cherbourg, 171

Chiang Kai-shek, Generalissimo, 293, 296

Chiefs of Staff Committee, 15-16, 19-20; Combined, 20, 219-20; on ability of Britain to fight alone, 78-9; minutes to, 242, 251, 290, 302; on defence against invasion, 260-1; makes for good teamwork, 277

China, Japanese war against, 293

Church bells, ringing of, a false alarm, 276

Churchill, Rt. Hon. Winston S., forms Government, 8 *et seq.*; Leader of Commons, 9; as Minister of Defence, 15, 19, 219-21; minutes of, 17, 144-54, 234-237, 281 *et seq.*; personal messages of, to heads of Governments, 21, 128-30; his personal relations with President 21-2; correspondence with President, 22, 50-1, 116, 127, 135, 157-8, 163, 166, 223; speeches to Commons, 24, 83-4, 87, 102-3, 197-9, 210-11, 213, 250, 303; in France, 40-6, 56-9, 96-100, 135-40, 158-62; and evacuation of French troops, 94-5, 97-8; letter to Stalin, 119; lucky escape of, 141; arranges to meet Reynaud, 182, 185-6; broadcasts of, 191, 303; Darlan's letter to, 203-5; original plans of (1917) for tank landingcraft and artificial islands, 214-17; takes over Joint Planning Committee, 219-221; visits coastal defences, 232-3; minutes of, on Invasion, 252-4, 256-260

Ciano, Count, and Italian entry into war, 108, 111, 113-14; his letter to Churchill, 115; diaries of, quoted, 230; *Diplomatic Papers* of, quoted, 228, 230

City of Benares, the, 292 n.

Civil Defence Service (A.R.P.), duties of, in invasion, 298, 303

Clemenceau, Georges, 162

Coal reserves, 301-2; of railways, 304

Colijn, Dr., 31

Combined Operations Command, 219, 222

Comines, 84

Commandos, origin of, 147, 218; plans for raids by, 214, 217, 288; in Home Defence, 251-2

Commons, House of, absentee members of, 289-90

Communists, effect of, on French Army 26; in Britain, internment of, 50

Compiègne, the Armistice at, 272

Conseil Supérieur de l'Air, 140 n.

Conservative Party, attitude of, to Churchill, 8-9, 211

Convoys, of arms from America, 237-8, 291; Channel, attacks on, 283, 288

Cooper, Rt. Hon. Alfred Duff, Minister of Information, 13; minutes to, 151, 301-2; at Rabat, 194

Cooper, Rt. Hon. T. M., Lord Advocate, 14

Corap, General, 33, 39

Corbin, Pierre, 180, 182, 184

Cork and Orrery, Admiral of the Fleet Earl of, 48

Corregidor, evacuation of American garrison at, 96

Corvettes, at Dunkirk, 89

Courtrai, 73

Coventry, aircraft industries at, 78

Cranborne, Viscount (5th Marquis of Salisbury), Paymaster-General, 14

Crete, mentioned, 40, 112

Cripps, Rt. Hon. Sir Stafford, Ambassador to Moscow, 118-20

"Cromwell", code word, 276

Cross, Rt. Hon. Sir Ronald, Minister of Shipping, 14

Cross-Channel guns, British, 218, 240-5; German, 238, 240-2, 244

Cruisers, at Dunkirk, 89, 94; *rôle* of, in invasion, 253

"Cultivator No. 6", 282

Cunningham of Hyndhope, Admiral of the Fleet Viscount, 210; minutes to, 308

Cunningham, Admiral Sir John, at Dakar, 304

Cuxhaven, attacks on shipping in, 271

Czech troops in France, 182; contingent in Britain, 291, 295 n.

Dakar, *Richelieu* at, 206, 210; choice of day for occupation of, 304

Daladier, Edouard, 42, 46; Foreign Minister, 51; proclaims French administration in Africa, 193

Dalton, Rt. Hon. Hugh, Minister of Economic Warfare, 14

Darlan, Admiral, at Supreme War Council, 97-8; promises not to surrender French Fleet, 141, 142, 158, 191, 202; 208n; Minister of Marine, 190, 202, sends *Massilia* to Africa, 192; his opportunities and failure at Bordeaux, 201-3; his letter to Churchill, 203; in Africa, 204; mentioned, 163, 209

Deal, 269-70

Defence, Minister of, 15-16, 19; takes over control of Joint Planning Committee 219-21

Defence of Realm Act, 56-7

Delayed-action bombs, 307

Denmark, agents in, 217; occupation of, 231

Destroyers, loan of American, 22-3, 50, 117, 167, 286; at Dunkirk, 89, 92, 94; for Mediterranean, 97; report on, called for, 124; Canadian, 129; *rôle* of, in Home Defence, 252-3; in Channel, 274-275

Dieppe, 134

Dill, Field-Marshal Sir John, C.I.G.S., 19 65; with Churchill in Paris, 40, 45-6, 56,

58; sent to Georges' H.Q., 52; with Lord Gort, 64, 72; signs Chiefs of Staff's report on war situation, 79; minutes to, 94, 282, 301; at Supreme War Council, 96-7, 136, 139; and functions of Joint Planning Committee, 220

Dinant, 35, 36

Dive-bombers, and German advance, 28-9, 36; in invasion preparations, 275

Dominions, informed of British position, 157, 172-4

Dover, defences of, 232, 240, 299; cross-Channel guns at, 240; bombardment of, 241; planned capture of, 270; mentioned, 88, 122, 244, 248, 264

Dover, Straits of, movement of German ships through, 235, 254-5, 261-2; minefield in, 237; German attempt to dominate, 240-5, 248, 267, 269; invasion army to cross, 269

Dowding, Air Chief Marshal Lord, on defence of Britain, 38, 249; mentioned, 129, 137

Duncan, Rt. Hon. Sir Andrew, President of Board of Trade, 13

Dunkerque, the, 206, 209, 210

Dunkirk, 28; withdrawal of Army to, 52, 68, 78, 80-6; evacuation from, 53, 88 *et seq.*; German threat to, 64; bridge-head at, 68, 76-7, 86; failure of German armour to attack, 69; Allied troops' arrival at, 86, 90; shipping losses at, 89-90, 100-1; air attacks on beaches, 91-2, 101-2, 173; evacuation of French from, 94-5, 97-8, 100-1

Dutch Army, 26, 28; Government in Britain, 31, 144; vessels used at Dunkirk, 53, 89-90; brigade in Britain, 144, 291, 295 *n.*

Dyle, river, 25, 32

"Dynamo", Operation, 53, 88-102

East Africa, Union brigade for, 111

Eastbourne, 270

E-boats, 288

Economic Warfare, Ministry of, 294

Eden, Rt. Hon. Anthony, War Minister, 13, 127; proposes formation of Local Defence Volunteers, 48; and defence of Calais, 73; minutes, telegrams, etc., to, 94, 145-8, 151, 220, 233, 236,-7, 288, 290, 294, 301, 304, 306-7; at Supreme War Council, 136, 139; and Franco-British Union 182, 185-6; mentioned, 80, 108, 171

Egypt, Indian troops for, 146, 153, 285, 308

Eire, possibility of German attack on, 23, 153, 254; suggested visit of U.S. squadron to, 23-4, 129, 136

Eisenhower, General Dwight David, 4, 169

Emden, attacks on shipping in, 271

English Channel, heavy batteries on coasts of, 238, 240-5, 267; invasion across, 250, 254-6, 261-2 266 *et seq.*; tides and currents of, 268, 270; German need for air superiority over, 272. *See also* Channel ports; Cross-Channel guns; Dover, Straits of

Erebus, H.M.S., 241-2, 245

Estonia, annexed by Russia, 120-1

Evacuation of invasion areas, 232, 235-6; of children abroad, 292 *n.*

Excess Profits Tax, 56

Fascists, in Britain, internment of, 50

Fayolle, Marshal, 97

Flame-throwers, 304-5

Fleet Air Arm, transfer of pilots from, to Fighter Command, 144

Foch, Marshal, 32

Folkestone, 262, 270

Fonblanque, Major-General E. B. de, 172

Food supplies, 299

Forbes, Admiral of the Fleet Sir C. M., 257

Force H, Oran, 207

Foreign corps in Great Britain, 291, 294-5

Foreign Legion, of anti-Nazi Germans, 291-2, 294-5

Fortune, Major-General Sir Victor, 134

France, collapse of, 3, 115, 142; gap in defences of, 33-4; aircraft for aid of, 45-6, 126, 137, 139, 189; possibility of capitulation of, 50, 78, 81, 100, 108-9, 116, 128, 138-9, 141-2, 158; Belgians in, 81; new B.E.F. for, 94-5, 103, 117, 123-124, 127-30; attempts to appease Italy, 108-11; Italy at war with, 111, 114-15; British bombers in Southern, 112-14, 139; troops sent to, 130; seeks Britain's sanction for separate peace, 159-64, 176, 179, 181; sacrifices of, 159-61; restoration of, 161, 165, 198; union between Britain and, 165, 180, 182-4, 186-8; asks for armistice, 171, 177-180, 192-3, 205; Laval's plans for, 178; scheme to help Frenchmen escape from, 193-4; conjectural effects of British union with, 195-6; attitude of, to British action at Oran 212; occupation of all, 204; agents in, 217, 300; weakening effect of continued fighting in, 227; German batteries on coast of, 238, 240 *et seq.*, 262, 267; raids on coast of, 294; information from unoccupied, 299-300. *See also* Channel ports, Free French, Vichy Government

Franco-British Union, draft declaration of, 183-4, 186; conjectural results of, 195

Franco-Italian campaign, 114-15

François-Poncet, André, 114

Franklyn, General Sir H. E., 61-2

Free French, in Britain, 291, 295 *n.*; equipment for, 295, 299

French Air Force, 47, 182

French Army, collapse of, 4, 29, 52-3; deterioration in, 26; deployment of, 28; fancied superiority of, 32, 34; faults in disposition of, 33-4, 42-3, 45, 66-7; in Belgium, 35; driven back, 35, 36 *et seq.*, 40, 67; no strategic reserve of, 42, 137; southward retreat of Northern, 51, 55; lack of co-ordination in, 60-1; withdrawal of Northern to Dunkirk, 76-8, 81-2, 85; evacuation of, 82-3, 86, 94-5, 97-8, 100-1, 130; evacuation of, from Norway, 97, 130; success of Alpine troops against Italy, 114-15; final defeat of, 130, 131, 134, *et seq.*, 167 *et seq.*; repatriation of troops in England, 150; exhausted state of, 159; "Cease Fire" offered to, 177-8; supplies for, 287; regimental badges of, 290

French Empire, France retains obligation to defend, 204; in India, 310. *See also* Africa, North Africa

French Navy, Darlan promises not to surrender, 140, 142, 158, 202-3; possible fate of, 166, 287; removal to safe ports, 176, 179, 181-2, 184-5, 187-8, 190-1, 203; Darlan's work for, 201-2; voluntary destruction of Toulon fleet, 203; Armistice conditions concerning, 205; disposition of, 206; British action to eliminate, 207 *et seq.*, 286

Frère, General, 57, 59, 63-4

Furnes, 77, 86

Gamelin, General, Plan D of, 25-6, 30; retains supreme direction of armies, 33; announces French defeat, 42, 47; on disposition of troops, 44; asks for R.A.F.

fighters, 45; final order of, 51, 67; dismissed from Supreme Command, 67; on Britain's help in the air battle, 140 *n.*; mentioned, 36, 40

Gaulle, General de, at Supreme War Council at Briare, 136, 138; favours carrying on a guerrilla war, 142; aid for, 150, 288; supports Franco-British Union, 180, 182-4, 186; in London, 189; escapes from France, 191-2; broadcasts of, 192, 301; and action against French Fleet, 212; mentioned, 158, 162, 194, 310

Genoa, preparations for air attacks on, 98

Gensoul, Admiral, 209

George, Rt. Hon. David Lloyd (Earl Lloyd George), 214-15

Georges, General, in Battle of France, 31, 33, 36, 40, 48, 169; Dill sent to, 52; Churchill wishes to visit, 59; at Supreme War Council, 137-8, 158; evidence of, at Pétain trial, 196; and Darlan, 202

German Air Force, in France, 29; dive-bombers of, 28-9; losses of, 47, 50, 91; raids Dunkirk and beaches, 89, 91-2, 101-2; hope of breaking, 129-30; pilots of, prisoners in France, 161, 286; R.A.F. superiority over, 249, 264; part of, in invasion, 269, 273-4; increase in fighting strength of, 275

German Army, new technique of, 22; in 1940, 26-7; Panzer divisions of, 27-8, 38-9, 51, 53, 66, 131, 168; deployment of, in attack on France, 27, 34-5, 66-7; advances through Belgium, 35, 36, 48; advances through France, 36-42, 45-6, 131, 134, 167-8; husbanding of Panzer divisions of, 68-9; pincers movement of, 77, 86; at French rear in South, 114-15; strength of, 140, 225; assembly of, for invasion, 262; views of, on invasion, 268-71, 277; marches through Paris, 272

German Navy, losses by, 5, 7, 268; plans invasions of Britain, 266-71; battleships of, 296-7, 300. *See also* U-boats

Germany, invades Low Countries, 25-32; possible invasion of Britain by, 78-9; Italian relations with, 106, 108; against interference in Balkans, 113; friendly relations of, with Russia, 117-19, 121; attacks Russia, 119, 268; use of captured countries for war production, 152; air raids on, 173, 228, 287, 289, 292; French armistice with, 192-3; disappointed in British reception of Peace Offer, 230;

crimes of Nazi, 231; lack of co-ordination between Services in, 277; agents in countries occupied by, 294

Gibraltar, evacuation of civilians from, 40; factor in the appeasement of Italy, 109; Italian ships detained at, 114; French bombs on, 211; Spain and, 226, 286; Germany and, 228; alternative base to, danger to ships in harbour of, 285, 293

Giraud, General, 25, 44

Glasgow, mentioned, 290

Glasgow, H.M.S., guns from, for Dover defences, 244

Glass, supply of, 310, 318

Gneisenau, the, 253 *n.*, 300

Godefroy, Admiral, 210

Goering, Hermann, confident of German success in air, 272, 277; fails to co-operate in invasion plans, 277

Gort, Field-Marshal Viscount, in command of B.E.F., 31, 43, 55, 72; considers possibility of withdrawal to coast, 48, 52, 67-8; on dangers of southward march, 55-6, 67; Churchill's telegrams and letters to, 58, 80; left without orders, 59; proposes to attack, 60, 62; southward move of, 64, 71, 74-6; withdraws to Dunkirk, 68, 75-8, 80-6; and relief of Calais, 71-3, 80; abandons Weygand plan, 74-6, 86; ordered to embark, 95-6, 98; and new B.E.F., 103, 124, 169; at Rabat, 194

Gravelines, 77, 86; waterline, 70, 73-4

Gravesend, 270

Graziani, Marshal, 113

Great Britain, magnitude of war effort of, 4-8; air squadrons needed to defend, 38, 45, 78-9, 137, 173; defences of, 78-9, 123-5, 127, 129, 146 *et seq.*, 232 *et seq.*, 247 *et seq.* (*see also* Home Defence); ability of, to fight alone, 78-80, 128, 138, 227-8; morale in, 79, 81, 146, 211, 226, 278; determined to fight on, 88, 99, 103-4, 127, 138, 146, 160-1, 163, 165, 191, 197-9, 226-7; threat of invasion of, 103, 117, 125, 146, 152, 172-3, 200, 214, 232, 234 *et seq.*, 245-6, 247 *et seq.*; Italy at war with, 114, 225; relations of, with Russia, 117-20; refuses to agree to France making separate peace, 159-64, 176; danger of air-borne attack on, 127, 146, 172-3, 214; proposed union between France and, 180, 182-4, 186-8; strength of position of, 172-4, 211; agrees conditionally to French asking terms of

armistice, 179, 181, 190; fights alone, 191, 225 *et seq.*; prepares to attack, 201, 213 *et seq.*; danger to, of loss of French Fleet, 205; German air attacks on, 230 (*see also* Air raids); possibility of invasion of (1914), 247-8; power of Navy to protect, 248; British air mastery over, 264; team-work between Services in, 277

Greece, Italian threat to, 112

Greenwood, Rt. Hon. Arthur, 11; in War Cabinet, 13; and Production Council, 56; minute to 293

Griffiths, Lieutenant P.M.K., 207 *n.*

Gris-Nez, Cape, gun batteries at, 238, 240 *et seq.*

Guernsey, 288, 294

Guerrilla warfare, possibility of, in France. 128, 137-8, 142, 160

Gunboats, at Dunkirk, 89

Haakon, King of Norway, 97

Halder, General, on the reduced German forces facing Russia, 27; on Hitler's intervention in the Battle of France, 68; invasion plans of, 269-71, 277

Halifax, Earl of, Foreign Secretary, 13; in the attempt to appease Italy, 106, 108, 110; at Tours, 158, 161; supports union with France, 180; broadcast of, on Peace Offer, 229-30; minutes to, 286, 288, 293, mentioned, 10, 203

Hankey, Lord, Chancellor of Duchy of Lancaster, 14

Harwich, 232, 244, 248, 263

Hastings, 270

Havre, war materials moved from, 64; withdrawal to, 134; burning of, 141

Hendon, aircraft at, 308

Hermes, H.M.S., 210

Hermione, the, 298

Herriot, Edouard, 162, 179; goes to Africa, 193

Himmler, Heinrich, 228

Hitler, Adolf, his agreement with Stalin, 27; military initiative rests with, 66; and conservation of armoured forces at Dunkirk, 68-70; secures postponement of Italy's entry into war, 108; meetings with Mussolini, 114; Ciano on, 115; and Stalin, 117-18; decides on war with Russia, 119, 200; possible effects of Franco-British Union upon, 196; might have offered tempting peace terms, 198;

mistakes of, in strategy, 227, 255; invasion plans of, 228, 230, 267-70; Peace Offer of, 229-30; jubilation of, on fall of Paris, 272; postpones invasion, 274

Hoare, Rt. Hon. Sir Samuel (Viscount Templewood), mentioned, 10, 106

Holidays, 298, 299

Holland, resistance by, 11, 30; French help for, 25, 30, 35; invasion of, 27, 30, 31; inundation of, 31; capitulation of, 39; agents in, 217; occupation of, 231; possible invasion from, 254, 263. *See also* Dutch

Holland, Captain C. S., at Oran, 207, 209

Hollis, Colonel Sir Leslie, 19

Home Defence, air squadrons needed for, 38, 45, 78-9, 137, 173; troops needed for, 49-50; against air-borne attack, 49, 156, 238, 251; Navy's *rôle* in, 78-9, 167, 172, 248-53, 255-7; Air Force's *rôle* in, 78-9, 129, 172, 249, 252, 257; B.E.F. available for, 103, 123-5, 173; coastal, 127, 147, 240, 245, 251, 258, 264; guns for, 147, 218, 236 *et seq.*; tanks for, 147, 245; Home Guard and, 147, 238, 252, 254; against tanks, 148, 251-2; Churchill inspects the defences, 232-3; bus transport for, 233; Southern Command of, 233; protection of civilians in invasion areas, 235-6; reserves of mobile troops in, 251-2, 255, 258, 261-2, 301; lines of, 257-8; distribution of troops in, 259-62; German recognition of effectiveness of, 274-5; civilian labour for, 287; and delayed-action bombs, 307

Home Guard, start of, 48-9, 147; manning of, 148; employment of 154-5, 252, 254; arms for, 235 *et seq.*, 246, 295, 302; called out in error, 276; uniforms for, 297; Reserve, 304; "Auxiliary Units" of, 306

Hood, H.M.S., at Oran, 207; guns from, 245; at Gibraltar, 285, 293; mentioned, 296, 297

Hopkins, C. J. W., 218, 219

Hore-Belisha, Rt. Hon. Leslie, 33

Horn Reef, plan to build island in (1917), 215-16

Hudson, Rt. Hon. Robert, Minister of Agriculture, 14

Hull, Cordell, on Britain's will to fight, 126-7

Humber, defences of, 232; cruisers in, 253; mentioned, 302

Huy, 35

Hythe, 270

Iceland, Canadian troops in, 232, 236, 294

Imports, programme for 1941, 301, 306; and closing of ports, 302-3

India, exchange of Territorials for Regulars in, 50, 124, 145, 154; employment of troops from, 151-2; French India must recognise de Gaulle, 310

Indian troops, for Palestine, 124, 145-6, 153; use of, 153;

Intelligence, British, 261

Invasion, outlook regarding, 78-9; threat of, 103, 117, 125, 152, 172-3, 200, 214, 232; defence against, 146, 167, 234, 236, 238; 240, 245-6, 247 *et seq.*; of Ireland, 153, 254; protection of civilians in case of, 235-6; naval defence against, 247-253; air-power and, 248-9, 267-9, 272-4, 278; plan of action in case of, 251-2, 257-8; likely areas of attack, 253-6, 261-3; German plan of, 254-5, 261-2, 266 *et seq.*; estimated scales of attack, 256, 258-61; assembly of shipping for, 261-2, 271, 275; time of attack, 263-4, 269, "scare", 264-5; postponement of, 274, 276; rumours concerning, 275-6; declaration of imminence of, 276; laying mines behind landing in, 295; duties of police in case of, 298, 303. *See aslo* Sea Lion

Iraq, Indian troops for, 153

Ireland—*see* Eire, Northern Ireland

Iron Duke, H.M.S., guns from, 245

Ironside, Field-Marshal Lord, sent to Gort, 52, 55; relinquishes C.I.G.S., 64-65; minutes to, 72-3; defence plans of, 155; Brooke succeeds in Home Defence, 233-4; mentioned, 73, 79

Ismay, General Lord, head of the Military Wing of the War Cabinet Secretariat, 19; minutes to, 17, 49 71-2, 94, 111-12, 123-5, 147, 149, 152-3, 193, 207, 214, 217-20, 235, 237, 242, 244, 281-2, 286-8, 290-4, 297, 299, 302, 304-6, 308-10; with Churchill in Paris, 40, 43 *n.*, 45; at Supreme War Council, 96-7, 196, 199; at Tours, 198; and Joint Planning Committee, 220; mentioned, 21, 65

Italian Air Force, squadrons of, attack Britain 228

Italian Army, divisions of, offered to Hitler, for the invasion of Britain, 228
Italian Navy, losses of, 5, 7; importance of attacking, 112
Italy, expected intervention of, 23; preparations for such intervention, 40, 97-99, 111-144; British relations with, 105-6; results of neutrality of, 106; Churchill's approach to, 107-8; declares war, 108, 111, 114, 225; French attempts to appease, 108-11; plans attack on Yugoslavia, 113; campaign of, against France, 114-15; air raids on, 114, 139; conjectural effect on, of Franco-British Union, 195; ships for attack on, 305

Jacob, Hon. Major-General Sir E. I. C., in the Military Wing of the War Cabinet Secretariat, 19; minutes to, 289
Japan, and U.S., 23; and closing of Burma Road, 225-6, 293; possible war against, 296-7, 300
Jean Bart, the, 206, 288
Jeanneney, Jules, 162, 179, 188; goes to Africa, 193
Jefferis, Major-General Sir M. R., 148-9, 305
Jersey, 288
Jews, in Palestine, arming of, 153-4, 281, 286
Jodl, General, 272, 277;
Joint Intelligence Staff, 289
Joint Planning Committee, Churchill takes over, 219-21; minute to, 308
Jowitt, Rt. Hon. Sir William (Viscount), Solicitor-General, 14

Karlsruhe, 36
Keitel, Marshal, in the Battle of France, 68-9; on difficulty of attacking England, 228; and Operation "Sea Lion," 272
Kenley Air Station, 306
Kennedy, J. P., U.S. Ambassador, 162-5
Kent, defence of, 242, 244; attacks on airfields of, 272; miners of, 302
Keyes, Admiral of the Fleet Sir Roger (Baron), and King Leopold, 61; telegram to, 80; on surrender of King Leopold, 80-1; Director of Combined Operations, 219; studying subject of raids, 294

Kiel, attacks on shipping in, 271; bombing of canal, 292; mentioned, 242, 300
Kind, Admiral E. J. (U.S.N.), 20
King, Rt. Hon. W L. Mackenzie, Churchill's correspondence with, 128, 199; informed of British position, 172-3; mentioned, 292
Kleist, General von, 28, 36
Kluge, General von, 69

Labour Party, seeks purge of "guilty men", 9-10
Labour Supply, Director of, 56
Lancastria, the, loss of, 172
Landing-Craft Tank, genesis of, 215, 217-19; development and use of, 221
Landing Ships Infantry, 223
Landing Ships Tank, 222
Langley Aerodrome, 290
Laon, 40
Latvia, annexed by Russia, 120-1
Laval, Pierre, policy of, 178; and Ministry of Foreign Affairs, 190; against Government in N. Africa, 192
Leahy, Admiral W. D. (U.S.N.), 20
Lebrun, Albert, 179-80, 184, 192, 212
Leeb, Marshal von, 27, 131
Lend-Lease, 7
Leopold, King of Belgians, conference of Weygand with, 55; capitulation of, 67, 74, 80-1; Churchill's message to, 80-1; Churchill on surrender of, 83-4
Liberty Ships, 8
Lille, 76-7, 84; surrender of, 86
Lindemann, Prof. F. A. (Baron Cherwell). minutes to, 152, 236, 282-4, 287, 299; mentioned, 149, 281-2, 301
Lithuania, annexed by Russia, 120-1
Liverpool, mentioned, 290
Lloyd, Lord, of Dolobran, Colonial Secretary, 13; anti-Jewish attitude of, 153-4; minutes to, 154, 281, 285; in Bordeaux, 191, 203; mentioned, 146
Local Defence Volunteers, 48-9, 147; renaming of, 148. See also Home Guard
Loire, river, 168
London, defence of, 235, 244, 256, 258, 293; bombing of, 272; delayed-action bombs in, 307; imports through Port of, 302; blak-out in, 309
Longwy, 28, 34
Loraine, Rt. Hon. Sir Percy, Ambassador to Rome, 115

Lothian, Marquess of, Churchill's correspondence with, 201; mentioned, 50, 199, 229
Louis of Battenberg, Prince, 248
Louvain, 26
Luxembourg, invasion of, 30; mentioned, 36
Lyme Regis, 269
Lys, river, 55, 77, 82

MacArthur, General D. (U.S.A.), at Corregidor, 96
Macdonald, Rt. Hon. Malcolm, Minister of Health, 13
McNaughton, General the Hon. A.G.L. (Can), 236
Maginot Line, 28, 30; gap at end of, 33; troops in, 34, 43; surrender of, 168
Malta, shipping at, 144; air defences for, 290-1; mentioned, 195
Mandel, Georges, Minister of Interior, 158-9; and Franco-British Union, 184, 188; in Africa, 192-3; imprisonment and death, 193
Manston airfield, 309
Margerie, Captain Roland de, 97, 100
Margesson, Rt. Hon. David (Viscount), minute to, 303
Marin, Louis, 184
Marne, river, 168
Marseilles, British bombers, at, 114, 139
Marshall, General G. C. (U.S.A.), 19-20; and arms for Britain, 125-6
Martel, Lieut.-General Sir G. Le Q., 61
Martinique, 206
Massilia, the, 193-4
Mayfield, 270
Meat supplies, 287
Mediterranean, U-boats destroyed in, 5; shipping diverted from, 40, 112; destroyers for, 97; Italian grievances in, 108-11; Allied mastery of, 111-12; conjectural effect of Franco-British Union in, 195; elimination of French Fleet in, 208 et seq.
Mediterranean Fleet, rôle of, 285; and defence of Egypt, 308
Merchant ships, losses in, 5; conversion of, to tankcarrying, 223-4
Mersa Matruh, defence position at, 308; troops at, 308
Mers-el-Kebir, 206, 208
Mersey, the, volume of imports through, 302

Meuse, river, 26, 29, 33, 35; Germans cross, 35, 36
Middle East, position in, 146; possible spread of war in, 153; landing-craft tanks in, 221; training centres for amphibious warfare in, 222; reinforcements for 223, 310
Milan, preparations for air attacks on, 98, 109, 139; air raids on, 114
Minefield(s), off French coast, 237, 262; to cover invasion, 250, 267, 269, 272; to cover South-Western Approaches, 259; aerial, 290
Mines, fluvial, 36, 285; aerial, 290; laying of, behind invaders landing, 295; in enemy harbours, 296
Minesweepers, at Dunkirk, 90
Molinié, General, 86
Molotov, M., praises German victories, 117-19
"Monday Cabinet Parade", 18
Monnet, Jean, 180, 182, 189
Montgomery, Field-Marshal Sir Bernard (Viscount), in Battle of France, 36, 68, 130; and Home Defences, 232; mentioned, 4
Monthermé, 28
Morgenthau, Henry, Jr., 302
Morice, M., Deputy-Governor of Rabat, 194
Morocco, evacuated French forces repatriated in, 150; plan to land force in, 288
Morrison, Rt. Hon. Herbert, Minister of Supply, 13, 144; suggests a new name for the Local Defence Volunteers, 148; minutes to, as M. of S., 286, 298
Morrison, Rt. Hon. W. S., Postmaster-General, 14
Morton, Major Sir Desmond, and the proposed Franco-British Union, 180, 182, 184; to receive secret reports from France, 299, 300
Motor torpedo-boats, at Dunkirk, 90
Mottistone, Lord, 298
"Mulberry", genesis of, 215-17
Munich, Hitler and Mussolini meet at, 114
Munitions, minute on, 283
Murray, Dr. Charles, quoted, 135
Mussolini, Benito, expected intervention of, 22-3; relations of, with Britain, 105-107; Churchill's correspondence with, 107-8; determines on war, 108, 111, 113-14; French attempts to buy off, 108-111; plans attack on Yugoslavia, 113; his meetings with Hitler, 114; Ciano on,

116 ; offers army and air force to Hitler, 228; wants war with Britain, 230

Oran, French fleet at, 206; British action against the French fleet, 208 et seq.
Ostend, 80
"Overlord," Operation 234

Namur, 26
Narvik, evacuation of, decided upon, 97; mentioned, 47, 124, 144, 150, 218
National Coalition Government, formation of, 8 et seq,; composition of, 13–14
Nazi-Soviet Relations, quoted, 117–18
Nelson, H.M.S., 206, 253, 285,
New Zealand, informed of British position, 172–4
Newall, Marshal of the Royal Air Force Sir C. L. N. (Baron), Chief of Air Staff, 19; and Britain's ability to fight on, 79, 174; minutes to, 284, 305, 309
Newcastle, H.M.S., guns from, 244
Newfoundland, internees to be sent to, 283
Nicholson, Brigadier Claude, 73
Nieuport, 77, 86, 91
Noguès, General, 193–4
Nore, the, 248
Normandy, invasion troops in, 262
North Africa, possibility of carrying on warm from, 100, 138, 159–60, 162, 172; French troops transported to, 150; Britain offers transport for French Government to, 176; scheme to transfer the French Government to, 176–7, 184–5, 187, 192; Frenchmen arrested in, 193–4; conjectured results in, of Franco-British Union, 195–6; Darlan and the landing of Allied troops in, 204; plan for co-operating with French in, 288
North Foreland, 269
North Sea, invasion across, 253
Northern Ireland, troop movements to, 153
Norway, no further reinforcements for 47; evacuation of troops from, 97; Russian congratulations on invasion of, 117–18; French troops evacuated from, 130; destruction of British aerodromes in, 144; Commandos in, 218; German occupation of, 231; Germany transfers bombers from, 275
Norwegian contingent in Britain, 295 n.

Oil imports, mentioned, 306
Oise, river, 167

Pacific Ocean, the war in, 5, 8; American Fleet in, 24;
P.A.C. rockets, 307
Palestine, Regular troops from, 49, 112, 124, 281; Indian troops for, 124, 145–6, 153; difficulty in drawing troops from, 145, 153–4; arming Jews of, 153–4, 281, 286
Parachute mines, and cable rockets, 307
Parachute troops, danger from, in England, 127, 146, 172, 293; British, 218
Paris, Churchill's visits to, 40 et seq., 56–9, 96–100; preparations to evacuate the Government from, 42; air raids on, 59, 100; seat of government moved from, 135; defence of, 136, 140; fall of, 139, 158, 168; Armée de, 167–8; German Army in, 272
Pas de Calais, invasion troops in, 262; dive-bombers in, 275
Pasteur, the, 189
P.E. fuzes—see Photo-electric fuzes
Pearl Harbour, American fleet at, 24
Peirse, Air Chief Marshal Sir R. E. C., Vice-Chief of Air Staff, 79; minutes to, 292, 305
Personnel ships, at Dunkirk, 53, 90, 92
Pétain, Marshal, and the Ardennes, 33; Vice-Président of Council, 51; at Supreme War Council, 97, 100, 136, 140; and French surrender, 100, 139, 141–2, 158; supports Weygand's demand for armistice, 178–80, 188; threatens to resign, 179–80; opposes Franco-British Union 187; "Armistice" Government of, 189–90; message from Churchill to, 190–1; and North African Government, 192; trial of, 196; and the French Fleet, 208 n.; becomes President, 212
Petersfield, 271
"Petreforce," 48
P.F. fuze—see Proximity fuze
Phillips, Admiral Sir Tom, Vice-Chief of Naval Staff, 79; minutes to, 295, 296
Photo-electric (P. E.) fuzes, 290, 300
Pim, Captain Sir R. P., 89
Pleven, René, 180, 182

Plymouth, French naval ships at, 206, 207; a possible invasion point, 263, 264
Police, duties in invasion, 298, 303
Polish troops evacuated from France, 171; Government in Britain, 182; contingent in Britain, 291, 295
Portal, Marshal of the Royal Air Force Sir Charles (Viscount), Chief of Air Staff, 19
Portland, 248, 263
Portsmouth, French naval ships at, 206, 207; shortage of troop transport at, 233; a possible invasion point, 263; mentioned, 248, 271
Pound, Admiral of the Fleet Sir Dudley, death of, 20; a Chief of Naval Staff, 79; at Bordeaux, 191, 211; minutes to, 223, 236, 295-6, 306, 308; on invasion forces 255-6
Pownall, Lt.-General Sir Henry 81
Prayer, Day of, 291
Press, treatment of air raids by, 151; rejection of Peace Offer announced in, 230; Churchill's statement to, on the possibility of invasion, 231-2
Prételat, General, 2
Prioux, General 82-3
Production Council, 56, 299
Provence, the, 210
Proximity (P.F.) fuzes, 144, 281, 284
Purvis, Arthur, 23

Quo Tai-chi, Mr., 296

Rabat, Mandel at, 194
Raeder, Admiral, invasion plans of, 266-270; realises difficulties, 268, 274-5, 277
Railways, coal reserves of, 304; question of ready adaptability of, 305
Ramsay, Admiral Sir B. H., and evacuation from Dunkirk, 52, 88, 96, 101; at Dover, 240
Ramsbotham, Rt. Hon. Herwald (Baron Soulbury), President of Board of Education, 14
Ramsgate, 269-70
Refugees, blocking roads in France, 71, 78, 137, 159; in Tours, 158; U.S. aid to French, 166
Reibel, Charles, 187
Reid, Rt. Hon. J. S. C., Solicitor-General for Scotland, 14
Reigate, 271
Reith, Sir John (Baron), Minister of Transport, 14; minutes to, 302, 304

Renown, H.M.S., at Scapa, 285; mentioned, 297
Repulse, H.M.S., 285
Resolution, H.M.S., at Oran, 207; at Gibraltar, 285, 293
Revenge, H.M.S., 264
Reynaud, Paul, announces French defeat, 38; Churchill meets at his conference in Paris, 42-3, 46; Cabinet changes by, 51, 57, 178; Churchill's letters and telegrams to, 60-1, 109-11, 164-5, 181; reproachful telegrams from, 62-3; told of the intended evacuation of the B.E.F., 77; on surrender of King Leopold, 83-4; at Supreme War Councils, 97-9, 135-6, 138-40; seeks to buy off Mussolini, 108-11; and capitulation, 139 *et seq.*; determined to fight on, 142, 158; seeks release from obligations, 159-61, 163, 181; appeals to Roosevelt, 162-6, 176; seeks to carry on war from N. Africa, 176-7, 179; fails to carry Cabinet, 177-180, 186-8; and Franco-British Union, 180, 182-8; Churchill proposes to meet, 183, 185-6, 188; resignation, 188; and sending to Britain of German prisoner pilots, 286
Rhine, fluvial mines in, 36
Ribbentrop, Herr von, on British defences, 246
Richelieu, the, at Dakar, 206, 210
Riggs, H. C., 89
Rockets, projectors, 281, 300; aerial mines laid by, 299; for proximity fuzes, 284; parachute-and-cable, 307; distress, 307
Rodney, H.M.S., 285
Rommel, Marshal, 61; and the surrender at St. Valery, 134; in the pursuit in the Cherbourg peninsula, 171
Roosevelt, President Franklin D., Chiefs of Staff of, 20; Churchill's personal relations with, 21-2; Churchill's correspondence with, 22, 50-1, 116, 135, 157-158, 163, 166, 223; reads order to Lord Gort, 96; asked to intervene with Italy, 109-10; speech of, on Italian entry into war, 116; sends arms to Britain, 125-7; his faith in Britain's will to fight, 127, 226; French appeals to, 159, 161-6, 176; interest of, in Mediterranean, 196
Rotterdam, German brutality in, 31, 231
Rouen, 131, 134, 168
Roumania, Russian ultimatum to, 120-1; financial retaliation on, 296
Royal Air Force, achievements of, 7; in 1940, 29; proves its superiority, 35, 47,

50, 91, 102-3, 128, 173, 249, 264; attacks bridges, 36, 38; losses of, in Battle of France, 38; needed for Britain's defence, 38, 45, 78-9, 137, 173, 227, 257-8; French demands for, 45-6, 137, 139, 189; in freeing of Amiens, 58; at Dunkirk, 91-2, 94, 102-3, 173, 249; bombers of, at Marseilles, 114, 139; Fleet Air Arm pilots transferred to, 144; German fear of, 228; shortage of pilots in, 228, 283; reconnaissance by, 257, 274; attacks invasion ships, 257, 271, 274; damage to airfields of, 309; shortage of aircraft in, 305; losses of bombers of, 289; plans attacks on German capital ships, 296-7, 300; communication squadrons of, 307; waste of resources of, 308

"Royal Marine," Operation, 36, 284

Royal Marines, Commandos raised from, 218-19; coastal guns manned by, 245

Royal Navy, as "bargaining counter," 51, 126, 201; and Britain's defence 78-79, 172-3, 247-50, 255-7, 264; transports troops from Norway, 97; strategy of Mediterranean fleets, 111-12; fate of, in event of German victory, 166-167, 174, 200; U.S. anxiety for, 199-200, 286; coastal guns manned by, 245; guarantees protection against invasion (1914), 248; patrolling vessels of, 248-9, 253, 257, 275; heavy ships of, in invasion, 253, 257; disposition of ships of, 285; use of P.E. fuzes in, 300; capital ship construction for, 305. See also Force H. Mediterranean Fleet

Royal Sovereign class, reconstruction of, 305

Ruhr, bombing attacks on, 173

Rundstedt, Marshal von, in the Battle of France, 27-8, 131; and conservation of the armoured forces, 68-70; in command of "Sea Lion," 270

Russia, Soviet, German agreement with, 27, 117-19, 226; Cripps Ambassador to, 118-20; Churchill's approach to, 119; annexes Baltic States, 120; demands Roumanian territories, 121; German antagonism to, 199; attack on, 200, 268

Russian Army, invades Baltic States, 120

Rye, 270

St. Helena, internees to be sent to, 283

St. Malo, 171

St. Nazaire, 171-2

St. Valery, 134

Scharnhorst, the, 253 *n.,* 300

Scheldt, river, withdrawal to, 40, 48, 52; rearguard action from, 55; Germans cross, 60; mentioned, 26, 30 39

Schulenburg, Count, receives Russia's congratulations on Germany's war success, 117-19

"Sea Lion," Operation, preparations for, 261-2, 268 *et seq.*; air superiority required for, 267-9, 272; disagreement between Services on, 269-70, 277; shipping for, 271; postponement of, 274; Goering disregards plans of, 277

Second Front, Russian demands for, 27, 119; preparations for, 223-4

Sedan, German break-through at, 36, 39, 40, 42, 43 *n.,* 44-6, 51; mentioned, 28, 33, 35

Seine, river, 131, 134; Lower, 140, 167

Shipping, analysis of losses in, 8; kinds of, used at Dunkirk, 89-90, 92, 100-1; detention of Italian, 112, 114; for assault, 218; German invasion, attacks on, 235-6, 257, 271, 274; assembly of invasion, 261-2, 271, 275; losses in merchant, 306; rockets to protect, 281; sinking of captured, 298; shortage of port facilities for, 303. See also Merchant ships

Simon, Viscount, 10; Lord Chancellor, 13

Sinclair, Rt. Hon. Sir Archibald, Air Minister, 11-13; and the suggested Anglo-French Union, 183; minutes to, 235, 282-4, 288-9, 300, 306-7, 309

Singapore, lack of defences at, 156; reinforcements for, 296; mentioned, 23

Skaarnlands aerodrome, 144

Sloops, at Dunkirk, 89

Slough, 306

Smetona, President, 120

Smoke-screens for factories, 285

Smuts, Field-Marshal the Rt. Hon. J. C., and movement of a Union brigade to East Africa and the Delta, 111; Churchill's correspondence with, 129, 200; informed of British position, 172-4

Somervell, Rt. Hon. Sir Donald, Attorney-General, 14

Somerville, Admiral of the Fleet Sir James F., at Oran, 207 *et seq. See also* Force H

Somme, river, retreat to, 51-2, 56; German forces on, 53; front along, 57, 100, 125, 130, 131

South Beveland, 35, 39

Southampton, imports through, 302, 306

Spain, approach to Africa through, 193, 196; possibilities of danger from, 226, 285; "discussing" Gibraltar with, 286

Spears, Major-General Sir Edward, envoy to M. Reynaud, 64; minute to, 94; at Supreme War Council in Paris, 96-7, 100; at Bordeaux, 188; leaves Bordeaux with de Gaule, 191-2

Spies, German, capture of, 275

Spitfire fighters, 158, 162

Sprague, Commander D. V., 207 n.

Stalin, Generalissimo, Hitler and, 117-18, 464; Churchill's letter to, 119-20

Steel, British need for, 23; from U.S., 286

Stettinius, E.R., Jr., his *Lend-Lease* quoted, 125, 126

Stimson, Henry L., 96

Strasbourg, the, 206, 210

Submarines, Italian, 117; reconnaissance by, 257. *See also* U-boats

Suez, and appeasement of Italy, 109

Supreme War Council, meets in Paris, 96-100, 112; meets at Briare, 135-40

Surcouf, French submarine, 206, 207

Sussex, attacks on airfields of, 272

Swayne, Lt.-General Sir J. G., 59

Sweden, peace overtures through, 229-230

Sylt, scheme to capture (1917), 215

Tangier, 99; International Zone occupied by Spain, 226

Tanks, German, 27-8, 34, 36, 53, 61; French, 28; British shortage of, 29, 128; methods of combating, 54; British, at Arras, 61-2; British, at Calais, 70-2; German, danger of, in Britain, 127, 146 148, 251-2; British, in Home Defence, 147, 245; vessels for landing, 214-222, 249; for raiding, 215, 217; retained in Britain, 310; minutes on, 282-3; production of, to give place to aircraft, 301. *See also* Armoured divisions

Teitgen, Pierre, 212

Tennant, Vice-Admiral Sir W. G., at Dunkirk, 92

Territorial Army, dispatched to India, 50, 124, 145, 154; for B.E.F., 124, 127-8; for Home Defence, 246; mentioned, 152

Thames, cruisers in, 253

Timber supply, 144-5, 293, 303

Tirpitz, the, value of air attack on, 296-7, 300

Tory Island, 297

Toulon, French Fleet at, 206, 226; voluntary destruction of Fleet at, 203, 204

Tours, French seat of government, 135; Churchill in, 158-62

Transport and General Workers' Union, 12

Trondheim, 253

Tunis, and appeasement of Italy, 109; feat of Italian seizure of, 184

Turin, preparations for air attacks on, 98, 109, 139; air raids on, 114

Turkey, friendly relations with, 154; attitude dependent on maintenance of strong British fleet in Eastern Mediterranean, 285

Tyneside, defences of, 232; danger of invasion at, 259

U-boats, losses of, 5, 7; danger of, to Britain, 167; to protect invasion fleet, 267

Umberto, Crown Prince of Italy, 114

United States, magnitude of war effort of, 4-8; British co-ordination with, 19; Chiefs of Staff of, 20; top-level transactions with, 21-2; Britain seeks destroyers from, 22-3, 50, 117, 167; likely effect of British defeat on, 51, 128-9, 166-7, 174, 198; help required from, 99-100, 116, 129, 152, 201; and Italy, 106, 109-10, 114; sends arms, 125-7, 189, 237-8, 291-302; declaration of war sought from, 159-60, 163-6, 176; anxiety of, for British Fleet, 199-200; and immobilisation of French ships, 207-8; tank landing-craft built in, 222-4, 249; fears for Britain in, 226; peace overtures through, 229; coast defence weapons of, 244; steel from, 286; evacuation of children to, 292 n.

United States Air Force, 7

United States Army, fighting forces of, 5-6

United States Navy, in Pacific, 5, 24; visit of squadron to Ireland, 23-4, 129, 136

Unrotated Projectile—*see* Rockets

U.P. weapon—*see* Rockets

Valiant, H.M.S., 207, 285, 293

Vansittart, Rt. Hon. Sir Robert (Baron), 180, 182, 184

Vatican, the, peace moves from, 152, 229

Vichy Government, Mandel and, 194;
Darlan disavowed by, 204; breaks off
relations with Britain, 212
Vincennes, conference at, 57
Volpi, Count, 106
Vuillemin, General, 136
Vyshinsky, M., in Latvia, 120

Wake-Walker, Admiral Sir William, 95
Walcheren, island of, 35, 39, 60
War Cabinet, Sir Archibald Sinclair and,
11; size of, 12; composition of, 13;
meetings of, 15, 18; Secretariat of, 17-
19; on need to retain air defences, 38;
prepares for evacuation of Army, 52-3;
determined to fight on, 80, 157; and
Italian appeasement, 109-11; in consul-
tation on fall of France, 175-6, 180-1;
decides on suggesting union with
France, 180, 182-4; decides on seizure
of French Fleet, 205 et seq.; mentioned,
20, 47, 52, 60, 67, 141, 194, 220, 306
War Cabinet Defence Committee, 16, 18,
40, 220
War Office, to deal with delayed-action
bombs, 307
Wavell, Field-Marshal Sir A. P. (Earl), in
Palestine, 145
Webb, Leading Seaman A., 207 n.
Wedgwood, Hon. Josiah, 235, 281, 293
Wesson, Major-General Charles M.
(U.S.A.), 126
West Indies, raising regiment in, 285
Western Approaches, losses in, 207
Western Prince, the, 291
Westminster Abbey, service of Inter-
cession and Prayer in, 87
Weygand, General, appointed Com-
mander-in-Chief, 51, 54, 67; visits
Northern Army, 54-5; plan of, 57-60;

62-3, 67, 69, 85; Gort abandons plan of,
74-6, 86; at Supreme War Councils, 97,
136-40; Churchill's letter to, 100; demands Britain's air squadrons, 137, 139;
on state of French Army, 137, 141, 158,
159, 169, 177; seeks armistice, 159, 163,
176-9, 188; considers England lost, 187;
Minister of National Defence, 189; and
Laval, 190; messages to, 190-1; against
evacuation of Government to Africa,
192; and the British ultimatum at Oran,
209
Weymouth, 271
Whitchurch, experimental station at, 148
Whitehall, scheme of defence for, 293
Wight, Isle of, 269
Wilhelmina, Queen, 31
Wilhelmshaven, attacks on shipping in,
271
Wilson, Admiral of the Fleet Sir A. K.
("Tug"), 247
Wilson, Sir Horace, mentioned, 299
"Winette," the, 222, 223
Womersley, Rt. Hon. Sir W. J., Minister
of Pensions, 14
Wood, Rt. Hon. Sir Kingsley, Chancellor
of Exchequer, 13; minutes to, 296
Woolton, Lord, Minister of Food, 13
Worthing, 270

Ybarnegaray, Jean, 187
Ypres, conference at, 55; mentioned, 75,
77, 82, 83
Ypres-Comines canal, 76
Yser, river, 84; withdrawal to, 55, 58;
opened sluices of, 58
Yugoslavia, Italy plans attack on, 113,
144

Zhdanov, M., in Estonia, 121

SOURCES OF THE ILLUSTRATIONS

1 Holland flooded. (B.N. Prints)
2 The Germans ford a river in Belgium. (Ullstein, Berlin)
3 A French plane shot down in Belgium, 14th May, 1940. (War Museum)
4 The exodus of the Belgium population. (Army Cinematographic Service)
5 The bombing of the aerodrome at Gilze-Rijen (Holland). (War Museum)
6 A Belgian house on fire after a bombardment. (B.N. Prints)
7 A German rifleman. (Staffel Propaganda)
8 German infantry in action. (War Museum)
9 A flame-thrower. (German Archives)
10 Going through barbed-wire. (Staffel Propaganda)
11 The town after the bombardment. (Army Cinematographic Service)
12 Soldiers wading with difficulty through the water to the nearest craft. (British Information Service)
13 The extraordinary crowding of ships in port. (Safara)
14 British and French soldiers waiting their turn on the beaches for embarkation. (Radio Times, London)
15 A bomb explodes at Dunkirk. (Army Cinematographic Service)
16 What was left of the town on the 4th June, 1940. (German Archives)
17 The beach at Torquay in 1940. (Radio-Times)
18 A fast patrol launch on the Thames. (B.N. Prints)
19 The Blitz of London: scenes of destruction around Saint Paul's Cathedral. (Keystone)
20 The intensive manufacture of shells in British factories. (British Official Photograph)
21 The return of British war wounded from Flanders. (Topical Press)
22 A French 75 mm. gun. (Safara)
23-24 The German advance in Northern France. (Ullstein, Berlin)
25 British Mark VI light tanks during the battle for France. (War Office)
26 Street fighting in a northern French town. (Ullstein)
27 The French rout. (Ullstein)
28 Rouen burning. (Ullstein)
29 A German outpost in Ile-de-France. (German Archives)
30 The enemy at the gates of Paris. (Army Cinematographic Service)
31 A parade of German amphibious vehicles along the Champs-Elysées. (B.N. Prints)
32 A German soldier standing guard on the Place de la Concorde. (World and Camera)
33 A depth-charge explodes as a British destroyer attacks a U-Boat. (War Museum)
34 The German submarine prepares to attack. (War Museum)

35 A German vessel on fire after an attack by the R.A.F. (War Museum)
36 The first photo of an attack on a convoy in the English Channel, 14th July, 1940. (War Museum)
37 The "Home Fleet" patrolling the North Sea. (War Museum)
38 A British freighter escorted by a warship. (Army Cinematographic Service)
39 Hitler and his generals in July 1940. From left to right: Keitel, von Rundstedt, von Bock, Goering, von Brauchitsch, Ritter von Leeb, List, von Kluge, von Witsleben, von Reichenau. (B.N. Prints)
40 The armistice is signed the 22nd June, 1940 at Compiègne. (German Archives)
41 De Gaulle broadcasting from London his famous appeal to the French people, 18th June, 1940. (Army Cinematographic Service)
42 Churchill broadcasting over the B.B.C.: "I have nothing to offer but blood, sweat and tears." (War Museum)
43 The Reynaud government of June 6th, 1940 (at the extreme right, General de Gaulle). (Keystone)
44 The first Pétain government: at Pétain's right Pierre Laval and at his left General Weygand. (Keystone)

This book, designed by
Werner Schelling
is a production of
Edito-Service S.A., Geneva

Printed in Switzerland